D0207646

Guide to
BRITISH POETRY EXPLICATION
Volume 1

Old English – Medieval

A
Reference
Publication
in
Literature

Guide to
BRITISH POETRY EXPLICATION
Volume 1

Old English – Medieval

NANCY C. MARTINEZ
and
JOSEPH G. R. MARTINEZ

G.K.HALL &CO.
70 LINCOLN STREET, BOSTON, MASS.

First published 1991
by G.K. Hall & Co.
70 Lincoln Street
Boston, Massachusetts 02111

10 9 8 7 6 5 4 3 2 1

Library of Congress Cataloging-in-Publication Data

Martinez, Nancy C. (Nancy Conrad)
Guide to British poetry explication / Nancy C. Martinez and
Joseph G. R. Martinez.
p. cm.
Includes bibliographical references.
Contents: v. 1. Old English-medieval
ISBN 0-8161-8921-8
1. English poetry – Explication – Bibliography.
I. Martinez, Joseph G. R., 1946- . II. Title.
Z2014.P7M34 1991
[PR311]
016.821009 – dc20 90-49129
CIP

The paper used in this publication meets the minimum requirements of American National Standard for Information Sciences – Permanence of Paper for Printed Library Materials. ANSI Z39.48-1984. ∞™
MANUFACTURED IN THE UNITED STATES OF AMERICA

For George Arms and Joseph M. Kuntz

Contents

The Authors

Nancy C. Martinez received her degrees from Southern Oregon State College and the University of New Mexico. She has taught at the UNM Main Campus and Valencia Branch and at the University of Albuquerque, where she was Dean of General Studies and Vice President for Academic Affairs. She coauthored *Poetry Explication: A Checklist*, 3d ed., with Joseph M. Kuntz and is currently consulting editor and chair of the Checklist bibliography committee for *The Explicator* as well as editor for the Guides to Explication series.

Joseph G. R. Martinez is Associate Professor and Chair of Educational Foundations at the University of New Mexico. He has served on *The Explicator* Checklist committee since 1988 and is also coauthoring volumes 2, 3, and 4 of the Guides to British Poetry Explication.

Preface

The Guides to Poetry Explication, American and British, continue and expand the list published in *Poetry Explication: A Checklist of Interpretation*, 3d ed. (Joseph M. Kuntz and Nancy C. Martinez, G. K. Hall, 1980). Like *Poetry Explication: A Checklist*, the Guides survey interpretations of primarily English-language poetry in journals and books. Unlike the earlier work, however, the Guides include explications for poems of all lengths and interpretations published in books about single authors as well as collections surveying periods or several poets. Because of this expanded coverage, we have moved away from the single-volume format of *Poetry Explication: A Checklist* to individual volumes devoted to various periods of American and British literature. The *Guides to American Poetry Explication* (Volume 1 by James Ruppert and Volume 2 by John Leo) were published by G. K. Hall in 1989. With this *Guide to British Poetry Explication: Old English-Medieval*, we begin a series of four volumes devoted to interpretations of British poetry, with Guides to the Renaissance, Restoration through Victorian, and Modern through Contemporary periods to follow.

Of the four Guides to British poetry explication, the current volume shows the most dramatic differences from our "parent" work. Because *Poetry Explication: A Checklist* limited entries to poems of five hundred lines or less, much Old English and Medieval poetry was excluded, including most major works such as *Beowulf*, *Piers Plowman*, *Sir Gawain and the Green Knight*, and the *Canterbury Tales*. *Poetry Explication: A Checklist*, 3d ed., cited a total of 384 explications for Old English and Medieval poetry with only 18 explications for Chaucer. The *Guide to British Poetry Explication: Old

English-Medieval cites approximately 4500 explications (plus several hundred reprints) with 1636 entries for Chaucer, and it adds more than 400 poems to those listed in *Poetry Explication: A Checklist*.

Coverage begins circa 1925, the date chosen by George Arms and Joseph M. Kuntz, authors of *Poetry Explication: A Checklist*, 1st ed., as sufficiently predating the general acceptance of explication as a critical tool to ensure the inclusion of most significant work. Extending coverage through 1989, with some excursions into 1990, involved a two-part process: first, updating lists for poems included in *Poetry Explication: A Checklist*, 3d ed., and, second, resurveying the critical canon of journals, periodicals, and books published during the past sixty-five years for explications of longer poems and for explications published in books about single authors. The effects of the critical explosion of the past fifty years was most evident in the second part of this process. A sprinkling of significant books and articles in the thirties and forties grew into a downpour in the late fifties and sixties and into a deluge in the seventies and eighties. Of course, not all of the thousands of books and articles surveyed could or should be listed here; instead, we have selected those that most effectively use explication as a critical tool, those that seem to us most essential to scholars as well as to students in the field, and those that might be difficult to find in existing bibliographies.

A starting point for our selection of entries was the definition of explication in the first edition of *Poetry Explication: A Checklist*: "an examination of a work of literature for a knowledge of each part, for the relations of these parts to each other, and for their relations to the whole." Implicitly, this definition calls for examining a poem as a literary artifact rather than as a biographical or historical document. It does not necessarily exclude the use of biographical or historical information that contributes to our understanding of the work as literature, nor does it demand that explication be an end in itself. Consequently, we have included here philological studies that use close-reading to demonstrate Old-English poets' craftsmanship; new historical studies that explicate within historical, religious, or cultural contexts; Marxist, psychological, linguistic, stylistic, deconstructionist, and rhetorical criticism when the writers' primary concern is interpretation and primary method is close-reading; and even some source studies in which source and poem are both explicated. As Cleanth Brooks has said, "We are all New Critics now"; the pages of this bibliography amply attest to the diversity and pervasiveness of explication in Old-English and Medieval studies.

Space limitations have necessitated our excluding very short explications and explications of single lines and words when the interpretation does not bear significantly upon our understanding of the poem as a whole. We have generally omitted metrical analysis and paraphrase unless the authors relate their analyses to the total effect of the poem. We have tended, however, to include rather than exclude borderline explications. In this first edition we have also limited citations for reasons of time and space to criticism written in English (we hope to include French- and German-language criticism in the second edition of this *Guide* and other languages in future editions).

Users of this *Guide* and others in the series will find the organization simple:

1. Poets are listed alphabetically by last name – or in the case of Thomas of Hales or King James I, by major name – and running heads at the top of the pages identify sections devoted to individual poets as well as individual poems.

2. Poems are listed alphabetically by title or first line (excluding articles *a*, *and*, and *the*) after the name of the poet.

3. Criticism is listed alphabetically by name of the author following each poem. Full publication information is included within the Checklist for all periodical and journal articles and for most books. Reprints and subsequent editions are cited following the major entry.

4. Books in which many explications appear (usually five or more and occasionally as many as fifty) are cited in shortened note form within the Checklist, with full publication information given in the Main Sources Consulted section. Also listed in the Main Sources section are periodicals and journals that frequently publish explications of Old-English or Medieval poetry.

5. Names of periodicals and journals are abbreviated in the Checklist following the standard MLA abbreviations; these are listed immediately after this Preface.

Identifying names of poets and titles of poems presented some special problems. Because the authors of so many Old-English and Medieval poems are unknown, we have in a few cases used the names of the poems themselves to identify the poets. Therefore, explications for *Beowulf* are listed under *Beowulf*-poet and explications of *Pearl*, *Patience*, *Cleanness*, and *Sir Gawain and the Green Knight*, under *Pearl*-poet. This practice helps break up the long section headed Anonymous and allows us to use the running heads more effectively. Since many poems of the period are untitled, we have tried to follow the critics' practice, wherever possible listing alternative titles from various editions. Similarly, when faced with various spellings for titles, we have generally adopted the one that appears most frequently in the criticism.

We would like to express our appreciation to the many people who have helped us with the preparation of this volume. The staff of the Interlibrary

Loan Office at the University of New Mexico's Zimmerman Library has been indefatigable in tracking down obscure and out-of-print books and articles, and the research and circulation staffs have been equally untiring in answering innumerable questions and conducting countless searches. Our editors at G. K. Hall have been both supportive and patient. Henriette Campagne has never failed to provide quick editorial assistance as well as encouragement; Ara Salibian's careful instructions have been invaluable in preparing the notes and manuscript; and Jan Wager's copyediting was both thorough and sensitive. Finally, we appreciate our family's understanding during the long evenings and weekends spent in the library and during the equally long days spent organizing note cards and entering citations on the computer.

N.C.M.
J.R.G.M.

Abbreviations

ABR	American Benedictine Review
AI	American Imago: A Psychoanalytic Journal for Culture, Science, and the Arts
Allegorica	
Anglia	Anglia: Zeitschrift für Englische Philologie
AnM	Annuale Mediaevale
AN&Q	American Notes and Queries
ArielE	Ariel: A Review of International English Literature

ASE	Anglo-Saxon England
Assays	Assays: Critical Approaches to Medieval and Renaissance Texts
BRMMLA	Bulletin of the Rocky Mountain Modern Language Association
BSUF	Ball State University Forum
BuR	Bucknell Review
CE	College English
CEA	CEA Critic: An Official Journal of the College English Association
CEJ	California English Journal
CentR	The Centennial Review
ChauR	The Chaucer Review
CimR	Cimarron Review
CL	Comparative Literature
CLAJ	College Language Association Journal

Classica and Medievalia

CollL	College Literature
CompD	Comparative Drama
CP	Concerning Poetry
CQ	The Cambridge Quarterly
CRAS	The Centennial Review of Arts and Science
Criticism	Criticism: A Quarterly for Literature and the Arts
CritQ	Critical Quarterly
DR	Dalhousie Review
E&S	Essays and Studies
EA	Études Anglaises: Grande-Bretagne, États-Unis
EIC	Essays in Criticism
EJ	English Journal
ELH	ELH: A Journal of English Literary History
ELN	English Language Notes
ELR	English Literary Renaissance

ELWIU	Essays in Literature (Macomb, IL)
EM	English Miscellany
English	English: The Journal of the English Association
ES	English Studies
ESA	English Studies in Africa
ESC	English Studies in Canada
Expl	The Explicator
FCS	Fifteenth-Century Studies
Genre	(University of Oklahoma, Norman)
HLQ	Huntington Library Quarterly
HudR	The Hudson Review
JAAC	Journal of Aesthetics and Art Criticism
JEGP	Journal of English and Germanic Philology
JMRS	Journal of Medieval and Renaissance Studies
JNT	Journal of Narrative Technique

KR	The Kenyon Review
L&P	Literature and Psychology
Lang&S	Language and Style
LangQ	USF Language Quarterly
LeedsSE	Leeds Studies in English
LitR	Literary Review: An International Journal of Contemporary Writing
LSE	Lund Studies in English
M&H	Medievalia et Humanistica: Studies in Medieval and Renaissance Culture
MÆ	Medium Ævum
Mediaevalia	Mediaevalia: A Journal of Mediaeval Studies
MLN	Modern Language Notes
MLQ	Modern Language Quarterly
MLR	Modern Language Review
Mosaic	Mosaic: A Journal for the Interdisciplinary Study of Literature

MP	Modern Philology
MQ	Midwest Quarterly: A Journal of Contemporary Thought
MS	Mediaeval Studies
N&Q	Notes and Queries
Neophil	Neophilologus
NLH	New Literary History: A Journal of Theory and Interpretation
NM	Neuphilologische Mitteilungen
PBA	Proceedings of the British Academy
PLL	Papers on Language and Literature
PMLA	Publications of the Modern Language Association of America
PQ	Philological Quarterly
Renascence	
Rendezvous	Rendezvous: A Journal of Arts and Letters
RES	Review of English Studies: A Quarterly Journal of English Literature and the English Language

Romania	Romania: Revue Consacrée à l'Etude des Langues et des Littératures Romanes
RS	Research Studies (Washington State University)
RUO	Revue de l'Université d'Ottawa
RUS	Rice University Studies
SAQ	South Atlantic Quarterly
SCRev	South Central Review
Scrutiny	
SHR	Southern Humanities Review
SLitI	Studies in the Literary Imagination
SN	Studia Neophilologica
SoRA	Southern Review (Australia)
SP	Studies in Philology
Speculum	Speculum: A Journal of Medieval Studies
SAC	Studies in the Age of Chaucer

SSF	Studies in Short Fiction
SSL	Studies in Scottish Literature
Style	
THOTH	(Department of English, Syracuse University, N.Y.)
Thought	Thought: A Review of Culture and Idea
TLS	Times Literary Supplement (London)
TQ	Texas Quarterly
Traditio	Traditio: Studies in Ancient and Medieval History, Thought, and Religion
Tristania	Tristania: A Journal Devoted to Tristan Studies
TSE	Tulane Studies in English
TSL	Tennessee Studies in Literature
TSLL	Texas Studies in Literature and Language: A Journal of the Humanities
UMSE	University of Mississippi Studies in English
UTQ	University of Toronto Quarterly

Viator	Viator: Medieval and Renaissance Studies
W&L	Women and Literature
WF	Western Folklore
YES	Yearbook of English Studies

Checklist of Interpretation

ALDHELM

"Lorica"
(OE version)

Huppé, *Doctrine and Poetry*, 75-77.

ANONYMOUS

"Adam Lay I-bowndyn"

Manning, *Wisdom and Number*, 6-7.

Reiss, *The Art of the Middle English Lyric*, 138-42.

Savage, *The Personal Principle*, 48-49.

Sarah Stanbury Smith, "'Adam Lay I-Bowndyn' and the *Vinculum Amoris*," *ELN* 15 (December 1977): 98-101.

Speirs, *Medieval English Poetry*, 65-66.

Woolf, *The English Religious Lyric*, 290-91.

"Æcerbot" Charm

Greenfield and Calder, *A New Critical History*, 258.

Thomas D. Hill, "The Æcerbot Charm and Its Christian User," *ASE* 6 (1977): 213-21.

John D. Niles, "The *Æcerbot* Ritual in Context," in *Old English Literature in Context*, ed. John D. Niles (Cambridge: D. S. Brewer; Totowa, N.J.: Rowman and Littlefield, 1980), 44-56.

"After Mydnyght, When Dremes Dothe Fawll"

Davidoff, *Beginning Well*, 181-82.

"Al Gold Janet Is Thin Her"

J. A. Burrow, "Poems Without Contexts: The Rawlinson Lyrics," *EIC* 29 (1979): 9-10. Reprinted in Burrow, *Essays on Medieval Literature*, 4-5.

Alliterative *Morte Arthure*

W. R. J. Barron, "Arthurian Romances: Traces of An English Tradition," *ES* 61 (February 1980): 10-14.

Barron, *English Medieval Romance*, 138-42.

Boitani, *English Medieval Narrative*, 43-46 and *passim*.

James Lewis Boren, "Narrative Design in the *Alliterative Morte Arthure*," *PQ* 56 (Summer 1977): 310-19.

James Lewis Boren, "A Reading of the Alliterative *Morte Arthure*," Ph.D. diss., University of Iowa, 1970.

W.G. Cooke, "Notes on the Alliterative *Morte Arthure*," *ES* 67 (August 1986): 304-7.

Christopher Dean, "Sir Gawain in the Alliterative *Morte Arthure*," *PLL* 22 (Spring 1986): 115-25.

John Eadie, "The Alliterative *Morte Arthure*: Structure & Meaning," *ES* 63 (February 1982): 1-12.

Jörg O. Fichte, "The Figure of Sir Gawain," in Göller, *Alliterative Morte Arthure*, 106-16.

John Finlayson, "Arthur and the Giant of St. Michael's Mount," *MÆ* 33 (1964): 112-20.

John Finlayson, "The Concept of the Hero in *Morte Arthure*," in *Chaucer und seine Zeit: Symposion für Walter* F. *Schirmer*, ed. Arno Esch (Tübingen: Max Niemeyer, 1968), 249-74.

Karl Heinz Göller, "The Dream of the Dragon and Bear," in Göller, *Alliterative Morte Arthure*, 130-39.

Karl Heinz Göller, "Reality Versus Romance: A Reassessment of the Alliterative *Morte Arthure*," in Göller, *Alliterative Morte Arthure*, 15-29.

Renate Haas, "The Laments for the Dead," in Göller, *Alliterative Morte Arthure*, 117-29.

Mary Hamel, "The 'Christening' of Sir Priamus in the Alliterative *Morte Arthure*," *Viator* 13 (1982): 295-307.

Anke Janssen, "The Dream of the Wheel of Fortune," in Göller, *Alliterative Morte Arthure*, 140-52.

George R. Keiser, "The Theme of Justice in the Alliterative *Morte Arthure*," *AnM* 16 (1975), 94-109.

H. A. Kelly, "The Non-Tragedy of Arthur," in *Medieval English Religious and Ethical Literature*: *Essays in Honour of G. H. Russell*, ed. Gregory Kratzmann and James Simpson (Cambridge: D. S. Brewer, 1986), 92-114.

David A. Lawton, "The Unity of Middle English Alliterative Poetry," *Speculum* 58 (1983): 84-89.

Robert M. Lumiansky, "The Alliterative *Morte Arthure*, the Concept of Medieval Tragedy, and the Cardinal Virtue Fortitude," in *Medieval and Renaissance Studies*: *Proceedings of the Southeastern Institute of Medieval and Renaissance Studies*, *Summer, 1967*, ed. John M. Headley (Chapel Hill: University of North Carolina Press, 1968), 95-118.

William Matthews, *The Tragedy of Arthur*: *A Study of the Alliterative Morte Arthure* (Berkeley: University of California Press, 1960).

Gratia H. Murphy, "Arthur as King: A Reading of the Alliterative *Morte Arthure* in the Light of the Fürstenspiegel Tradition," Ph.D. diss., Kent State University, 1976.

Eithne M. O'Sharkey, "King Arthur's Prophetic Dreams and the Role of Modred in Layamon's *Brut* and the Alliterative *Morte Arthure*," *Romania* 99 (1978): 347-62.

Lee W. Patterson, "The Historiography of Romance and the Alliterative *Morte Arthure*," *JMRS* 13 (Spring 1983): 11-32.

Lee W. Patterson, *Negotiating the Past: The Historical Understanding* of *Medieval Literature* (Madison: University of Wisconsin Press, 1987), 197-230.

Russell A. Peck, "Willfulness and Wonders: Boethian Tragedy in the Alliterative *Morte Arthure*," in Levy and Szarmach, *The Alliterative Tradition*, 153-82.

Richmond, *The Popularity*, 47-56.

Jean Ritzke Rutherford, "Formulaic Macrostructure: The Theme of Battle," in Göller, *Alliterative Morte Arthure*, 83-95.

Schmidt and Jacobs, *Medieval English Romances*, Vol. 2, 29-39.

R. A. Shoaf, "The Alliterative *Morte Arthure*: The Story of Britain's David," *JEGP* 81 (1982): 204-26.

Spearing, *Readings in Medieval Poetry*, 148-65.

M. F. Vaughan, "Consecutive Alliteration, Strophic Patterns and the Composition of the Alliterative *Morte Arthure*," *MP* 77 (August 1979): 1-9.

Jan Ziolkowski, "A Narrative Structure in the Alliterative *Morte Arthure*, 1-1221 and 3150-4346," *ChauR* 22 (1988): 234-45.

"Almsgiving"

Anderson, *Two Literary Riddles*, 126-29.

Carl T. Berkhout, "Some Notes on the Old English 'Almsgiving,'" *ELN* 10 (December 1972): 81-85.

Greenfield and Calder, *A New Critical History*, 260.

"Alnight by the Rose"

J. A. Burrow, "Poems Without Contexts: The Rawlinson Lyrics," *EIC* 29 (1979): 11-12. Reprinted in Burrow, *Essays on Medieval Literature*, 6-7.

"Als I Lay in a Winteris Nyt"

Wenzel, *Preachers, Poets*, 137-39.

Woolf, *English Religious Lyric*, 98-102.

"Als I Lay vp-on a Nith"

Fowler, *The Bible in Middle English Literature*, 60-61.

Weber, *Theology and Poetry in the Middle English Lyric*, 73-86.

Woolf, *The English Religious Lyric*, 151-52.

"Alysoun"

Peter Heidtmann, "The *Reverdie* Convention and 'Lenten Is Come with Love to Toune,'" *AnM* 12 (1971): 81-83.

Moore, *The Secular Lyric in Middle English*, 68-79.

Oliver, *Poems without Names*, 22-23, 37.

Theo Stemmler, "An Interpretation of *Alysoun*," in Rowland, *Chaucer and Middle English Studies*, 111-18.

Amis and Amiloun

Barron, *English Medieval Romance*, 200-204.

Susan Dannenbaum, "Insular Tradition in the Story of Amis and Amiloun," *Neophil* 67 (October 1983): 611-22.

Kathryn Hume, "*Amis and Amiloun* and the Aesthetics of Middle English Romance," *SP* 70 (1973): 19-41.

Dale Kramer, "Structural Artistry in *Amis and Amiloun*," *AnM* 9 (1968): 103-22.

Mehl, *The Middle English Romances*, 105-11.

Ramsey, *Chivalric Romances*, 118-22.

Richmond, *The Popularity*, 92-105.

"An a Byrchyn Bonke þer Bous Arne Bryȝt"

Woolf, *The English Religious Lyric*, 346-47.

Andreas

Frederick M. Biggs, "The Passion of Andreas: *Andreas* 1398-1491," *SP* 85 (1988): 413-27.

Bridges, *Generic Contrast*, 56-68, 179-211.

Daniel G. Calder, "Figurative Language and Its Contexts in *Andreas*: A Study in Medieval Expressionism," in Brown, Crampton, and Robinson, *Modes of Interpretation*, 115-36.

Cherniss, *Ingeld and Christ*, 171-93.

James W. Earl, "The Typological Structures of *Andreas*," in *Old English Literature in Context*, ed. John D. Niles (Cambridge: D. S. Brewer; Totowa, N.J.: Rowman and Littlefield, 1980), 66-89.

Wallace G. Gober, "*Andreas*, Lines 360-62," *NM* 73 (1972): 672-74.

Greenfield and Calder, *A New Critical History*, 159-63.

David Hamilton, "The Diet and Digestion of Allegory in *Andreas*," *ASE* 1 (1972): 147-58.

Hermann, *Allegories of War*, 119-49.

Constance B. Hieatt, "The Harrowing of Mermedonia: Typological Patterns in the Old English 'Andreas,'" *NM* 77 (1976): 49-62.

Thomas D. Hill, "Figural Narrative in *Andreas*: The Conversion of the Meremedonians," *NM* 70 (1969): 261-73.

Edward B. Irving, Jr., "A Reading of *Andreas*: The Poem as Poem," *ASE* 12 (1983): 215-37.

Kennedy, *The Earliest English Poetry*, 267-81.

Lisa J. Kiser, "*Andreas* and the *Lifes Wey*: Convention and Innovation in Old English Metaphor," *NM* 85 (1984): 65-75.

Lee, *The Guest-Hall*, 87-95.

Alexandra Hennessey Olsen, *Speech, Song, and Poetic Craft*: *The Artistry of the Cynewulf Canon* (New York: Peter Lang, 1984), 129-54.

Schaar, *Critical Studies*, 12-24, 49-60, 128-35.

Penn R. Szittya, "The Living Stone and the Patriarchs: Typological Imagery in *Andreas*, Lines 706-810," *JEGP* 72 (1973): 167-74.

Marie Michelle Walsh, "The Baptismal Flood in the Old English 'Andreas': Liturgical and Typological Depths," *Traditio* 33 (1977): 137-58.

Ruth Waterhouse, "Self-Reflexivity and 'Wraetlic word' in *Bleak House* and *Andreas*," *JNT* 18 (Fall 1988): 217-23.

"Annot and John"

Daniel J. Ransom, "'Annot and John' and the Ploys of Parody," *SP* 75 (April 1978): 121-41.

Daniel J. Ransom, *Poets at Play: Irony and Parody in the Harley Lyrics* (Norman, Okla.: Pilgrim Books, 1985), 31-48.

"A Prayer"

Raw, *The Art and Background of Old English Poetry*, 123-26.

"As I Walkyd Vppone a Day"

Wenzel, *Preachers, Poets*, 244-50.

"As Reson Rywlyde My Rechyles Mynde"

Woolf, *The English Religious Lyric*, 261-62.

Assembly of Ladies

Davidoff, *Beginning Well*, 146-59.

"At a Sprynge-wel under a Thorn"

Dronke, *The Medieval Lyric*, 69-70.

Fowler, *The Bible in Middle English Literature*, 55-57.

Gray, *Themes and Images*, 92-94.

Wenzel, *Preachers, Poets*, 210-11, 230-32.

Athelston

A. Inskip Dickerson, "The Subplot of the Messenger in *Athelston*," *PLL* 12 (Spring 1976): 115-24.

Mehl, *The Middle English Romances*, 146-52.

Richmond, *The Popularity*, 88-92.

Schmidt and Jacobs, *Medieval English Romances*, Vol. 2, 15-21.

The Avowing of King Arthur

Bennett, *Middle English Literature*, 175-78.

J. A. Burrow, "*The Avowing of King Arthur*," in Stokes and Burton, *Medieval Literature*, 99-109.

The Awntyrs off Arthure

Ralph Hanna III, "*The Awntyrs off Arthure*, An Interpretation" *MLQ* 31 (September 1970): 275-97.

David N. Klausner, "Exempla and the *Awntyrs off Arthure*," *MS* 34 (1972): 307-25.

Helen Phillips, "The Ghost's Baptism in *The Awntyrs off Arthure*,"*MÆ* 58 (1989): 49-58.

A. C. Spearing, "The Awntyrs off Arthure," in Levy and Szarmach, *The Alliterative Tradition*, 183-202.

A. C. Spearing, "Central and Displaced Sovereignty in Three Medieval Poems," *RES*, n.s. 33 (August 1982): 248-52.

Spearing, *Medieval to Renaissance*, 122-42.

Speirs, *Medieval English Poetry*, 252-62.

Azarias

James W. Kirkland and Charles E. Modlin, "The Art of *Azarias*," *MÆ* 41 (1972): 9-15.

"The Bargain of Judas"

J. D. W. Crowther, "'The Bargain of Judas,'" *ELN* 13 (June 1976): 245-49.

"The Battle of Brunanburh"

W. F. Bolton, "'Variation' in *The Battle of Brunanburh*," *RES*, n.s. 19 (November 1968): 363-72.

Dolores Warwick Frese, "Poetic Prowess in *Brunanburh* and *Maldon*: Winning, Losing, and Literary Outcome," in Brown, Crampton, and Robinson, *Modes of Interpretation*, 83-99.

Donald K. Fry, "Launching Ships in *Beowulf* 210-16 and *Brunanburh* 32b-36," *MP* 79 (August 1981), 61-66.

Neil D. Isaacs, "Battlefield Tour: 'Brunanburg,'" *NM* 63 (1962): 236-44.

Isaacs, *Structural Principles in Old English Poetry*, 118-26.

Ann S. Johnson, "The Rhetoric of Brunanburh," *PQ* 47 (October 1968): 487-93.

Frances Randall Lipp, "Contrast and Point of View in *The Battle of Brunanburh*," *PQ* 48 (April 1969): 166-77.

"The Battle of Maldon"

Earl R. Anderson, "Flyting in *The Battle of Maldon*," *NM* 71 (1970): 197-202.

F. J. Battaglia, "Notes on 'Maldon': Toward a Definitive *Ofermod*," *ELN* 2 (June 1965): 247-49.

N. F. Blake, "The Flyting in *The Battle of Maldon*," *ELN* 13 (June 1976): 242-45.

W. F. Bolton, "Byrhtnoth in the Wilderness," *MLR* 64 (July 1969): 481-90.

W. G. Busse and R. Holtei, "*The Battle of Maldon*: A Historical, Heroic and Political Poem," *Neophil* 65 (October 1981): 614-21.

George Clark, "The Battle in *The Battle of Maldon*," *NM* 69 (1968): 374-79.

George Clark, "*The Battle of Maldon*: A Heroic Poem," *Speculum* 43 (January 1968): 52-71.

George Clark, "The Hero of *Maldon*: *Vir Pius et Strenuus*," *Speculum* 54 (April 1979): 257-82.

J. E. Cross, "Mainly on Philology and the Interpretive Criticism of *Maldon*," in Burlin and Irving, *Old English Studies*, 235-53.

Crossley-Holland and Mitchell, *The Battle of Maldon*, 28-29.

A. N. Doane, "Legend, History and Artifice in *The Battle of Maldon*," *Viator* 9 (1978): 39-66.

Alan J. Fletcher, "Cald Wæter, Scir Wæter: A Note on Lines 91 and 98 of 'The Battle of Maldon,'" *NM* 85 (1984): 435-37.

Dolores Warwick Frese, "Poetic Prowess in *Brunanburh* and *Maldon*: Winning, Losing, and Literary Outcome," in Brown, Crampton, and Robinson, *Modes of Interpretation*, 83-99.

Greenfield and Calder, *A New Critical History*, 150-53.

David G. Hale, "Structure and Theme in *The Battle of Maldon*," *N&Q* 15 (July 1968): 242-43.

Thomas D. Hill, "History and Heroic Ethic in *Maldon*," *Neophil* 54 (July 1970): 291-96.

Bernard F. Huppé, "The Concept of the Hero in the Early Middle Ages," in *Concepts of the Hero in the Middle Ages and the Renaissance*, ed. Norman T. Burns and Christopher J. Reagan (Albany: State University of New York Press, 1975), 9-13.

Edward B. Irving, Jr., "The Heroic Style in *The Battle of Maldon*," *SP* 58 (1961): 457-67.

Isaacs, *Structural Principles in Old English Poetry*, 159-66.

Kennedy, *The Earliest English Poetry*, 340-48.

Louis G. Locke, *Expl* 1 (November 1942): 9. Reprinted in *The Explicator Cyclopedia* 2:1.

O. D. Macrae-Gibson, "How Historical Is *The Battle of Maldon*?" *MÆ* 39 (1970): 89-107.

O. D. Macrae-Gibson, "*Maldon*: The Literary Structure of the Later Part," *NM* 71 (1970): 192-96.

A. D. Mills, "Bryhtnoð's Mistake in Generalship," *NM* 67 (1966): 14-27.

Marie Nelson, "*The Battle of Maldon* and *Juliana*: The Language of Confrontation," in Brown, Crampton, and Robinson, *Modes of Interpretation*, 137-50.

Fred C. Robinson, "God, Death, and Loyalty in *The Battle of Maldon*," in Salu and Farrell, *J. R. R. Tolkien*, 76-98.

Geoffrey G. Russom, "Artful Avoidance of the Useful Phrase in *Beowulf*, *The Battle of Maldon*, and *Fates of the Apostles*," *SP* 75 (October 1978): 371-90.

T. A. Shippey, *Old English Verse* (London: Hutchinson University Library, 1972), 107-10.

Heather Stuart, "The Meaning of *Maldon*," *Neophil* 66 (January 1982): 126-39.

Michael J. Swanton, "*The Battle of Maldon*: A Literary Caveat," *JEGP* 67 (1968): 441-50.

Swanton, *English Literature*, 165-74.

"Bird Us Neure Bliþe Be"

Thomas J. Heffernan, "Four Middle English Lyrics from the Thirteenth Century," *MS* 43 (1981): 134-37.

"Blodles and Bonles, Blod Has Nou Bon"

Manning, *Wisdom and Number*, 145.

"Blow, Northerne Wynd"

Georgia Ronan Crampton, "'Blow, Northerne Wynd' and the Heart's Health," *ChauR* 15 (1981): 183-203.

Leo Spitzer, "*Explication de Texte* Applied to Three Great Middle English Poems," in Spitzer, *Essays on English and American Literature by Leo Spitzer*, 195-216.

"Bryd One Brere, Brid, Brid One Brere"

Dronke, *The Medieval Lyric*, 145-46.

"Bryng Vs in No Browne Bred"

Oliver, *Poems without Names*, 104-5.

"Bytuene Mersh and Aueril"

Reiss, *The Art of the Middle English Lyric*, 58-65.

The Carle of Carlile

Speirs, *Medieval English Poetry*, 206-11.

Chevalere Assigne

Ramsey, *Chivalric Romances*, 171-72.

Christ I, Advent Lyrics

Earl R. Anderson, *Cynewulf: Structure, Style, and Theme in His Poetry* (Cranbury, N.J.; London; Mississauga, Ontario: Associated University Presses, 1983), 45-67.

Earl R. Anderson, "Mary's Role as *Eiron* in *Christ I*," *JEGP* 70 (1971): 230-40.

George Hardin Brown, "Old English Verse as a Medium for Christian Theology," in Brown, Crampton, and Robinson, *Modes of Interpretation*, 15-28.

Robert B. Burlin, *The Old English "Advent": A Typological Commentary* (New Haven, Conn.: Yale University Press, 1968).

Jackson J. Campbell, "Structural Patterns in the Old English Advent Lyrics," *ELH* 23 (1956): 239-55.

J. E. Cross, "*Halgu Hyht* and Poetic Stimulus in the Advent Poem (*Christ I*), 50-70," *Neophil* 53 (April 1968): 194-99.

Gardner, *The Construction of Christian Poetry in Old English*, 107-10.

Greenfield, *A Critical History*, 124-28.

Greenfield, *Hero and Exile*, 197-204.

Stanley B. Greenfield, "The Theme of Spiritual Exile in 'Christ I,'" *PQ* 32 (1953): 321-28.

Greenfield and Calder, *A New Critical History*, 183-88.

Thomas D. Hill, "The Seraphim's Song: The 'Sanctus' in the Old English 'Christ I,' Lines 403-415," *NM* 83 (1982): 26-30.

Kennedy, *The Earliest English Poetry*, 235-41.

Roger Lass, "Poem as Sacrament: Transcendence of Time in the *Advent Sequence* from the Exeter Book," *AnM* 7 (1966): 3-15.

Douglas Moffat, "Tonal Development in the *Advent Lyrics*," *Neophil* 69 (January 1985): 134-41.

Raw, *The Art and Background of Old English Poetry*, 39-40 and *passim*.

Schaar, *Critical Studies*, 35-37, 71-75, 137-39.

Christ I, Lyric 1

George Hardin Brown, "Old English Verse as a Medium for Christian Theology," in Brown, Crampton, and Robinson, *Modes of Interpretation*, 19-21.

Greenfield, *Hero and Exile*, 205-8.

Greenfield and Calder, *A New Critical History*, 184-86.

Christ I, Lyric 2

George Hardin Brown, "Old English Verse as a Medium for Christian Theology," in Brown, Crampton, and Robinson, *Modes of Interpretation*, 21-24.

Chance, *Woman as Hero*, 17-20.

Greenfield, *Hero and Exile*, 208-9.

Greenfield and Calder, *A New Critical History*, 186.

Christ I, Lyric 3

Chance, *Woman as Hero*, 20.

Christ I, Lyric 4

Earl R. Anderson, "Mary's Role as *Eiron* in *Christ I*," *JEGP* 70 (1971): 234-39.

Chance, *Woman as Hero*, 20-24.

Christ I, Lyric 7

Earl R. Anderson, "Mary's Role as *Eiron* in *Christ I*," *JEGP* 70 (1971): 234-39.

Earl R. Anderson, "The Spcech Boundaries in Advent Lyric VII," *Neophil* 63 (October 1979): 611-18.

Jackson J. Campbell, "Structural Patterns in the Old English Advent Lyrics," *ELH* 23 (1956): 249-52.

Chance, *Woman as Hero*, 24-26.

John Miles Foley, "*Christ* 164-213: A Structural Approach to the Speech Boundaries in 'Advent Lyric VII,'" *Neophil* 59 (January 1975): 114-18.

Judith N. Garde, "*Christ I* (164-195a): The Mary Joseph Dialogue in Medieval Christian Perspective," *Neophil* 74 (January 1990): 122-30.

Greenfield and Calder, *A New Critical History*, 187.

Isaacs, *Structural Principles in Old English Poetry*, 93-99.

Neil D. Isaacs, "Who Says What in 'Advent Lyric VII'? (*Christ*, lines 164-213)," *PLL* (Spring 1966): 162-66.

Anne L. Klinck, "Female Characterisation in Old English Poetry and the Growth of Psychological Realism: *Genesis B* and *Christ I*," *Neophil* 63 (October 1979): 601-4.

Christ I, Lyric 9

Earl R. Anderson, "Mary's Role as *Eiron* in *Christ I*," *JEGP* 70 (1971): 239-40.

Chance, *Woman as Hero*, 26-28.

Christ I, Lyric 10

Robert C. Rice, "Hreowcearig 'Penitent, Contrite,'" *ELN* 12 (June 1975): 246-47.

Christ I, Lyric 12

Chance, *Woman as Hero*, 28-30.

Christ III

Christopher L. Chase, "'Christ III,' 'The Dream of the Rood,' and Early Christian Passion Piety," *Viator* 11 (1980): 11-33.

Greenfield and Calder, *A New Critical History*, 193-94.

Thomas D. Hill, "Further Notes on the Eschatology of the Old English *Christ III*," *NM* 72 (1971): 691-98.

Thomas D. Hill, "Notes on the Eschatology of the Old English *Christ III*," *NM* 70 (1969): 672-79.

Thomas D. Hill, "Vision and Judgement in the Old English *Christ III*," *SP* 70 (July 1973): 233-42.

Lois R. Kuznets and Martin Green, "Voice and Vision in the Old English *Christ III*," *PLL* 12 (Summer 1976): 227-45.

Schaar, *Critical Studies*, 139-43.

Christ and Satan

Spencer Cosmos, "Old English 'Limwaestin' ('Christ and Satan' 129)," *N&Q* 22 (May 1975): 196-98.

Robert Emmett Finnegan, *Expl* 31 (October 1972): 10.

Robert Emmett Finnegan, *"Christ and Satan": A Critical Edition* (Waterloo, Ont.: Wilfrid Laurier University Press, 1977), 22-36.

Gardner, *The Construction of Christian Poetry in Old English*, 37-38.

Greenfield, *A Critical History*, 142-44.

Greenfield and Calder, *A New Critical History*, 200-202.

Constance D. Harsh, "*Christ and Satan*: The Measured Power of Christ," *NM* 90 (1989): 243-53.

Thomas D. Hill, "The Measure of Hell: *Christ and Satan* 695-722," *PQ* 60 (Summer 1981): 409-14.

Huppé, *Doctrine and Poetry*, 227-31.

Isaacs, *Structural Principles in Old English Poetry*, 127-44.

Kennedy, *The Earliest English Poetry*, 188-97.

Lee, *The Guest-Hall*, 20-22 and *passim*.

Geoffrey Shepherd, "Scriptural Poetry," in Stanley, *Continuations and Beginnings*, 33-35.

Charles R. Sleeth, *Expl* 42 (Fall 1983): 2-4.

Charles R. Sleeth, *Studies in "Christ and Satan"* (Toronto: University of Toronto Press, 1982).

"Continvaunce/Of Remembraunce"

Oliver, *Poems without Names*, 29-30.

"Corpus Christi Carol" ("Lully, lullay, lully, lullay")

Fowler, *The Bible in Middle English Literature*, 92-93.

Gray, *Themes and Images* , 164-67.

Richard Leighton Greene, "The Burden and the Scottish Variant of the Corpus Christi Carol," *MÆ* 38 (1964): 53-60.

Richard Leighton Greene, "The Meaning of the Corpus Christi Carol," *MÆ* 29 (1960): 10-21.

Speirs, *Medieval English Poetry*, 76-78.

"Crabbed Age and Youth"

Edward F. Nolan, *Expl* 30 (May 1972): 76.

"Cristes Milde Moder, Seynte Marie" ("On God Ureisun of Ure Lefde")

Manning, *Wisdom and Number*, 94-96.

"Crist Makith to Man a Fair Present"

Manning, *Wisdom and Number*, 27, 146-50.

Florence Newman, "'Christ Maketh to Man,' Stanza Four: A Case for Interpolation," *NM* 85 (1984): 454-61.

Cursor Mundi

Miriam Skey, "The Death of Herod in the *Cursor Mundi*," *MÆ* 57 (1988): 74-80.

"Cyning Sceal Rice Healdan"

J. K. Bollard, "The Cotton Maxims," *Neophil* 57 (April 1973): 179-87.

"Dame Sirith and the Weeping Bitch

Swanton, *English Literature*, 216-25.

Nicolai von Kreisler, "Satire in Dame Sirith and the Weeping Bitch," in *Essays in Honor of Esmond Linworth Marilla*, ed. Thomas Austin Kirby and William John Olive (Baton Rouge: Louisiana State University Press, 1970), 379-87.

Daniel

Earl R. Anderson, "Style and Theme in the Old English *Daniel*," *ES* 68 (1987): 1-23.

Robert E. Bjork, "Oppressed Hebrews and the Song of Azarias in the Old English *Daniel*," *SP* 77 (Summer 1980): 213-26.

Graham D. Caie, "The Old English *Daniel*: A Warning Against Pride," *ES* 59 (February 1978): 1-9.

Robert T. Farrell, "The Structure of Old English *Daniel*," *NM* 69 (1968): 533-59.

Robert T. Farrell, "The Unity of Old English *Daniel*," *RES*, n.s. 18 (May 1967): 117-35.

Gardner, *The Construction of Christian Poetry in Old English*, 34-37.

Greenfield and Calder, *A New Critical History*, 216-18.

J. R. Hall, *Expl* 45 (Winter 1987): 3-4.

Huppé, *Doctrine and Poetry*, 223-27.

Isaacs, *Structural Principles in Old English Poetry*, 145-51.

Lee, *The Guest-Hall*, 50-55.

Gillian R. Overing, "Nebuchadnezzar's Conversion in the Old English *Daniel*: A Psychological Portrait," *PLL* 20 (Winter 1984): 3-14.

Harry Jay Solo, "The Twice-told Tale: A Reconsideration of the Syntax and Style of the Old English *Daniel*, 245-429," *PLL* 9 (Fall 1973): 347-64.

"Death and Life"

W. A. Davenport, "Patterns in Middle English Dialogues," in *Medieval English Studies Presented to George Kane*, ed. Edward Donald Kennedy, Ronald Waldron, and Joseph S. Wittig (Suffolk: D. S. Brewer, 1988), 133-34.

David V. Harrington, "The Personifications in *Death and Liffe*, a Middle-English Poem," *NM* 68 (1967), 35-47.

Spearing, *Medieval Dream-Poetry*, 166-70.

"The Death of Edgar"

Isaacs, *Structural Principles in Old English Poetry*, 89-93.

"De Clerico et Puella"

Patricia Abel, "The Cleric, the Kitchie Boy, and the Returned Sailor," *PQ* 44 (October 1965): 552-55.

Moore, *The Secular Lyric in Middle English*, 70-72.

De Erkenwaldo

Sandra Cairns, "Fact and Fiction in the Middle English *De Erkenwaldo*," *NM* 83 (1982): 430-38.

Deor

Anderson, *Two Literary Riddles*, 19-44.

Jacqueline Banerjee, *Expl* 42 (Summer 1984): 4-7.

Morton W. Bloomfield, "*Deor* Revisited," in Brown, Crampton, and Robinson, *Modes of Interpretation*, 273-86.

Morton W. Bloomfield, "The Form of *Deor*," *PMLA* 79 (1964): 534-41. Reprinted in Stevens and Mandel, *Old English Literature*, 212-28.

James L. Boren, "The Design of the Old English *Deor*," in Nicholson and Frese, *Anglo-Saxon Poetry*, 264-76.

Edward I. Condren, "Deor's Artistic Triumph," *SP* 78 (Early Winter 1981): 62-76.

Norman E. Eliason, "*Deor* – a Begging Poem?" in *Medieval Literature and Civilization: Studies in Memory of G. N. Garmonsway*, ed. D. A. Pearsall and R. A. Waldron (London: Athlone Press, 1969), 55-61.

P. J. Frankis, "*Deor* and *Wulf and Eadwacer*: Some Conjectures," *MÆ* 31 (1962): 165-72.

Greenfield, *Hero and Exile*, 111-14.

Stanley B. Greenfield, "The Old English Elegies," in Stanley, *Continuations and Beginnings*, 160-63.

Hansen, *The Solomon Complex*, 84-88.

Joseph Harris, "'Deor' and Its Refrain: Preliminaries to an Interpretation," *Traditio* 43 (1987): 23-53.

Isaacs, *Structural Principles in Old English Poetry*, 107-114.

Kennedy, *The Earliest English Poetry*, 30-35.

Kevin S. Kiernan, "*Deor*: The Consolation of an Anglo-Saxon Boethius," *NM* 79 (1978): 333-40.

Kevin S. Kiernan, "A Solution to the Maedhild-Geat Crux in *Deor*," *ES* 56 (April 1975): 97-99.

Anne L. Klinck, "The Old English Elegy as a Genre," *ESC* 10 (June 1984): 129-40.

Lee, *The Guest-Hall*, 161-68.

Kemp Malone, "Introduction" to *Deor* (London: Methuen & Co., 1933, 1949, 1961), 1-22 *passim*.

Mandel, *Alternative Readings*, 109-47.

Jerome Mandel, "Audience Response Strategies in the Opening of *Deor*," *Mosaic* 15 (December 1982): 127-32.

Jerome Mandel, "Exemplum and Refrain: The Meaning of *Deor*," *YES* 7 (1977): 1-9.

Murray F. Markland, *"Deor: thaes Ofereode; thisses swa maeg," AN&Q* 11 (November 1972): 35-36.

T. A. Shippey, *Old English Verse* (London: Hutchinson University Library, 1972), 75-78.

Swanton, *English Literature*, 39-43.

Thomas T. Tuggle, "The Structure of *Deor*," *SP* 74 (1977): 229-42.

L. Whitbread, "The Pattern of Misfortune in *Deor* and Other Old English Poems," *Neophil* 54 (April 1970): 167-72.

The Descent into Hell

Anderson, *Two Literary Riddles*, 116-26.

Patrick W. Conner, "The Liturgy and the Old English 'Descent into Hell,'" *JEGP* 79 (1980): 179-91.

Greenfield and Calder, *A New Critical History*, 199-200.

Thomas D. Hill, "Cosmic Stasis and the Birth of Christ: The Old English *Descent into Hell*, Lines 99-106," *JEGP* 71 (1972): 382-89.

Shippey, *Poems of Wisdom and Learning*, 36-43.

Richard M. Trask, "*The Descent into Hell* of the Exeter Book," *NM* 72 (1971): 419-35.

"A Disputacion Betwyx þe Body and Wormes"

Marjorie M. Malvern, "An Earnest 'Monyscyon' and 'þinge Delectabyll' Realized Verbally and Visually in 'A Disputacion Betwyx þe Body and Wormes,' a Middle English Poem Inspired by Tomb Art and Northern Spirituality," *Viator* 13 (1982): 415-43.

"The Dream of the Rood"

Earl R. Anderson, "Liturgical Influence in *The Dream of the Rood*," *Neophil* 73 (April 1989): 293-304.

J. A. W. Bennett, *Poetry of the Passion: Studies in Twelve Centuries of English Verse* (Oxford: Clarendon Press, 1982), 1-27.

Carl T. Berkhout, "The Problem of OE *Holmwudu*," *MS* 36 (1974): 429-33.

Robert Boenig, "The *Engel Dryhtnes* and Mimesis in 'The Dream of the Rood,'" *NM* 86 (1985): 442-46.

Monica Brzezinski, "The Harrowing of Hell, the Last Judgment, and *The Dream of the Rood*," *NM* 89 (1988): 252-65.

Robert B. Burlin, "The Ruthwell Cross, *The Dream of the Rood* and the *Vita Contemplativa*," *SP* 65 (January 1968): 23-43.

J. A. Burrow, "An Approach to *The Dream of the Rood*," *NM* 43 (1959): 123-33. Reprinted in Stevens and Mandel, *Old English Literature*, 253-67.

John Canuteson, "The Crucifixion and the Second Coming in *The Dream of the Rood*," *MP* 66 (May 1969): 293-97.

Christopher L. Chase, "'Christ III,' 'The Dream of the Rood,' and Early Christian Passion Piety," *Viator* 11 (1980): 11-33.

Michael D. Cherniss, "The Cross as Christ's Weapon: The Influence of Heroic Literary Tradition on *The Dream of the Rood*," *ASE* 2 (1973): 250-51.

Crossley-Holland and Mitchell, *The Battle of Maldon*, 124-27.

M. L. del Mastro, "*The Dream of the Rood* and the *Militia Christi*: Perspective in Paradox," *ABR* 27 (June 1976): 171-86.

Kathleen E. Dubs, "*Hæleð*: Heroism in 'The Dream of the Rood,'" *Neophil* 59 (October 1975): 614-15.

Robert R. Edwards, "Narrative Technique and Distance in *The Dream of the Rood*," *PLL* 6 (Summer 1970): 291-301.

Alison Finlay, "The Warrior Christ and the Unarmed Hero," in *Medieval English Religious and Ethical Literature: Essays in Honour of G. H. Russell*, ed. Gregory Kratzmann and James Simpson (Cambridge: D. S. Brewer, 1986), 20-21.

John V. Fleming, "'The Dream of the Rood' and Anglo-Saxon Monasticism," *Traditio* 22 (1966): 43-72.

Andrew Galloway, "*Beowulf* and the Varieties of Choice," *PMLA* 105 (1990): 200-201.

Gardner, *The Construction of Christian Poetry in Old English*, 98-105.

Robert V. Graybill, "'The Dream of the Rood': Apotheosis of Anglo-Saxon Paradox," in *Proceedings of the Illinois Medieval Association*, ed. Roberta Bux Bosse *et al*. (Macomb, Ill.: IMA, 1984), 1-12.

Greenfield, *A Critical History*, 136-41.

Greenfield and Calder, *A New Critical History*, 194-98.

Willem Helder, "The *Engel Dryhtnes* in *The Dream of the Rood*," *MP* 73 (November 1975): 148-50.

John P. Hermann, "*The Dream of the Rood*, 19A: *Earmra Ærgewin*," *ELN* 15 (June 1978): 241-44.

Constance B. Hieatt, "Dream Frame and Verbal Echo in the *Dream of the Rood*," *NM* 72 (1971): 250-63.

Carolyn Holdsworth, "Frames: Time Level and Variation in 'The Dream of the Rood,'" *Neophil* 66 (October 1982): 622-28.

Julia B. Holloway, "'The Dream of the Rood' and Liturgical Drama," *CompD* 18 (Spring 1984): 19-37.

A. D. Horgan, "'The Dream of the Rood' and Christian Tradition," *NM* 79 (1978): 11-20.

David R. Howlett, "The Structure of *The Dream of the Rood*," *SN* 48 (1976): 301-6.

Bernard F. Huppé, "The Concept of the Hero in the Early Middle Ages," in *Concepts of the Hero in the Middle Ages and the Renaissance*, ed. Norman Burns and Christopher Reagan (Albany: State University of New York Press, 1975), 6-8.

Bernard F. Huppé, *The Hero in the Earthly City: A Reading of "Beowulf,"* Medieval & Renaissance Texts & Studies, no. 33 (Binghamton: State University of New York at Binghamton, 1984), 29-30.

Martin Irvine, "Anglo-Saxon Literary Theory Exemplified in Old English Poems: Interpreting the Cross in *The Dream of the Rood* and *Elene*," *Style* 20 (Summer 1986): 171-74.

Edward B. Irving, Jr., "Crucifixion Witnessed, or Dramatic Interaction in *The Dream of the Rood*," in Brown, Crampton, and Robinson, *Modes of Interpretation*, 101-13.

Isaacs, *Structural Principles in Old English Poetry*, 3-18.

Kennedy, *The Earliest English Poetry*, 259-66.

Eugene R. Kintgen, "Echoic Repetition in Old English Poetry, Especially 'The Dream of the Rood,'" *NM* 75 (1974): 215-23.

Lee, *The Guest-Hall*, 60-64.

Alvin A. Lee, "Toward a Critique of *The Dream of the Rood*," in Nicholson and Frese, *Anglo-Saxon Poetry*, 163-91.

N. A. Lee, "The Unity of 'The Dream of the Rood,'" *Neophil* 56 (October 1972): 469-86.

Louis H. Leiter, "*The Dream of the Rood*: Patterns of Transformation," in *Old English Poetry: Fifteen Essays*, ed. Robert P. Creed (Providence, R.I.: Brown University Press, 1967), 93-127.

O. D. Macrae-Gibson, "Christ the Victor-Vanquished in *The Dream of the Rood*," *NM* 70 (1969): 667-72.

Éamonn Ó Carragáin, "Crucifixion as Annunciation: The Relation of 'The Dream of the Rood' to the Liturgy Reconsidered," *ES* 63 (December 1982): 487-505.

Alexandra Hennessey Olsen, *Speech, Song, and Poetic Craft: The Artistry of the Cynewulf Canon* (New York: Peter Lang, 1984), 113-15.

Carol Braun Pasternack, "Stylistic Disjunctions in *The Dream of the Rood*," *ASE* 13 (1984): 167-86.

Faith H. Patten, "Structure and Meaning in *The Dream of the Rood*," *ES* 49 (October 1968): 385-401.

Richard C. Payne, "Convention and Originality in the Vision Framework of *The Dream of the Rood*," *MP* 73 (May 1976): 329-41.

Derek Pearsall, *Old English and Middle English Poetry*, The Routledge History of English Poetry, Vol. 1 (London: Routledge & Kegan Paul, 1977), 46-48.

T. E. Pickford, "Another Look at the *Engel Dryhtnes* in 'The Dream of the Rood,'" *NM* 77 (1976): 565-68.

Raw, *The Art and Background of Old English Poetry* , 127-32.

Barbara C. Raw, "*The Dream of the Rood* and Its Connections with Early Christian Art," *MÆ* 39 (1970): 239-56.

Schaar, *Critical Studies*, 135-37.

Margaret Schlauch, "*The Dream of the Rood* as Prosopopoeia," in *Essays and Studies in Honor of Carleton Brown* (New York: New York University Press, 1940), 23-34. Reprinted in Bessinger and Kahrl, *Essential Articles*, 428-41.

Geoffrey Shepherd, "Scriptural Poetry," in Stanley, *Continuations and Beginnings*, 15-17.

James Smith, "The Garments That Honour the Cross in *The Dream of the Rood*," *ASE* 4 (1975): 29-35.

M[ichael] Swanton, "Ambiguity and Anticipation in 'The Dream of the Rood,'" *NM* 70 (1969): 407-25.

Swanton, *English Literature*, 94-101.

Michael Swanton, "Introduction" to *The Dream of the Rood* (Manchester: University of Manchester; New York: Barnes & Noble, 1970), 62-78.

George S. Tate, "Chiasmus as Metaphor: The 'Figura Crucis' Tradition and 'The Dream of the Rood,'" *NM* 79 (1978): 114-25.

P. B. Taylor, "Text and Texture of 'The Dream of the Rood,'" *NM* 75 (1974): 193-201.

Raymond P. Tripp, Jr., "*The Dream of the Rood*: 9b and Its Context," *MP* 69 (November 1971): 136-37.

F. H. Whitman, *Expl* 33 (May 1975): 70.

Williamson, *A Feast of Creatures*, 41-42.

Carol Jean Wolf, "Christ as Hero in 'The Dream of the Rood,'" *NM* 71 (1970): 202-10.

Rosemary Woolf, "Doctrinal Influences on the Dream of the Rood," *MÆ* 27 (1958): 137-53. Reprinted in Woolf, *Art and Doctrine*, 29-48.

Durham

Calvin B. Kendall, "Let Us Now Praise a Famous City: Wordplay in the OE *Durham* and the Cult of St. Cuthbert," *JEGP* 87 (October 1988): 507-21.

"The Duty of Prelates"

Davidoff, *Beginning Well*, 51-52.

The Earl of Toulouse

Mehl, *The Middle English Romances*, 85-93.

Ramsey, *Chivalric Romances*, 172-76.

Robert Reilly, "*The Earl of Toulouse*: A Structure of Honor," *MS* 37 (1975): 515-23.

"Edi Beo Thu Heuene Quene"

Manning, *Wisdom and Number*, 97-100.

Rogers, *Image and Abstraction*, 43-51.

Woolf, *The English Religious Lyric*, 124-28.

"Edward"

Abad, *A Formal Approach to Lyric Poetry*, 75-76, 77-78.

Beaty and Matchett, *Poetry: From Statement to Meaning*, 145-49.

Brooks, Purser, and Warren, *An Approach to Literature*, 435-37; 3d ed., 288-90; 4th ed., 290-92.

Daniels, *The Art of Reading Poetry*, 151-54.

Arthur K. Moore, "The Literary Status of the English Popular Ballad," *CL* 10 (Winter 1958): 16.

"The Epitaph of Lobe, the King's Fool"

Fowler, *The Bible in Middle English Literature*, 81-83.

Eger and Grime

Ramsey, *Chivalric Romances*, 133-50 *passim*.

Emare

Mortimer J. Donovan, "Middle English *Emare* and the Cloth Worthily Wrought," in Benson, *The Learned and the Lewed*, 337-42.

Mehl, *The Middle English Romances*, 135-40.

Ramsey, *Chivalric Romances*, 181-84.

Richmond, *The Popularity*, 61-65.

Speirs, *Medieval English Poetry*, 157-61.

"Envy"

Bruce Moore, "The Reeve's 'Rusty Blade,'" *MÆ* 58 (1989): 307-8.

"Erþe Toc of Erþe"

Russell A. Peck, "Public Dreams and Private Myths: Perspective in Middle English Literature," *PMLA* 90 (1975): 465-66.

Reiss, *The Art of the Middle English Lyric*, 50-56.

Woolf, *The English Religious Lyric*, 84-85.

Exeter Book, Riddle 1
"Hwylc is hæleþa þæs horsc"

Jackson J. Campbell, "A Certain Power," *Neophil* 59 (January 1975): 128-38.

John Miles Foley, "'Riddle I' of the *Exeter Book*: The Apocalyptical Storm," *NM* 77 (1976): 347-57.

Gardner, *The Construction of Christian Poetry in Old English*, 42-44.

Laurence K. Shook, C. S. B., "Old-English Riddle I: 'Fire,'" *MS* 8 (1946): 316-18.

Erika von Erhardt-Siebold, "The Old English Storm Riddles," *PMLA* 64 (1949): 884-88.

Williamson, *A Feast of Creatures*, 158-62.

Exeter Book, Riddle 2
"Hwilum ic gewite, swa ne wenaþ men"

Gardner, *The Construction of Christian Poetry in Old English*, 44-49.

Exeter Book, Riddle 3
"Hwilum mec min frea fæste genearwað"

John F. Adams, "The Anglo-Saxon Riddle as Lyric Mode," *Criticism* 7 (Fall 1965): 345-47.

Gardner, *The Construction of Christian Poetry in Old English*, 44-49.

Marie Nelson, "Time in the Exeter Book Riddles," *PQ* 54 (Spring 1975): 512-13.

Exeter Book, Riddle 4
"Ic Sceal þragbysig þegne minum"

A. N. Doane, "Three Old English Implement Riddles: Reconsiderations of Numbers 4, 49, and 73," *MP* 84 (February 1987): 244-49.

Matthew Marino, "The Literariness of the Exeter Book Riddles," *NM* 79 (1978): 264.

Ann Harleman Stewart, "The Solution to Old English Riddle 4," *SP* 78 (Early Winter 1981): 52-61.

Exeter Book, Riddle 5
"Ic eom anhaga iserne wund"

Marie Nelson, "Time in the Exeter Book Riddles," *PQ* 54 (Spring 1975): 514-15.

Exeter Book, Riddle 7
"Hrægl min swigað þonne ic hrusan trede"

John F. Adams, "The Anglo-Saxon Riddle as Lyric Mode," *Criticism* 7 (Fall 1965): 343-45.

Matthew Marino, "The Literariness of the Exeter Book Riddles," *NM* 79 (1978): 264-65.

Exeter Book, Riddle 8
"Ic þurh muþ sprece mongum reordum"

Jean I. Young, "Riddle 8 of the Exeter Book," *RES* 18 (July 1942): 308-12.

Exeter Book, Riddle 15
"Hals is min hwit ond heafod fealo"

Marie Nelson, "Old English Riddle No. 15: The 'Badger': An Early Example of Mock Heroic," *Neophil* 59 (July 1975): 447-50.

Jean I. Young, "Riddle 15 of *The Exeter Book*," *RES* 20 (October 1944): 304-06.

Exeter Book, Riddle 16
"Oft ic sceal wiþ wæge winnan"

John F. Adams, "The Anglo-Saxon Riddle as Lyric Mode," *Criticism* 7 (Fall 1965): 342-43.

Exeter Book, Riddle 19
"Ic on siþe seah"

N. E. Eliason, "Four Old English Cryptographic Riddles," *SP* 49 (1952): 557-61.

Exeter Book, Riddle 20
"Ic eom wunderlicu wiht, on gewin sceapen"

Michael D. Cherniss, "The Cross as Christ's Weapon: The Influence of Heroic Literary Tradition on *The Dream of the Rood*," *ASE* 2 (1973): 246-47.

Donald Kay, "Riddle 20: A Reevaluation," *TSL* 13 (1968): 133-38.

Marie Nelson, "Old English Riddle 18(20): A Description of Ambivalence," *Neophil* 66 (April 1982): 291-99.

Lawrence K. Shook, "Old English Riddle No. 20: *Heoruswealwe*," in *Medieval and Linguistic Studies in Honor of Francis Peabody Magoun, Jr.*, ed. Jess B. Bessinger, Jr., and Robert P. Creed (London: George Allen and Unwin, 1965), 194-204.

F. H. Whitman, "The Christian Background to Two Riddle Motifs," *SN* 41 (1969): 93-98.

Williamson, *A Feast of Creatures*, 174-75.

Exeter Book, Riddle 22
"Ætsomne cwom sixtig monna"

L. Blakely, "Riddles 22 and 58 of the Exeter Book," *RES*, n.s. 9 (May 1958): 242-47.

Exeter Book, Riddle 23
"Agof is min noma eft onhwyrfed"

Ann Harleman Stewart, "Kenning and Riddle in Old English," *PLL* 15 (Spring 1979): 131-33.

Exeter Book, Riddle 25
"Ic eom wunderluci wiht, wifum on hyhte"

Gardner, *The Construction of Christian Poetry in Old English*, 41-42.

Williamson, *A Feast of Creatures*, 38-39, 177-78.

Exeter Book, Riddle 28
"Biþ foldan dæl fægre gegierwed"

Marie Nelson, "The Rhetoric of the Exeter Book Riddles," *Speculum* 49 (1974): 436-39.

Laurence K. Shook, C. S. B., "Old-English Riddle 28 – Testudo (Tortoise-Lyre)," *MS* 20 (1958): 93-97.

Ann Harleman Stewart, "Kenning and Riddle in Old English," *PLL* 15 (Spring 1979): 133-35.

Williamson, *A Feast of Creatures*, 180-81.

Exeter Book, Riddle 29
"Ic wiht geseah wundorlice"

John J. Joyce, "Natural Process in *Exeter Book* Riddle 29: 'Sun and Moon,'" *AnM* 14 (1973): 5-8.

Williamson, *A Feast of Creatures*, 28-29, 181-82.

Exeter Book, Riddle 30
"Ic eom legbysig lace mid winde"

Roy M. Liuzza, "The Texts of the Old English *Riddle 30*," *JEGP* 87 (1988): 1-15.

Arnold Talentino, "Riddle 30: The Vehicle of the Cross," *Neophil* 65 (January 1981): 129-36.

Exeter Book, Riddle 30b
"Ic eom ligbysig, lace mid winde"

Anderson, *Two Literary Riddles*, 138-44.

Exeter Book, Riddle 36
"Ic wiht geseah on wege feran"

N. E. Eliason, "Four Old English Cryptographic Riddles," *SP* 49 (1952): 562-65.

Williamson, *A Feast of Creatures*, 185.

Exeter Book, Riddle 39
"Gewritu secgað þæt seo wiht sy"

Greenfield, *Hero and Exile*, 223-28.

Christopher B. Kennedy, "Old English Riddle No. 39," *ELN* 13 (December 1975): 81-85.

Paul Meyvaert, "The Solution to Old English Riddle 39," *Speculum* 51 (1976): 195-201.

Marie Nelson, "The Rhetoric of the Exeter Book Riddles," *Speculum* 49 (1974): 428-31.

Exeter Book, Riddle 43
"Ic wat indryhtne æþelum deorne"

Matthew Marino, "The Literariness of the Exeter Book Riddles," *NM* 79 (1978): 260-61.

Williamson, *A Feast of Creatures*, 190-91.

Exeter Book, Riddle 45
"Ic on wincle gefrægn weaxan nathwæt"

Edith Whitehurst Williams, "What's So New about the Sexual Revolution?" *TQ* 18 (Summer 1975): 49-50.

Exeter Book, Riddle 46
"Wær sæt æt wine mid his wifum twam"

Williamson, *A Feast of Creatures*, 192.

Exeter Book, Riddle 47
"Moððe word fræt – me þæt þuhte"

John F. Adams, "The Anglo-Saxon Riddle as Lyric Mode," *Criticism* 7 (Fall 1965): 337-40.

Matthew Marino, "The Literariness of the Exeter Book Riddles," *NM* 79 (1978): 259.

Fred C. Robinson, "Artful Ambiguities in the Old English 'Book-Moth' Riddle," in Nicholson and Frese, *Anglo-Saxon Poetry*, 355-62.

Ann Harleman Stewart, "Old English Riddle 47 as Stylistic Parody," *PLL* 11 (Summer 1975): 227-41.

Exeter Book, Riddle 48
"Ic Gefrægn for hæleðum hring gyddian"

Marie Nelson, "The Paradox of Silent Speech in the Exeter Book Riddles," *Neophil* 62 (October 1978): 611-12.

Exeter Book, Riddle 49
"Ic wat eardfæstne anne standan"

A. N. Doane, "Three Old English Implement Riddles: Reconsiderations of Numbers 4, 49, and 73," *MP* 84 (February 1987): 249-54.

Exeter Book, Riddle 50
"Wiga is on eorþan wundrum acenned"

Matthew Marino, "The Literariness of the Exeter Book Riddles," *NM* 79 (1978): 263-64.

Exeter Book, Riddle 53
"Ic seah on bearwe beam hlifian"

F. H. Whitman, "Significant Motifs in Riddle 53," *MÆ* 46 (1977): 1-11.

Exeter Book, Riddle 54
"Hyse cwom gangan þær he hie wisse"

Williamson, *A Feast of Creatures*, 196.

Exeter Book, Riddle 55
"Ic seah in healle, þær hæleð druncon"

Tim William Machan and Robyn G. Peterson, "The Crux of Riddle 53," *ELN* 24 (March 1987): 7-14.

Exeter Book, Riddle 56
"Ic wæs þær inne þær ic ane geseah"

Williamson, *A Feast of Creatures*, 197-98.

Exeter Book, Riddle 58
"Ic wat anfete ellen dreogan"

L. Blakeley, "Riddles 22 and 58 of the *Exeter Book*," *RES*, n.s. 9 (May 1958): 247-52.

Exeter Book, Riddle 59
"Ic seah in healle hring gyldenne"

Williamson, *A Feast of Creatures*, 200.

Exeter Book, Riddle 60
"Ic wæs be sonde, sæwealle neah"

Margaret E. Goldsmith, "The Enigma of *The Husband's Message*," in Nicholson and Frese, *Anglo-Saxon Poetry*, 242-46.

R. E. Kaske, "A Poem of the Cross in the Exeter Book: 'Riddle 60' and 'The Husband's Message,'" *Traditio* 23 (1967): 41-71.

Roy F. Leslie, "The Integrity of Riddle 60," *JEGP* 67 (1968): 451-57.

Marie Nelson, "The Paradox of Silent Speech in the Exeter Book Riddles," *Neophil* 62 (October 1978): 612-14.

F. H. Whitman, "Riddle 60 and Its Source," *PQ* 40 (January 1971): 108-15.

Exeter Book, Riddle 61
"Oft mec fæste bileac freolicu meowle"

Edith Whitehurst Williams, "What's So New about the Sexual Revolution?" *TQ* 18 (Summer 1975): 50-51.

Exeter Book, Riddle 64
"Ic seah ᚹ ond ᛁ ofer wong faran"

N. E. Eliason, "Four Old English Cryptographic Riddles," *SP* 49 (1952): 557-61.

Exeter Book, Riddle 72
"Ic wæs lytel"

Marie Nelson, "Time in the Exeter Book Riddles," *PQ* 54 (Spring 1975): 513-14.

Exeter Book, Riddle 73
"Ic on wonge aweox, wunode þær mec feddon"

A. N. Doane, "Three Old English Implement Riddles: Reconsiderations of Numbers 4, 49, and 73," *MP* 84 (February 1987): 254-57.

Exeter Book, Riddle 74
"Ic wæs fæmne geong, feaxhar cwene"

E. S. Kiernan, "The Mysteries of the Sea-eagle in Exeter Riddle 74," *PQ* 54 (Spring 1975): 518-22.

Exeter Book, Riddle 75
"Ic swiftne geseah on swaþe feran"

N. E. Eliason, "Four Old English Cryptographic Riddles," *SP* 49 (1952): 554-56.

Thomas A. Reisner, *Expl* 28 (May 1970): 78.

Exeter Book, Riddle 83
"Frod wæs min fromcynn"

Marie Nelson, "The Rhetoric of the Exeter Book Riddles," *Speculum* 49 (1974): 426-28.

Exeter Book, Riddle 85
"Nis min sele swige, ne ic sylfa hlud"

John F. Adams, "The Anglo-Saxon Riddle as Lyric Mode," *Criticism* 7 (Fall 1965): 340-41.

Marie Nelson, "The Paradox of Silent Speech in the Exeter Book Riddles," *Neophil* 62 (October 1978): 610-11.

Exeter Book, Riddle 91
"Min heafod is homere geþuren"

Edith Whitehurst Williams, "What's So New about the Sexual Revolution?" *TQ* 18 (Summer 1975): 51-54.

Exeter Book, Riddle 92
"Ic wæs brunra beot, beam on holte"

Williamson, *A Feast of Creatures*, 10-11, 214-15.

Exeter Book, Riddle 95
"Ic eom indryhten ond eorlum cuð"

E. S. Kiernan, "Cwene: The Old Profession of Exeter Riddle 95," *MP* 72 (May 1975): 384-89.

"An Exhortation to Christian Living"

Hansen, *The Solomon Complex*, 102-8.

Exodus

Daniel G. Calder, "Two Notes on the Typology of the OE *Exodus*," *NM* 74 (1973): 85-89.

J. E. Cross and S. I. Tucker, "Allegorical Tradition and the Old English *Exodus*," *Neophil* 44 (1960): 122-27.

James W. Earl, "Christian Traditions in the Old English *Exodus*," *NM* 71 (1970): 541-70.

Robert T. Farrell, "A Reading of OE *Exodus*," *RES*, n.s. 20 (1969): 401-17.

Paul F. Ferguson, "Noah, Abraham, and the Crossing of the Red Sea," *Neophil* 65 (April 1981): 282-87.

Greenfield and Calder, *A New Critical History*, 212-16.

J. R. Hall, "The Building of the Temple in *Exodus*: Design for Typology," *Neophil* 59 (October 1975): 616-21.

J. R. Hall, *Expl* 39 (Spring 1981): 26-27.

J. R. Hall, *Expl* 41 (Summer 1983): 2-3.

J. R. Hall, "'Niwe Flodas': Old English 'Exodus' 362," *N&Q* 22 (June 1975): 243-44.

Stanley R. Hauer, "The Patriarchal Digression in the Old English *Exodus*, Lines 362-446," *SP* 78 (Early Winter 1981): 77-90.

William Helder, "Etham and the Ethiopians in the Old English *Exodus*," *AnM* 16 (1975): 5-23.

Hermann, *Allegories of War*, 57-89.

John P. Hermann, "The Selection of Warriors in the Old English *Exodus*, Lines 233-240A," *ELN* 14 (September 1976): 1-5.

Thomas D. Hill, "The *Virga* of Moses and the Old English *Exodus*," in *Old English Literature in Context*, ed. John D. Niles (Cambridge: D. S. Brewer; Totowa, N.J.: Rowman and Littlefield, 1980), 57-65.

Huppé, *Doctrine and Poetry*, 220-23.

Edward Burroughs Irving, Jr., "*Exodus* Retraced," in Burlin and Irving, *Old English Studies*, 203-23.

Edward Burroughs Irving, Jr., "Introduction" to *The Old English "Exodus"* (New Haven, Conn.: Yale University Press, 1953), 28-35.

Isaacs, *Structural Principles in Old English Poetry*, 151-59.

Kennedy, *The Earliest English Poetry*, 175-83.

Lee, *The Guest-Hall*, 41-48 and *passim*.

Peter J. Lucas, "The Cloud in the Interpretation of the Old English *Exodus*," *ES* 51 (August 1970): 297-311.

Peter J. Lucas, "Old English Christian Poetry: The Cross in *Exodus*," in *Famulus Christi: Essays in Commemoration of the Thirteenth Centenary of the Birth of the Venerable Bede*, ed. Gerald Banner (London: SPCK, 1976), 193-209.

Maxwell Luria, "The Old English *Exodus* as a Christian Poem: Notes Toward a Reading," *Neophil* 65 (October 1981): 600-606.

Ellen E. Martin, "Allegory and the African Woman in the Old English *Exodus*," *JEGP* 81 (1982): 1-15.

Phillip Rollinson, "Some Kinds of Meaning in Old English Poetry," *AnM* 11 (1970): 16-18.

Swanton, *English Literature*, 84-93.

Zacharias P. Thundy, "*Afisc Meowle* and the Old English *Exodus*," *Neophil* 64 (April 1980): 297-306.

Richard M. Trask, "Doomsday Imagery in the Old English *Exodus*," *Neophil* 57 (July 1973): 295-97.

John F. Vickrey, "'Exodus' and the Battle in the Sea," *Traditio* 28 (1972): 119-40.

John F. Vickrey,"'Exodus' and the 'Herba Humilis,'" *Traditio* 31 (1975): 25-54.

John F. Vickrey, "*Exodus* and the Robe of Joseph," *SP* 86 (Winter 1989): 1-17.

John F. Vickrey, "*Exodus* and the Treasure of Pharoah," *ASE* 1 (1972): 159-65.

"The Fair Maid of Ribblesdale"

Bennett, *Middle English Literature*, 401-2.

T. L. Burton, "'The Fair Maid of Ribblesdale' and the Problem of Parody," *EIC* 31 (October 1981): 282-98.

Michael J. Franklin, "'Fyngres heo haþ feir to folde': Trothplight in Some of the Love Lyrics of MS Harley 2253," *MÆ* 55 (1986): 179-80.

David Jauss, "The Ironic Use of Medieval Poetic Conventions in 'The Fair Maid of Ribblesdale,'" *Neophil* 67 (April 1983): 293-304.

F. Jones, "A Note on *Harley Lyrics* 7," *NM* 87 (1986): 142-43.

Daniel J. Ransom, *Poets at Play: Irony and Parody in the Harley Lyrics* (Norman, Okla.: Pilgrim Books, 1985), 49-63.

Swanton, *English Literature*, 243-45.

The Fight at Finnsburh

Swanton, *English Literature*, 45-49.

Floris and Blauncheflour

G. Barnes, "Cunning and Ingenuity in the Middle English *Floris and Blauncheflur*," *MÆ* 53 (1984): 10-24.

Ramsey, *Chivalric Romances*, 114-18.

Edmund Reiss, "Symbolic Detail in Medieval Narrative: *Floris and Blancheflour*," *PLL* 7 (1971): 339-50.

Swanton, *English Literature*, 216-25.

Karl P. Wentersdorf, "Iconographic Elements in *Floris and Blancheflour*," *AnM* 20 (1981): 76-96.

"Floure and the Leafe"

Alexandra T. Barratt, "'The Flower and the Leaf' and 'The Assembly of Ladies': Is There a (Sexual) Difference?" *PQ* 66 (1987): 1-24.

Davidoff, *Beginning Well*, 159-65.

David V. Harrington, "The Function of Allegory in the *Flower and the Leaf*," *NM* 71 (1970): 244-53.

D. A. Pearsall, "Introduction" to *The Floure and the Leafe and The Assembly of Ladies* (Nashville, Tenn.: Thomas Nelson & Sons, 1962; reprint, Manchester: Manchester University Press, 1980), 29-52.

"For Ou That Is So Feir ant Brist"

Manning, *Wisdom and Number*, 126-31, 172.

"For a Swarm of Bees"

Greenfield, *A Critical History*, 194.

Greenfield and Calder, *A New Critical History*, 256.

Marie Nelson, "'Wordsige and Worcsige': Speech Acts in Three Old English Charms," *Lang&S* 17 (Winter 1984): 57-59.

The Fortunes of Men

Greenfield and Calder, *A New Critical History*, 263-64.

Raw, *The Art and Background of Old English Poetry* , 73-74.

Shippey, *Poems of Wisdom and Learning*, 10-11.

"For Unfruitful Land"

Marie Nelson, "'Wordsige and Worcsige': Speech Acts in Three Old English Charms," *Lang&S* 17 (Winter 1984): 59-63.

Fouke Fitzwarin

Ramsey, *Chivalric Romances*, 89-93.

"Foweles in þe Frith"

Howell D. Chickering, Jr., "'Foweles in the frith': A Religious Art-Song," *PQ* 50 (January 1971): 115-20.

Daiches, *A Study of Literature*, 151-52.

Dronke, *The Medieval Lyric*, 144-45.

Fowler, *The Bible in Middle English Literature*, 83-84.

David Luisi, *Expl* 25 (February 1967): 47

Thomas C. Moser, Jr., "'And I Mon Waxe Wod': The Middle English 'Foweles in the Frith,'" *PMLA* 102 (1987): 326-37.

Richard H. Osberg, "Collocation and Theme in the Middle English Lyric 'Foweles in þe Frith,'" *MLQ* 46 (June 1985): 115-27.

Reiss, *The Art of the Middle English Lyric, 18-22.*

Edmund Reiss, "A Critical Approach to the Middle English Lyrics," *CE* 27 (February 1966): 376-77.

"The Fox and the Wolf"

Sacvan Bercovitch, "Clerical Satire in þe *Vox and* þe *Wolf*," *JEGP* 65 (1966): 287-94.

Boitani, *English Medieval Narrative*, 30-32.

Franks Casket Poems

Marijane Osborn, "The Grammar of the Inscription on the Franks Casket, Right Side," *NM* 73 (1972): 663-71.

Marijane Osborn, "The Picture-poem on the Front of the Franks Casket," *NM* 75 (1974): 50-65.

"Gabriel, Fram Evene-King"

Swanton, *English Literature*, 250-52.

Weber, *Theology and Poetry in the Middle English Lyric*, 32-46.

Gamelyn

Ramsey, *Chivalric Romances*, 93-95.

Genesis

Lee, *The Guest-Hall*, 17-41 and *passim*.

Thomas H. Ohlgren, "The Illustrations of the Cædmonian Genesis: Literary Criticism Through Art," *M&H*, n.s. 3 (1972): 199-212.

Geoffrey Shepherd, "Scriptural Poetry," in Stanley, *Continuations and Beginnings*, 24-30.

Swanton, *English Literature*, 77-84.

Genesis A

Bennett A. Brockman, "'Heroic' and 'Christian' in *Genesis A*: The Evidence of the Cain and Abel Episode," *MLQ* 35 (1974): 115-28.

Alan Crozier, "Old English *Drēogan*," *ES* 68 (1987): 297-304.

Gardner, *The Construction of Christian Poetry in Old English*, 18-32.

J. R. Hall, *Expl* 35 (Spring 1977): 17.

Constance B. Hieatt, "Divisions: Theme and Structure of *Genesis A*," *NM* 81 (1980): 243-51.

Huppé, *Doctrine and Poetry*, 131-216.

Genesis B

Pat Belanoff, "The Fall (?) of the Old English Female Poetic Image," *PMLA* 104 (1989): 822-31.

Michael Benskin, "An Argument for an Interpolation in the Old English *Later Genesis*," *NM* 72 (1971): 224-45.

G. C. Britton, "Repetition and Contrast in the Old English Later Genesis," *Neophil* 58 (January 1974): 66-73.

Susan Burchmore, "Traditional Exegesis and the Question of Guilt in the Old English 'Genesis B,'" *Traditio* 41 (1985): 117-44.

Chance, *Woman as Hero*, 65-79.

Karen Cherewatuk, "Standing, Turning, Twisting, Falling: Posture and Moral Stance in 'Genesis B,'" *NM* 87 (1986): 537-44.

Cherniss, *Ingeld and Christ*, 151-70.

Rachel Crabtree, "Ladders and Lines of Connection in Anglo-Saxon Religious Art and Literature," in Stokes and Burton, *Medieval Literature*, 45-51.

Kathleen E. Dubs, "*Genesis B*: A Study in Grace," *ABR* 33 (March 1982): 47-64.

Margaret J. Ehrhart, "Tempter as Teacher: Some Observations on the Vocabulary of the Old English *Genesis B*," *Neophil* 59 (July 1975): 435-46.

Robert Emmett Finnegan, "Eve and 'Vincible Ignorance' in *Genesis B*," *TSLL* 18 (Summer 1976): 329-39.

Robert Emmett Finnegan, *Expl* 37 (Summer 1979): 20-21.

Gardner, *The Construction of Christian Poetry in Old English*, 32-34.

Greenfield and Calder, *A New Critical History*, 209-12.

J. R. Hall, "Duality and the Dual Pronoun in *Genesis B*," *PLL* 17 (Spring 1981): 139-145.

J. R. Hall, "*Geongordom* and *Hyldo* in *Genesis B*: Serving the Lord for the Lord's Favor," *PLL* 11 (Summer 1975): 302-7.

John P. Hermann, "The Recurrent Motifs of Spiritual Warfare in Old English Poetry," *AnM* 22 (1982): 26-28.

Thomas D. Hill, "The Fall of Angels and Man in the Old English *Genesis B*," in Nicholson and Frese, *Anglo-Saxon Poetry*, 279-90.

Eric Jager, "A *Miles Diaboli* in the Old English *Genesis B*," *ELN* 27 (March 1990): 1-5.

Eric Jager, "Tempter as Rhetoric Teacher: The Fall of Language in the Old English *Genesis B*," *Neophil* 72 (July 1988): 434-48.

Kennedy, *The Earliest English Poetry*, 164-70.

Anne K. Klinck, "Female Characterisation in Old English Poetry and the Growth of Psychological Realism: *Genesis B* and *Christ I*," *Neophil* 63 (October 1979): 598-601.

Alain Renoir, "The Self-Deception of Temptation: Boethian Psychology in *Genesis B*," in *Old English Poetry: Fifteen Essays*, ed. Robert P. Creed (Providence, R.I.: Brown University Press, 1967): 47-67.

Eric Smith, *Some Versions of the Fall: The Myth of the Fall of Man in English Literature* (Pittsburgh, Penn.: University of Pittsburgh, 1973), 69-91.

John F. Vickrey, "The Vision of Eve in *Genesis B*," *Speculum* 44 (1969): 86-102.

The Gest Hystoriale of the Destruction of Troy

Richmond, *The Popularity*, 29-34.

"A Gest of Robyn Hode"

Jess B. Bessinger, Jr., "*The Gest of Robin Hood* Revisited," in Benson, *The Learned and the Lewed*, 355-69.

Dean A. Hoffman, "'With the Shot Y Wyll/Alle Thy Lustes to Full-fyl': Archery as Symbol in the Early Ballads of Robin Hood," *NM* 86 (1985): 498-500.

David Parker, "Popular Protest in 'A Gest of Robyn Hode,'" *MLQ* 32 (March 1971): 3-20.

The Gifts of Men

Greenfield and Calder, *A New Critical History*, 262-63.

Raw, *The Art and Background of Old English Poetry* , 69-73.

Douglas D. Short, "*Leoþocræftas* and the Pauline Analogy of the Body in the Old English *Gifts of Men*," *Neophil* 59 (July 1975): 463-65.

Douglas D. Short, "The Old English 'Gifts of Men,' Line 13," *MP* 71 (May 1974): 388-89.

"Gif Wif Ne Mæge Bearn Beran"

George Hardin Brown, "Solving the 'Solve' Riddle in B. L. MS Harley 585," *Viator* 18 (1987): 45-51.

"Glade Us Maiden, Moder Milde"

Weber, *Theology and Poetry in the Middle English Lyric*, 156-64.

Golagrus and Gawain

W. R. J. Barron, "Arthurian Romances: Traces of an English Tradition," *ES* 61 (February 1980): 14-17.

"Gold and Al This Werdis Wyn"

Reiss, *The Art of the Middle English Lyric*, 132-36.

"The Grave"

Lee, *The Guest-Hall*, 153-55.

Douglas D. Short, "Aesthetics and Unpleasantness: Classical Rhetoric in the Medieval English Lyric *The Grave*," *SN* 48 (1976): 291-99.

Guthlac

John P. Hermann, "The Recurrent Motifs of Spiritual Warfare in Old English Poetry," *AnM* 22 (1982): 20-24.

Alexandra Hennessey Olsen, *Guthlac of Croyland: A Study of Heroic Hagiography* (Washington, D.C.: University Press of America, 1981), 111-34.

Guthlac A

Bridges, *Generic Contrast*, 36-47, 117-46.

Daniel G. Calder, "*Guthlac A* and *Guthlac B*: Some Discriminations," in Nicholson and Frese, *Anglo-Saxon Poetry*, 65-80.

Cherniss, *Ingeld and Christ*, 226-33.

Kathleen E. Dubs, "*Guthlac A* and the Acquisition of Wisdom," *Neophil* 65 (October 1981): 607-13.

Greenfield, *A Critical History*, 119-20.

Greenfield and Calder, *A New Critical History*, 176-77.

Thomas D. Hill, "The Age of Man and the World in the Old English *Guthlac A*," *JEGP* 80 (1981): 13-21.

Thomas D. Hill, "The Middle Way: *Idel-Wuldor* and *Egesa* in the Old English Guthlac A," *RES*, n.s. 30 (May 1979): 182-87.

Kennedy, *The Earliest English Poetry*, 250-55.

Lee, *The Guest-Hall*, 103-9.

Frances Randall Lipp, "*Guthlac A*: An Interpretation," *MS* 33 (1971): 46-62.

Alexandra Hennessey Olsen, *Guthlac of Croyland: A Study of Heroic Hagiography* (Washington, D.C.: University Press of America, 1981), 15-67.

Paul F. Reichardt, "*Guthlac A* and the Landscape of Spiritual Perfection," *Neophil* 58 (July 1974): 331-38.

Jane Roberts, "Introduction" to *The Guthlac Poems of the Exeter Book* (Oxford: Clarendon Press, 1979), 29-36.

Schaar, *Critical Studies*, 143-46.

Laurence K. Shook, [C. S. B.,] "The Burial Mound in *Guthlac A*," *MP* 58 (1960): 1-10.

Laurence K. Shook, C. S. B., "The Prologue of the Old-English 'Guthlac *A*,'" *MS* 23 (1961): 294-304.

Robert D. Stevick, "The Length of *Guthlac A*," *Viator* 13 (1982): 15-48.

Swanton, *English Literature*, 145-54.

Karl P. Wentersdorf, "*Guthlac A*: The Battle for the *Beorg*," *Neophil* 62 (January 1978): 135-42.

Charles D. Wright, "The Three Temptations and the Seven Gifts of the Holy Spirit in 'Guthlac A,' 160b-169," *Traditio* 38 (1982): 341-43.

Guthlac B

Frederick M. Biggs, "Unities in the Old English *Guthlac B*," *JEGP* 89 (1990): 155-65.

Bridges, *Generic Contrast*, 48-55, 147-78.

Daniel G. Calder, "*Guthlac A* and *Guthlac B*: Some Discriminations," in Nicholson and Frese, *Anglo-Saxon Poetry*, 65-80.

Daniel G. Calder, "Theme and Strategy in *Guthlac B*," *PLL* 8 (Summer 1972): 227-42.

Greenfield and Calder, *A New Critical History*, 177-79.

Thomas D. Hill, "The Typology of the Week and the Numerical Structure of the Old English *Guthlac B*," *MS* 37 (1975): 531-36.

Kennedy, *The Earliest English Poetry*, 255-59.

Lee, *The Guest-Hall*, 109-13.

Sally Mussetter, "Type as Prophet in the Old English *Guthlac B*," *Viator* 14 (1983): 41-58.

Alexandra Hennessey Olsen, *Guthlac of Croyland: A Study of Heroic Hagiography* (Washington, D.C.: University Press of America 1981), 69-109.

Alexandra Hennessey Olsen, "Guthlac on the Beach," *Neophil* 64 (April 1980): 290-95.

Jane Roberts, "Introduction" to *The Guthlac Poems of the Exeter Book* (Oxford: Clarendon Press, 1979), 43-48.

James L. Rosier, "Death and Transfiguration: *Guthlac B*," in *Philological Essays: Studies in Old and Middle English Language and Literature in Honour of Herbert Dean Merritt*, ed. James L. Rosier (The Hague and Paris: Mouton, 1970), 82-92.

Schaar, *Critical Studies*, 146-48.

Guy of Warwick

Barron, *English Medieval Romance*, 74-80.

David N. Klausner, "Didacticism and Drama in *Guy of Warwick*," *M&H*, n.s. 6 (1975): 103-19.

Mehl, *The Middle English Romances*, 220-27.

Ramsey, *Chivalric Romances*, 45-68 and *passim*.

Richmond, *The Popularity*, 149-93.

"Haile Be Thu, Mari, Maiden Bright"

Manning, *Wisdom and Number*, 75-77.

"Half-Waking, Half-Sleeping"

Thomas D. Hill, "'Half-Waking, Half-Sleeping': A Tropological Motif in a Middle English Lyric and Its European Context," *RES*, n.s. 29 (February 1978): 50-56.

"Hand by Hand We Shall Us Take"

Fowler, *The Bible in Middle English Literature*, 59-60.

Havelok the Dane

Barron, *English Medieval Romance*, 69-74.

Boitani, *English Medieval Narrative*, 50-52.

John M. Ganim, *Style and Consciousness in Middle English Narrative* (Princeton, N.J.: Princeton University Press, 1983), 16-37 and *passim*.

Robert W. Hanning, "*Havelock the Dane*: Structure, Symbols, Meaning," *SP* 64 (July 1967): 586-605.

Dayton Haskin, S. J., "Food, Clothing and Kingship in *Havelok the Dane*," *ABR* 24 (June 1973): 204-13.

Mehl, *The Middle English Romances*, 161-72.

Maldwyn Mills, "Havelok and the Brutal Fisherman," *MÆ* 36 (1967): 219-30.

Maldwyn Mills, "Havelok's Return," *MÆ* 46 (1976): 20-35.

Ramsey, *Chivalric Romances*, 26-43 and *passim*.

Schmidt and Jacobs, *Medieval English Romances*, Vol. 2, 7-15.

Spearing, *Readings in Medieval Poetry*, 43-55.

Speirs, *Medieval English Poetry*, 191-200.

D. Staines, "*Havelok the Dane*: A Thirteenth-century Handbook for Princes," *Speculum* 51 (1976): 602-23.

Swanton, *English Literature*, 195-203.

Judith Weiss, "Structure and Characterisation in *Havelok the Dane*," *Speculum* 44 (1969): 247-57.

"Hayl Mari!/Hic Am Sori"

Woolf, *The English Religious Lyric*, 120-24.

"He Bare Him Vp, He Bare Hym Down"

Manning, *Wisdom and Number*, 115-18.

"He Iesus Is Myth"

Wenzel, *Preachers, Poets*, 212-14.

"Herodes, Thou Wikked Fo"

Manning, *Wisdom and Number*, 118-20, 132.

"He Yaf Himself as Good Felowe"

Manning, *Wisdom and Number*, 121-22.

"Heyl Be Thou, Marie, Milde Quene of Hevene"

Weber, *Theology and Poetry in the Middle English Lyric*, 182-86.

"Heȝe Louerd, Thou Here My Bone"

Manning, *Wisdom and Number*, 51-55.

"Hi Sike, Al Wan Hi Singe"

John E. Hallwas, "The Two Versions of 'Hi Sike, Al Wan Hi Singe,'" *NM* 77 (1976): 360-64.

"Homiletic Fragment I"

Greenfield and Calder, *A New Critical History*, 267-68.

Isaacs, *Structural Principles in Old English Poetry*, 99-106.

Phillip Pulsiano, "Bees and Backbiters in the Old English *Homiletic Fragment I*," *ELN* 25 (December 1987): 1-6.

"Homiletic Fragment II"

Anderson, *Two Literary Riddles*, 136-38.

Greenfield and Calder, *A New Critical History*, 267.

Joseph S. Wittig, "'Homiletic Fragment II' and the Epistle to the Ephesians," *Traditio* 25 (1969): 358-63.

"How Christ Shall Come"

Fowler, *The Bible in Middle English Literature*," 126-27.

"The Hunting of the Cheviot"

Douglas Hamer, "Towards Restoring *The Hunting of the Cheviot*," *RES*, n.s. 20 (February 1969): 1-21.

"The Husband's Message"

Earl R. Anderson, "The Husband's Message: Persuasion and the Problem of Genre," *ES* 56 (August 1975): 289-94.

Anderson, *Two Literary Riddles*, 144-63.

Earl R. Anderson, "Voices in 'The Husband's Message,'" *NM* 74 (1973): 238-46.

A. C. Bouman, *Patterns in Old English and Old Icelandic Literature* (Leiden: Universitaire Pers Leiden, 1962), 61-72.

Crossley-Holland and Mitchell, *The Battle of Maldon*, 88-89.

Gardner, *The Construction of Christian Poetry in Old English*, 52.

Margaret E. Goldsmith, "The Enigma of *The Husband's Message*," in Nicholson and Frese, *Anglo-Saxon Poetry*, 247-63.

Greenfield, *Hero and Exile*, 120-22.

Stanley B. Greenfield, *The Interpretation of Old English Poems* (London: Routledge & Kegan Paul, 1972), 145-54.

Stanley B. Greenfield, "The Old English Elegies," in Stanley, *Continuations and Beginnings*, 169-71.

D. R. Howlett, "'The Wife's Lament' and 'The Husband's Message,'" *NM* 79 (1978): 7-10.

Robert E. Kaske, "A Poem of the Cross in *The Exeter Book*: 'Riddle 60' and 'The Husband's Message,'" *Traditio* 23 (1967): 41-71.

Kennedy, *The Earliest English Poetry*, 121-26.

Anne L. Klinck, "The Old English Elegy as a Genre," *ESC* 10 (June 1984): 129-40.

Peter Orton, "The Speaker in *The Husband's Message*," *LeedsSE*, n.s. 12, *Essays in Honour of A. C. Cowley*, ed. Peter Meredith (1981), 43-56.

M. J. Swanton, "*The Wife's Lament* and *The Husband's Message*: A Reconsideration," *Anglia* 82 (1964): 269-90.

L. Whitbread, "The Pattern of Misfortune in *Deor* and Other Old English Poems," *Neophil* 54 (April 1970): 176, 178.

"I Am a Fol, I Can No God"

John E. Hallwas, "The Identity of the Speaker in 'I am a fol, i can no god,'" *PLL* 10 (Fall 1974): 415-17.

"I am Iesu, That Cum to Fith"

John E. Hallwas, *Expl* 32 (March 1974): 51.

"Ich Am of Irlaunde"

J. A. Burrow, "Poems Without Contexts: The Rawlinson Lyrics," *EIC* 29 (1979): 18-20. Reprinted in Burrow, *Essays on Medieval Literature*, 13-16.

Norman Holland, *Expl* 15 (June 1957): 5. Reprinted in *The Explicator Cyclopedia* 2: 3-4.

Speirs, *Medieval English Poetry*, 60-61.

"Iesu Cristes Milde Moder"

Weber, *Theology and Poetry in the Middle English Lyric*, 137-45.

"If Man Him Biəocte"

Oliver, *Poems without Names*, 113-14.

"I Have Laborede Sore and Suffered Deyȝth"

Manning, *Wisdom and Number*, 46.

"I Have a Lady Where So She Be"

Jan Ziolkowski, "Avatars of Ugliness in Medieval Literature," *MLR* 79 (January 1984): 14-15.

"I Herd an Harping on a Hille"

Margaret Emblom, "'I Herd an Harping on a Hille': Its Text and Context," in *Proceedings of the Illinois Medieval Association*, ed. Roberta Bux Bosse *et al.* (Macomb, Ill.: IMA, 1984), 49-61.

"Ihesu for Thy Holy Name"

John C. Hirsh, "A Fifteenth-Century Commentary on 'Ihesu for thy holy name,'" *N&Q* 17 (February 1970): 44-45.

"Ihesu, Swete Sone Dere"

Woolf, *The English Religious Lyric*, 152-54.

"In All This Worlde Ys None So Tru"

Oliver, *Poems without Names*, 30.

"In þe Ceson of Huge Mortalite"

Woolf, *The English Religious Lyric*, 328-30.

"In a Fryht as Y Con Fare Fremede"

Michael J. Franklin, "'Fyngres heo haþ feir to folde': Trothplight in Some of the Love Lyrics of MS Harley 2253," *MÆ* 55 (1986): 181-82.

Rosemary Woolf, "The Construction of 'In a Fryht as Y Con Fare Fremede,'" *MÆ* 38 (1969): 55-59. Reprinted in Woolf, *Art and Doctrine*, 125-30.

"In May Hit Murgeth When Hit Dawes"

Andrew J. Howell, "Reading the Harley Lyrics: A Master Poet and the Language of Conventions," *ELH* 47 (1980): 635-39.

"Instructions for Christians"

Hansen, *The Solomon Complex*, 108-14.

"In Summer Before the Ascension"

Fowler, *The Bible in Middle English Literature*, 99.

"In That Blisful Bearnes Buirde"

Dronke, *The Medieval Lyric*, 67.

"In a þestri Stude"

Woolf, *The English Religious Lyric*, 97-98.

"In a Tabernacle of Atoure"

J. E. Cross, "The Virgin's *Quia Amore Langueo*," *NM* 73 (1972): 37-44.

"In a Valey of þis Restles Mynde"

Bennett, *Middle English Literature*, 382-83.

Davidoff, *Beginning Well*, 179-80.

Gray, *Themes and Images*, 143-44.

Thomas D. Hill, "Androgyny and Conversion in the Middle English Lyric 'In the Vaile of Restles Mynd,'" *ELH* 53 (1986): 459-70.

Manning, *Wisdom and Number*, 59-62.

Speirs, *Medieval English Poetry*, 80-81.

Mary-Ann Stouck, "'In a valey of þis restles mynde': Contexts and Meaning," *MP* 85 (August 1987): 1-11.

Woolf, *The English Religious Lyric*, 187-91.

Ipomedon

Schmidt and Jacobs, *Medieval English Romances*, Vol. 2, 40-49.

Ipomedon A

Mehl, *The Middle English Romances*, 58-68.

Ipomedon B

Mehl, *The Middle English Romances*, 58-68.

"I Sayh Hym Wiþ Fless al Bi-sprad"

Thomas D. Hill, "The Middle English Lyric 'How Christ Shall Come': An Interpretation," *MÆ* 52 (1983): 239-46.

Manning, *Wisdom and Number*, 19-21.

Reiss, *The Art of the Middle English Lyric*, 116-22.

"I Seche a Youthe"

John C. Hirsh, "'I Seche a Youthe': A Late Middle English Lyric," *ELN* 17 (March 1980): 163-65.

The Isle of Ladies or *The Ile of Pleasaunce*

Anthony Jenkins, "Introduction" to *The Isle of Ladies or The Ile of Pleasaunce* (New York and London: Garland Publishing, 1980), 31-52.

"I Syng of a Myden That Is Makeles"

Derek Brewer, *English Gothic Literature* (London and Basingstoke: Macmillan, 1983), 50-52.

Fowler, *The Bible in Middle English Literature*, 57-58.

Gray, *Themes and Images*, 102-6.

David G. Halliburton, "The Myden Makeles," *PLL* 4 (Spring 1968): 115-20.

Thomas Jemielity, "'I Sing of a Maiden': God's Courting of Mary," *CP* 2 (Spring 1969): 53-59.

Stephen Manning, "I Syng of a Myden," *PMLA* 75 (1960): 8-12.

Manning, *Wisdom and Number*, 158-67.

Reiss, *The Art of the Middle English Lyric*, 158-64.

Speirs, *Medieval English Poetry*, 67-69.

Leo Spitzer, "*Explication de Texte* Applied to Three Great Middle English Poems," in Spitzer, *Essays on English and American Literature by Leo Spitzer*, 233-46.

Weber, *Theology and Poetry in the Middle English Lyric*, 55-60.

Woolf, *The English Religious Lyric*, 287.

"It Was on a Holy Thursday That Our Lord Arose"

Fowler, *The Bible in Middle English Literature*, 86-88.

"I Walk with Sorrow"

Swanton, *English Literature*, 238-41.

"I Wende to Dede"

Oliver, *Poems without Names*, 107-8.

Reiss, *The Art of the Middle English Lyric*, 152-56.

"I Wolde Witen of Sum Wys Wiht"

Gray, *Themes and Images*, 212-26.

"Jacob and Joseph"

Oscar Sherwin, "Art's Spring-Birth: The Ballad of Iacob and Iosep," *SP* 42 (January 1945): 1-18.

"Joly Jankyn"

J. D. W. Crowther, "The Middle English Lyric 'Joly Jankyn,'" *AnM* 12 (1971): 123-25.

"A Journey Charm"

Marie Nelson, "'Wordsige and Worcsige': Speech Acts in Three Old English Charms," *Lang&S* 17 (Winter 1984): 63-64.

Heather Stuart, "'Ic me on þisse gyrde beluce': The Structure and Meaning of the Old English *Journey Charm*," *MÆ* 50 (1981): 259-73.

Judas

Donald G. Schueler, "The Middle English *Judas*: An Interpretation," *PMLA* 91 (1976): 840-45.

Mary-Ann Stouck, "A Reading of the Middle English *Judas*," *JEGP*, 80 (1981): 188-98.

Judgment Day I

Anderson, *Two Literary Riddles*, 99-108.

Graham D. Caie, *The Judgment Day Theme in Old English Poetry* (Copenhagen: Nova, 1976), 95-114.

Karma Lochrie, "The Structure and Wisdom of *Judgment Day I*," *NM* 87 (1986): 201-10.

Karma Lochrie, "*Wyrd* and the Limits of Human Understanding: A Thematic Sequence in the *Exeter Book*," *JEGP* 85 (1986): 323-31.

Judgment Day II

Graham D. Caie, *The Judgment Day Theme in Old English Poetry* (Copenhagen: Nova, 1976), 95-114.

Greenfield, *A Critical History*, 133-35.

Greenfield and Calder, *A New Critical History*, 238-40.

Richard L. Hoffman, "Structure and Symbolism in the *Judgment Day II*," *Neophil* 52 (April 1968): 170-78.

Richard L. Hoffman, "The Theme of *Judgment Day II*," *ELN* 6 (March 1969): 161-64.

Lee, *The Guest-Hall*, 79-80.

Judith

Jackson J. Campbell, "Schematic Technique in *Judith*," *ELH* 38 (1971): 155-72.

Chance, *Woman as Hero*, 36-40.

James F. Doubleday, "The Principle of Contrast in *Judith*," *NM* 72 (1971): 436-41.

Donald K. Fry, "The Heroine on the Beach in *Judith*," *NM* 68 (1967): 168-84.

Donald K. Fry, "Type-Scene Composition in *Judith*," *AnM* 12 (1971): 110-19.

Fredrik J. Heinemann, "*Judith* 266-291a: A Mock Heroic Approach-to-Battle Type Scene," *NM* 71 (1970): 83-96.

Hermann, *Allegories of War*, 173-98.

John P. Hermann, "The Theme of Spiritual Warfare in the Old English *Judith*," *PQ* 55 (Winter 1976): 1-9.

Huppé, *The Web of Words*, 136-89.

R. E. Kaske, "*Sapientia et Fortitudo* in the Old English *Judith*," in Benson and Wenzel, *The Wisdom of Poetry*, 13-29.

Lee, *The Guest-Hall*, 48-50 and *passim*.

Hugh Magennis, "Adaptation of Biblical Detail in the Old English *Judith*: The Feast Scene," *NM* 84 (1983): 331-37.

Alexandra Hennessey Olsen, "Inversion and Political Purpose in the Old English *Judith*," *ES* 65 (August 1982): 289-93.

Ian Pringle, "'Judith': The Homily and the Poem," *Traditio* 31 (1975): 83-97.

Alain Renoir, "*Judith* and the Limits of Poetry," *ES* 43 (1962): 145-55.

Swanton, *English Literature*, 155-65.

"Kemp Owyne"

Ribner and Morris, *Poetry*, 112-14.

King Hart

Sheila Delany, "*King Hart*: Rhetoric and Meaning in a Middle Scots Allegory," *Neophil* 55 (July 1971): 328-41.

King Horn

Barron, *English Medieval Romance*, 65-69, 72-74.

Boitani, *English Medieval Narrative*, 48-50.

D. M. Hill, "An Interpretation of *King Horn*," *Anglia* 75 (1957): 157-72.

Mary Hynes-Berry, "Cohesion in *King Horn* and *Sir Orfeo*," *Speculum* 50 (1975): 652-54, 656-63.

Timothy D. O'Brien, "Word Play in the Allegory of *King Horn*," *Allegorica* 7 (Winter 1982): 110-22.

Ramsey, *Chivalric Romances*, 26-43 *passim*.

Anne Scott, "Plans, Predictions, and Promises: Traditional Story Techniques and the Configuration of Word and Deed in *King Horn*," in *Studies in Medieval English Romances: Some New Approaches*, ed. Derek Brewer (Cambridge: D. S. Brewer, 1988), 37-68.

Spearing, *Readings in Medieval Poetry*, 28-43.

Speirs, *Medieval English Poetry*, 178-91.

Anne Wilson, *Traditional Romance and Tale: How Stories Mean* (Cambridge and Ipswich: D. S. Brewer, 1976), 59-62.

Georgianna Ziegler, "Structural Repetition in *King Horn*," *NM* 81 (1980): 403-8.

The King of Tars

Ramsey, *Chivalric Romances*, 216-18.

"Kyndeli Is Now Mi Coming"

Oliver, *Poems without Names*, 47-48.

Kyng Alisaunder

Richmond, *The Popularity*, 35-42.

The Land of Cockayne

Boitani, *English Medieval Narrative*, 32-33.

Clifford Davidson, "The Sins of the Flesh in the Fourteenth-Century Middle English 'Land of Cokaygne,'" *BSUF* 11 (Autumn 1970): 21-26.

Le Bone Florence of Rome

Anne Thompson Lee, "*Le Bone Florence of Rome*: A Middle English Adaptation of a French Romance," in Benson, *The Learned and the Lewed*, 343-54.

Mehl, *The Middle English Romances*, 140-46.

Legend of the Seven Sleepers

Hugh Magennis, "Style and Method in the Old English Version of the *Legend of the Seven Sleepers*," *ES* 66 (August 1985): 285-95.

"Lenten Ys Come with Loue to Toune"

Peter Heidtmann, "The *Reverdie* Convention and 'Lenten Is Come with Love to Toune,'" *AnM* 12 (1971): 83-89.

Andrew J. Howell, "Reading the Harley Lyrics: A Master Poet and the Language of Conventions," *ELH* 47 (1980): 621-35.

Reiss, *The Art of the Middle English Lyric*, 66-73.

Swanton, *English Literature*, 241-43.

"Ler to Louen as I Loue The"

Manning, *Wisdom and Number*, 48-49.

"Leuedi Sainte Marie, Moder and Meide"

Manning, *Wisdom and Number*, 42.

"Levedi, for Thare Blisse! That Thu Heddest at the Frume"

Weber, *Theology and Poetry in the Middle English Lyric*, 167-74, 186-91.

Libeas Desconus

Stephen Thomas Knight, "The Social Function of the Middle English Romances, in Aers, *Medieval Literature*, 105-8.

Anne Wilson, *Traditional Romance and Tale: How Stories Mean* (Cambridge and Ipswich: D. S. Brewer, 1976), 85-88.

"Littel Geste of Robyn Hode and his Meiny"

Maurice Keen, *The Outlaws of Medieval Legend* (Toronto: University of Toronto Press, 1961), 100-115.

"Lo! Lemman Swete, Now May þou Se"

Woolf, *The English Religious Lyric*, 49-50.

"London Lickpenny"

Moore, *The Secular Lyric in Middle English*, 164-65.

"Lord Randall"

Abad, *A Formal Approach to Lyric Poetry*, 75-77.

E. W. Baughman, "'Eels Boiled in Broo' or What Killed Lord Randall?" *BRMMLA* 10 (May 1957): 3.

Brooks and Warren, *Understanding Poetry*, 122-25; rev. ed., 48-51.

Arthur K. Moore, "The Literary Status of the English Popular Ballad," *CL* 10 (Winter 1958): 16.

"The Lord's Prayer I"

Anderson, *Two Literary Riddles*, 134-35.

"Louerd Thu Clepedest Me"

Manning, *Wisdom and Number*, 36-38.

"Luf Es Lyf That Lastes Ay"

Manning, *Wisdom and Number*, 58-59.

"Lullay, Lullay, Litel Child"

Wenzel, *Preachers, Poets*, 164-66.

"The Maid and the Palmer"

Fowler, *The Bible in Middle English Literature*, 115-18.

"Maiden in the Mor Lay"

J. A. Burrow, "Poems Without Contexts: The Rawlinson Lyrics," *EIC* 29 (1979): 20-25. Reprinted in Burrow, *Essays on Medieval Literature*, 16-20.

Jane L. Curry, "Waking the Well," *ELN* 2 (September 1964): 1-4.

Fowler, *The Bible in Middle English Literature*, 113-14.

Richard Leighton Greene, "Troubling the Well-Waters," *ELN* 4 (September 1966): 4-6.

Joseph Harris," 'Maiden in the Mor Lay' and the Medieval Magdalene Tradition," *JMRS* 1 (1971): 59-87.

Reiss, *The Art of the Middle English Lyric*, 98-106.

D. W. Robertson, Jr., "Historical Criticism," in *English Institute Essays 1950*, ed. Alan S. Downer (New York: Columbia University Press, 1951), 26-27. Reprinted in Robertson, *Essays in Medieval Culture*, 3-20.

Speirs, *Medieval English Poetry*, 62-64.

"Man Folwe Seintt Berardes Trace"

Oliver, *Poems without Names*, 121.

"Marye, Mayde Mylde and Fre"

Gray, *Themes and Images*, 84-86.

"Mary, The Rose-Bush"

Thomas D. Hill, "'Mary, The Rose-Bush' and the Leaps of Christ," *ES* 67 (1986): 478-82.

"Maxims I"

Greenfield and Calder, *A New Critical History*, 260-61.

Raw, *The Art and Background of Old English Poetry* , 74-81.

Shippey, *Poems of Wisdom and Learning*, 15-18.

"Maxims IA"
"Frige mec frodum wordum!"

Hansen, *The Solomon Complex*, 157-63, 170-71, 172-73.

"Maxims IB"
"Forst sceal freosan"

Hansen, *The Solomon Complex*, 163-67, 170, 173-74.

"Maxims IC"
"Ræd sceal mon secgan"

Hansen, *The Solomon Complex*, 167-70, 170-72, 174-75.

"Maxims II"

Greenfield and Calder, *A New Critical History*, 261-62.

Stanley B. Greenfield and Richard Evert, "*Maxims II*: Gnome and Poem," in Nicholson and Frese, *Anglo-Saxon Poetry*, 337-54.

Fred C. Robinson, "Understanding an Old English Wisdom Verse: *Maxims II*, Lines 10ff," in Benson and Wenzel, *The Wisdom of Poetry*, 1-11.

Shippey, *Poems of Wisdom and Learning*, 13-15.

"The Meeting in the Wood"

J. J. Anderson, "Two Difficulties in *The Meeting in the Wood*," *MÆ* 49 (1980): 258-59.

"The Menologium"

Hansen, *The Solomon Complex*, 115-22.

"Methinkit"

John C. Hirsh, *Expl* 35 (Spring 1977): 11.

"Metrical Epilogue to the Pastoral Care"

Isaacs, *Structural Principles in Old English Poetry*, 83-89.

"Middelerd for Mon Wes Mad"

Ralph Hanna, "A Note on a Harley Lyric," *ELN* 7 (June 1970): 243-46.

Celia Townsend Wells, "Line 21 of 'Middelerd for Mon Wes Mad,'" *ELN* 10 (March 1973): 167-69.

"The Milde Lomb Isprad O Rode"

Weber, *Theology and Poetry in the Middle English Lyric*, 94-109.

"Mirie It Is Whilc Sumer Ilast"

David L. Jeffrey, *The Early English Lyric & Franciscan Spirituality* (Lincoln: University of Nebraska Press, 1975), 12-15.

Reiss, *The Art of the Middle English Lyric*, 2-6.

Edmund Reiss, "The Art of the Middle English Lyric: Two Poems on Winter," *AnM* 11 (1970): 22-26.

The Mirror of the Periods of Man's Life

Brian S. Lee, "A Poem 'Clepid the Sevene Ages,'" in *An English Miscellany Presented to W. S. Mackie*, ed. Brian S. Lee (London: Oxford University Press, 1977), 85-92.

"Mon in the Mone"

Frank Bessai, "A Reading of 'The Man in the Moon,'" *AnM* 12 (1971): 120-22.

Moore, *The Secular Lyric in Middle English*, 95-97.

Rogers, *Image and Abstraction*, 53-68.

Speirs, *Medieval English Poetry*, 92-94.

MS Junius II

J. R. Hall, "The Old English Epic of Redemption: The Theological Unity of MS Junius II," *Traditio* 32 (1976): 185-208.

Mum & the Sothsegger

Alcuin G. Blamires, "*Mum & the Sothsegger* and Langlandian Idiom" *NM* 76 (1975): 583-604.

D. A. Lawton, "Lollardy and the 'Piers Plowman' Tradition," *MLR* 76 (1981): 780-93.

Spearing, *Medieval Dream-Poetry*, 162-66.

"Naueth My Saule Bute Fur and Ys"

Reiss, *The Art of the Middle English Lyric*, 24-28.

"Ne Saltou Neuer, Leuedi"

T. L. Burton, *Expl* 39 (Spring 1981): 19-21.

"Nine Herbs Charm"

L. M. C. Weston, "The Language of Magic in Two Old English Metrical Charms," *NM* 86 (1985): 181-85.

"Nou Goth Sonne under Wod"

John L. Cutler, *Expl* 4 (October 1945): 7. Reprinted in *The Explicator Cyclopedia* 2:4-5; Locke, Gibson, and Arms, *Readings for Liberal Education*, 506-7.

Dronke, *The Medieval Lyric*, 64-65.

Gradon, *Form and Style*, 185-87.

Stephen Manning, "Nou Goth Sonne Under Wod," *MLN* 74 (November 1959): 578-81.

Manning, *Wisdom and Number*, 80-84.

Reiss, *The Art of the Middle English Lyric*, 14-17.

Edmund Reiss, "A Critical Approach to the Middle English Lyrics," *CE* 27 (February 1966): 375-76.

William Elford Rogers, *The Three Genres and the Interpretation of Lyric* (Princeton, N.J.: Princeton University Press, 1983), 70-72.

C. G. Thayer, *Expl* 11 (February 1953): 25. Reprinted in *The Explicator Cyclopedia* 2: 5-6.

"Nou Sprinketh Rose ant Lylie Flour"

Manning, *Wisdom and Number*, 100-105.

"Nou Sprinkes the Sprai"

Reiss, *The Art of the Middle English Lyric*, 44-49.

"Nutbrowne Mayde"

Moore, *The Secular Lyric in Middle English*, 182-88.

"Nu This Fules Singet Hand Maket Hure Blisse"

Weber, *Theology and Poetry in the Middle English Lyric*, 48-55.

"Nv Yh She Blost Me Sprynge"

Manning, *Wisdom and Number*, 22-23.

Wenzel, *Preachers, Poets*, 54-59.

"Of a Rose, a Lovely Rose"

Speirs, *Medieval English Poetry*, 70-72.

Leo Spitzer, "*Explication de Texte* Applied to Three Great Middle English Poems," in Spitzer, *Essays on English and American Literature by Leo Spitzer*, 216-33.

"Of Everykune Tree"

J. A. Burrow, "Poems Without Contexts: The Rawlinson Lyrics," *EIC* 29 (1979): 10-11. Reprinted in Burrow, *Essays on Medieval Literature*, 5-6.

"O Man Vnkynde"

Oliver, *Poems without Names*, 24-25.

Woolf, *The English Religious Lyric*, 185-86.

"The Order of the World" or "Wonders of Creations"

Greenfield and Calder, *A New Critical History*, 266-67.

Hansen, *The Solomon Complex*, 80-84.

Ida Masters Hollowell, "*Scop* and *Woðbora* in OE Poetry," *JEGP* 77 (1978): 317-29.

Huppé, *The Web of Words*, 34-61.

Isaacs, *Structural Principles in Old English Poetry*, 71-82.

"Oure Ladi Freo"

Woolf, *The English Religious Lyric*, 252-54.

"O Western Wind"

Abad, *A Formal Approach to Lyric Poetry*, 363-64.

Bateson, *English Poetry*, 81. Abridged in Gwynn, Condee, and Lewis, *The Case for Poetry*, 13.

Brooks and Warren, *Understanding Poetry*, rev. ed., 177-78.

Ciardi, *How Does a Poem Mean?*, 996-98.

Roberts W. French, "'Western Wind' and the Complexity of Poetry," *EJ* 60 (February 1971): 212-14.

Charles Frey, "Interpreting 'Western Wind," *ELH* 43 (1976): 259-78.

Walter Gierasch, *Expl* 14 (April 1956): 43. Reprinted in *The Explicator Cyclopedia* 2:6.

Greenfield and Weatherhead, "The Experience of a Poem," in Greenfield and Weatherhead, *The Poem: An Anthology*, xxvii-xxxi.

Richard R. Griffith, *Expl* 21 (May 1963): 69.

Nat Henry, *Expl* 16 (October 1957): 5. Reprinted in *The Explicator Cyclopedia* 2:7.

Arthur O. Lewis, Jr., *Expl* 15 (February 1957): 28. Reprinted in *The Explicator Cyclopedia* 2:6-7.

Moore, *The Secular Lyric in Middle English*, 29-30.

Sanders, *The Discovery of Poetry*, 163-64.

Douglas D. Short and Porter Williams, Jr., "'Westron Wynde': A Problem in Syntax and Interpretation," *PLL* 13 (Spring 1977): 187-92.

Stauffer, *The Nature of Poetry*, 63. Abridged in Gwynn, Condee, and Lewis, *The Case for Poetry*, 13.

Patrick M. Sweeney, *Expl* 14 (October 1955): 6. Reprinted in *The Explicator Cyclopedia* 2:6.

Unger and O'Connor, *Poems for Study*, 12-13.

Chad Walsh, *Doors into Poetry* (Englewood Cliffs, N.J.: Prentice Hall, 1962), 4, 127.

R. P. Warren, "Pure and Impure Poetry," *KR* 5 (Spring 1943): 233-35. Reprinted in Schorer, Miles, and McKenzie, *Criticism*, 369; Stallman, *Critiques*, 89-90; *Essays in Modern Literary Criticism*, ed. Ray B. West, Jr. (New York: Rinehart & Company, 1952), 250-51; Ransom, *The Kenyon Critics*, 22-24. Abridged in Gwynn, Condee, and Lewis, *The Case for Poetry*, 13.

The Owl and the Nightingale

(See Nicholas of Guilford)

The Parlement of the Thre Ages

David V. Harrington, "Indeterminacy in *Winner and Waster* and *The Parliament of the Three Ages*," *ChauR* 20 (1986): 246-57.

Anne Kernan, "Theme and Structure in *The Parlement of the Thre Ages*," *NM* 75 (1974): 253-78.

Lisa Kiser, "Elde and His Teaching in *The Parlement of the Thre Ages*," *PQ* 66 (Summer 1987): 303-14.

David E. Lampe, "The Poetic Strategy of the *Parlement of the Thre Ages*," *ChauR* 7 (1973): 173-83.

David A. Lawton, "The Unity of Middle English Alliterative Poetry," *Speculum* 58 (1983): 81-82.

Marie Nelson, "*The Parlement of the Thre Ages*: Meaning and Design," *Neophil* 62 (October 1978): 620-33.

Russell A. Peck, "The Careful Hunter in *The Parlement of the Thre Ages*," *ELH* 39 (1972): 333-41.

V. J. Scattergood, "*The Parlement of the Thre Ages*," *LeedsSE*, n.s. 14 (1983): 167-81.

Spearing, *Medieval Dream-Poetry*, 134-37.

Speirs, *Medieval English Poetry*, 289-301.

John Speirs, "'Wynnere and Wastoure' and 'The Parlement of the Thre Ages,'" *Scrutiny* 17 (Autumn 1950): 221-52.

Philippa Tristram, *Figures of Life and Death in Medieval English Literature* (London: Paul Elek, 1976), 85-86 and *passim*.

Thorlac Turville-Petre, "The Ages of Man in *The Parlement of the Thre Ages*," *MÆ* 46 (1977): 66-76.

R. A. Waldron, "The Prologue to 'The Parlement of the Thre Ages,'" *NM* 73 (1972): 786-94.

Partenay

Richmond, *The Popularity*, 75-84.

Partonope of Blois

Ramsey, *Chivalric Romances*, 135, 139-50 and *passim*.

"The Penitent's Prayer"

(See "Resignation")

Perceval of Galles

Ramsey, *Chivalric Romances*, 191-96.

"Pharoah"

Anderson, *Two Literary Riddles*, 129-34.

The Phoenix

N. F. Blake, "Introduction" to *The Phoenix* (Manchester: Manchester University Press, 1964), 24-35. Reprinted as "The Form of *The Phoenix*," in Stevens and Mandel, *Old English Literature*, 268-78.

N. F. Blake, "Some Problems of Interpretation and Translation in the OE *Phoenix*," *Anglia* 80 (1962): 50-62.

John Bugge, "The Virgin Phoenix," *MS* 38 (1976): 332-50.

Daniel G. Calder, "The Vision of Paradise: A Symbolic Reading of the Old English *Phoenix*," *ASE* 1 (1972): 167-81.

J. E. Cross, "The Conception of the Old English *Phoenix*," in *Old English Poetry: Fifteen Essays*, ed. Robert P. Creed (Providence, R.I.: Brown University Press, 1967), 129-52.

Greenfield, *A Critical History*, 183-86.

Stanley B. Greenfield, *The Interpretation of Old English Poems* (London: Routledge & Kegan Paul, 1972), 140-45.

Greenfield and Calder, *A New Critical History*, 242-45.

Carol Falvo Heffernan, "The Old English *Phoenix*: A Reconsideration," *NM* 83 (1982): 239-54.

Joanne S. Kantrowitz, "The Anglo-Saxon *Phoenix* and Tradition," *PQ* 43 (1964): 1-13.

Kennedy, *The Earliest English Poetry*, 290-300.

Lee, *The Guest-Hall*, 120-24.

Alexandra Hennessey Olsen, *Speech, Song, and Poetic Craft: The Artistry of the Cynewulf Canon* (New York: Peter Lang, 1984), 125-28.

Schaar, *Critical Studies*, 84-91, 149-51.

Robert D. Stevick, "Mathematical Proportions and Symbolism in 'The Phoenix,'" *Viator* 11 (1980): 95-121.

Swanton, *English Literature*, 129-38.

Janet Thormann, "Variations on the Theme of 'The Hero on the Beach' in *The Phoenix*," *NM* 71 (1970): 187-90.

Xun Lee Too, "The Appeal to the Senses in the Old English *Phoenix*," *NM* 91 (1990): 229-42.

Karl P. Wentersdorf, "On the Meaning of OE *heorodreorig* in *The Phoenix* and Other Poems," *SN* 45 (1973): 34-38.

"Physiologus"

Frederick M. Biggs, "The Eschatological Conclusion of the Old English *Physiologus*," *MÆ* 58 (1989): 286-97.

Crossley-Holland and Mitchell, *The Battle of Maldon*, 98-99.

Greenfield, *A Critical History*, 180-83.

Greenfield and Calder, *A New Critical History*, 240-42.

Bruce Ross, *Expl* 42 (Fall 1983): 4-5.

Pierce the Ploughman's Crede

Ritchie D. Kendall, *The Drama of Dissent: The Radical Poetics of Nonconformity, 1380-1590* (Chapel Hill and London: University of North Carolina Press, 1986), 73-80.

David Lampe, "The Satiric Strategy of *Peres the Ploughmans Crede*," in Levy and Szarmach, *The Alliterative Tradition*, 69-80.

D. A. Lawton, "Lollardy and the 'Piers Plowman' Tradition," *MLR* 76 (1981): 780-93.

The Plowman's Tale

Heiserman, *Skelton and Satire*, 224-27.

Andrew N. Wawn, "The Genesis of *The Plowman's Tale*," *YES* 2 (1972): 21-40 *passim*.

"The Poet's Repentance"

Daniel J. Ransom, *Poets at Play: Irony and Parody in the Harley Lyrics* (Norman, Okla.: Pilgrim Books, 1985), 1-29.

"Precepts"

Elaine Tuttle Hansen, "*Precepts*: An Old English Instruction," *Speculum* 56 (1981): 1-16.

Hansen, *The Solomon Complex*, 41-55.

Sandra McEntire, "The Monastic Context of Old English 'Precepts,'" *NM* 91 (1990): 243-49.

"Quanne Hic Se on Rode"

Reiss, *The Art of the Middle English Lyric*, 30-36.

"Resignation," or "The Penitent's Prayer"

Anderson, *Two Literary Riddles*, 108-15.

Thomas H. Bestul, "The Old English *Resignation* and the Benedictine Reform," *NM* 78 (1977): 18-23.

Allen Bliss and Allen J. Frantzen, "The Integrity of *Resignation*," *RES*, n.s. 27 (November 1976): 385-402.

Greenfield, *A Critical History*, 222.

P. L. Henry, Th*e Early English and Celtic Lyric* (London: George Allen & Unwin; New York: Barnes & Noble, 1966), 176-80.

Anne L. Klinck, "The Old English Elegy as a Genre," *ESC* 10 (June 1984): 129-40.

Anne L. Klinck, "*Resignation*: Exile's Lament or Penitent's Prayer," *Neophil* 71 (July 1987): 423-30.

Lee, *The Guest-Hall*, 147-49.

Marie Nelson, "On *Resignation*," in Green, *The Old English Elegies*, 133-47.

Raw, *The Art and Background of Old English Poetry* , 126-27.

E[ric] G[erald] Stanley, "Old English Poetic Diction and the Interpretation of *The Wanderer*, *The Seafarer*, and *The Penitent's Prayer*," *Anglia* 73 (1955): 456-62. Reprinted in Bessinger and Kahrl, *Essential Articles*, 494-98.

"Resignation A"

Greenfield and Calder, *A New Critical History*, 289.

Karma Lochrie, "*Wyrd* and the Limits of Human Understanding: A Thematic Sequence in the Exeter Book," *JEGP* 85 (1986): 325-26, 328-29.

"Resignation B"

Greenfield and Calder, *A New Critical History*, 289-90.

Karma Lochrie, "*Wyrd* and the Limits of Human Understanding: A Thematic Sequence in the Exeter Book," *JEGP* 85 (1986): 329-31.

Richard, Coer de Lyon

John Finlayson, "*Richard, Coer de Lyon*: Romance, History or Something in Between," *SP* 87 (Spring 1990): 156-80.

"The Riming Poem"

J. E. Cross, "Aspects of Microcosm and Macrocosm in Old English Literature," in *Studies in Old English Literature in Honor of Arthur G. Brodeur*, ed. Stanley B. Greenfield (Eugene: University of Oregon Books, 1963), 11-15.

James W. Earl, "Hisperic Style in the Old English 'Rhyming Poem,'" *PMLA* 102 (1987): 187-96.

Greenfield, *A Critical History*, 222-23.

John P. Hermann, *Expl* 34 (September 1975): 4.

Isaacs, *Structural Principles in Old English Poetry*, 56-70.

Anne L. Klinck, "Growth and Decay in The Riming Poem, Lines 51-54," *ELN* 23 (March 1986): 1-3.

Anne L. Klinck, "The Old English Elegy as a Genre," *ESC* 10 (June 1984): 129-40.

Anne L. Klinck, "*The Riming Poem*: Design and Interpretation," *NM* 89 (1988): 266-79.

Lee, *The Guest-Hall*, 149-50.

Ruth P. M. Lehmann, "The Old English *Riming Poem*: Interpretation, Text, and Translation," *JEGP* 69 (1970): 437-49.

O. D. Macrae-Gibson, "Introduction" to *The Old English "Riming Poem"* (Cambridge: D. S. Brewer, 1983), 5-11.

O. D. Macrae-Gibson, "The Literary Structure of 'The Riming Poem,'" *NM* 74 (1973): 62-84.

Karl P. Wentersdorf, "The Old English *Rhyming Poem*: A Ruler's Lament," *SP* 82 (Summer 1985): 265-94.

"Robin Hood and the Potter"

Dean A. Hoffman, "'With the Shot Y Wyll/Alle Thy Lustes to Full-fyl': Archery as Symbol in the Early Ballads of Robin Hood," *NM* 86 (1985): 501-2.

"The Ruin"

Anderson, *Two Literary Riddles*, 163-81.

Janet Bately, "Time and the Passing of Time in 'The Wanderer' and Related OE Texts," *E&S* 37 (1984): 1-15.

Daniel G. Calder, "Perspective and Movement in *The Ruin*," *NM* 72 (1971): 442-45.

James F. Doubleday, "*The Ruin*: Structure and Theme," *JEGP* 71 (1972): 369-81.

Greenfield, *A Critical History*, 214-15.

Greenfield, *Hero and Exile*, 94-97.

Stanley B. Greenfield, "The Old English Elegies," in Stanley, *Continuations and Beginnings*, 144-46.

Greenfield and Calder, *A New Critical History*, 281-82.

Kathryn Hume, "The 'Ruin Motif' in Old English Poetry," *Anglia* 94 (1976): 352-53.

Edward B. Irving, Jr., "Image and Meaning in the Elegies," in *Old English Poetry: Fifteen Essays*, ed. Robert B. Creed (Providence, R.I.: Brown University Press, 1967), 154-57.

William C. Johnson, Jr., "*The Ruin* as Body-City Riddle," *PQ* 59 (Fall 1980): 397-411.

Anne L. Klinck, "The Old English Elegy as a Genre," *ESC* 10 (June 1984): 129-40.

Lee, *The Guest-Hall*, 151-53.

Anne Thompson Lee, "'The Ruin': Bath or Babylon?" *NM* 74 (1973): 443-55.

John C. Pope, "The Existential Mysteries as Treated in Certain Passages of Our Older Poets," in Carruthers and Kirk, *Acts of Interpretation*, 354-56.

Alain Renoir, "The Old English *Ruin*: Contrastive Structure and Affective Impact," in Green, *The Old English Elegies*, 148-73.

Swanton, *English Literature*, 122-28.

Arnold V. Talentino, "Moral Irony in *The Ruin*," *PLL* 14 (Winter 1978): 3-10.

Karl P. Wentersdorf, "Observations on *The Ruin*," *MÆ* 46 (1977): 171-80.

"Rune Poem"

J. R. Hall, "Perspective and Wordplay in the Old English *Rune Poem*," *Neophil* 61 (July 1977): 453-60.

Frederick G. Jones, "The Hypermetric Lines of the *Rune Poem*," *NM* 74 (1973): 224-31.

Saint Erkenwald

Boitani, *English Medieval Narrative*, 21-23.

S. L. Clark and Julian N. Wasserman, "*St. Erkenwald*'s Spiritual Itinerary," *ABR* 33 (September 1982): 257-69.

Arnold E. Davidson, "Mystery, Miracle, and Meaning in *Saint Erkenwald*," *PLL* 16 (Winter 1980): 37-44.

Lester L. Faigley, "Typology and Justice in *St. Erkenwald*," *ABR* 29 (December 1978): 381-90.

Fowler, *The Bible in Middle English Literature*, 194-200.

Ruth Morse, "Introduction" to *St. Erkenwald* (Cambridge: D. S. Brewer; Totowa, N.J.: Rowman and Littlefield, 1975), 34-44.

Russell A. Peck, "Number Structure in *St. Erkenwald*," *AnM* 14 (1973): 9-21.

Vincent F. Petronella, "*St. Erkenwald*: Style as the Vehicle for Meaning," *JEGP* 66 (1967): 532-40.

William A. Quinn, "The Psychology of *St. Erkenwald*," *MÆ* 53 (1984): 180-93.

G. Whatley, "Heathens and Saints: *St. Erkenwald* in Its Legendary Context," *Speculum* 61 (1986): 330-63.

Saint Michael

Gregory M. Sadlek, "The Archangel and the Cosmos: The Inner Logic of the *South English Legendary*'s 'St. Michael,'" *SP* 85 (Spring 1988): 177-91.

"The Seafarer"

O. Arngart, "*The Seafarer*: A Postscript," *ES* 60 (June 1979): 249-253.

Janet Bately, "Time and the Passing of Time in 'The Wanderer' and Related OE Texts," *E&S* 37 (1984): 11-13.

Roberta Bux Bosse, "Aural Aesthetic and the Unity of The Seafarer," *PLL* 9 (Winter 1973): 3-14.

Daniel G. Calder, "Setting and Mode in 'The Seafarer' and 'The Wanderer,'" *NM* 72 (1971): 264-70.

Cherniss, *Ingeld and Christ*, 207-17.

Peter Clemoes, "*Mens absentia cogitans* in *The Seafarer* and *The Wanderer*," in *Medieval Literature and Civilization: Studies in Memory of G. N. Garmonsway*, ed. D. A. Pearsall and R. A. Waldron (London: Athlone Press, 1969), 62-77.

Muriel Cornell, "Varieties of Repetition in Old English Poetry, Especially in *The Wanderer* and *The Seafarer*," *Neophil* 65 (April 1981): 292-307 *passim*.

J. E. Cross, "Aspects of Microcosm and Macrocosm in Old English Literature," in *Studies in Old English Literature in Honor of Arthur G. Brodeur*, ed. Stanley B. Greenfield (Eugene: University of Oregon Books, 1963), 15-20 *passim*.

James Cross, "On the Allegory in *The Seafarer*–Illustrative Notes," *MÆ* 28 (1959): 104-6.

Crossley-Holland and Mitchell, *The Battle of Maldon*, 114-16.

W. A. Davenport, "The Modern Reader and the Old English *Seafarer*," *PLL* 10 (Summer 1974): 227-40.

F. N. M. Diekstra, "*The Seafarer* 58-66a: The Flight of the Exiled Soul to Its Fatherland," *Neophil* 55 (October 1971): 433-46.

Andrew Galloway, "1 Peter and *The Seafarer*," *ELN* 25 (June 1988): 1-10.

I. L. Gordon, "Introduction" to *The Seafarer* (New York: Appleton-Century-Crofts, 1966), 1-12.

I. L. Gordon, "Traditional Themes in *The Wanderer* and *The Seafarer*," *RES*, n.s. 5 (January 1954): 1-13.

Gradon, *Form and Style*, 117-18.

Brian K. Green, "*Spes Viva*: Structure and Meaning in *The Seafarer*," in *An English Miscellany Presented to W. S. Mackie*, ed. Brian S. Lee (London: Oxford University Press, 1977), 28-45.

Martin Green, "Man, Time, and Apocalypse in *The Wanderer*, *The Seafarer*, and *Beowulf*," *JEGP* 75 (1975): 506-12.

Stanley B. Greenfield, "Attitudes and Values in *The Seafarer*," *SP* 51 (1954): 15-20.

Greenfield, *A Critical History*, 219-21.

Greenfield, *Hero and Exile*, 104-11, 155-69, 171-83.

Stanley B. Greenfield, "The Old English Elegies," in Stanley, *Continuations and Beginnings*, 153-60.

Stanley B. Greenfield, "*Sylf*, Seasons, Structure and Genre in *The Seafarer*," *ASE* 9 (1981): 199-211.

Greenfield and Calder, *A New Critical History*, 285-88.

P. L. Henry, *The Early English and Celtic Lyric* (London: George Allen & Unwin; New York: Barnes & Noble, 1966), 133-60.

Joyce M. Hill, "'This Deade Lif': A Note on *The Seafarer*, Lines 64-66," *ELN* 15 (December 1977): 95-97.

Frederick S. Holton, "Old English Sea Imagery and the Interpretation of *The Seafarer*," *YES* 12 (1982): 208-17.

A. D. Horgan, "The Structure of *The Seafarer*," *RES*, n.s. 30 (February 1979): 41-49.

D. R. Howlett, "The Structures of 'The Wanderer' and 'The Seafarer,'" *SN* 47 (1975): 313-17.

Edward B. Irving, Jr., "Image and Meaning in the Elegies," in *Old English Poetry: Fifteen Essays*, ed. Robert B. Creed (Providence, R.I.: Brown University Press, 1967), 158-59.

Neil D. Isaacs, "Image, Metaphor, Irony, Allusion, and Moral: The Shifting Perspective of 'The Seafarer,'" *NM* 67 (1966): 266-82.

Isaacs, *Structural Principles in Old English Poetry*, 19-34.

Nicolas Jacobs, "Syntactical Connection and Logical Disconnection: The Case of *The Seafarer*," *MÆ* 58 (1989): 105-13.

W. F. Klein, "Purpose and the 'Poetics' of *The Wanderer* and *The Seafarer*," in Nicholson and Frese, *Anglo-Saxon Poetry*, 218-23.

Anne L. Klinck, "The Old English Elegy as a Genre," *ESC* 10 (June 1984): 129-40.

Lee, *The Guest-Hall*, 143-46.

Roy F. Leslie, "The Meaning and Structure of *The Seafarer*," in Green, *The Old English Elegies*, 96-122.

Clair McPherson, "The Sea a Desert: Early English Spirituality and *The Seafarer*," *ABR* 38 (June 1987): 115-26.

Mandel, *Alternative Readings*, 71-108.

Jerome Mandel, "The Seafarer," *NM* 77 (1976): 538-51.

Bruce Moore, *Expl* 35 (Fall 1976): 11-12.

P. R. Orton, "*The Seafarer*, 58-64a," *Neophil* 66 (July 1982): 450-59.

Marijane Osborn, "Venturing upon Deep Waters in 'The Seafarer,'" *NM* 79 (1978): 1-6.

John C. Pope, "Dramatic Voices in *The Wanderer* and *The Seafarer*," in *Franciplegius: Medieval and Linguistic Studies in Honor of Francis Peabody Magoun, Jr.*, ed. Jess B. Bessinger, Jr., and Robert P. Creed (London: George Allen & Unwin; New York: New York University Press, 1965), 73-88. Reprinted in Bessinger and Kahrl, *Essential Articles*, 533-70; Stevens and Mandel, *Old English Literature*, 163-97.

John C. Pope, "Second Thoughts on the Interpretation of *The Seafarer*," *ASE* 3 (1974): 75-86.

T. A. Shippey, *Old English Verse* (London: Hutchinson University Library, 1972), 68-71.

Kenneth Sisam, "*Seafarer*, Lines 97-102," *RES* 21 (October 1945): 316-17.

G. V. Smithers, "The Meaning of *The Seafarer* and *The Wanderer*," *MÆ* 26 (1957): 137-53.

G. V. Smithers, "The Meaning of *The Seafarer* and *The Wanderer* (continued)," *MÆ* 28 (1959): 1-22.

G. V. Smithers, "The Meaning of *The Seafarer* and *The Wanderer*: Appendix," *MÆ* 28 (1959): 99-104.

Eric Gerald Stanley, "Old English Poetic Diction and the Interpretation of *The Wanderer*, *The Seafarer*, and *The Penitent's Prayer*," *Anglia* 73 (1955): 453-55. Reprinted in Bessinger and Kahrl, *Essential Articles*, 492-94.

Swanton, *English Literature*, 114-21.

Raymond P. Tripp, Jr., "The Narrator as Revenant: A Reconsideration of Three Old English Elegies," *PLL* 8 (Fall 1972): 352-57.

L. Whitbread, "The Pattern of Misfortune in *Deor* and Other Old English Poems," *Neophil* 54 (April 1970): 174-76.

Dorothy Whitelock, "The Interpretation of *The Seafarer*," in *Chadwick Memorial Studies, Early Cultures of North West Europe*, ed. Sir Cyril Fox and Bruce Dickens (Cambridge: Cambridge University Press, 1950), 261-72. Reprinted in Bessinger and Kahrl, *Essential Articles*, 442-57; Stevens and Mandel, *Old English Literature*, 198-211.

Phyllis Gage Whittier, "Spring in 'The Seafarer' 48-50," *N&Q* 15 (November 1968): 407-9.

Rosemary Woolf, "'The Wanderer,' 'The Seafarer,' and the Genre of *Planctus*," in Nicholson and Frese, *Anglo-Saxon Poetry*, 202-6. Reprinted in Woolf, *Art and Doctrine*, 168-72.

"The Seasons for Fasting"

Hansen, *The Solomon Complex*, 122-25.

"The Sex Werkdays and Agis"

Luuk Houwen, "*The Sex Werkdays and Agis*: Text and Context," *ES* 69 (October 1988): 372-85.

Sir Amadace

Bennett, *Middle English Literature*, 165-67.

Sir Beues of Hamtoun

Mehl, *The Middle English Romances*, 211-20.

Ramsey, *Chivalric Romances*, 45-67 *passim*.

Sire Degarre

Derek Brewer, *Symbolic Stories: Traditional Narratives of the Family Drama in English Literature* (Cambridge: D. S. Brewer; Totowa, N.J.: Rowman & Littlefield, 1980), 66-71.

Mortimer J. Donovan, "*Sir Degare*: ll. 992-997," *MS* 15 (1953), 206-8.

Ramsey, *Chivalric Romances*, 159-62.

Bruce A. Rosenberg, "The Three Tales of *Sir Degaré*," *NM* 76 (1975): 39-51.

Schmidt and Jacobs, *Medieval English Romances*, Vol. 2, 7-11.

Speirs, *Medieval English Poetry*, 150-57.

Sir Degrevant

Mehl, *The Middle English Romances*, 93-99.

Ramsey, *Chivalric Romances*, 172-76.

Sir Eglamour of Artois

Stephen Knight, "The Social Function of the Middle English Romances," in Aers, *Medieval Literature*, 99-122.

Ramsey, *Chivalric Romances*, 165-68.

Wim Tigges, "*Sir Eglamour*: The Knight Who Could Not Say No," *Neophil* 72 (January 1988): 107-15.

Sir Gowther

Shirley Marchalonis, "*Sir Gowther*: The Process of a Romance," *ChauR* 6 (1971): 14-29.

Ramsey, *Chivalric Romances*, 218-19.

Richmond, *The Popularity*, 65-68.

Sir Launfal

Earl R. Anderson, "The Structure of *Sir Launfal*," *PLL* 2 (Spring 1977): 115-24.

Daryl Lane, "Conflict in *Sir Launfal*," *NM* 74 (1973): 283-87.

Peter J. Lucas, "Towards an Interpretation of *Sir Launfal* with Particular Reference to Line 683," *MÆ* 39 (1970): 291-300.

Sir Orfeo

Dorena Allen, "Orpheus and Orfeo: The Dead and the *Taken*," *MÆ* 33 (1964): 102-11.

Barron, *English Medieval Romance*, 186-90.

Bennett, *Middle English Literature*, 138-48.

Michael D. Bristol, "The Structure of the Middle English *Sir Orfeo*," *PLL* 6 (Fall 1970): 339-47.

Francis P. Carpinelli, *Expl* 19 (November 1960): 13. Reprinted in *The Explicator Cyclopedia* 2: 9-10.

A. S. G. Edwards, *Expl* 29 (January 1971): 43.

A. S. G. Edwards, "Marriage, Harping and Kingship: The Unity of *Sir Orfeo*," *ABR* 32 (September 1981): 282-91.

Kenneth R. R. Gros Louis, "The Significance of Sir Orfeo's Self-Exile," *RES*, n.s. 18 (August 1967): 245-52.

Thomas B. Hanson, "*Sir Orfeo*: Romance as Exemplum," *AnM* 13 (1972): 135-54.

D. M. Hill, "The Structure of 'Sir Orfeo,'" *MS* 23 (1961): 136-53.

Mary Hynes-Berry, "Cohesion in *King Horn* and *Sir Orfeo*," *Speculum* 50 (1975): 654-56, 663-69.

David Lyle Jeffrey, "The Exiled King: Sir Orfeo's Harp and the Second Death of Eurydice," *Mosaic* 9 (Winter 1976): 45-60.

David L. Jeffrey, "Literature in an Apocalyptic Age; or, How to End a Romance," *DR* 61 (Autumn 1981): 426-46.

N. H. Keeble, "The Narrative Achievement of *Sir Orfeo*," *ES* 56 (June 1975): 193-206.

Edward D. Kennedy, "Sir Orfeo as *Rex Inutilis*," *AnM* 17 (1976): 88-110.

Seth Lerer, "Artifice and Artistry in *Sir Orfeo*," *Speculum* 60 (1985): 92-109.

Robert M. Longsworth, "*Sir Orfeo*, the Minstrel, and the Minstrel's Art," *SP* 79 (Winter 1982): 1-11.

Christina J. Murphy, "*Sir Orfeo*: The Self and the Nature of Art," *UMSE* 13 (1972): 19-30.

Lewis J. Owen, "The Recognition Scene in *Sir Orfeo*," *MÆ* 40 (1971): 249-53.

Ramsey, *Chivalric Romances*, 150-56.

Felicity Riddy, "The Uses of the Past in *Sir Orfeo*," *YES* 6 (1976): 5-15.

E. C. Ronquist, "The Powers of Poetry in *Sir Orfeo*," *PQ* 64 (Winter 1985): 99-117.

Schmidt and Jacobs, *Medieval English Romances*, Vol. 2, 23-28.

Spearing, *Readings in Medieval Poetry*, 56-82.

Speirs, *Medieval English Poetry*, 139-50.

"Sir Patrick Spens"

Abad, *A Formal Approach to Lyric Poetry*, 106-7.

Adams, *The Contexts of Poetry*, 23-28.

Brooks, Purser, and Warren, *An Approach to Literature*, 429-31; 3d ed., 283-84; 4th ed., 285-86.

Daniels, *The Art of Reading Poetry*, 137-41.

Frankenberg, *Invitation to Poetry*, 112-13.

Louis L. Martz, "The Teaching of Poetry," in Gorden and Noyes, *Essays on the Teaching of English*, 254-55.

William H. Matchett, "The Integrity of 'Sir Patrick Spence,'" *MP* 68 (August 1970): 25-31.

Arthur K. Moore, "The Literary Status of the English Popular Ballad," *CL* 10 (Winter 1958): 1-13.

Van Doren, *Introduction to Poetry*, 127-29. Reprinted in Locke, Gibson, and Arms, *Introduction to Literature*, 3d ed., 6-8; 4th ed., 8-10; 5th ed., 8-10.

Wheeler, *The Design of Poetry*, 280-82, 283-87.

Sir Perceval of Galles

F. Xavier Baron, "Mother and Son in *Sir Perceval of Galles*," *PLL* 8 (Winter 1972): 3-14.

Caroline D. Eckhardt, "Arthurian Comedy: The Simpleton-Hero in *Sir Perceval of Galles*," *ChauR* 8 (1974): 205-20.

Speirs, *Medieval English Poetry*, 122-38.

Sir Triamour

Ramsey, *Chivalric Romances*, 162-65.

Sir Tristrem

Donald L. Hoffman, "Cult and Culture: 'Courtly Love' in the Cave and Forest," *Tristania* 4 (November 1978): 15-34.

Thomas C. Rumble, "The Middle English *Sir Tristrem*: Toward a Reappraisal," *CL* 11 (1959): 221-28.

Swanton, *English Literature*, 203-15.

Ernest C. York, *Expl* 25 (May 1967): 76.

Sir Ysumbras

Laurel Braswell, "'Sir Isumbras' and the Legend of Saint Eustace," *MS* 27 (1965): 128-51.

ANONYMOUS, "SITH IT CONCLUDID WAS IN THE TRINITE"

Mehl, *The Middle English Romances*, 128-35.

"Sith It Concludid Was in the Trinite"

Woolf, *The English Religious Lyric*, 267-68.

"Sodenly Afraide/Half-waking, Half-slepyng"

Reiss, *The Art of the Middle English Lyric*, 144-50.

Solomon and Saturn

Kennedy, *The Earliest English Poetry*, 311-18.

Solomon and Saturn II

Joseph A. Dane, "The Structure of the Old English *Solomon and Saturn II*," *Neophil* 64 (October 1980): 592-603.

Greenfield and Calder, *A New Critical History*, 273-76.

Hansen, *The Solomon Complex*, 147-52.

"Somer Is Comen and Winter Gon"

Peter Dronke, "Two Thirteenth-Century Religious Lyrics," in Rowland, *Chaucer and Middle English Studies*, 398-403.

Manning, *Wisdom and Number*, 114-15.

Woolf, *The English Religious Lyric*, 64-65.

"Somer Soneday"

T. M. Smallwood, "The Interpretation of *Somer Soneday*," *MÆ* 42 (1973): 238-43.

"Song of the Husbandman"

Moore, *The Secular Lyric in Middle English*, 85-87.

"A Song of Lewes"

Swanton, *English Literature*, 256-58.

Soul and Body I

Allen J. Frantzen, "The Body in *Soul and Body I*," *ChauR* 17 (1982): 76-88.

Kennedy, *The Earliest English Poetry*, 319-21.

P. R. Orton, "Disunity in the Vercelli Book *Soul and Body*," *Neophil* 63 (July 1979): 450-60.

Shippey, *Poems of Wisdom and Learning*, 29-36.

Cyril Smetana, O. S. A., "Second Thoughts on 'Soul and Body I,'" *MS* 29 (1967): 193-205.

Soul and Body II

Anderson, *Two Literary Riddles*, 44-52.

Mary Heyward Ferguson, "The Structure of the *Soul's Address to the Body* in Old English," *JEGP* 69 (1970): 72-73.

Greenfield and Calder, *A New Critical History*, 235-37.

Speculum Misericordie

Davidoff, *Beginning Well*, 83-86.

"The Squyr of Lowe Degre"

Huston Diehl, "'For No Theves Shall Come Thereto': Symbolic Detail in *The Squyr of Lowe Degre*," *ABR* 32 (June 1981): 140-55.

Stanzaic *Morte Arthur*

Barron, *English Medieval Romance*, 142-47.

Sherron E. Knopp, "Artistic Design in the *Stanzaic Morte Arthur*," *ELH* 45 (1978): 563-82.

ANONYMOUS, "STOD HO THERE NEH"

Mehl, *The Middle English Romances*, 186-93.

Ramsey, *Chivalric Romances*, 127-30.

Richmond, *The Popularity*, 129-42.

Schmidt and Jacobs, *Medieval English Romances*, Vol. 2, 20-28.

Richard A. Wertime, "The Theme and Structure of the Stanzaic *Morte Arthur*," *PMLA* 87 (1972): 1075-82.

"Stod Ho There Neh"

Manning, *Wisdom and Number*, 150-54.

"Stond Wel, Moder, Vnder Rode"

Manning, *Wisdom and Number*, 77-80.

Weber, *Theology and Poetry in the Middle English Lyric*, 125-45.

Wenzel, *Preachers, Poets*, 48-52.

"Suete Sone, Reu on Me, & Brest out of Thi Bondis"

Weber, *Theology and Poetry in the Middle English Lyric*, 117-21.

"Sumer Is Icumen In"

Huntington Brown, *Expl* 3 (February 1945): 34. Reprinted in *The Explicator Cyclopedia* 2: 11-12.

Peter Heidtmann, "The *Reverdie* Convention and 'Lenten Is Come with Love to Toune,'" *AnM* 12 (1971): 79-80.

Jeffrey A. Helterman, "The Antagonistic Voices of 'Sumer Is Icumen In,'" *TSL* 18 (1973): 13-17.

Theodore C. Hoepfner, *Expl* 3 (December 1944): 18 and 3 (June 1945): 59. Reprinted in *The Explicator Cyclopedia* 2:10-11, 12.

John S. Kenyon, *Expl* 3 (March 1945): 40. Reprinted in *The Explicator Cyclopedia* 2: 12.

Stephen Manning, *Expl* 18 (October 1959): 2. Reprinted in *The Explicator Cyclopedia* 2: 12-13.

Moore, *The Secular Lyric in Middle English*, 50-52.

Reiss, *The Art of the Middle English Lyric*, 8-12.

Ribner and Morris, *Poetry*, 35-36.

"Swarte-Smekyd Smethes, Smateryd wyth Smoke"

Reiss, *The Art of the Middle English Lyric*, 166-70.

Syre Gawene and the Carle of Carelyle

Anne Wilson, *Traditional Romance and Tale: How Stories Mean* (Cambridge and Ipswich: D. S. Brewer, 1976), 90-93.

Tale of Beryn

Bradley Darjes and Thomas Rendall, "A Fabliau in the *Prologue to the Tale of Beryn*," *MS* 47 (1985): 416-31.

The Tale of Gamelyn

Richard W. Kaeuper, "An Historian's Reading of *The Tale of Gamelyn*," *MÆ* 52 (1983): 51-62.

Maurice Keen, *The Outlaws of Medieval Legend* (Toronto: University of Toronto Press, 1961), 78-94.

Edward Z. Menkin, "Comic Irony and the Sense of Two Audiences in the *Tale of Gamelyn*," *THOTH* 10 (Winter 1969): 41-53.

"Tam Lin"

John D. Niles, "Tam Lin: Form and Meaning in a Traditional Ballad," *MLQ* 38 (December 1977): 336-47.

"That Lovely Lady Sat and Song"

Manning, *Wisdom and Number*, 49-50.

" þene Latemeste Dai"

Woolf, *The English Religious Lyric*, 95-97.

"There Is a Floure Sprung of a Tree"

Speirs, *Medieval English Poetry*, 72-74.

"Ther Is No Rose of Swych Vertu"

Gray, *Themes and Images*, 88-89.

Manning, *Wisdom and Number*, 155-58.

Thomas of Ercildoune and the Quene of Elf-land

Speirs, *Medieval English Poetry*, 168-77.

"Thomas Rymer"

Daniels, *The Art of Reading Poetry*, 144-47.

The Three Kings

Susanna G. Fein, "The Ghoulish and the Ghastly: A Moral Aesthetic in Middle English Alliterative Verse," *MLQ* 48 (March 1987): 9-11.

"The Three Ravens"

Brooks and Warren, *Understanding Poetry*, 118-22; rev. ed., 45-48.

Daniels, *The Art of Reading Poetry*, 133-37. Reprinted in Locke, Gibson, and Arms, *Readings for Liberal Education*, Vol. 2, 363-66.

Anthony Easthope, *Poetry as Discourse* (London and New York: Methuen, 1983), 83-93.

Tyrus Hillway, *Expl* 5 (March 1947): 36. Reprinted in *The Explicator Cyclopedia* 2: 14.

Seymour Lainoff, *Expl* 17 (May 1959): 55. Reprinted in *The Explicator Cyclopedia* 2: 14-15.

Louis G. Locke, *Expl* 4 (June 1946): 54. Reprinted in *The Explicator Cyclopedia* 2: 13-14.

Rosenthal and Smith, *Exploring Poetry*, 311-14.

"The Thrush and the Nightingale"

Michael J. Franklin, "The Fieldfase and the Nightingale: A Note on *The Thrush and the Nightingale*," *MÆ* 47 (1978): 308-11.

Swanton, *English Literature*, 258-62.

" þu Sikest Sore"

John E. Hallwas, *Expl* 35 (Spring 1977): 12-13.

Wenzel, *Preachers, Poets*, 135-37.

"To My Dere Herte Variant and Mutable"

Jan Ziolkowski, "Avatars of Ugliness in Medieval Literature," *MLR* 79 (January 1984): 13-14.

"To My Trew Loue and Able"

Jan Ziolkowski, "Avatars of Ugliness in Medieval Literature," *MLR* 79 (January 1984): 13-14.

Torrent of Portyngale

Vincent A. Dunn, *Cattle-Raids and Courtships: Medieval Narrative Genres in a Traditional Context* (New York and London: Garland Publishing, 1989), 167-85.

The Turk and Gawain

Speirs, *Medieval English Poetry*, 202-5.

"The Twa Corbies"

Abad, *A Formal Approach to Lyric Poetry*, 347-49.

Daniels, *The Art of Reading Poetry*, 133-37. Reprinted in Locke, Gibson, and Arms, *Readings for Liberal Education*, Vol. 2, 363-66.

Bert Case Diltz, *Sense or Nonsense: Contemporary Education at the Crossroads* (Toronto: McClelland and Stewart, 1972), 63-69.

Drew, *Poetry: A Modern Guide*, 93-94.

Arthur K. Moore, "The Literary Status of the English Popular Ballad," *CL* 10 (Winter 1958): 15-16.

"Ubi Sount Qui Ante Nas Fueront"

Swanton, *English Literature*, 252-54.

"Vainglory"

Greenfield and Calder, *A New Critical History*, 265-66.

Hansen, *The Solomon Complex*, 69-80.

John P. Hermann, "The Recurrent Motifs of Spiritual Warfare in Old English Poetry," *AnM* 22 (1982): 16-17, 32-33.

Huppé, *The Web of Words*, 8-26.

Catharine A. Regan, "Patristic Psychology in the Old English 'Vainglory,'" *Traditio* 26 (197): 324-35.

Shippey, *Poems of Wisdom and Learning*, 7-10.

Valentine and Orson

Richmond, *The Popularity*, 105-18.

"Verses on a Chained Horae"

Oliver, *Poems without Names*, 23-24.

"Vndo Thi Dore, My Spuse Dere"

Fowler, *The Bible in Middle English Literature*, 85-86.

Manning, *Wisdom and Number*, 125-26.

Reiss, *The Art of the Middle English Lyric*, 124-30.

"The Wanderer"

William Alfred, "The Drama of *The Wanderer*," in Benson and Wenzel, *The Wisdom of Poetry*, 31-44.

Janet Bately, "Time and the Passing of Time in 'The Wanderer' and Related OE Texts," *E&S* 37 (1984): 1-15 *passim*.

Robert E. Bjork, "*Sundor æt rune*: The Voluntary Exile of the Wanderer," *Neophil* 73 (January 1989): 119-29.

Robert O. Bowen, *Expl* 13 (February 1955): 26. Reprinted in *The Explicator Cyclopedia* 2: 15-16.

George Hardin Brown, "An Iconographic Explanation of 'The Wanderer,' Lines 81b-82a," *Viator* 9 (1978): 31-38.

Daniel G. Calder, "Setting and Mode in 'The Seafarer' and 'The Wanderer,'" *NM* 72 (1971): 270-75.

S. L. Clark and Julian N. Wasserman, "The Imagery of *The Wanderer*," *Neophil* 63 (April 1979): 291-96.

Peter Clemoes, "*Mens absentia cogitans* in *The Seafarer* and *The Wanderer*," in *Medieval Literature and Civilization: Studies in Memory of G. N. Garmonsway*, ed. D. A. Pearsall and R. A. Waldron (London: Athlone Press, 1969), 62-77.

Muriel Cornell, "Varieties of Repetition in Old English Poetry, Especially in *The Wanderer* and *The Seafarer*," *Neophil* 65 (April 1981): 292-307 *passim*.

J. E. Cross, "On the Genre of *The Wanderer*," *Neophil* 45 (January 1961): 63-75. Reprinted in Bessinger and Kahrl, *Essential Articles*, 515-32.

Crossley-Holland and Mitchell, *The Battle of Maldon*, 106-8.

F. N. M. Dickstra, "*The Wanderer* 65b-72: The Passions of the Mind and the Cardinal Virtues," *Neophil* 55 (January 1971): 73-88.

James F. Doubleday, "The Three Faculties of the Soul in *The Wanderer*," *Neophil* 53 (April 1969): 189-94.

T. P. Dunning and A. J. Bliss, "Introduction" to *The Wanderer* (New York: Appleton-Century-Crofts, 1969), 78-102.

Ralph W. V. Elliott, "The Wanderer's Conscience," *ES* 39 (1958): 193-200.

Roger Fowler, "A Theme in *The Wanderer*," *MÆ* 36 (1967): 1-14.

P. J. Frankis, "The Thematic Significance of *Enta Geweorc* and Related Imagery in *The Wanderer*," *ASE* 2 (1973): 253-69.

Gradon, *Form and Style*, 115-16, 162-64.

I. L. Gordon, "Traditional Themes in *The Wanderer* and *The Seafarer*," *RES*, n.s. 5 (January 1954): 1-13.

B. K. Green, "The Twilight Kingdom: Structure and Meaning in *The Wanderer*," *Neophil* 60 (July 1976): 442-51.

Martin Green, "Man, Time, and Apocalypse in *The Wanderer*, *The Seafarer*, and *Beowulf*," *JEGP* 74 (1975): 506-12.

Greenfield, *A Critical History*, 215-19.

Greenfield, *Hero and Exile*, 97-104, 133-47, 161-69.

Stanley B. Greenfield, *The Interpretation of Old English Poems* (London: Routledge & Kegan Paul, 1972), 117-22.

Stanley B. Greenfield, "The Old English Elegies," in Stanley, *Continuations and Beginnings*, 146-53.

Stanley B. Greenfield, "*The Wanderer*: A Reconsideration of Theme and Structure," *JEGP* 50 (1951): 451-65.

Greenfield and Calder, *A New Critical History*, 282-85.

Elizabeth A. Hait, "The Wanderer's Lingering Regret: A Study of Patterns of Imagery," *Neophil* 68 (April 1984): 278-91.

P. L. Henry, *The Early English and Celtic Lyric* (London: George Allen & Unwin; New York: Barnes & Noble, 1966), 161-75.

John P. Hermann, *Expl* 37 (Spring 1979): 23.

Ida Masters Hollowell, "On the Identity of the Wanderer," in Green, *The Old English Elegies*, 82-95.

A. D. Horgan, "*The Wanderer* – A Boethian Poem," *RES*, n.s. 38 (February 1987): 40-46.

D. R. Howlett, "The Structures of 'The Wanderer' and 'The Seafarer,'" *SN* 47 (1975): 313-17.

Kathryn Hume, "The 'Ruin Motif' in Old English Poetry," *Anglia* 94 (1976): 353-54.

Huppé, *Doctrine and Poetry*, 233-35.

Bernard F. Huppé, "*The Wanderer*: Theme and Structure," *JEGP* 42 (1943): 516-38.

Edward B. Irving, Jr., "Image and Meaning in the Elegies," in *Old English Poetry: Fifteen Essays*, ed. Robert B. Creed (Providence, R.I.: Brown University Press, 1967), 159-63.

Isaacs, *Structural Principles in Old English Poetry*, 35-55.

Kennedy, *The Earliest English Poetry*, 105-8.

Eugene R. Kintgen, "Wordplay in *The Wanderer*," *Neophil* 59 (January 1975): 119-27.

W. F. Klein, "Purpose and the 'Poetics' of *The Wanderer* and *The Seafarer*," in Nicholson and Frese, *Anglo-Saxon Poetry*, 212-18.

Anne L. Klinck, "The Old English Elegy as a Genre," *ESC* 10 (June 1984): 129-40.

Lee, *The Guest-Hall*, 136-43.

R. F. Leslie, "Introduction" to *The Wanderer* (New York: Barnes & Noble, 1966), 1-25. Reprinted as "*The Wanderer*: Theme and Structure," in Stevens and Mandel, *Old English Literature*, 139-62.

Lars Malmberg, "'The Wanderer': *Waþema Gebind*," *NM* 71 (1970): 96-99.

Mandel, *Alternative Readings*, 11-69.

Graham Midgley, "*The Wanderer*, Lines 49-55," *RES*, n.s. 10 (February 1959): 53-54.

Tony Millns, "*The Wanderer* 98: 'Weal Wundrum Heah Wyrmlicum Fah,'" *RES*, n.s. 28 (November 1977): 431-38.

Karen A. Mullen, "*The Wanderer*: Considered Again," *Neophil* 58 (January 1974): 74-81.

R. A. Peters, "Philosophy and Theme of the Old English Poem 'The Exile,'" *Neophil* 65 (April 1981): 288-91.

John C. Pope, "Dramatic Voices in *The Wanderer* and *The Seafarer*," in *Franciplegius: Medieval and Linguistic Studies in Honor of Francis Peabody Magoun, Jr.*, ed. Jess B. Bessinger, Jr., and Robert P. Creed (London: George Allen & Unwin; New York: New York University Press, 1965), 164-93. Reprinted in Stevens and Mandel, *Old English Literature*, 163-97; Bessinger and Kahrl, *Essential Articles*, 533-70.

John C. Pope, "The Existential Mysteries as Treated in Certain Passages of Our Older Poets," in Carruthers and Kirk, *Acts of Interpretation*, 347-50.

Raw, *The Art and Background of Old English Poetry* , 66-68.

John Richardson, "The Hero at the Wall in *The Wanderer*," *NM* 89 (1988): 280-85.

D. W. Robertson, Jr., "Historical Criticism," in *English Institute Essays, 1950*, ed. Alan S. Downer (New York: Columbia University Press, 1951), 18-22. Reprinted in Robertson, *Essays in Medieval Culture*, 3-20.

Mary Rohrberger, "A Psychoanalytical Reading of 'The Wanderer,'" *CimR* 2 (December 1967): 70-74.

James L. Rosier, "The Literal-Figurative Identity of the Wanderer," *PMLA* 79 (1964): 366-69.

Thomas C. Rumble, "From *Eardstapa* to *Snotter on Mode*: The Structural Principle of 'The Wanderer,'" *MLQ* 19 (September 1958): 225-30.

John L. Salzer, "*The Wanderer* and the Meditative Tradition," *SP* 80 (Spring 1983): 227-37.

T. A. Shippey, *Old English Verse* (London: Hutchinson University Library, 1972), 56-60.

G. V. Smithers, "The Meaning of *The Seafarer* and *The Wanderer*," *MÆ* 26 (1957): 137-53.

G. V. Smithers,"The Meaning of *The Seafarer* and *The Wanderer* (continued)," *MÆ* 28 (1959): 1-22.

G. V. Smithers, "The Meaning of *The Seafarer* and *The Wanderer*: Appendix," *MÆ* 28 (1959): 99-104.

Eric Gerald Stanley, "Old English Poetic Diction and the Interpretation of *The Wanderer*, *The Seafarer*, and *The Penitent's Prayer*," *Anglia* 73 (1955): 462-66. Reprinted in Bessinger and Kahrl, *Essential Articles*, 499-503.

Swanton, *English Literature*, 105-14, 121-22.

Raymond P. Tripp, Jr., "The Narrator as Revenant: A Reconsideration of Three Old English Elegies," *PLL* 8 (Fall 1972): 345-52.

Susie I. Tucker, "Return to *The Wanderer*," *EIC* 8 (July 1958): 229-37.

Karl P. Wentersdorf, "*The Wanderer*: Notes on Some Semantic Problems," *Neophil* 59 (April 1975): 287-92.

L. Whitbread, "The Pattern of Misfortune in *Deor* and Other Old English Poems," *Neophil* 54 (April 1970): 173-74.

Rosemary Woolf, "'The Wanderer,' 'The Seafarer,' and the Genre of *Planctus*," in Nicholson and Frese, *Anglo-Saxon Poetry*, 196-202. Reprinted in Woolf, *Art and Doctrine*, 159-68.

"Wanne Mine Eyhnen Misten"

Manning, *Wisdom and Number*, 15-17.

Reiss, *The Art of the Middle English Lyric*, 88-92.

"A Wayle Whyt ase Whalles Bon"

Moore, *The Secular Lyric in Middle English*, 64-65.

Daniel J. Ransom, *Poets at Play: Irony and Parody in The Harley Lyrics* (Norman, Okla.: Pilgrim Books, 1985), 65-79.

"We Ben Chapmen"

James Hala, *Expl* 46 (Spring 1988): 3-4.

William Ian Miller, *Expl* 42 (Summer 1984): 2-4.

The Weddynge of Sir Gawen and Dame Ragnell

Susan Dannenbaum, *Expl* 40 (Spring 1982): 3-4.

Anne Wilson, *Traditional Romance and Tale: How Stories Mean* (Cambridge and Ipswich: D. S. Brewer, 1976), 88-90.

"Weep You No More, Sad Fountains"

Laurence Perrine, *Expl* 34 (April 1976): 61.

"Wel Who Shal Thire Hornes Blowe"

Russell A. Peck, "Public Dreams and Private Myths: Perspective in Middle English Literature," *PMLA* 90 (1975): 462-63.

Reiss, *The Art of the Middle English Lyric*, 94-97.

Edmund Reiss, "A Critical Approach to the Middle English Lyrics," *CE* 27 (February 1966): 377-79.

"Wenne Hic Soe on Rode Idon"

Woolf, *The English Religious Lyric*, 33-34.

"Wen the Turuf Is Thi Tuur"

Reiss, *The Art of the Middle English Lyric*, 83-87.

Ribner and Morris, *Poetry*, 29-30.

"Wer Ther Outher in This Toun"

J. A. Burrow, "Poems Without Contexts: The Rawlinson Lyrics," *EIC* 29 (1979): 14-16. Reprinted in Burrow, *Essays on Medieval Literature*, 9-10.

"What Ys He, Thys Lordling, That Cometh vrom the Vyht"

J. A. W. Bennett, *Poetry of the Passion: Studies in Twelve Centuries of English Verse* (Oxford: Clarendon Press, 1982), 76-77.

"When Thi Hed Whaketh"

Manning, *Wisdom and Number*, 17-19.

"When Y Se Blosmes Springe"

Woolf, *The English Religious Lyric*, 63-64.

"Who Can the Sorow Conceyve Allas"

Woolf, *The English Religious Lyric*, 268.

Widsith

Ray Brown, "The Begging Scop and the Generous King in *Widsith*," *Neophil* 73 (April 1989): 281-92.

Chance, *Woman as Hero*, 85.

Norman E. Eliason, "Two Old English Scop Poems," *PMLA* 81 (1966): 185-92.

Greenfield and Calder, *A New Critical History*, 146-48.

Hansen, *The Solomon Complex*, 88-95.

Ida Masters Hollowell, "Was Widsið a Scop?" *Neophil* 64 (October 1980): 583-91.

David R. Howlett, "Form and Genre in *Widsith*," *ES* 55 (1974): 505-11.

Kemp Malone, *Widsith* (Copenhagen: Rosenkilde and Bagger, 1962), 27-105 *passim*.

David A. Rollman, "*Widsith* as an Anglo-Saxon Defense of Poetry," *Neophil* 66 (July 1982): 431-39.

Swanton, *English Literature*, 32-39.

Lamar York, "A Reading of 'Widsith,'" *MQ* 20 (Summer 1979): 325-31.

"The Wife's Lament"

Anderson, *Two Literary Riddles*, 84-99.

Rudolph C. Bambas, "Another View of the Old English *Wife's Lament*," *JEGP* 62 (1963): 303-9. Reprinted in Stevens and Mandel, *Old English Literature*, 229-36.

A. C. Bouman, *Patterns in Old English and Old Icelandic Literature* (Leiden: Universitaire Pers Leiden, 1962), 43-60.

Chance, *Woman as Hero*, 90-94.

Dennis Chase, "'The Wife's Lament': An Eighth-Century Existential Cry," *LangQ* 24 (Spring-Summer 1986): 18-20.

Cherniss, *Ingeld and Christ*, 117-18.

Crossley-Holland and Mitchell, *The Battle of Maldon*, 82-83.

Jane L. Curry, "Approaches to a Translation of the Anglo-Saxon *The Wife's Lament*," *MÆ* 35 (1966): 187-98.

Clifford Davidson, "Erotic 'Women's Songs' in Anglo-Saxon England," *Neophil* 59 (July 1975): 456-59.

Thomas M. Davis, "Another View of 'The Wife's Lament,'" *PLL* 1 (Fall 1965): 291-304.

A. N. Doane, "Heathen Form and Christian Function in 'The Wife's Lament,'" *MS* 28 (1966): 77-91.

Gareth W. Dunleavy, "Possible Irish Analogues for 'The Wife's Lament,'" *PQ* 35 (July 1956): 211-13.

Robert P. Fitzgerald, "'The Wife's Lament' and 'The Search for the Lost Husband,'" *JEGP* 62 (1963): 769-77.

Martin Green, "Time, Memory, and Elegy in *The Wife's Lament*," in Green, *The Old English Elegies*, 123-32.

Greenfield, *A Critical History*, 225-26.

Greenfield, *Hero and Exile*, 116-20, 149-54.

Stanley B. Greenfield, "The Old English Elegies," in Stanley, *Continuations and Beginnings*, 165-69.

Stanley B. Greenfield, "'The Wife's Lament' Reconsidered," *PMLA* 68 (1953): 907-12.

Greenfield and Calder, *A New Critical History*, 292-94.

Joseph Harris, "A Note on *eorthscr aef/eorthsele* and Current Interpretations of *The Wife's Lament*," *ES* 58 (June 1977): 204-8.

Patrick Leo Henry, *The Early English and Celtic Lyric* (London: Unwin, 1967), 23.

D. R. Howlett, "'The Wife's Lament' and 'The Husband's Message,'" *NM* 79 (1978): 7-10.

Lee Ann Johnson, "The Narrative Structure of 'The Wife's Lament,'" *ES* 52 (December 1971): 497-501.

William C. Johnson, Jr., "The Wife's Lament as Death-Song," in Green, *The Old English Elegies*, 69-81.

Anne L. Klinck, "The Old English Elegy as a Genre," *ESC* 10 (June 1984): 129-40.

William Witherle Lawrence, "The Banished Wife's Lament," *MP* 5 (January 1908): 387-405.

Angela M. Lucas, "The Narrator of *The Wife's Lament* Reconsidered," *NM* 70 (1969): 282-97.

Kemp Malone, "Two English *Frauenlieder*," in *Studies in Old English Literature in Honor of Arthur G. Brodeur*, ed. Stanley B. Greenfield (Eugene: University of Oregon Books, 1963), 111-17.

Mandel, *Alternative Readings*, 149-85.

Audrey L. Meaney, "The *Ides* of the Cotton Gnomic Poem," *MÆ* 48 (1979): 36-37.

Michael D. Patrick, *Expl* 28 (February 1970): 50.

Alain Renoir, "Christian Inversion in 'The Wife's Lament,'" *SN* 49 (1977): 19-24.

Alain Renoir, "A Reading Context for *The Wife's Lament*," in Nicholson and Frese, *Anglo-Saxon Poetry*, 224-41.

Alain Renoir, "A Reading of *The Wife's Lament*," *ES* 58 (February 1977): 4-19.

Matti Rissanen, "The Theme of 'Exile' in *The Wife's Lament*," *NM* 70 (1969): 90-104.

Thomas J. Rountree, *Expl* 29 (November 1970): 24.

T. A. Shippey, *Old English Verse* (London: Hutchinson University Library, 1972), 73-75.

Douglas D. Short, "The Old English *Wife's Lament*: An Interpretation," *NM* 71 (1970): 585-603.

Martin Stevens, "The Narrator of *The Wife's Lament*," *NM* 69 (1968): 72-90.

Robert D. Stevick, Formal Aspects of 'The Wife's Lament,'" *JEGP* 59 (1960): 21-25.

Michael Swanton, "*The Wife's Lament* and *The Husband's Message*: A Reconsideration," *Anglia* 82 (1964): 269-90.

Raymond P. Tripp, Jr., "The Narrator as Revenant: A Reconsideration of Three Old English Elegies," *PLL* 8 (Fall 1972): 356-60.

J. A. Ward, "'The Wife's Lament': An Interpretation," *JEGP* 59 (January 1960): 26-33.

Karl P. Wentersdorf, "The Situation of the Narrator in the Old English *Wife's Lament*," *Speculum* 56 (1981): 492-516.

Karl P. Wentersdorf, "The Situation of the Narrator's Lord in *The Wife's Lament*," *NM* 71 (1970): 604-10.

L. Whitbread, "The Pattern of Misfortune in *Deor* and Other Old English Poems," *Neophil* 54 (April 1970): 176-78.

"The Wife of Usher's Well"

Abad, *A Formal Approach to Lyric Poetry*, 108-9.

Charles Barber, *Poetry in English: An Introduction* (London and Basingstoke: Macmillan, 1983), 148-51.

Brooks and Warren, *Understanding Poetry*, 42-45; rev. ed., 16-20.

Arthur K. Moore, "The Literary Status of the English Popular Ballad," *CL* 10 (Winter 1958): 13-14.

William of Palerne

Barron, *English Medieval Romance*, 196-99.

Erik Kooper, "*Grace*: The Healing Herb in *William of Palerne*," *LeedsSE*, n.s. 15 (1984): 83-93.

Ramsey, *Chivalric Romances*, 123-27.

"Wið Færstice," or "Against a Sudden Stitch"

Howell D. Chickering, Jr., "The Literary Magic of 'Wið Færstice,'" *Viator* 2 (1971): 83-104.

Minna Doskow, "Poetic Structure and the Problem of the Smiths in 'With Faerstice,'" *PLL* 12 (Summer 1976): 321-26.

Greenfield and Calder, *A New Critical History*, 257.

Stanley R. Hauer, "Structure and Unity in the Old English Charm *Wið Færstice*," *ELN* 15 (June 1978): 250-57.

L. M. C. Weston, "The Language of Magic in Two Old English Metrical Charms," *NM* 86 (1985): 177-80.

"With Favoure in Hir Face Ferr Passyng My Reason"

Woolf, *The English Religious Lyric*, 265-66.

"Worldes Blisce, Haue God Day"

Reiss, *The Art of the Middle English Lyric*, 38-42.

"Wulf and Eadwacer"

John F. Adams, "'Wulf and Eadwacer': An Interpretation," *MLN* 73 (1958): 1-5.

Anderson, *Two Literary Riddles*, 19-44.

Peter S. Baker, "The Ambiguity of *Wulf and Eadwacer*," *SP* 78 (Early Winter 1981): 39-51.

Chance, *Woman as Hero*, 86-90.

Crossley-Holland and Mitchell, *The Battle of Maldon*, 78-79.

Arnold E. Davidson, "Interpreting *Wulf and Eadwacer*," *AnM* 16 (1975): 24-32.

Clifford Davidson, "Erotic 'Women's Songs' in Anglo-Saxon England," *Neophil* 59 (July 1975): 459-60.

Norman E. Eliason, "On *Wulf and Eadwacer*," in Burlin and Irving, *Old English Studies*, 225-34.

John M. Fanagan, "*Wulf and Eadwacer*: A Solution to the Critics' Riddle," *Neophil* 60 (January 1976): 130-37.

P. J. Frankis, "*Deor* and *Wulf and Eadwacer*: Some Conjectures," *MÆ* 31 (1962): 172-75.

Donald K. Fry, "*Wulf and Eadwacer*: A Wen Charm," *ChauR* 5 (Spring 1971): 247-63.

Richard F. Giles, "'Wulf and Eadwacer': A New Reading," *Neophil* 65 (April 1981): 468-72.

Greenfield, *Hero and Exile*, 114-16, 185-94.

Stanley B. Greenfield, "The Old English Elegies," in Stanley, *Continuations and Beginnings*, 164-65.

Stanley B. Greenfield, "*Wulf and Eadwacer*: All Passion Spent," *ASE* 15 (1986): 5-14.

Isaacs, *Structural Principles in Old English Poetry*, 114-17.

Emily Jensen, "Narrative Voice in the Old English *Wulf*," *ChauR* 13 (Spring 1979): 373-83.

F. Jones, "A Note on the Interpretation of *Wulf and Eadwacer*," *NM* 86 (1985): 323-27.

Harry E. Kavros, "A Note on 'Wulf and Eadwacer,'" *ELN* 15 (December 1977): 83-84.

Johan Kerling, "Another Solution to the Critics' Riddle: *Wulf and Eadwacer* Revisited," *Neophil* 64 (January 1980): 140-43.

Anne L. Klinck, "Animal Imagery in *Wulf and Eadwacer*," *PLL* 23 (Winter 1987): 3-13.

Anne L. Klinck, "The Old English Elegy as a Genre," *ESC* 10 (June 1984): 129-40.

Terrence Kough, "The Tension of Separation in *Wulf and Eadwacer*," *NM* 77 (1976): 552-60.

Ruth P. M. Lehmann, "The Metrics and Structure of 'Wulf and Eadwacer,'" *PQ* 48 (April 1968): 151-65.

Janemarie Luecke, "*Wulf and Eadwacer*: Hints for Reading from *Beowulf* and Anthropology," in Green, *The Old English Elegies*, 190-203.

Kemp Malone, "Two English *Frauenlieder*," in *Studies in Old English Literature in Honor of Arthur G. Brodeur*, ed. Stanley B. Greenfield (Eugene: University of Oregon Books, 1963), 107-10.

Wesley S. Mattox, "Encirclement and Sacrifice in *Wulf and Eadwacer*," *AnM* 16 (1975): 33-40.

Marijane Osborn, "The Text and Context of *Wulf and Eadwacer*," in Green, *The Old English Elegies*, 174-89.

Alan Renoir, "*Wulf and Eadwacer*: A Noninterpretation," in *Franciplegius: Medieval and Linguistic Studies in Honor of Francis Peabody Magoun, Jr.*, ed. Jess B. Bessinger, Jr., and Robert P. Creed (London: George Allen & Unwin; New York: New York University Press, 1965), 147-63.

James B. Spamer, "The Marriage Concept in *Wulf and Eadwacer*," *Neophil* 62 (January 1978): 143-44.

Seiichi Suzuki, "'*Wulf and Eadwacer*': A Reinterpretation and Some Conjectures," *NM* 88 (1987): 175-85.

L. Whitbread, "The Pattern of Misfortune in *Deor* and Other Old English Poems," *Neophil* 54 (April 1970): 179.

"Wy Have Ye No Reuthe on My Child?"

Weber, *Theology and Poetry in the Middle English Lyric*, 111-17.

"Wynnere and Wastoure"

Thomas H. Bestul, *Satire and Allegory in "Wynnere and Wastour"* (Lincoln: University of Nebraska Press, 1974).

Derek Brewer, *English Gothic Literature* (London and Basingstoke: Macmillan, 1983), 142-46.

Davidoff, *Beginning Well*, 63-66.

David V. Harrington, "Indeterminacy in *Winner and Waster* and *The Parliament of the Three Ages*," *ChauR* 20 (1986): 246-57.

Nicolas Jacobs, "The Typology of Debate and the Interpretation of *Wynnere and Wastoure*," *RES*, n.s. 36 (November 1985): 481-500.

Jerry D. James, "The Undercutting of Conventions in 'Wynnere and Wastoure,'" *MLQ* 25 (September 1964): 243-58.

Bruce Moore, "The Dominicans' Banner in *Wynnere and Wastoure*," *ELN* 26 (December 1988): 7-12.

Spearing, *Medieval Dream-Poetry*, 130-34.

Speirs, *Medieval English Poetry*, 272-89.

John Speirs, "'Wynnere and Wastoure' and 'The Parlement of the Three Ages,'" *Scrutiny* 17 (Autumn 1950): 221-52.

Gardiner Stillwell, "*Wynnere and Wastoure* and the Hundred Years' War," *ELH* 8 (1941): 241-47.

Thorlac Turville-Petre, "The Prologue of *Wynnere and Wastoure*," *LeedsSE* 18 (1987): 23-27.

"Wynter Wakeneþ Al My Care"

David L. Jeffrey, *The Early English Lyric & Franciscan Spirituality* (Lincoln: University of Nebraska Press, 1975), 257-59.

Manning, *Wisdom and Number*, 105-6, 133.

Lewis H. Miller, Jr., "Two Poems of Winter," *CE* 28 (January 1967): 316-17.

Reiss, *The Art of the Middle English Lyric*, 74-81.

Edmund Reiss, "The Art of the Middle English Lyric: Two Poems on Winter," *AnM* 11 (1970): 27-34.

Ann Shannon, "The Meaning of *grein* in 'Winter wakeneth al my care,'" *PQ* 53 (Summer 1974): 425-27.

"Young Waters"

Hardy, *The Curious Frame*, 3-21.

Ywain and Gawain

John Finlayson, "*Ywain and Gawain* and the Meaning of Adventure," *Anglia* 87 (1969): 312-37.

Gayle K. Hamilton, "The Breaking of the Troth in *Ywain and Gawain*," *Mediaevalia* 2 (1976): 111-35.

Mehl, *The Middle English Romances*, 180-85.

Richmond, *The Popularity*, 121-29.

Schmidt and Jacobs, *Medieval English Romances*, Vol. 2, 11-19.

Speirs, *Medieval English Poetry*, 114-21.

AUDELAY, JOHN

"Gaude! Felix Anna, þe Moder of Mari"

Woolf, *The English Religious Lyric*, 296.

BARBOUR, JOHN

Bruce

Bernice W. Kliman, "The Idea of Chivalry in John Barbour's *Bruce*," *MS* 35 (1972): 477-508.

Bernice W. Kliman, "John Barbour and Rhetorical Tradition," *AnM* 18 (1977): 106-35.

Kurt Wittig, *The Scottish Tradition in Literature* (Westport, Conn.: Greenwood Press, 1958; reprinted 1972), 11-32 *passim*.

BARCLAY, ALEXANDER

"The Towre of Vertue and Honoure," Eclogue 4

R. J. Lyall, "Tradition and Innovation in Alexander Barclay's 'Towre of Vertue and Honoure,'" *RES*, n.s. 23 (February 1972): 1-18.

BEDE

"Death-Song"

Howell D. Chickering, Jr., "Some Contexts for Bede's *Death-Song*," *PMLA* 91 (1976): 91-100.

Greenfield and Calder, *A New Critical History*, 264-65.

Huppé, *Doctrine and Poetry*, 78-79.

Michael W. Twomey, "On Reading 'Bede's Death Song,'" *NM* 84 (1983): 171-81.

"Be Domes Dæge"
(OE version of *De die Judicii*)

Huppé, *Doctrine and Poetry*, 80-82, 86-93.

BEOWULF-POET

Beowulf

Roberta Adams Albrecht, *Expl* 40 (Summer 1982): 4-6.

Judson Boyce Allen, "God's Society and Grendel's Shoulder Joint," *NM* 78 (1977): 239-40.

Earl R. Anderson, "A Submerged Metaphor in the Scyld Episode," *YES* 2 (1972): 1-4.

Earl R. Anderson, "Treasure Trove in *Beowulf*: A Legal View of the Dragon's Hoard," *Mediaevalia* 3 (1978): 141-64.

George K. Anderson, *The Literature of the Anglo-Saxons* (Princeton, N.J.: Princeton University Press, 1949), 63-85.

J. J. Anderson, "The *cuþ e folme* in *Beowulf*," *Neophil* 67 (January 1983): 126-30.

Theodore M. Andersson, "Tradition and Design in Beowulf," in *Old English Literature in Context*, ed. John D. Niles (Cambridge: D. S. Brewer; Totowa, N.J.: Rowman and Littlefield, 1980), 90-106.

Malcolm Andrew, "Grendel in Hell," *ES* 62 (October 1981): 401-10.

Joseph L. Baird, "Grendel the Exile," *NM* 67 (1966): 375-81.

Stephen C. Bandy, "*Beowulf*: The Defense of Heorot," *Neophil* 56 (January 1972): 86-92.

Stephen C. Bandy, "Cain, Grendel, and the Giants of *Beowulf*," *PLL* 9 (Summer 1973): 235-49.

Daniel R. Barnes, "Folktale Morphology and the Structure of *Beowulf*," *Speculum* 45 (1970): 416-34.

Paull F. Baum, "The *Beowulf* Poet," *PQ* 39 (1960): 389-99. Reprinted in Nicholson, *An Anthology of Beowulf Criticism*, 353-65.

P. Beekman, "The Traditional Language of Treasure in *Beowulf*," *JEGP* 85 (1986): 191-205.

Harry Berger, Jr., and H. Marshall Leicester, Jr., "Social Structure as Doom: The Limits of Heroism in *Beowulf*," in Burlin and Irving, *Old English Studies*, 37-79.

A. J. Bliss, "*Beowulf*, Lines 3074-3075," in Salu and Farrell, *J. R. R. Tolkien*, 41-63.

Joan Blomfeld, "The Style and Structure of *Beowulf*," *RES* 14 (1938): 396-403. Reprinted in Fry, *The Beowulf Poet*, 57-65.

Morton W. Bloomfield, "*Beowulf* and Christian Allegory: An Interpretation of Unferth," *Traditio* 7 (1949-1951): 410-15. Reprinted in Nicholson, *An Anthology of Beowulf Criticism*, 155-64; Fry, *The Beowulf Poet*, 68-75.

W. F. Bolton, *Alcuin and "Beowulf": An Eighth-Century View* (New Brunswick, N.J.: Rutgers University Press, 1978), 95-178 *passim*.

Adrien Bonjour, "Beowulf and the Beasts of Battle," *PMLA* 72 (September 1957): 563-73. Reprinted in Adrien Bonjour, *Twelve Beowulf Papers, 1940-1960: With Additional Comments* (Neuchâtel: Faculté des Lettres; Genève: Librairie E. Droz, 1962), 135-49.

Adrien Bonjour, "Beowulf and Heardred," *ES* 32 (1951): 193-200. Reprinted in Adrien Bonjour, *Twelve Beowulf Papers, 1940-1960: With Additional Comments* (Neuchâtel: Faculté des Lettres; Genève: Librairie E. Droz, 1962), 67-76.

Adrien Bonjour, *The Digressions in "Beowulf,"* Medium Ævum Monographs, no. 5 (Oxford: Basil Blackwell, 1950, 1965).

Adrien Bonjour, "Grendel's Dam and the Composition of *Beowulf*," *ES* 30 (1949): 113-24.

Adrien Bonjour, "Monsters Crouching and Critics Rampant: Or the Beowulf Dragon Debated," *PMLA* 68 (1953): 304-12. Reprinted in Adrien Bonjour, *Twelve Beowulf Papers, 1940-1960: With Additional Comments* (Neuchâtel: Faculté des Lettres; Genève: Librairie E. Droz, 1962), 97-113.

Adrien Bonjour, "The Technique of Parallel Descriptions in Beowulf," *RES*, n.s. 2 (1951): 1-10. Reprinted in Adrien Bonjour, *Twelve Beowulf Papers, 1940-1960: With Additional Comments* (Neuchâtel: Faculté des Lettres; Genève: Librairie E. Droz, 1962), 51-65.

G. C. Britton, "Unferth, Grendel, and the Christian Meaning of *Beowulf*," *NM* 72 (1971): 246-50.

Arthur G. Brodeur, *The Art of Beowulf* (Berkeley and Los Angeles: University of California Press, 1959).

Arthur G. Brodeur, "Design for Terror in the Purging of Heorot," *JEGP* 53 (1954): 503-13.

Arthur G. Brodeur, "The Structure and Unity of *Beowulf*," *PMLA* 68 (1953): 1183-95.

Alan K. Brown, "The Firedrake in *Beowulf*," *Neophil* 64 (July 1980): 439-60.

Robert B. Burlin, "Gnomic Indirection in *Beowulf*," in Nicholson and Frese, *Anglo-Saxon Poetry*, 41-49.

Robert B. Burlin, "Inner Weather and Interlace: A Note on the Semantic Value of Structure in *Beowulf*," in Burlin and Irving, *Old English Studies*, 81-89.

Richard Butts, "The Analogical Mere: Landscape and Terror in *Beowulf*," *ES* 68 (1987): 113-21.

Allen Cabaniss, "*Beowulf* and the Liturgy," *JEGP* 54 (April 1955): 195-201. Reprinted in Nicholson, *An Anthology of Beowulf Criticism*, 223-32.

Daniel G. Calder, "Setting and Ethos: The Pattern of Measure and Limit in *Beowulf*," *SP* 69 (January 1972): 21-37.

Martin Camargo, "The Finn Episode and the Tragedy of Revenge in *Beowulf*," *SP* 78 (Early Winter 1981): 120-34.

A. P. Campbell, "The Time Element of Interlace Structure in *Beowulf*," *NM* 70 (1969): 425-35.

Thomas A. Carnicelli, "The Function of the Messenger in *Beowulf*," *SP* 72 (July 1975): 246-57.

Paul Cavill, "A Note on *Beowulf*, Lines 2490-2509," *Neophil* 67 (October 1983): 599-604.

Chance, *Woman as Hero*, 95-108.

William A. Chaney, "Grendel and the *Gifstol*: A Legal View of Monsters," *PMLA* 77 (1962): 520.

Cherniss, *Ingeld and Christ*, *passim*.

Michael D. Cherniss, "The Progress of the Hoard in *Beowulf*," *PQ* 47 (1968): 473-86.

George Clark, "Beowulf's Armor," *ELH* 32 (1965): 409-41.

Carol J. Clover, "The Germanic Context of the Unferþ Episode," *Speculum* 55 (1980): 444-68.

Hennig Cohen, *Expl* 16 (April 1958): 40.

Spenser Cosmos, "Kuhn's Law and the Unstressed Verbs in *Beowulf*," *TSLL* 18 (Summer 1976): 306-28.

André Crépin, "Wealhtheow's Offering of the Cup to Beowulf: A Study in Literary Structure," in *Saints, Scholars, and Heroes: Studies in Medieval Culture in Honour of Charles W. Jones*, ed. Margot H. King and Wesley M. Stevens, Vol. 2 (Collegeville, Minn.: Hill Monastic Manuscript Library and Saint John's Abbey and University, 1979), 45-68.

Eugene J. Crook, "Pagan Gold in *Beowulf*," *ABR* 25 (June 1974): 218-34.

Taylor Culbert, "The Narrative Functions of Beowulf's Swords," *JEGP* 59 (1960): 13-20.

Charles Dahlberg, *The Literature of Unlikeness* (Hanover and London: University Press of New England, 1988), 26-54 *passim*.

Helen Damico, *Beowulf's Wealhtheow and the Valkyrie Tradition* (Madison: University of Wisconsin Press, 1984).

Rodney Delasanta and James Slevin, "Beowulf and the Hypostatic Union," *Neophil* 52 (October 1968): 409-16.

Laurence N. de Looze, "Frame Narratives and Fictionalization: Beowulf as Narrator," *TSLL* 26 (Summer 1984): 145-56.

Harvey De Roo, "*Beowulf* 2223b: A Thief by Any Other Name?" *MP* 79 (February 1982): 297-304.

Charles Donahue, "*Beowulf* and Christian Tradition: A Reconsideration from a Celtic Stance," *Traditio* 21 (1965): 55-116.

Charles Donahue, "Potlatch and Charity: Notes on the Heroic in *Beowulf*," in Nicholson and Frese, *Anglo-Saxon Poetry*, 23-40.

S. L. Dragland, "Monster-Man in *Beowulf*," *Neophil* 61 (October 1977): 606-18.

Arthur E. Du Bois, "The Dragon in *Beowulf*," *PMLA* 72 (1957): 819-22.

Arthur E. Du Bois, "The Unity of *Beowulf*," *PMLA* 49 (1934): 374-405.

Katherine Duncan-Jones, "'For *Metode*': *Beowulf* 169," *ES* 49 (October 1968): 418-25.

James W. Earl, "Apocalypticism and Mourning in *Beowulf*," *Thought* 57 (1982): 362-70.

James W. Earl, "Beowulf's Rowing Match," *Neophil* 63 (April 1979): 285-90.

Norman E. Eliason, "The Arrival at Heorot," in *Studies in Language, Literature, and Culture of the Middle Ages and Later*, ed. E. Bagby Atwood and Archibald A. Hill (Austin: University of Texas at Austin, 1969), 235-42.

Norman E. Eliason, "Beowulf's Inglorious Youth," *SP* 76 (Spring 1979): 101-8.

Norman E. Eliason, "The Burning of Heorot," *Speculum* 55 (1980): 75-83.

Norman E. Eliason, "The 'Thryth-Offa Digression' in *Beowulf*," in *Franciplegius: Medieval and Linguistic Studies in Honor of Francis Peabody Magoun, Jr.*, ed. Jess B. Bessinger, Jr., and Robert P. Creed (London: George Allen & Unwin; New York: New York University Press, 1965), 124-38.

Norman E. Eliason, "The þyle and Scop in *Beowulf*," *Speculum* 38 (1963): 267-84. Reprinted in Norman E. Eliason, *English Essays Literary and Linguistic*, ed. Robert G. Benson and Erika C. D. Lindemann (Grand Prairie, Tex.: Scholars Guild, 1975), 59-81.

George J. Engelhardt, "*Beowulf* 3150," *MLN* 68 (1953): 535-38.

George J. Engelhardt, "On the Sequence of Beowulf's *Geogoð*," *MLN* 68 (1953): 91-95.

Donald Fanger, "Three Aspects of Beowulf and His God," *NM* 59 (1958): 172-79.

Lawrence E. Fast, "Hygelac: A Centripetal Force in *Beowulf*," *AnM* 12 (1971): 90-99.

Thalia Phillies Feldman, "A Comparative Study of *Feond*, *Deofl*, *Syn* and *Hel* in *Beowulf*," *NM* 88 (1987): 159-74.

Robert Emmett Finnegan, "Beowulf at the Mere (and Elsewhere)," *Mosaic* 11 (Summer 1978): 45-54.

Peter F. Fisher, "The Trials of the Epic Hero in *Beowulf*," *PMLA* 73 (June 1958): 171-83.

John M. Foley, "*Beowulf* and the Psychohistory of Anglo-Saxon Culture," *AI* 34 (Summer 1977): 133-53.

Donald K. Fry, "*Finnsburh*: A New Interpretation," *ChauR* 9 (1974): 1-14.

Donald K. Fry, "Launching Ships in *Beowulf* 210-16 and *Brunanburh* 32b-36," *MP* 79 (August 1981): 61-66.

Andrew Galloway, "*Beowulf* and the Varieties of Choice," *PMLA* 105 (1990): 202-6.

Gardner, *The Construction of Christian Poetry in Old English*, 54-84.

John Gardner, "Fulgentius's *Expositio Vergiliana Continentia* and the Plan of *Beowulf*: Another Approach to the Poem's Style and Structure," *PLL* 6 (Summer 1970): 227-262.

John Gardner, "Guilt and the World's Complexity: The Murder of Ongentheow and the Slaying of the Dragon," in Nicholson and Frese, *Anglo-Saxon Poetry*, 14-22.

Linda Georgianna, "King Hrethel's Sorrow and the Limits of Heroic Action in *Beowulf*," *Speculum* 64 (1987): 829-50.

Robert S. Gingher, "The Unferth Perplex," *THOTH* 14, no. 2-3 (1974): 19-28.

John Golden, "A Typological Approach to the *Gifstol* of *Beowulf* 168," *NM* 77 (1976): 190-204.

Margaret E. Goldsmith, "The Christian Perspective in *Beowulf*," *CL* 14 (Winter 1962): 71-80. Reprinted in Nicholson, *An Anthology of Beowulf Criticism*, 373-85; *Studies in Old English Literature in Honor of Arthur G. Brodeur*, ed. Stanley B. Greenfield (Eugene: University of Oregon Books, 1963), 71-90.

Margaret E. Goldsmith, "The Christian Theme of *Beowulf*," *MÆ* 29 (1960): 81-101.

Margaret E. Goldsmith, *The Mode and Meaning of Beowulf* (London: University of London, Athlone Press, 1970).

Gradon, *Form and Style*, 127-31.

Martin Green, "Man, Time, and Apocalypse in *The Wanderer*, *The Seafarer*, and *Beowulf*," *JEGP* 74 (1975): 512-17.

Stanley B. Greenfield, "The Authenticating Voice in *Beowulf*," *ASE* 5 (1976): 51-62.

Greenfield, *A Critical History*, 81-92.

Stanley B. Greenfield, "The Extremities of the *Beowulf*ian Body Politic," in *Saints, Scholars, and Heroes: Studies in Medieval Culture in Honour of Charles W. Jones*, Vol. 2, ed. Margot H. King and Wesley M. Stevens (Collegeville, Minn.: Hill Monastic Manuscript Library and Saint John's Abbey and University, 1979), 1-14.

Stanley B. Greenfield, "'Gifstol' and Goldhoard in *Beowulf*," in Burlin and Irving, *Old English Studies*, 107-17.

Stanley B. Greenfield, "Grendel's Approach to Heorot: Syntax and Poetry," in *Old English Poetry: Fifteen Essays*, ed. Robert B. Creed (Providence, R.I.: Brown University Press, 1967): 275-84.

Greenfield, *Hero and Exile*, 19-89.

Stanley B. Greenfield, *The Interpretation of Old English Poems* (London: Routledge & Kegan Paul, 1972), 122-30.

Stanley B. Greenfield, "Of Words and Deeds: The Coastguard's Maxim Once More," in Benson and Wenzel, *The Wisdom of Poetry*, 45-51.

Stanley B. Greenfield, "A Touch of the Monstrous in the Hero, or Beowulf Re-Marvellized," *ES* 63 (August 1982): 294-300.

Greenfield and Calder, *A New Critical History*, 136-46.

John Halverson, "*Beowulf* and the Pitfalls of Piety," *UTQ* 35 (April 1966): 260-78.

John Halverson, "The World of *Beowulf*," *ELH* 36 (1969): 593-608.

Marie P. Hamilton, "The Religious Principle in *Beowulf*," *PMLA* 61 (1946): 309-30.

Robert W. Hanning, "*Beowulf* as Heroic History," *M&H*, n.s. 5 (1974): 88-99.

Robert W. Hanning, "Sharing, Dividing, Depriving – The Verbal Ironies of Grendel's Last Visit to Heorot," *TSLL* 15 (Summer 1973): 203-13.

Elaine Tuttle Hansen, "Hrothgar's 'Sermon' in *Beowulf* as Parental Wisdom," *ASE* 10 (1982): 53-67.

Hansen, *The Solomon Complex*, 55-67.

Adelaide Hardy, "The Christian Hero Beowulf and Unferð þyle," *Neophil* 53 (January 1969): 55-69.

A. Leslie Harris, "Litotes and Superlative in *Beowulf*," *ES* 69 (February 1988): 1-11.

William Helder, "*Beowulf* and the Plundered Hoard," *NM* 78 (1977): 317-25.

Jeffrey Helterman," *Beowulf*: The Archetype Enters History," *ELH* 35 (1968): 1-20.

John P. Herman, *Expl* 37 (Spring 1979): 24-25.

John M. Hill, "Beowulf and the Danish Succession: Gift Giving as an Occasion for Complex Gesture," *M&H*, n.s. 11 (1982): 177-97.

John M. Hill, "*Beowulf*, Value, and the Frame of Time," *MLQ* 40 (March 1979): 3-16.

John M. Hill, "Revenge and Superego Mastery in *Beowulf*," *Assays* 5 (1989): 3-36.

Sylvia Huntley Horowitz, "The Interrupted Battles in *Beowulf*," *NM* 85 (1984): 295-304.

Sylvia Huntley Horowitz, "The Ravens in *Beowulf*," *JEGP* 80 (1981): 502-11.

David R. Howlett, "Form and Genre in *Beowulf*," *SN* 46 (1974): 309-25.

Geoffrey Hughes, "*Beowulf*, Unferth and Hrunting: An Interpretation," *ES* 58 (October 1977): 385-95.

Kathryn Hume, "The Theme and Structure of *Beowulf*," *SP* 72 (1975): 1-27.

Bernard F. Huppé, "The Concept of the Hero in the Early Middle Ages," in *Concepts of the Hero in the Middle Ages and the Renaissance*, ed. Norman T. Burns and Christopher J. Reagan (Albany: State University of New York Press, 1975), 19-23.

Bernard F. Huppé, *The Hero in the Earthly City: A Reading of Beowulf*, Medieval & Renaissance Texts & Studies, no. 33 (Binghamton: State University of New York at Binghamton, 1984).

Edward B. Irving, Jr., "Beowulf Comes Home: Close Reading in Epic Context," in Carruthers and Kirk, *Acts of Interpretation*, 129-43.

Edward B. Irving, Jr., *Introduction to "Beowulf"* (Englewood Cliffs, N.J.: Prentice-Hall, 1969.).

Edward B. Irving, Jr., "The Nature of Christianity in *Beowulf*," *ASE* 13 (1984): 7-21.

Edward B. Irving, Jr., *A Reading of "Beowulf"* (New Haven and London: Yale University Press, 1968).

Edward B. Irving, Jr., *Rereading "Beowulf"* (Philadelphia: University of Pennsylvania Press, 1989).

W. T. H. Jackson, *The Hero and the King: An Epic Theme* (New York: Columbia University Press, 1982), 26-36, 126-27.

J. G. Johansen, "Grendel the Brave? *Beowulf*, Line 834," *ES* 63 (June 1982): 193-97.

Samuel F. Johnson, *Expl* 9 (1951): 52.

Stanley Kahrl, "Feuds in *Beowulf*: A Tragic Necessity," *MP* 69 (February 1972): 189-98.

R. E. Kaske, "Beowulf," in *Critical Approaches to Six Major English Works: "Beowulf" Through "Paradise Lost,"* ed. R. M. Lumiansky and Herschel Baker (Philadelphia: University of Pennsylvania Press, 1968), 3-40.

R. E. Kaske, "*Sapientia et fortitudo* as the Controlling Theme of *Beowulf*," *SP* 60 (July 1958): 423-57. Reprinted in Nicholson, *An Anthology of Beowulf Criticism*, 269-310.

Robert E. Kaske, "The Sigemund-Heremod and Hama-Hygelac Passages in *Beowulf*," *PMLA* 74 (1959): 489-94.

Robert E. Kaske, "Weohstan's Sword," *MLN* 75 (1960): 465-68.

Harry E. Kavros, "*Swefan æfter Symble*: The Feast Sleep Them in *Beowulf*," *Neophil* 65 (January 1981): 120-28.

Kennedy, *The Earliest English Poetry*, 53-100.

Robert L. Kindrick, "Germanic *Sapientia* and the Heroic Ethos of Beowulf," *M&H*, n.s. 10 (1981): 1-17.

Clare Kinney, "The Needs of the Moment: Poetic Foregrounding as a Narrative Device in *Beowulf*," *SP* 82 (Summer 1985): 295-314.

Johann Köberl, "The Magic Sword in *Beowulf*," *Neophil* 71 (January 1987): 120-28.

Norma Kroll, "*Beowulf*: The Hero as Keeper of Human Polity," *MP* 84 (November 1986): 117-29.

Sherman M. Kuhn, "*Beowulf* and the Life of Beowulf: A Study in Epic Structure," in *Studies in Language, Literature, and Culture of the Middle Ages and Later in Honor of Rudolph Willard*, ed. Elmer Bagby Atwood and Archibald A. Hill (Austin: University of Texas at Austin, 1969): 243-64.

Lawrence, Seifter, and Ratner, *McGraw-Hill Guide*, 8-10.

William W. Lawrence, "The Dragon and His Lair in *Beowulf*," *PMLA* 33 (1918): 547-83.

Lee, *The Guest-Hall*, 171-223.

Winfred P. Lehmann, "*Beowulf* 33, *īsig*," *MLN* 74 (November 1959): 577-78.

John Leyerle, "Beowulf the Hero and the King," *MÆ* 34 (1965): 89-102.

John Leyerle, "The Interlace Structure of *Beowulf*," *UTQ* 37 (October 1967): 1-17.

Elisabeth M. Liggins, "Revenge and Reward as Recurrent Motives in *Beowulf*," *NM* 74 (1973): 193-213.

Richard Lock, *Aspects of Time in Medieval Literature* (New York and London: Garland Publishing, 1985), 46-54, 142-71.

Albert Bates Lord, "Beowulf and Odysseus," in *Franciplegius: Medieval and Linguistic Studies in Honor of Francis Peabody Magoun, Jr.*, ed. Jess B. Bessinger, Jr., and Robert P. Creed (London: George Allen & Unwin; New York: New York University Press, 1965), 86-92.

Albert Bates Lord, "Interlocking Mythic Patterns in *Beowulf*," in *Old English Literature in Context*, ed. John D. Niles (Cambridge: D. S. Brewer; Totowa, N.J.: Rowman and Littlefield, 1980): 137-42.

R. M. Lumiansky, "The Dramatic Audience in *Beowulf*," *JEGP* 51 (1952): 545-550. Reprinted in Fry, *The Beowulf Poet*, 76-82.

Robert M. Lumiansky, "Wiglaf," *CE* 14 (January 1953): 202-6.

John C. McGalliard, "The Poet's Comment in *Beowulf*," *SP* 75 (July 1978): 243-70.

Daniel McGuiness, "Beowulf's Byrnies," *ELN* 26 (March 1989): 1-3.

John McNamara, *Expl* 32 (April 1974): 62.

M. B. McNamee, S. J., "*Beowulf*–An Allegory of Salvation?" *JEGP* 59 (1960): 190-207. Reprinted in Nicholson, *An Anthology of Beowulf Criticism*, 331-52.

Lars Malmberg, "Grendel and the Devil," *NM* 78 (1977): 241-43.

Kemp Malone, "*Beowulf*," *ES* 29 (1948): 161-72. Reprinted in Nicholson, *An Anthology of Beowulf Criticism*, 137-54; *Literary Masterpieces of the Western World*, ed. F. H. Horn (Baltimore, Md: Johns Hopkins University Press, 1953).

Kemp Malone, "Beowulf the Headstrong," *ASE* 1 (1972): 139-45.

Kemp Malone, "Coming Back from the Mere," *PMLA* 69 (1954): 1292-99.

Kemp Malone, "The Finn Episode in *Beowulf*," *JEGP* 25 (1926): 157-72.

Kemp Malone, "Ingeld," *MP* 27 (1930): 257-76.

Kemp Malone, "Young Beowulf," *JEGP* 36 (1937): 21-23.

Douglas S. Mead, *Expl* 2 (October 1943): 2.

Allan Metcalf, "Ten Natural Animals in *Beowulf*," *NM* 64 (1963): 378-89.

Bruce Moore, "The Relevance of the Finnsburh Episode," *JEGP* 75 (1976): 317-29.

Bruce Moore, "The Thryth-Offa Digression in *Beowulf*," *Neophil* 64 (January 1980): 127-33.

Gerald Morgan, "The Treachery of Hrothulf," *ES* 53 (February 1972): 23-39.

Lewis E. Nicholson, "Hunlafing and the Point of the Sword," in Nicholson and Frese, *Anglo-Saxon Poetry*, 50-61.

Lewis E. Nicholson, "The Literal Meaning and Symbolic Structure of *Beowulf*," *Classica and Medievalia* 25 (1964): 151-201.

John D. Niles, *Beowulf: The Poem and Its Tradition* (Cambridge, Mass., and London: Harvard University Press, 1983), 179-247.

John D. Niles, "Ring Composition and the Structure of *Beowulf*," *PMLA* 94 (1979): 924-35.

John A. Nist, *The Structure and Texture of "Beowulf"* (São Paulo, Brasil: Universidade de São Paulo, 1959).

John A. Nist, "The Structure of *Beowulf*," *Papers of the Michigan Academy of Science, Arts, and Letters* 43 (1958): 307-14.

Jane C. Nitzsche, "The Structural Unity of *Beowulf*: The Problem of Grendel's Mother," *TSLL* 22 (Fall 1980): 287-303.

Jerome Oetgen, "Order and Chaos in the World of *Beowulf*," *ABR* 29 (June 1978): 134-52.

Jack D. A. Ogilvy, "Unferth: Foil to Beowulf?" *PMLA* 79 (1964): 370-75.

Jack D. A. Ogilvy and Donald C. Baker, *Reading "Beowulf": An Introduction to the Poem, Its Background and Its Style* (Norman: University of Oklahoma Press, 1983).

Katherine O'Brian O'Keefe, "*Beowulf*, Lines 702b-836: Transformations and the Limits of the Human," *TSLL* 23 (Winter 1981): 484-94.

J. L. N. O'Loughlin, "*Beowulf*–Its Unity and Purpose," *MÆ* 21 (1952): 1-13.

Marijane Osborn, "The Great Feud: Scriptural History and Strife in *Beowulf*," *PMLA* 93 (1978): 973-81.

Marijane Osborn, "Some Uses of Ambiguity in *Beowulf*," *THOTH* 10, no. 1 (1969): 18-35.

Gillian R. Overing, "Patterning, Time and Nietzsche's 'Spirit of Revenge' in *Beowulf* and the *Mayor of Casterbridge*," *UMSE*, n.s. 7 (1989): 41-50.

R. Barton Palmer, "In His End Is His Beginning: *Beowulf*, 2177-2199 and the Question of Unity," *AnM* 17 (1976): 5-21.

F. Anne Payne, "The Danes' Prayers to the 'Gastbona' in *Beowulf*," *NM* 80 (1979): 308-14.

F. Anne Payne, "Three Aspects of Wyrd in *Beowulf*," in Burlin and Irving, *Old English Studies*, 15-35.

Thomas Pettitt, "*Beowulf*: The Mark of the Beast and the Balance of Frenzy," *NM* 77 (1976): 526-35.

John C. Pope, "*Beowulf* 505 *gehedde* and the Pretensions of Unferth," in Brown, Crampton, and Robinson, *Modes of Interpretation*, 173-211.

John C. Pope, "Beowulf's Old Age," in *Philological Essays: Studies in Old and Middle English Language and Literature in Honour of Herbert Dean Merritt*, ed. James L. Rosier (The Hague and Paris: Mouton, 1970), 55-64.

John C. Pope, "The Existential Mysteries as Treated in Certain Passages of Our Older Poets," in Carruthers and Kirk, *Acts of Interpretation* 350-54.

Strother B. Purdy, "Beowulf and Hrothgar's Dream," *ChauR* 21 (1986): 257-73.

Lee C. Ramsey, "The Sea Voyages in *Beowulf*," *NM* 72 (1971): 51-59.

Raw, *The Art and Background of Old English Poetry* , 84-96 *passim*.

Alain Renoir, *A Key to Old Poems: The Oral-Formulaic Approach to the Interpretation of West-Germanic Verse* (University Park and London: Pennsylvania State University Press, 1988), 107-32.

Alain Renoir, "Point of View and Design for Terror in *Beowulf*," *NM* 63 (1962): 154-67. Reprinted in Fry, *The Beowulf Poet*, 154-66.

Samuel M. Riley, *Expl* 40 (Summer 1982): 2-3.

Richard N. Ringler, "*Him Seo Wen Geleah*: The Design for Irony in Grendel's Last Visit to Heorot," *Speculum* 41 (1966): 49-67.

D. W. Robertson, Jr., "The Doctrine of Charity in Mediaeval Literary Gardens: A Topical Approach through Symbolism and Allegory," *Speculum* 26 (1951): 24-49. Reprinted in Nicholson, *An Anthology of Beowulf Criticism*, 165-88; Robertson, *Essays in Medieval Culture*, 21-50.

Fred C. Robinson, *"Beowulf" and the Appositive Style* (Knoxville: University of Tennessee Press, 1985).

Fred C. Robinson, "Elements of the Marvellous in the Characterization of Beowulf: A Reconsideration of the Textual Evidence," in Burlin and Irving, *Old English Studies*, 119-37.

H. L. Rogers, "Beowulf's Three Great Fights," *RES*, n.s. 6 (October 1955): 339-55. Reprinted in Nicholson, *An Anthology of Beowulf Criticism*, 233-56.

Alan H. Roper, "Boethius and the Three Fates of *Beowulf*," *PQ* 41 (1962): 386-400.

J. L. Rosier, "Design for Treachery: The Unferth Intrigue," *PMLA* 77 (1962): 1-7.

Geoffrey R. Russom, "Artful Avoidance of the Useful Phrase in *Beowulf*, *The Battle of Maldon*, and *Fates of the Apostles*," *SP* 75 (October 1978): 371-90.

Geoffrey R. Russom, "A Germanic Concept of Nobility in *The Gifts of Men* and *Beowulf*," *Speculum* 53 (1978): 1-15.

Jay Ruud, "Gardner's Grendel and *Beowulf*: Humanizing the Monster," *THOTH* 14, no. 2/3 (1974): 3-17.

Walter Scheps, "The Sequential Nature of Beowulf's Three Fights," *Rendezvous* 9 (1974-75): 41-50.

Brian A. Shaw, "The Speeches in *Beowulf*: A Structural Study," *ChauR* 13 (1978): 86-92.

Thomas A. Shippey, *Beowulf*, Studies in English Literature, no. 76 (London: Edward Arnold, 1978).

Patricia Silber, "Gold and Its Significance in *Beowulf*," *AnM* 18 (1977): 5-19.

Patricia Silber, "Rhetoric as Prowess in the Unferð Episode," *TSLL* 23 (Winter 1981): 471-83.

Kenneth Sisam, *The Structure of "Beowulf"* (Oxford: Clarendon Press, 1965).

G. V. Smithers, "Destiny and the Heroic Warrior in *Beowulf*," in *Philological Essays: Studies in Old and Middle English Language and Literature in Honour of Herbert Dean Merritt*, ed. James L. Rosier (The Hague and Paris: Mouton, 1970), 65-81.

James Smith, "*Beowulf*-I," *English* 25 (Autumn 1976): 203-29.

James Smith, "*Beowulf*-II," *English* 26 (Spring 1977): 3-22.

Sarah Stanbury Smith, "*Folce to Frofre*: The Theme of Consolation in *Beowulf*," *ABR* 30 (June 1979): 191-204.

James B. Spamer, "*Beowulf* 1-2: An Argument for a New Reading," *ES* 65 (June 1981): 210-14.

Martin Stevens, "The Structure of *Beowulf*: From Gold-Hoard to Word-Hoard," *MLQ* 39 (September 1978): 219-38.

Godfrid Storms, "The Figure of Beowulf in the O. E. Epic," *ES* 60 (1959): 3-13.

Godfrid Storms, "Grendel the Terrible," *NM* 78 (1972): 427-36.

Swanton, *English Literature*, 49-67.

Paul Beekman Taylor, "*Searoniðas*: Old Norse Magic and Old English Verse," *SP* 80 (Spring 1983): 109-25.

Paul Beekman Taylor, "Themes of Death in *Beowulf*," in *Old English Poetry: Fifteen Essays*, ed. Robert B. Creed (Providence, R.I.: Brown University Press, 1967), 249-74.

M. K. Temple, "*Beowulf* 1258-1266: Grendel's Lady-Mother," *ELN* 23 (March 1986): 10-15.

Mary C. Wilson Tietjen, "God, Fate, and the Hero of *Beowulf*," *JEGP* 74 (1975): 159-71.

J. R. R. Tolkien, "*Beowulf*: The Monsters and the Critics," *PBA* 22 (1936): 245-95. Reprinted in Fry, *The Beowulf Poet*, 8-56; Nicholson, *An Anthology of Beowulf Criticism*, 51-103.

H. Ward Tonsfeldt, "Ring Structure in *Beowulf*," *Neophil* 61 (July 1977): 443-52.

Raymond P. Tripp, Jr., "Lifting the Curse on *Beowulf*," *ELN* 23 (December 1985): 1-8.

Raymond P. Tripp, Jr., *More About the Fight with the Dragon: "Beowulf" 2208b-3182, Commentary, Edition, and Translation* (Lanham, N.Y., and London: University Press of America, 1983), 1-366.

Raymond P. Tripp, Jr., "The Restoration of *Beowulf* 2781a: *Hāt ne forhogode* ('Did Not Despise Heat')," *MP* 78 (November 1980): 153-58.

J. C. van Meurs, "*Beowulf* and Literary Criticism," *Neophil* 39 (1955): 114-30.

John F. Vickrey, "The Narrative Structure of Hengest's Revenge in *Beowulf*," *ASE* 6 (1977): 91-103.

John F. Vickrey, "Un[h]litme 'Voluntarily' in *Beowulf* Line 1097," *JEGP* 87 (1988): 315-28.

Karl P. Wentersdorf, "Beowulf's Adventure with Breca," *SP* 72 (April 1975): 140-66.

Karl P. Wentersdorf, "Beowulf's Withdrawal from Frisia: A Reconsideration," *SP* 68 (July 1971): 395-415.

F. H. Whitman, "The Kingly Nature of Beowulf," *Neophil* 61 (April 1977): 277-86.

David Williams, *Cain and Beowulf: A Study in Secular Allegory* (Toronto, Buffalo, and London: University of Toronto Press, 1982).

R. A. Williams, *The Finn Episode in Beowulf: An Essay in Interpretation* (Cambridge: Cambridge University Press, 1924).

Henry B. Woolf, "Unferth," *MLQ* 10 (1949): 145-52.

C. L. Wrenn, "Introduction" to *Beowulf: With the Finnesburg Fragment*, (Boston: D. C. Heath; London: George G. Harrap, 1953), 65-76; 3d ed., 1973, 62-87.

Herbert G. Wright, "Good and Evil; Light and Darkness; Joy and Sorrow in *Beowulf*," *RES*, n.s. 8 (1957): 1-11. Abridged in Nicholson, *An Anthology of Beowulf Criticism*, 257-67.

CAEDMON

"Hymn"

Greenfield and Calder, *A New Critical History*, 227-31.

Huppé, *Doctrine and Poetry*, 99-130. Reprinted in Stevens and Mandel, *Old English Literature*, 117-38.

K. O. O'Keeffe, "Orality and the Developing Text of Caedmon's *Hymn*," *Speculum* 62 (1987): 1-20.

Swanton, *English Literature*, 73-74.

CAXTON, WILLIAM

Paris and Vienne (Eng. trans.)

Richmond, *The Popularity*, 142-48.

CHARLES OF ORLEANS

"Honure, Ioy, Helthe and Plesaunce"

Gradon, *Form and Style*, 346-47.

"The Smylyng Mouth and Laughyng Eyen Gray"

Gradon, *Form and Style*, 336-38.

CHAUCER, GEOFFREY

"An A B C"

Georgia Ronan Crampton, "Of Chaucer's ABC," *Chaucer Newsletter* 1 (Winter 1979): 8-10.

Alfred David, "An ABC to the Style of the Prioress," in Carruthers and Kirk, *Acts of Interpretation*, 147-54.

Ralph A. Klinefelter, *Expl* 23 (September 1965): 5.

Rogers, *Image and Abstraction*, 94-106.

Anelida and Arcite

Wolfgang Clemen, *Chaucer's Early Poetry*, trans. C. A. M. Sym (London: Methuen, 1963; New York: Barnes & Noble, 1964), 197-209.

Davenport, *Chaucer: Complaint and Narrative*, 24-33.

Gardner, *The Poetry of Chaucer*, 74-78.

Doreen Gillam, "Lovers and Riders in Chaucer's *Anelida and Arcite*," *ES* 63 (October 1982): 394-401.

Gwendolyn Morgan, *Expl* 47 (Winter 1989): 3-5.

Book of the Duchess

Donald C. Baker, "Imagery and Structure in Chaucer's *Book of the Duchess*," *SN* 30 (1958): 17-26.

Normand Berlin, "Chaucer's *The Book of the Duchess* and Spenser's *Daphnaida*: A Contrast," *SN* 38 (1966): 282-89.

Earle Birney, *Essays on Chaucerian Irony*, ed. Beryl Rowland (Toronto: University of Toronto Press, 1985), 60-64.

Ian Bishop, "Chaucer and the Rhetoric of Consolation," *MÆ* 52 (1983): 39-41.

N. F. Blake, "*The Book of the Duchess* Again," *ES* 67 (1986): 122-25.

Philip C. Boardman, "Courtly Language and the Strategy of Consolation in the *Book of the Duchess*," *ELH* 44 (1977): 567-79.

Boitani, *English Medieval Narrative*, 140-49, 183-92, and *passim*.

Piero Boitani, "Old Books Brought to Life in Dreams: The *Book of the Duchess*, the *House of Fame*, the *Parliament of Fowls*," in Boitani and Mann, *The Cambridge Chaucer Companion*, 44-47.

Brewer, *An Introduction to Chaucer*, 57-61 *passim*.

Bertrand H. Bronson, "The *Book of the Duchess* Re-opened," *PMLA* 67 (1952): 863-81. Reprinted in Wagenknecht, *Chaucer*, 271-94.

D. Brunley, "Some Terminology of Perception in the *Book of the Duchess*," *ELN* 23 (March 1986): 15-22.

Burlin, *Chaucerian Fiction*, 59-74.

M. Angela Carson, O. S. U., "Easing of the 'Hert' in the *Book of the Duchess*," *ChauR* 1 (1967): 157-60.

Cherniss, *Boethian Apocalypse*, 169-91.

Michael D. Cherniss, "The Narrator Asleep and Awake in Chaucer's *Book of the Duchess*," *PLL* 8 (Spring 1972): 115-26.

Wolfgang Clemen, *Chaucer's Early Poetry*, trans. C. A. M. Sym (New York: Barnes & Noble, 1964), 23-66.

Corsa, *Chaucer: Poet of Mirth*, 4-19.

Georgia Ronan Crampton, "Transitions and Meaning in *The Book of the Duchess*," *JEGP* 62 (July 1963): 486-500.

Davidoff, *Beginning Well*, 101-14.

James Dean, "Chaucer's *Book of the Duchess*: A Non-Boethian Interpretation," *MLQ* 46 (September 1985): 235-49.

Rodney Delasanta, "Christian Affirmation in *The Book of the Duchess*," *PMLA* 84 (1969): 245-51.

Raymond D. Dilorenzo, "Wonder and Words: Paganism, Christianity, and Consolation in Chaucer's *Book of the Duchess*," *UTQ* 52 (Fall 1982): 20-39.

Colleen Donnelly, "Challenging the Conventions of Dream Vision in *The Book of the Duchess*," *PQ* 66 (Fall 1987): 421-35.

Dove, *The Perfect Age*, 141-47.

Julia G. Ebel, "Chaucer's *The Book of the Duchess*," *CE* 29 (December 1967): 197-206.

Robert R. Edwards, "The *Book of the Duchess* and the Beginnings of Chaucer's Narrative," *NLH* 13 (Winter 1982): 189-204.

Robert R. Edwards, *The Dream of Chaucer: Representation and Reflection in the Early Narratives* (Durham and London: Duke University Press, 1989), 65-91 and *passim*.

Judith Ferster, *Chaucer on Interpretation* (Cambridge: Cambridge University Press, 1985), 69-93.

Judith Ferster, "Intention and Interpretation in *The Book of the Duchess*," *Criticism* 22 (Winter 1980): 1-24.

Joerg O. Fichte, "*The Book of the Duchess* – A Consolation?" *SN* 45 (1973): 53-67.

John Block Friedman, "The Dreamer, the Whelp, and Consolation in the *Book of the Duchess*," *ChauR* 3 (1969): 145-62.

Fyler, *Chaucer and Ovid*, 65-81.

John M. Fyler, "Irony and the Age of Gold in the *Book of the Duchess*," *Speculum* 52 (1977): 314-28.

Gardner, *The Poetry of Chaucer*, 1-41.

John Gardner, "Style as Meaning in the *Book of the Duchess*," *Lang&S* 2 (Spring 1969): 143-71.

Joseph E. Grennen, "*Hert-huntying* in the *Book of the Duchess*," *MLQ* 25 (June 1964): 131-39.

Robert W. Hanning, "Chaucer's First Ovid: Metamorphosis and Poetic Tradition in the *Book of the Duchess* and the *House of Fame*," in Arrathoon, *Chaucer and the Craft*, 134-41.

Duncan Harris and Nancy L. Steffen, "The Other Side of the Garden: An Interpretive Comparison of Chaucer's *Book of the Duchess* and Spenser's *Daphnaida*," *JMRS* 8 (1978): 17-36.

Carol Falvo Heffernan, "That Dog Again: *Melancholia Caning* and Chaucer's *Book of the Duchess*," *MP* 84 (November 1986): 185-90.

Michael B. Herzog, "*The Book of the Duchess*: The Vision of the Artist as a Young Dreamer," *ChauR* 22 (1988): 269-81.

Hieatt, *The Realism of Dream Visions*, 67-73.

John M. Hill, "*The Book of the Duchess*, Melancholy, and that Eight-Year Sickness," *ChauR* 9 (1974): 35-50.

Edwin J. Howard, *Geoffrey Chaucer* (New York: Twayne, 1964), 54-60.

Bernard F. Huppé and D. W. Robertson, Jr., *Fruyt and Chaf: Studies in Chaucer's Allegories* (Princeton, N.J.: Princeton University Press, 1963), 32-100.

Hussey, *Chaucer*, 29-36.

Robert M. Jordan, "The Compositional Structure of the *Book of the Duchess*," *ChauR* 9 (1974): 99-117.

Kean, *Love Division and Debate*, 52-66.

Alfred L. Kellogg, *Chaucer, Langland, Arthur: Essays in Middle English Literature* (New Brunswick, N.J.: Rutgers University Press, 1972), 83-95.

Lisa J. Kiser, "Sleep, Dreams, and Poetry in Chaucer's *Book of the Duchess*," *PLL* 19 (Winter 1983): 3-12.

George Lyman Kittredge, *Chaucer and His Poetry* (Cambridge, Mass.: Harvard University Press, 1915; reprint, 1946), 37-72.

James R. Kreuzer, "The Dreamer in *The Book of the Duchess*," *PMLA* 66 (1951): 543-47.

Allen D. Lackey, *Expl* 32 (May 1974): 74.

John Lawlor, "The Earlier Poems," in *Chaucer & Chaucerians: Critical Studies in Middle English Literature*, ed. D. S. Brewer (University: University of Alabama Press, 1966), 42-45.

John Lawlor, "The Pattern of Consolation in *The Book of the Duchess*," *Speculum* 31 (1956): 626-48. Reprinted in Schoeck and Taylor, *Chaucer Criticism, II*, 230-60.

Leonard, *Laughter in the Courts of Love*, 34-38.

John Leyerle, "The Heart and the Chain," in Benson, *The Learned and the Lewed*, 114-18.

David Luisi, "The Hunt Motif in *The Book of the Duchess*," *ES* 52 (August 1971): 309-11.

R. M. Lumiansky, "The Bereaved Narrator in Chaucer's *The Book of the Duchess*," *TSE* 9 (1959): 5-17.

Andrew Lynch, "'Taking Keep' of the *Book of the Duchess,*" in *Medieval English Religious and Ethical Literature: Essays in Honour of G. H. Russell*, ed. Gregory Kratzmann and James Simpson (Cambridge: D. S. Brewer, 1986), 167-78.

Kathryn L. Lynch, "The *Book of the Duchess* as a Philosophical Vision: The Argument of Form," *Genre* 21 (Fall 1988): 279-306.

McCall, *Chaucer among the Gods*, 18-22, 44-45.

Kemp Malone, *Chapters on Chaucer* (Baltimore, Md.: Johns Hopkins Press, 1951), 22-41.

Ellen E. Martin, "Spenser, Chaucer, and the Rhetoric of Elegy," *JMRS* 17 (Spring 1987): 84-88.

Mehl, *Geoffrey Chaucer*, 22-36.

Mogan, *Chaucer and the Theme*, 94-99.

Ruth Morse, "Understanding the Man in Black," *ChauR* 15 (1981): 204-8.

Barbara Nolan, "The Art of Expropriation: Chaucer's Narrator in *The Book of the Duchess*," in *New Perspectives in Chaucer Criticism*, ed. Donald M. Rose (Norman, Okla.: Pilgrim Books, 1981), 203-22.

North, *Chaucer's Universe*, 342-48.

Payne, *The Key of Remembrance*, 121-29.

Robert O. Payne, *Geoffrey Chaucer*, 2d ed. (Boston: Twayne Publishers, 1986), 57-61.

Helen Phillips, "The *Book of the Duchess*, Lines 31-96: Are They a Forgery?" *ES* 67 (1986): 113-21.

Sandra Pierson Prior, "*Routhe* and *Hert-Huntyng* in the *Book of the Duchess*," *JEGP* 85 (1986): 3-19.

Edmund Reiss, "Chaucer's Parodies of Love," in Mitchell and Provost, *Chaucer the Love Poet*, 34-36.

D. W. Robertson, Jr., "The Historical Setting of Chaucer's *Book of the Duchess*," in *Medieval Studies in Honor of Urban Tigner Holmes, Jr.,* ed. John Mahoney and John Esten Keller (Chapel Hill: University of North Carolina Press, 1965), 169-95. Reprinted in Robertson, *Essays in Medieval Culture*, 235-56.

D. W. Robertson, Jr., *A Preface to Chaucer* (London: Oxford University Press, 1962), 463-66.

Anne Rooney, "*The Book of the Duchess*: Hunting and the 'Ubi Sunt' Tradition," *RES*, n.s. 38 (August 1987): 299-314.

Diane M. Ross, "The Play of Genres in the *Book of the Duchess*," *ChauR* 19 (1984): 1-13.

Beryl Rowland, "The Chess Problem in Chaucer's *Book of the Duchess*," *Anglia* 80 (1962): 384-89.

Beryl Rowland, "The Horse and Rider Figure in Chaucer's Works," *UTQ* 35 (April 1966): 250-52.

Beryl Rowland, "The Whelp in Chaucer's *Book of the Duchess*," *NM* 66 (1965): 148-60.

J. Stephen Russell, *The English Dream Vision: Anatomy of a Form* (Columbus: Ohio State University Press, 1988), 142-59.

Lynn Veach Sadler, "Chaucer's *The Book of the Duchess* and the 'Law of Kinde,'" *AnM* 11 (1970): 51-64.

Gale C. Schricker, "On the Relation of Fact and Fiction in Chaucer's Poetic Endings," *PQ* 60 (Winter 1981): 13-27.

David Scott-Macnab, "A Re-examination of Octovyen's Hunt in *The Book of the Duchess*," *MÆ* 56 (1987): 183-99.

J. Burke Severs, "Chaucer's Self-Portrait in the *Book of the Duchess*," *PQ* 43 (January 1964): 27-39.

R. A. Shoaf, "'Mutatio Amoris': 'Penitentia' and the Form of *The Book of the Duchess*," *Genre* 14 (Summer 1981): 163-89.

R. A. Shoaf, "Stalking the Sorrowful H(e)art: Penitential Love and the Hunt Scene in Chaucer's *The Book of the Duchess*," *JEGP* 78 (1979): 313-24.

Sklute, *Virtue of Necessity*, 23-34.

Spearing, *Medieval Dream-Poetry*, 49-73.

Spearing, *Readings in Medieval Poetry*, 94-106.

Martin Stevens, "Narrative Focus in *The Book of the Duchess*: A Critical Reevaluation," *AnM* 7 (1966): 16-32.

Kay Gilliland Stevenson, "Readers, Poets, and Poems Within the Poem," *ChauR* 24 (1989): 1-19.

Charles P. R. Tisdale, "Boethian 'Hert-Huntyng': The Elegiac Pattern of *The Book of the Duchess*," *ABR* 24 (September 1973): 365-80.

Derek Traversi, *Chaucer, the Earlier Poetry: A Study in Poetic Development* (London and Toronto: Associated University Presses; Newark: University of Delaware Press, 1987), 33-53.

Denis Walker, "Narrative Inconclusiveness and Consolatory Dialectic in the *Book of the Duchess*," *ChauR* 18 (1983): 1-17.

F. H. Whitman, "Exegesis and Chaucer's Dream Visions," *ChauR* 3 (1969): 229-38.

G. R. Wilson, Jr., "The Anatomy of Compassion: Chaucer's *Book of the Duchess*," *TSLL* 14 (Fall 1972): 381-88.

Wimsatt, *Allegory and Mirror*, 61-84 *passim*.

James I. Wimsatt, "*The Book of the Duchess*: Secular Elegy or Religious Vision?" in Hermann and Burke, *Signs and Symbols*, 113-29.

James I. Wimsatt, *Chaucer and the French Love Poets: The Literary Background of the "Book of the Duchess"* (Chapel Hill: University of North Carolina Press, 1968), 12-29.

James Winny, *Chaucer's Dream-Poems* (New York: Barnes & Noble, 1973), 44-75.

Rose A. Zimbardo, "The *Book of the Duchess* and the Dream of Folly," *ChauR* 18 (1984): 329-46.

Canon's Yeoman's Tale

R. G. Baldwin, "The Yeoman's Canons: A Conjecture," *JEGP* 61 (1962): 232-43.

Bishop, *The Narrative Art*, 113-18.

Peter Brown, "Is the 'Canon's Yeoman's Tale' Apocryphal?" *ES* 64 (December 1983): 481-90.

Burlin, *Chaucerian Fiction*, 175-80.

Robert Cook, "The Canon's Yeoman and His Tale," *ChauR* 22 (1987): 28-40.

James Dean, "Dismantling the Canterbury Book," *PMLA* 100 (1985): 749-52.

Donald R. Dickson, "The 'Slidynge' Yeoman: The Real Drama in the *Canon's Yeoman's Tale*," *SCRev* 2 (1985): 10-22.

Karl E. Felsen, *Expl* 41 (Fall 1982): 2.

John Gardner, "The *Canon's Yeoman's Prologue and Tale*: An Interpretation," *PQ* 46 (1967): 1-17.

Gardner, *The Poetry of Chaucer*, 323-31.

Bruce L. Grenberg, "The *Canon's Yeoman's Tale*: Boethian Wisdom and the Alchemists," *ChauR* 1 (Summer 1966): 37-54.

Joseph Edward Grennan, "The Canon's Yeoman's Alchemical 'Mass,'" *SP* 62 (July 1965): 546-60.

Joseph Edward Grennan, "The Canon's Yeoman and the Cosmic Furnace: Language and Meaning in the 'Canon's Yeoman's Tale,'" *Criticism* 4 (Summer 1962): 225-40.

David V. Harrington, "Dramatic Irony in the *Canon's Yeoman's Tale*," *NM* 66 (1965): 160-66.

David V. Harrington, "The Narrator of the *Canon's Yeoman's Tale*," *AnM* 9 (1968): 85-97.

Britton J. Harwood, "Chaucer and the Silence of History: Situating the *Canon's Yeoman's Tale*," *PMLA* 102 (1987): 338-50.

Ann S. Haskell, *Essays on Chaucer's Saints* (The Hague and Paris: Mouton, 1976), 26-29.

Ann S. Haskell, "The St. Giles Oath in the *Canon's Yeoman's Tale*," *ChauR* 7 (1973): 221-26.

Knight, *The Poetry of the Canterbury Tales*, 180-87.

Stoddard Malarkey, "Chaucer's Yeoman Again," *CE* 24 (January 1963): 289-95.

Charles Muscatine, *Chaucer and the French Tradition* (Berkeley and Los Angeles: University of California Press, 1957), 213-21.

K. Michael Olmert, "*The Canon's Yeoman's Tale*: An Interpretation," *AnM* 8 (1967): 70-94.

John Reidy, "Chaucer's Canon and the Unity of *The Canon's Yeoman's Tale*," *PMLA* 80 (1965): 31-37.

Rogers, *Upon the Ways*, 113-16.

Bruce A. Rosenberg, "The Contrary Tales of the Second Nun and the Canon's Yeoman," *ChauR* 2 (Spring 1968): 278-91.

Bruce A. Rosenberg, "Swindling Alchemist, Antichrist," *CRAS* 6 (Spring 1962): 566-80.

Ruggiers, *The Art of the Canterbury Tales*, 131-41.

Lawrence V. Ryan, "The Canon's Yeoman's Desperate Confession," *ChauR* 8 (1974): 297-310.

Paul B. Taylor, "The Canon's Yeoman's Breath: Emanations of a Metaphor," *ES* 60 (August 1979): 380-88.

Traversi, *The Canterbury Tales*, 195-209.

Whittock, *A Reading of the Canterbury Tales*, 262-79.

The Canterbury Tales

David Aers, *Chaucer, Langland, and the Creative Imagination* (London, Boston, and Henley: Routledge & Kegan Paul, 1980), 143-73.

Judson Boyce Allen and Theresa Anne Moritz, *A Distinction of Stories: The Medieval Unity of Chaucer's Fair Chain of Narratives for Canterbury* (Columbus: Ohio State University Press, 1981), 119-241.

Ralph Baldwin, *The Unity of the Canterbury Tales*, Anglistica, no. 5 (Copenhagen: Rosenkilde and Bagger, 1955).

Paull F. Baum, *Chaucer: A Critical Appreciation* (New York: Octagon Books, 1982), 60-142.

C. David Benson, *Chaucer's Drama of Style: Poetic Variety and Contrast in The Canterbury Tales* (Chapel Hill and London: University of North Carolina Press, 1986).

Boitani, *English Medieval Narrative*, 236-72 *passim*.

D. S. Brewer, *Chaucer*, 3d ed. (London: Longman, 1973), *passim*.

Brewer, *An Introduction to Chaucer*, 161-243.

Nevill Coghill, *The Poet Chaucer* (London: Oxford University Press, 1949; reprint, 1960), 113-83.

Jon Cook, "Carnival and *The Canterbury Tales*: 'Only equals may laugh' (Herzen)," in Aers, *Medieval Literature*, 169-91.

Helen Cooper, *The Structure of the Canterbury Tales* (London: Duckworth, 1983).

Bruce Kent Cowgill, "'By *corpus dominus*': Harry Bailly as False Spiritual Guide," *JMRS* 15 (Fall 1985): 157-81.

Rodney Delasanta, "The Theme of Judgement in *The Canterbury Tales*," *MLQ* 31 (September 1970): 298-307.

George J. Engelhardt, "The Ecclesiastical Pilgrims of *The Canterbury Tales*: A Study in Ethology," *MS* 37 (1975): 287-315.

George J. Engelhardt, "The Lay Pilgrims of *The Canterbury Tales*: A Study in Ethology," *MS* 36 (1974): 278-330.

Judith Ferster, *Chaucer on Interpretation* (Cambridge: Cambridge University Press, 1985), 139-56.

William Frost, "The Unity of the Canterbury Tales," in *The Age of Chaucer*, English Masterpieces, Vol. 1 (New York: Prentice-Hall, 1950), 8-14.

Gardner, *The Poetry of Chaucer*, 216-337.

Katharine Slater Gittes, "*The Canterbury Tales* and the Arabic Frame Tradition," *PMLA* 98 (1983): 246-50.

Donald C. Green, "The Semantics of Power: *Maistrie* and *Soveraynetee* in *The Canterbury Tales*," *MP* 84 (August 1986): 18-23.

Robert W. Hanning, "The Theme of Art and Life in Chaucer's Poetry," in *Geoffrey Chaucer*, ed. George D. Economou (New York: McGraw-Hill, 1975), 24-36.

Norman T. Harrington, "Experience, Art, and the Framing of the *Canterbury Tales*," *ChauR* 10 (1976): 187-200.

Richard L. Hoffman, "The Canterbury Tales," in *Critical Approaches to Six Major English Works: "Beowulf" through "Paradise Lost,"* ed. R. M. Lumiansky and Herschel Baker (Philadelphia: University of Pennsylvania Press, 1968), 41-80.

Richard L. Hoffman, "Ovid and *The Canterbury Tales*," Ph.D. diss., Princeton University, 1964.

Donald R. Howard, *The Idea of the "Canterbury Tales"* (Berkeley, Los Angeles, and London: University of California Press, 1976).

Edwin J. Howard, *Geoffrey Chaucer* (New York: Twayne, 1964), 118-89.

Huppé, *A Reading of the "Canterbury Tales."*

Hussey, *Chaucer*, 96-188.

Emily Jensen, "Male Competition as a Unifying Motif in Fragment A of the Canterbury Tales," *ChauR* 24 (1990): 320-28.

Jordan, *Chaucer and the Shape of Creation*, 111-31.

G. D. Josipovici, "Fiction and Game in *The Canterbury Tales*," *CritQ* 7 (Summer 1965): 185-97.

R. E. Kaske, "Chaucer's Marriage Group," in Mitchell and Provost, *Chaucer the Love Poet*, 46-65.

Kean, *The Art of Narrative*, 53-185.

Laura Kendrick, *Chaucerian Play: Comedy and Control in the "Canterbury Tales"* (Berkeley: University of California Press, 1988), *passim*.

George Lyman Kittredge, *Chaucer and His Poetry* (Cambridge, Mass.: Harvard University Press, 1915; reprint, 1946), 146-218.

Stephen Thomas Knight, "Chaucer's Religious *Canterbury Tales*," in *Medieval English Religious and Ethical Literature: Essays in Honour of G. H. Russell*, ed. Gregory Kratzmann and James Simpson (Cambridge: D. S. Brewer, 1986), 156-66.

Traugott Lawler, *The One and the Many in the Canterbury Tales* (Hamden, Conn.: Shoe String Press, 1980).

L. M. Leitch, "Sentence and Solaas: The Function of the Hosts in the *Canterbury Tales*," *ChauR* 17 (Summer 1982): 5-20.

John Leyerle, "Thematic Interlace in 'The Canterbury Tales,'" *E&S* 29 (1976): 107-21.

Carl Lindahl, *Earnest Games: Folkloric Patterns in the Canterbury Tales* (Bloomington and Indianapolis: Indiana University Press, 1987).

Carl Lindahl, "The Festive Form of the *Canterbury Tales*," *ELH* 52 (1985): 531-66.

Lumiansky, *Of Sondry Folk*.

Rosemarie P. McGerr, "Retraction and Memory: Retrospective Structure in the *Canterbury Tales*," *CL* 37 (Spring 1985): 97-113.

Jerome Mandel, "Other Voices in the 'Canterbury Tales,'" *Criticism* 19 (Fall 1977): 338-49.

Jill Mann, "Parents and Children in the 'Canterbury Tales,'" in *Literature in Fourteenth-Century England*, ed. Piero Boitani and Anne Torti (Cambridge: D. S. Brewer, 1983), 165-83.

Mehl, *Geoffrey Chaucer*, 120-204.

Tony Millns, "Chaucer's Suspended Judgements," *EIC* 27 (January 1977): 13-18.

Marvin Mudrick, "Chaucer's Nightingales," *HudR* 10 (Spring 1957): 88-95.

North, *Chaucer's Universe*, 502-13.

Norton-Smith, *Geoffrey Chaucer*, 79-159.

Clair C. Olson, "The Interludes of the Marriage Group in the *Canterbury Tales*," in Rowland, *Chaucer and Middle English Studies*, 164-72.

Charles A. Owen, "The Alternative Reading of *The Canterbury Tales*: Chaucer's Text and the Early Manuscripts," *PMLA* 97 (1982): 237-56.

Owen, *Pilgrimage and Storytelling*, 87-217.

Robert O. Payne, *Geoffrey Chaucer*, 2d ed. (Boston: Twayne Publishers, 1986), 102-38.

Payne, *The Key of Remembrance*, 147-70.

Derek Pearsall, *The Canterbury Tales* (London, Boston, and Sydney: George Allen & Unwin, 1985), 53-71.

Russell A. Peck, "Biblical Interpretation: St. Paul and *The Canterbury Tales*," in *Chaucer and Scriptural Tradition*, ed. David Lyle Jeffrey (Ottawa: University of Ottawa Press, 1984), 143-70.

Raymond Preston, *Chaucer* (London and New York: Sheed and Ward, 1952), 149-285.

Esther C. Quinn, "Religion in Chaucer's *Canterbury Tales*: A Study in Language and Structure," in *Geoffrey Chaucer*, ed. George D. Economou (New York: McGraw-Hill, 1975), 55-73.

Cynthia C. Richardson, "The Function of the Host in *The Canterbury Tales*," *TSLL* 12 (Fall 1970): 325-44.

Rogers, *Upon the Ways*.

Ruggiers, *The Art of the Canterbury Tales*.

Gale C. Schricker, "On the Relation of Fact and Fiction in Chaucer's Poetic Endings," *PQ* 60 (Winter 1981): 13-27.

Marsha Siegel, "What the Debate Is and Why It Founders in Fragment A of *The Canterbury Tales*," *SP* 82 (Winter 1985): 1-24.

Sklute, *Virtue of Necessity*, 92-138.

Martin Stevens, "The Royal Stanza in Early English Literature," *PMLA* 94 (1979): 62-76.

William C. Stokoe, Jr., "Structure and Intention in the First Fragment of *The Canterbury Tales*," *MÆ* 21 (1952): 120-27.

Paul B. Taylor, "The Canon's Yeoman's Breath: Emanations of a Metaphor," *ES* 60 (August 1979): 380-88.

Zacharias Thundy, "Chaucer's Quest for Wisdom in *The Canterbury Tales*," *NM* 77 (1976): 582-98.

Traversi, *The Canterbury Tales*.

Julian N. Wasserman, "The Ideal and the Actual: The Philosophical Unity of *Canterbury Tales*, Ms. Group III," *Allegorica* 7 (Winter 1982): 65-99.

Karl P. Wentersdorf, "Chaucer's Worthless Butterfly," *ELN* 14 (March 1977): 167-72.

Whittock, *A Reading of the Canterbury Tales*.

David Eliot Williams, *The Canterbury Tales: A Literary Pilgrimage* (Boston: Twayne, 1987).

Chauncey Wood, "The April Date as a Structural Device in *The Canterbury Tales*," *MLQ* 25 (September 1964): 259-71.

The Clerk's Tale

Aers, *Chaucer*, 32-34.

Donald C. Baker, "Chaucer's Clerk and the Wife of Bath on the Subject of *Gentilesse*," *SP* 59 (October 1962): 631-40.

Barbara Bartholomew, *Fortuna and Natura: A Reading of Three Chaucer Narratives* (The Hague: Mouton, 1966), 58-72.

Thomas H. Bestul, "True and False *Cheere* in Chaucer's *Clerk's Tale*," *JEGP* 82 (1983): 500-14.

Bishop, *The Narrative Art*, 129-34.

Brewer, *An Introduction to Chaucer*, 214-21.

Bertrand H. Bronson, *In Search of Chaucer* (Toronto: University of Toronto Press, 1960), 103-13.

Burlin, *Chaucerian Fiction*, 140-46.

Mary J. Carruthers, "The Lady, the Swineherd, and Chaucer's Clerk," *ChauR* 17 (1983): 221-34.

Michael D. Cherniss, "The *Clerk's Tale* and *Envoy*, The Wife of Bath's Purgatory, and the *Merchant's Tale*," *ChauR* 6 (1972): 235-45.

Gloria Cigman, "Introduction" to *The Wife of Bath's Prologue and Tale and The Clerk's Prologue and Tale from The Canterbury Tales* (London: University of London Press, 1975), 15-26.

Corsa, *Chaucer: Poet of Mirth*, 149-55.

David, *The Strumpet Muse*, 158-69.

Judith Ferster, *Chaucer on Interpretation* (Cambridge: Cambridge University Press, 1985), 94-121.

Dolores Warwick Frese, "Chaucer's *Clerk's Tale*: The Monsters and the Critics Reconsidered," *ChauR* 8 (1973): 133-46.

John M. Ganim, "Carnival Voices and the Envoy to the *Clerk's Tale*," *ChauR* 22 (1987): 112-27.

Gardner, *The Poetry of Chaucer*, 282-85.

Kristine Gilmartin, "Array in the *Clerk's Tale*," *ChauR* 13 (1979): 234-46.

Warren Ginsberg, "'And Speketh so Pleyn': The *Clerk's Tale* and Its Teller," *Criticism* 20 (Summer 1978): 313-23.

Douglas Gray, "Chaucer and 'Pite,'" in Salu and Farrell, *J. R. R. Tolkien*, 195-203.

Joseph E. Grennen, "Science and Sensibility in Chaucer's Clerk," *ChauR* 6 (1971): 81-93.

Harriett Hawkins, *Poetic Freedom and Poetic Truth: Chaucer, Shakespeare, Marlowe, Milton* (Oxford: Clarendon Press, 1976), 29-51.

Carol Falvo Heffernan, "Tyranny and Commune Profit in the *Clerk's Tale*," *ChauR* 17 (1983): 332-40.

S. K. Heninger, Jr., "The Concept of Order in Chaucer's *Clerk's Tale*," *JEGP* 56 (1957): 382-95.

Huppé, *A Reading of the "Canterbury Tales,"* 136-47.

Hussey, *Chaucer*, 163-72.

Lynn Staley Johnson, "The Prince and His People: A Study of the Two Covenants in the *Clerk's Tale*," *ChauR* 10 (1975): 17-29.

Jordan, *Chaucer and the Shape of Creation*, 198-207.

Kean, *The Art of Narrative*, 123-29.

Alfred L. Kellogg, *Chaucer, Langland, Arthur: Essays in Middle English Literature* (New Brunswick, N.J.: Rutgers University Press, 1972), 291-316.

Peggy A. Knapp, "Knowing the Tropes: Literary Exegesis and Chaucer's Clerk," *Criticism* 27 (1986): 331-45.

Knight, *The Poetry of "The Canterbury Tales,"* 78-87.

Norman Lavers, "Freud, 'The Clerkes Tale,' and Literary Criticism," *CE* 26 (December 1964): 180-87.

Bernard S. Levy, "*Gentilesse* in Chaucer's *Clerk's* and *Merchant's Tales*," *ChauR* 11 (1977): 307-9.

Bernard S. Levy, "The Meaning of the *Clerk's Tale*," in Arrathoon, *Chaucer and the Craft*, 385-409.

Robert Longsworth, "Chaucer's Clerk as Teacher," in Benson, *The Learned and the Lewed*, 61-66.

John P. McCall, "The *Clerk's Tale* and the Theme of Obedience," *MLQ* 27 (September 1966): 260-69.

John McNamara, "Chaucer's Use of the Epistle of St. James in the *Clerk's Tale*," *ChauR* 7 (1973): 184-93.

Makarewicz, *The Patristic Influence*, 196-203.

Stephen Manning, "The Paradox of the Narrative Styles in Chaucer's *Clerk's Tale*," *JNT* 15 (Winter 1985): 29-41.

Robert P. Miller, "Allegory in *The Canterbury Tales*," in Rowland, *Companion to Chaucer Studies*, 280-81.

J. Mitchell Morse, "The Philosophy of the Clerk of Oxenford," *MLQ* 19 (March 1958): 14-20.

Owen, *Pilgrimage and Storytelling*, 184-89.

Roger Ramsey, "Clothing Makes a Queen in *The Clerk's Tale*," *JNT* 7 (Spring 1977): 104-15.

Donald H. Reiman, "The Real *Clerk's Tale*; or, Patient Griselda Exposed," *TSLL* 5 (Autumn 1963): 356-73.

Velma Bourgeois Richmond, "*Pacience in Adversitee*: Chaucer's Presentation of Marriage," *Viator* 10 (1979): 336-40.

Rogers, *Upon the Ways*, 61-65.

Irving N. Rothman, "Humility and Obedience in the *Clerk's Tale* with the Envoy Considered as an Ironic Affirmation," *PLL* 9 (Spring 1973): 115-27.

Ruggiers, *The Art of the Canterbury Tales*, 216-25.

Elizabeth Salter, *Chaucer: The Knight's Tale and The Clerk's Tale* (London: Edward Arnold, 1962), 37-65.

Speirs, *Chaucer the Maker*, 151-55.

David C. Steinmetz, "Late Medieval Nominalism and the *Clerk's Tale*," *ChauR* 12 (1977): 38-54.

Robert Stepsis, "*Potentia Absoluta* and the *Clerk's Tale*," *ChauR* 10 (1975): 129-47.

Traversi, *The Canterbury Tales*, 122-34.

Francis Lee Utley, "Five Genres in the *Clerk's Tale*," *ChauR* 6 (1972): 198-228.

Thomas A. Van, "Walter at the Stake: A Reading of Chaucer's *Clerk's Tale*," *ChauR* 22 (1988): 214-24.

Kristine Gilmartin Wallace, "Array as Motif in the *Clerk's Tale*," *RUS* 62 (1976): 99-110.

Karl P. Wentersdorf, "Chaucer's Clerk of Oxenford as Rhetorician," *MS* 51 (1989): 324-28.

Whittock, *A Reading of the Canterbury Tales*, 143-52.

"The Complaint of Mars"

D. S. Brewer, "Chaucer's 'Complaint of Mars,'" *N&Q*, n.s. 1 (November 1954): 462-63.

Wolfgang Clemen, *Chaucer's Early Poetry*, trans. C. A. M. Sym (New York: Barnes & Noble, 1964), 188-97.

Davenport, *Chaucer: Complaint and Narrative*, 33-40.

Nancy Dean, "Chaucer's *Complaint*, A Genre Descended from the *Heroides*," CL 19 (1967): 19-26.

Gardner, *The Poetry of Chaucer*, 82-89.

Neil C. Hultin, "Anti-Courtly Elements in Chaucer's *Complaint of Mars*," *AnM* 9 (1968): 58-75.

Edgar S. Laird, "Chaucer's *Complaint of Mars*, Line 145: 'Venus valaunse,'" *PQ* 51 (April 1972): 486-89.

Rodney Merrill, "Chaucer's *Broche of Thebes*: The Unity of 'The Complaint of Mars' and 'The Complaint of Venus,'" in *Literary Monographs*, no. 5, ed. Eric Rothstein (Madison: University of Wisconsin Press, 1973), 29-43.

North, *Chaucer's Universe*, 304-25.

Norton-Smith, *Geoffrey Chaucer*, 28-34.

Charles A. Owen, "The Problem of Free Will in Chaucer's Narratives," *PQ* 46 (1967): 433-39.

Rossell Hope Robbins, "The Lyrics," in Rowland, *Companion to Chaucer Studies*, 323-24.

Gardiner Stillwell, "Convention and Individuality in Chaucer's *Complaint of Mars*," *PQ* 35 (1956): 69-89.

M. Stokes, "The Moon in Leo in Book V of *Troilus and Criseyde*," *ChauR* 17 (1982): 123-26.

Melvin G. Storm, Jr., "The Mythological Tradition in Chaucer's *Complaint of Mars*," *PQ* 57 (1978): 323-35.

George Williams, "What Is the Meaning of Chaucer's *Complaint of Mars*?" *JEGP* 57 (1958): 167-73. Revised in George Williams, *A New View of Chaucer* (Durham, N.C.: Duke University Press, 1965), 56-65.

Chauncey Wood, *Chaucer and the Country of the Stars: Poetic Uses of Astrological Imagery* (Princeton, N.J.: Princeton University Press, 1970), 103-60.

"The Complaint of Venus"

Davenport, *Chaucer: Complaint and Narrative*, 15-18.

Gardner, *The Poetry of Chaucer*, 89-93.

Rodney Merrill, "Chaucer's *Broche of Thebes*: The Unity of 'The Complaint of Mars' and 'The Complaint of Venus,'" in *Literary Monographs*, no. 5, ed. Eric Rothstein (Madison: University of Wisconsin Press, 1973), 43-61.

"Complaint to His Lady"

John Stephens, "The Uses of Personae and the Art of Obliqueness in Some Chaucer Lyrics, Part III," *ChauR* 22 (1987): 41-42, 45-49.

"Complaint to His Purse"

Andres J. Finnel, "The Poet as Sunday Man: 'The Complaint of Chaucer to His Purse,'" *ChauR* 8 (1973): 147-58.

Gardner, *The Poetry of Chaucer*, 69-70.

Charles D. Ludlum, "Heavenly Word-Play in Chaucer's 'Complaint to His Purse,'" *N&Q* 23 (September 1976): 391-92.

Jay Ruud, *Expl* 41 (Spring 1983): 5-6.

John Stephens, "The Uses of Personae and the Art of Obliqueness in Some Chaucer Lyrics, Part III," *ChauR* 22 (1987): 49-51.

"The Complaint unto Pity"

Davenport, *Chaucer: Complaint and Narrative*, 18-20.

Gardner, *The Poetry of Chaucer*, 81-82.

Renate Haas, "Chaucer's Use of the Lament for the Dead," in Wasserman and Blanch, *Chaucer in the Eighties*, 24-25.

C. J. Nolan, "Structural Sophistication in 'The Complaint Unto Pity,'" *ChauR* 13 (1979): 363-72.

Malcolm Pittock, "Chaucer: The Complaint Unto Pity," *Criticism* 1 (Spring 1959): 160-68.

John Stephens, "The Uses of Personae and the Art of Obliqueness in Some Chaucer Lyrics, Part I," *ChauR* 21 (1987): 362-66, 368-70.

"Fortune"

Jane Chance, "Chaucerian Irony in the Boethian Short Poems: The Dramatic Tension Between Classical and Christian," *ChauR* 20 (1986): 237-38.

Davenport, *Chaucer: Complaint and Narrative*, 20-23.

Margaret Galway, "Chaucer Among Thieves," *TLS*, 20 April 1946, 187.

Mogan, *Chaucer and the Theme*, 81-85.

Edna Rideout, "Chaucer's 'Beste Frend,'" *TLS*, 8 February 1947, 79.

John Stephens, "The Uses of Personae and the Art of Obliqueness in Some Chaucer Lyrics, Part I," *ChauR* 21 (1987): 366-68, 370-72.

The Franklin's Tale

Aers, *Chaucer*, 85-91.

David Aers, *Chaucer, Langland, and the Creative Imagination* (London, Boston, and Henley: Routledge & Kegan Paul, 1980), 160-69.

W. Bryant Bachman, Jr., "'To Maken Illusioun': The Philosophy of Magic and the Magic of Philosophy in the *Franklin's Tale*," *ChauR* 12 (1977): 55-67.

Donald C. Baker, "A Crux in Chaucer's *Franklin's Tale*: Dorigen's Complaint," *JEGP* 60 (1961): 56-64.

Edwin B. Benjamin, "The Concept of Order in *The Franklin's Tale*," *PQ* 38 (January 1959): 119-24.

Harry Berger, Jr., "The F-Fragment of the *Canterbury Tales*: Part I," *ChauR* 1 (1966): 88-102.

Harry Berger, Jr., "The F-Fragment of the *Canterbury Tales*: Part II," *ChauR* 1 (1967): 135-56.

Ian Bishop, "Chaucer and the Rhetoric of Consolation," *MÆ* 52 (1983): 45-47.

Bishop, *The Narrative Art*, 139-46.

Morton W. Bloomfield, "*The Franklin's Tale*: A Story of Unanswered Questions," in Carruthers and Kirk, *Acts of Interpretation* 189-98.

D. S. Brewer, *Chaucer*, 3d ed. (London: Longman, 1973), 146-48, 178-80.

Brewer, *An Introduction to Chaucer*, 227-33.

Saul N. Brody, "The Comic Rejection of Courtly Love," in *In Pursuit of Perfection: Courtly Love in Medieval Literature*, ed. Joan M. Ferrante and George D. Economou (London: National University Publications; Port Washington, N.Y.: Kennikat Press, 1975), 252-54.

Douglas A. Burger, "The *Cosa Impossibile* of *Il Filocolo* and the Impossible of the *Franklin's Tale*," in Arrathoon, *Chaucer and the Craft*, 165-78.

Burlin, *Chaucerian Fiction*, 196-207.

Mary J. Carruthers, "The Gentilesse of Chaucer's Franklin," *Criticism* 23 (Fall 1981): 293-97.

Linda Charnes, "'This Werk Unresonable': Narrative Frustration and Generic Redistribution in Chaucer's *Franklin's Tale*," *ChauR* 23 (1989): 300-15.

Helen Cooper, "The Girl with Two Lovers: Four Canterbury Tales," in *Medieval Studies for J. A. W. Bennett*, ed. P. L. Heyworth (Oxford: Clarendon, 1981), 65-79.

Corsa, *Chaucer: Poet of Mirth*, 168-81.

Davenport, *Chaucer: Complaint and Narrative*, 178-97.

David, *The Strumpet Muse*, 182-92.

Judith Ferster, "Interpretation and Imitation in Chaucer's *Franklin's Tale*," in Aers, *Medieval Literature*, 148-68.

W. H. French, "*The Franklin's Tale*, Line 942," *MLN* 60 (November 1945): 477-80.

Gardner, *The Poetry of Chaucer*, 289-91.

Alan T. Gaylord, "The Promises in *The Franklin's Tale*," *ELH* 31 (1964): 331-65.

M. R. Golding, "The Importance of Keeping 'Trouthe' in *The Franklin's Tale*," *MÆ* 39 (1970): 306-12.

Paul Edward Gray, "Synthesis and the Double Standard in the *Franklin's Tale*," *TSLL* 7 (Autumn 1965): 213-24.

Carol Falvo Heffernan, "Wells and Streams in Three Chaucerian Gardens," *PLL* 15 (Fall 1979): 350-54.

Phyllis Hodgson, *The Franklin's Tale* (London: Athlone Press, 1960), 10-14, 71-105.

C. Hugh Holman, "Courtly Love in the Merchant's and the Franklin's Tales," *ELH* 18 (1951): 241-52. Reprinted in Wagenknecht, *Chaucer*, 240-49.

Hornsby, *Chaucer and the Law*, 51-55, 84-87.

Kathryn Hume, "The Pagan Setting of the *Franklin's Tale* and the Sources of Dorigen's Cosmology," *SN* 44 (1972): 289-94.

Kathryn Hume, "Why Chaucer Calls the *Franklin's Tale* a Breton Lai," *PQ* 51 (April 1972): 365-79.

Huppé, *A Reading of the "Canterbury Tales,"* 163-74.

Hussey, *Chaucer*, 132-36.

Kathryn Jacobs, "The Marriage Contract of the *Franklin's Tale*: The Remaking of Society," *ChauR* 20 (1985): 132-43.

Gerhard Joseph, "*The Franklin's Tale*: Chaucer's Theodicy," *ChauR* 1 (1966): 20-32.

R. E. Kaske, "Chaucer's Marriage Group," in Mitchell and Provost, *Chaucer the Love Poet*, 58-65.

Kean, *The Art of Narrative*, 141-48.

A. M. Kearney, "Truth and Illusion in *The Franklin's Tale*," *EIC* 19 (July 1969): 245-53.

Kenneth Kee, "Two Chaucerian Gardens," *MS* 23 (1961): 161-62.

Knight, *The Poetry of the Canterbury Tales*, 106-16.

Stephen Thomas Knight, *Rymyng Craftly: Meaning in Chaucer's Poetry* (Sydney and London: Angus and Robertson, 1973), 183-204.

Koff, *Chaucer*, 187-204.

Robert Lane, "*The Franklin's Tale*: Of Marriage and Meaning," in *Portraits of Marriage in Literature*, ed. Ann C. Hargrove and Maurine Magliocco (Macomb: Western Illinois University, 1984), 107-24.

Anne Thompson Lee, "'A Woman True and Fair': Chaucer's Portrayal of Dorigen in the *Franklin's Tale*," *ChauR* 19 (1984): 169-78.

Anthony E. Luengo, "Magic and Illusion in the *Franklin's Tale*," *JEGP* 77 (1978): 1-16.

R. M. Lumiansky, "The Character and Performance of Chaucer's Franklin," *UTQ* 20 (July 1951): 344-56.

Lumiansky, *Of Sondry Folk*, 187-93.

McCall, *Chaucer among the Gods*, 131-36 and *passim*.

Laury Magnus, "The Hem of Philosophy: Free and Bound Motifs in the *Franklin's Tale*," *Assays*, 2 (1983): 3-18.

Lindsay A. Mann, "'Gentilesse' and *The Franklin's Tale*," *SP* 63 (January 1966): 10-29.

Effie Jean Mathewson, "The Illusion of Morality in the *Franklin's Tale*," *MÆ* 52 (1983): 27-37.

Mehl, *Geoffrey Chaucer*, 165-71.

Robert P. Miller, "Allegory in *The Canterbury Tales*," in Rowland, *Companion to Chaucer Studies*, 283-85.

Gerald Morgan, "Boccaccio's *Filocolo* and the Moral Argument of the *Franklin's Tale*," *ChauR* 20 (1986): 285-306.

Gerald Morgan, "A Defence of Dorigen's Complaint," *MÆ* 46 (1977): 77-97.

North, *Chaucer's Universe*, 422-42.

Charles A. Owen, "The Crucial Passages in Five of *The Canterbury Tales*: A Study in Irony and Symbol," *JEGP* 52 (1953), 294-311. Reprinted in Wagenknecht, *Chaucer*, 252-68.

Owen, *Pilgrimage and Storytelling*, 203-10.

Roy J. Pearcy, "A Pun in the '*Franklin's Tale*' 942: 'Withouten Coppe He Drank Al His Penaunce,'" *N&Q* 22 (May 1975): 198.

Russell A. Peck, "Sovereignty and the Two Worlds of the *Franklin's Tale*," *ChauR* 1 (1967): 253-71.

Velma Bourgeois Richmond, "*Pacience in Adversitee*: Chaucer's Presentation of Marriage," *Viator* 10 (1979): 348-52.

D. W. Robertson, Jr., "Chaucer's Franklin and His Tale," *Costerus*, n.s. 1 (1974): 414-33. Reprinted in Robertson, *Essays in Medieval Culture*, 273-90.

D. W. Robertson, Jr., *A Preface to Chaucer* (London: Oxford University Press, 1962), 470-72 and *passim*.

Rogers, *Upon the Ways*, 73-78.

Wolfgang E. H. Rudat, "Aurelius' Quest for *Grace*: Sexuality and the Marriage Debate in the *Franklin's Tale*," *CEA* 45 (November 1982): 16-21.

Wolfgang E. H. Rudat, "*Gentillesse* and the Marriage Debate in the *Franklin's Tale*: Chaucer's Squires and the Question of Nobility," *Neophil* 68 (July 1984): 451-70.

Ruggiers, *The Art of the Canterbury Tales*, 226-37.

Gary D. Schmidt, "The Marriage Irony in the Tales of the Merchant and Franklin," in *Portraits of Marriage in Literature*, ed. Ann C. Hargrove and Maurine Magliocco (Macomb: Western Illinois University, 1984): 101-4.

James Sledd, "Dorigen's Complaint," *MP* 45 (August 1947): 36-46.

Speirs, *Chaucer the Maker*, 164-68.

John Stevens, *Medieval Romance: Themes and Approaches* (London: Hutchinson University Library, 1973), 62-66.

Derek Traversi, *The Literary Imagination: Studies in Dante, Chaucer, and Shakespeare* (Newark: University of Delaware Press; London and Toronto: Associated University Presses, 1982), 87-119.

Raymond P. Tripp, Jr., "The Darker Side to Absolon's Dawn Visit," *ChauR* 20 (1986): 208-10.

Gertrude M. White, "*The Franklin's Tale*: Chaucer or the Critics," *PMLA* 89 (1974): 454-62.

Whittock, *A Reading of the Canterbury Tales*, 170-78.

Chauncey Wood, *Chaucer and the Country of the Stars: Poetic Uses of Astrological Imagery* (Princeton, N.J.: Princeton University Press, 1970), 245-71.

Chauncey Wood, "Of Time and Tide in the *Franklin's Tale*," *PQ* 45 (October 1966): 688-711.

Rosemary Woolf, "Moral Chaucer and Kindly Gower," in Salu and Farrell, *J. R. R. Tolkien*, 239-43.

The Friar's Tale

Paul E. Beichner, C. S. C., "Baiting the Summoner," *MLQ* 22 (December 1961): 367-76.

Gail Ivy Berlin, "Speaking to the Devil: A New Context for the *Friar's Tale*," PQ 69 (Winter 1990): 1-12.

Earle Birney, "'After his Ymage': The Central Ironies of the *Friar's Tale*," *MS* 21 (1959): 17-35. Reprinted in Earle Birney, *Essays on Chaucer*, ed. Beryl Rowland (Toronto: University of Toronto Press, 1985), 85-108.

Bishop, *The Narrative Art*, 107-10.

Morton W. Bloomfield, "The *Friar's Tale* as a Liminal Tale," *ChauR* 17 (1983): 286-91.

Adrien Bonjour, "Aspects of Chaucer's Irony in 'The Friar's Tale,'" *EIC* 11 (April 1961): 121-27.

Craik, *The Comic Tales*, 98-115.

James Dean, "Spiritual Allegory and Chaucer's Narrative Style: Three Test Cases," *ChauR* 18 (1984): 275-77.

Gardner, *The Poetry of Chaucer*, 279-81.

Richard Hamilton Green, "Classical Fable and English Poetry in the Fourteenth Century," in *Critical Approaches to Medieval Literature: Selected Papers from the English Institute, 1958-1959*, ed. Dorothy Bethurum (New York and London: Columbia University Press, 1960), 125-28.

Martha Powell Harley, *Expl* 46 (Winter 1988): 4-5.

Tom Hatton, "Chaucer's Friar's 'Old Rebekke,'" *JEGP* 67 (1968): 266-71.

N. R. Havely, "Introduction" to *The Friar's, Summoner's and Pardoner's Tales from the Canterbury Tales* (London: University of London Press, 1975), 10-16.

Hugh L. Hennedy, "The Friar's Summoner's Dilemma," *ChauR* 5 (1971): 213-17.

Hornsby, *Chaucer and the Law*, 46-51.

Edward C. Jacobs and Robert E. Jungman, "His Mother's Curse: Kinship in *The Friar's Tale*," *PQ* 64 (Spring 1985): 256-59.

Knight, *The Poetry of the Canterbury Tales*, 65-69.

H. Marshall Leicester, Jr., "'No Vileyns Word': Social Context and Performance in Chaucer's *Friar's Tale*," *ChauR* 17 (1982): 21-39.

Daniel M. Murtaugh, "Riming Justice in *The Friar's Tale*," *NM* 74 (1973): 107-12.

Norman Nathan, "Pronouns of Address in the 'Friar's Tale,'" *MLQ* 17 (March 1956): 39-42.

Owen, *Pilgrimage and Storytelling*, 158-61.

Thomas W. Ross, *Expl* 34 (October 1975): 17.

Richardson, *Blameth Nat Me*, 73-85.

Ruggiers, *The Art of the Canterbury Tales*, 90-97.

A. C. Spearing, "*The Canterbury Tales* IV: Exemplum and Fable," in Boitani and Mann, *The Cambridge Chaucer Companion*, 161-65.

Penn R. Szittya, "The Green Yeoman as Loathly Lady: The Friar's Parody of the *Wife of Bath's Tale*," *PMLA* 90 (1975): 386-94.

Whittock, *A Reading of the Canterbury Tales*, 133-36.

General Prologue to the *Canterbury Tales*

Aers, *Chaucer*, 17-20.

Lawrence Besserman, "Girdles, Belts, and Cords: A Leitmotif in Chaucer's *General Prologue*," *PLL* 22 (Summer 1986): 322-25.

Muriel Bowden, *A Commentary on the General Prologue to the Canterbury Tales* (New York: Macmillan, 1948).

H. David Brumble III, *Expl* 37 (Fall 1978): 45.

Corsa, *Chaucer: Poet of Mirth*, 79-95.

David, *The Strumpet Muse*, 52-76.

Rodney Delasanta, *Expl* 38 (Spring 1980): 39-40.

E. T. Donaldson, "Commentary," in *Chaucer's Poetry: An Anthology for the Modern Reader*, ed. E. T. Donaldson, 2d ed. (New York: Ronald Press, 1975), 1036-61.

Gardner, *The Poetry of Chaucer*, 227-41.

David Leon Higdon, "Diverse Melodies in Chaucer's 'General Prologue,'" *Criticism* 14 (Spring 1972): 97-108.

Elton D. Higgs, "The Old Order and the 'Newe World' in the General Prologue to the *Canterbury Tales*," *HLQ* 45 (Spring 1982): 155-73.

Arthur W. Hoffman, "Chaucer's Prologue to Pilgrimage: The Two Voices," *ELH* 21 (1954): 1-16. Reprinted in Wagenknecht, *Chaucer*, 30-45.

Hornsby, *Chaucer and the Law*, 81-84.

Huppé, *A Reading of the "Canterbury Tales,"* 13-48.

R. E. Kaske, "The Summoner's Garleek, Oynons, and eek Lekes," *MLN* 74 (June 1959): 481-84.

Thomas A. Kirby, "The General Prologue," in Rowland, *Companion to Chaucer Studies*, 208-28.

Knight, *The Poetry of the Canterbury Tales,* 3-18.

Lawrence, Seifter, and Ratner, *McGraw-Hill Guide*, 38-41.

H. Marshall Leicester, Jr., "The Art of Impersonation: A General Prologue to the *Canterbury Tales*," *PMLA* 95 (1980): 213-24.

R. M. Lumiansky, *Expl* 5 (December 1946): 20.

Lumiansky, *Of Sondry Folk*, 15-28.

John McKee, *Expl* 32 (March 1974): 54.

Jill Mann, *Chaucer and Medieval Estates Satire: The Literature of Social Classes and the "General Prologue" to the "Canterbury Tales"* (Cambridge: Cambridge University Press, 1973).

Loy D. Martin, "History and Form in the *General Prologue* to the *Canterbury Tales*," *ELH* 45 (1978): 1-17.

Mehl, *Geoffrey Chaucer*, 130-43.

Gerald Morgan, "The Design of the *General Prologue* to the *Canterbury Tales*," *ES* 59 (December 1978): 481-98.

Gerald Morgan, "Rhetorical Perspectives in the *General Prologue* to the *Canterbury Tales*," *ES* 62 (October 1981): 411-22.

J. C. Nitzsche, "Creation in Genesis and Nature in Chaucer's *General Prologue* 1-18," *PLL* 4 (Fall 1978): 459-64.

Barbara Nolan, "'A Poet There Was': Chaucer's Voices in the *General Prologue* to the *Canterbury Tales*," *PMLA* 101 (1986): 154-69.

Charles A. Owen, Jr., "Development of the Art of Portraiture in Chaucer's *General Prologue*," *LeedsSE*, n.s. 14 (1983): 116-33.

Owen, *Pilgrimage and Storytelling*, 48-86.

T. M. Pearce, *Expl* 5 (March 1947): 38.

George A. Renn, III, *Expl* 46 (Spring 1988): 4-7.

Speirs, *Chaucer the Maker*, 99-121.

Margaret R. Stobie, "Chaucer's Shipman and the Wine," *PMLA* 64 (1949): 565-69.

Traversi, *The Canterbury Tales*, 19-36.

Wimsatt, *Allegory and Mirror*, 163-65, 170-78.

Chauncey Wood, "Chaucer's Use of Signs in His Portrait of the Prioress," in Hermann and Burke, *Signs and Symbols*, 81-101.

"Gentilesse"

Valerie Allen, "The 'Firste Stok' in Chaucer's *Gentilesse*: Barking up the Right Tree," *RES*, n.s. 40 (November 1989): 531-37.

Jane Chance, "Chaucerian Irony in the Boethian Short Poems: The Dramatic Tension between Classical and Christian," *ChauR* 20 (1986): 239-41.

The Hous of Fame

Robert J. Allen, "A Recurring Motif in Chaucer's *House of Fame*," *JEGP* 55 (1956): 393-405.

Paull F. Baum, "Chaucer's 'The House of Fame,'" *ELH* 8 (1941): 248-56.

J. A. W. Bennett, *Chaucer's Book of Fame: An Exposition of the House of Fame* (Oxford: Clarendon Press, 1968).

Dorothy Bethurum, "Chaucer's Point of View as Narrator in the Love Poems," *PMLA* 74 (1959): 514.

David M. Bevington, "The Obtuse Narrator in Chaucer's *House of Fame*," *Speculum* 36 (1961): 288-98.

Robert Boenig, "Chaucer's *House of Fame*, the Apocalypse, and Bede," *ABR* 36 (September 1985): 263-77.

Piero Boitani, *Chaucer and the Imaginary World of Fame* (Cambridge: D. S. Brewer; Totowa, N.J.: Barnes & Noble, 1984).

Boitani, *English Medieval Narrative*, 149-68, 183-92, and *passim*.

Piero Boitani, "Introduction: An Idea of Fourteenth-Century Literature," in *Literature in Fourteenth-Century England*, ed. Piero Boitani and Anna Torti (Cambridge: D. S. Brewer, 1983), 11-31.

Piero Boitani, "Old Books Brought to Life in Dreams: The *Book of the Duchess*, the *House of Fame*, the *Parliament of Fowls*," in Boitani and Mann, *The Cambridge Chaucer Companion*, 52-56.

Mary Flowers Braswell, "Architectural Portraiture in Chaucer's *House of Fame*," *JMRS* 11 (1981): 101-12.

Brewer, *An Introduction to Chaucer*, 73-77 *passim*.

Burlin, *Chaucerian Fiction*, 45-58.

Wolfgang Clemen, *Chaucer's Early Poetry*, trans. C. A. M. Sym (New York: Barnes & Noble, 1964), 67-121.

Corsa, *Chaucer: Poet of Mirth*, 29-35.

Joseph A. Dane, "Chaucer's Eagle's Ovid's Phaethon: A Study in Literary Reception," *JMRS* 11 (1981): 71-82.

Davidoff, *Beginning Well*, 114-23.

Sheila Delany, *Chaucer's "House of Fame": The Poetics of Skeptical Fideism* (Chicago and London: University of Chicago Press, 1972).

A. Inskip Dickerson, "Chaucer's *House of Fame*: A Skeptical Epistemology of Love," *TSLL* 18 (Summer 1976): 171-83.

Robert R. Edwards, *The Dream of Chaucer: Representation and Reflection in the Early Narratives* (Durham and London: Duke University Press, 1989), 93-121 and *passim*.

Lawrence Eldredge, "Chaucer's *Hous of Fame* and the *Via Moderna*," *NM* 71 (1970): 105-19.

Fyler, *Chaucer and Ovid*, 23-64.

Gardner, *The Poetry of Chaucer*, 148-90.

Joseph E. Grennen, "Chaucer and Chalcidius: The Platonic Origins of the *Hous of Fame*," *Viator* 15 (1984): 237-62.

Carrie Esther Hammil, *The Celestial Journey and the Harmony of the Spheres in English Literature, 1300-1700* (Fort Worth: Texas Christian University Press, 1980), 39-51.

Robert W. Hanning, "Chaucer's First Ovid: Metamorphosis and Poetic Tradition in the *Book of the Duchess* and the *House of Fame*," in Arrathoon, *Chaucer and the Craft*, 141-58.

Hieatt, *The Realism of Dream Visions*, 74-78.

Hussey, *Chaucer*, 36-41.

Eric Hyman, "'So Sely an Avisyon': Chaucer's *House of Fame* as Comic Monologue," *ELWIU* 16 (Fall 1989): 155-71.

Martin Irvine, "Medieval Grammatical Theory and Chaucer's *House of Fame*," *Speculum* 60 (1985): 850-76.

David Lyle Jeffrey, "Sacred and Secular Scripture: Authority and Interpretation in *The House of Fame*," in *Chaucer and Scriptural Tradition*, ed. David Lyle Jeffrey (Ottawa: University of Ottawa Press, 1984), 207-28.

William Joyner, "Parallel Journeys in Chaucer's *House of Fame*," *PLL* 12 (Winter 1976): 3-19.

Kean, *Love Division and Debate*, 85-111.

Lisa Kiser, "Eschatological Poetics in Chaucer's *House of Fame*," *MLQ* 49 (1988): 99-119.

George Lyman Kittredge, *Chaucer and His Poetry* (Cambridge, Mass.: Harvard University Press, 1915; reprint, 1946), 73-107.

B. G. Koonce, *Chaucer and the Tradition of Fame: Symbolism in "The House of Fame"* (Princeton, N.J.: Princeton University Press, 1966), 89-279.

John Lawlor, "The Earlier Poems," in *Chaucer & Chaucerians: Critical Studies in Middle English Literature*, ed. D. S. Brewer (University: University of Alabama Press, 1966), 45-50.

Leonard, *Laughter in the Courts of Love*, 38.

John Leyerle, "Chaucer's Windy Eagle," *UTQ* 40 (Spring 1971): 247-65.

McCall, *Chaucer among the Gods*, 48-58 and *passim*.

Kemp Malone, *Chapters on Chaucer* (Baltimore, Md.: Johns Hopkins Press, 1951), 42-60.

Mehl, *Geoffrey Chaucer*, 54-64.

Jacqueline T. Miller, "The Writing on the Wall: Authority and Authorship in Chaucer's *House of Fame*," *ChauR* 17 (1982): 95-115.

Tony Millns, "Chaucer's Suspended Judgements," *EIC* 27 (January 1977): 11-13.

Mogan, *Chaucer and the Theme*, 99-106.

Norton-Smith, *Geoffrey Chaucer*, 35-61.

Pat Trefzger Overbeck, "The 'Man of Gret Auctorite' in Chaucer's *House of Fame*," *MP* 73 (November 1975): 157-61.

Robert O. Payne, *Geoffrey Chaucer*, 2d ed. (Boston: Twayne, 1986), 61-68.

Payne, *The Key of Remembrance*, 129-39.

Edmund Reiss, "Chaucer's Parodies of Love," in Mitchell and Provost, *Chaucer the Love Poet*, 38-40.

Paul G. Ruggiers, "The Unity of Chaucer's *House of Fame*," *SP* 50 (1953): 16-29. Reprinted in Schoeck and Taylor, *Chaucer Criticism, II*, 261-74; Wagenknecht, *Chaucer*, 295-308.

J. Stephen Russell, *The English Dream Visions: Anatomy of a Form* (Columbus: Ohio State University Press, 1988), 174-94.

J. Stephen Russell, "A Seme in the Integument: Allegory in the *Hous of Fame*," in *Allegorisis: The Craft of Allegory in Medieval Literature*, ed. J. Stephen Russell (New York and London: Garland, 1988), 171-85.

Barry Sanders, "Love's Crack-up: *The House of Fame*," *PLL* 3 (Summer supplement 1967): 3-13.

R. J. Schoeck, "A Legal Reading of Chaucer's *Hous of Fame*," *UTQ* 23 (January 1954): 185-92.

Geoffrey T. Shepherd, "Make Believe: Chaucer's Rationale of Storytelling in *The House of Fame*," in Salu and Farrell, *J. R. R. Tolkien*, 204-20.

Lawrence K. Shook, "The House of Fame," in Rowland, *Companion to Chaucer Studies*, 341-54.

J. L. Simmons, "The Place of the Poet in Chaucer's *House of Fame*," *MLQ* 27 (June 1966): 125-35.

James Simpson, "Dante's 'Astripetam Aquilam' and the Theme of Poetic Discretion in the 'House of Fame,'" *E&S* 39 (1986): 1-18.

Sklute, *Virtue of Necessity*, 35-47.

Spearing, *Medieval Dream-Poetry*, 73-89.

Spearing, *Readings in Medieval Poetry*, 83-93.

Kay Stevenson, "The Endings of Chaucer's *House of Fame*," *ES* 59 (February 1978): 10-26.

Karla Taylor, *Chaucer Reads "The Divine Comedy"* (Stanford, Calif.: Stanford University Press, 1989), 20-39.

Charles P. R. Tisdale, "*The House of Fame*: Virgilian Rcason and Boethian Wisdom," *CL* 25 (Summer 1973): 247-61.

Derek Traversi, *Chaucer, the Earlier Poetry: A Study in Poetic Development* (London and Toronto: Associated University Presses; Newark: University of Delaware Presses, 1987), 54-77.

Ann C. Watts, "'Amor gloriae' in Chaucer's *House of Fame*," *JMRS* 3 (1973): 87-113.

George Williams, *A New View of Chaucer* (Durham, N.C.: Duke University Press, 1965), 105-29.

William S. Wilson, "Scholastic Logic in Chaucer's *House of Fame*," *ChauR* 1 (Winter 1967): 181-84.

Wimsatt, *Allegory and Mirror*, 42-45, 98-100.

James Winny, *Chaucer's Dream-Poems* (New York: Barnes & Noble, 1973), 76-112.

The Knight's Tale

Aers, *Chaucer*, 24-32, 76-82.

David Aers, *Chaucer, Langland, and the Creative Imagination* (London, Boston and Henley: Routledge & Kegan Paul, 1980), 174-95.

Barbara Bartholomew, *Fortuna and Natura: A Reading of Three Chaucer Narratives* (The Hague: Mouton, 1966), 73-107.

C. David Benson, *Chaucer's Drama of Style: Poetic Variety and Contrast in the "Canterbury Tales"* (Chapel Hill and London: University of North Carolina Press, 1986), 64-88.

Ian Bishop, "Chaucer and the Rhetoric of Consolation," *MÆ* 52 (1983): 43-44.

Bishop, *The Narrative Art*, 38-48.

Kathleen A. Blake, "Order and the Noble Life in Chaucer's *Knight's Tale*," *MLQ* 34 (March 1973): 3-19.

Robert J. Blanch and Julian N. Wasserman, "White and Red in the *Knight's Tale*: Chaucer's Manipulation of a Convention," in Wasserman and Blanch, *Chaucer in the Eighties*, 175-91.

E. D. Blodgett, "Chaucerian *Pryvetee* and the Opposition to Time," *Speculum* 51 (1976): 485-89.

W. F. Bolton, "The Topic of the *Knight's Tale*," *ChauR* 1 (1976): 217-27.

Brewer, *An Introduction to Chaucer*, 107-14.

Saul N. Brody, "The Comic Rejection of Courtly Love," in *In Pursuit of Perfection: Courtly Love in Medieval Literature*, ed. Joan M. Ferrante and George D. Economou (London: National University Publications; Port Washington, N.Y.: Kennikat Press, 1975), 248-50.

Douglas Brooks and Alastair Fowler, "The Meaning of Chaucer's *Knight's Tale*," *MÆ* 39 (1970): 123-46.

Burlin, *Chaucerian Fiction*, 97-111.

Burrow, *Essays on Medieval Literature*, 27-48.

Allen Barry Cameron, "The Heroine in *The Knight's Tale*," *SSF* 5 (Winter 1968): 119-27.

Paolo Cherichi, "'The Knight's Tale': Lines 1774-81," *MP* 76 (August 1978): 46-48.

Helen Cooper, "The Girl with Two Lovers: Four Canterbury Tales," in *Medieval Studies for J. A. W. Bennett*, ed. P. L. Heyworth (Oxford: Clarendon, 1981), 65-79.

Helen Cooper, *The Structure of the Canterbury Tales* (London: Duckworth, 1983), 91-107.

Corsa, *Chaucer: Poet of Mirth*, 95-108.

Georgia Ronan Crampton, *The Condition of Creatures: Suffering and Action in Chaucer and Spenser* (New Haven and London: Yale University Press, 1974), 45-112.

Davenport, *Chaucer: Complaint and Narrative*, 91-128.

David, *The Strumpet Muse*, 77-89.

Christopher Dean, "Imagery in the *Knight's Tale* and the *Miller's Tale*," *MS* 31 (1969): 149-63.

Rodney Delasanta, "Uncommon Commonplaces in *The Knight's Tale*," *NM* 70 (1969): 683-90.

E. Talbot Donaldson, "The Masculine Narrator and Four Women of Style," in Donaldson, *Speaking of Chaucer*, 48-50.

Philip Drew, *The Meaning of Freedom* (Aberdeen: Aberdeen University Press, 1982), 24-29.

Peter H. Elbow, "How Chaucer Transcends Oppositions in the *Knight's Tale*," *ChauR* 7 (1972): 97-112.

Peter H. Elbow, *Oppositions in Chaucer* (Middletown, Conn.: Wesleyan University Press, 1973), 73-94, 114-16.

Judith Ferster, *Chaucer on Interpretation* (Cambridge: Cambridge University Press, 1985), 23-45.

Joerg O. Fichte, "Man's Free Will and the Poet's Choice: The Creation of Artistic Order in Chaucer's *Knight's Tale*," *Anglia* 93 (1975): 335-60.

Merle Fifield, "*The Knight's Tale*: Incident, Idea, Incorporation," *ChauR* 3 (1968): 95-106.

Jerold C. Frakes, "'Ther Nis Namoore to Seye': Closure in the *Knight's Tale*," *ChauR* 22 (1987): 1-7.

William Frost, "An Interpretation of Chaucer's *Knight's Tale*," *RES* 25 (October 1949): 288-304.

Fyler, *Chaucer and Ovid*, 138-47.

Gardner, *The Poetry of Chaucer*, 241-53.

Alan T. Gaylord, "The Role of Saturn in the *Knight's Tale*," *ChauR* 8 (1974): 171-90.

Richard Firth Green, "Arcite at Court," *ELN* 18 (June 1981): 251-57.

Richard Hamilton Green, "Classical Fable and English Poetry in the Fourteenth Century," in *Critical Approaches to Medieval Literature: Selected Papers from the English Institute, 1958-1959*, ed. Dorothy Bethurum (New York and London: Columbia University Press, 1960), 128-33.

Robert S. Haller, "The *Knight's Tale* and the Epic Tradition," *ChauR* 1 (1966): 67-84.

John Halverson, "Aspects of Order in 'The Knight's Tale,'" *SP* 57 (October 1960): 606-21.

Robert W. Hanning, "'The Struggle Between Noble Designs and Chaos': The Literary Tradition of Chaucer's *Knight's Tale*," *LitR* 23 (Summer 1980): 519-41.

David V. Harrington, "Rhetoric and Meaning in Chaucer's *Knight's Tale*," *PLL* 3 (Summer supplement 1967): 71-79.

Joseph Harrison, "'Tears for Passing Things': The Temple of Diana in the *Knight's Tale*," *PQ* 63 (Winter 1984): 108-16.

Thomas J. Hatton, "Medieval Anticipations of Dryden's Stylistic Revolution: *The Knight's Tale*," *Lang&S* 7 (Fall 1974): 261-70.

Judith Scherer Herz, "Chaucer's Elegiac Knight," *Criticism* 6 (Summer 1964): 212-24.

Ronald B. Herzman, "The Paradox of Form: *The Knight's Tale* and Chaucerian Aesthetics," *PLL* 10 (Fall 1974): 339-52.

A. Kent Hieatt, *Chaucer, Spenser, Milton: Mythopoeic Continuities and Transformations* (Montreal and London: McGill-Queen's University Press, 1975), 32-44.

Richard L. Hoffman, "The Canterbury Tales," in *Critical Approaches to Six Major English Works: "Beowulf" through "Paradise Lost,"* ed. R. M. Lumiansky and Herschel Baker (Philadelphia: University of Pennsylvania Press, 1968), 61-70.

Huppé, *A Reading of the "Canterbury Tales,"* 49-74.

Hussey, *Chaucer*, 125-32.

Terry Jones, *Chaucer's Knight: The Portrait of a Medieval Mercenary* (London: Weidenfeld and Nicolson, 1980), 141-216.

Jordan, *Chaucer and the Shape of Creation*, 152-84.

Gerhard Joseph, "Chaucerian *Game-Earnest* and the Argument of Herbergage in *The Canterbury Tales*," *ChauR* 5 (1970): 84-88.

Kean, *The Art of Narrative*, 1-52.

Alfred L. Kellogg, *Chaucer, Langland, Arthur: Essays in Middle English Literature* (New Brunswick, N.J.: Rutgers University Press, 1972), 164-80.

Daniel Kempton, "Chaucer's Knight and the Knight's Theseus: 'And Though That He Were Worthy, He Was Wys,'" *JNT* 17 (Fall 1987): 237-58.

Laura Kendrick, *Chaucerian Play: Comedy and Control in the "Canterbury Tales"* (Berkeley: University of California Press, 1988), 118-21.

Knight, *The Poetry of the Canterbury Tales,* 19-29.

Stephen Thomas Knight, *Rymyng Craftily: Meaning in Chaucer's Poetry* (Sydney and London: Angus and Robertson, 1973), 98-160.

Koff, *Chaucer*, 173-84.

Kolve, *Chaucer and the Imagery of Narrative*, 85-157.

G. A. Lester, "Chaucer's Knight and the Medieval Tournament," *Neophil* 66 (July 1982): 460-68.

John Leyerle, "The Heart and the Chain," in Benson, *The Learned and the Lewed*, 118-21.

R. M. Lumiansky, "Chaucer's Philosophical Knight," *TSE* 3 (1952): 47-68.

Lumiansky, *Of Sondry Folk*, 29-49.

Thomas H. Luxon, "'Sentence' and 'Solaas': Proverbs and Consolation in the *Knight's Tale*," *ChauR* 22 (1987): 94-111.

T. McAlindon, "Cosmology, Contrariety and the *Knight's Tale*," *MÆ* 55 (1986): 41-57.

McCall, *Chaucer among the Gods*, 64-86, 88-92.

Garth A. McCann, "Chaucer's First Three Tales: Unity in Trinity," *BRMMLA* 27 (1973): 11-13.

Mehl, *Geoffrey Chaucer*, 158-62.

Charles Mitchell, "The Worthiness of Chaucer's Knight," *MLQ* 25 (March 1964): 66-75.

Mogan, *Chaucer and the Theme*, 145-60.

Charles Moorman, *A Knyght There Was* (Lexington: University of Kentucky Press, 1967), 76-95.

Charles Muscatine, *Chaucer and the French Tradition* (Berkeley and Los Angeles: University of California Press, 1957), 175-90.

Charles Muscatine, "Form, Texture, and Meaning in Chaucer's *Knight's Tale*," *PMLA* 65 (1950): 911-29. Reprinted in Wagenknecht, *Chaucer*, 60-82.

Richard Neuse, "The Knight: The First Mover in Chaucer's Human Comedy," *UTQ* 31 (April 1962): 299-315.

John Kevin Newman, *The Classical Epic Tradition* (Madison: University of Wisconsin Press, 1986), 340-71.

R. H. Nicholson, "Theseus's 'Ordinaunce': Justice and Ceremony in the *Knight's Tale*," *ChauR* 22 (1988): 192-213.

North, *Chaucer's Universe*, 402-21.

Norton-Smith, *Geoffrey Chaucer*, 123-36.

Paul A. Olson, "Chaucer's Epic Statement and the Political Milieu of the Late Fourteenth Century," *Mediaevalia* 5 (1979): 61-87.

Charles A. Owen, "Chaucer's *Canterbury Tales*: Aesthetic Design in the Stories of the First Day," *ES* 35 (1954): 48-51.

Owen, *Pilgrimage and Storytelling*, 88-96.

F. Anne Payne, *Chaucer and Menippean Satire* (Madison: University of Wisconsin Press, 1981), 207-58.

Judith C. Perryman, "The 'False Arcite' of Chaucer's *Knight's Tale*," *Neophil* 68 (January 1984): 121-33.

John Reidy, "The Education of Chaucer's Duke Theseus," in *The Epic in Medieval Society: Aesthetic and Moral Values*, ed. Harald Scholler (Tübingen: Max Niemeyer Verlag, 1977): 391-408.

D. W. Robertson, Jr., *A Preface to Chaucer* (London: Oxford University Press, 1962), 105-10, 466-68, and *passim*.

Rogers, *Upon the Ways*, 29-37.

Wolfgang E. H. Rudat, "Chaucer's Mercury and Arcite: *The Aeneid* and the World of the *Knight's Tale*," *Neophil* 64 (April 1980): 307-19.

Ruggiers, *The Art of the Canterbury Tales*, 151-66.

Paul C. Ruggiers, "Some Philosophical Aspects of 'The Knight's Tale,'" *CE* 19 (April 1958): 296-302.

T. C. Rumble, "Chaucer's 'Knight's Tale,' 2680-83," *PQ* 43 (January 1964): 130-33.

Elizabeth Salter, *Chaucer: The Knight's Tale and The Clerk's Tale* (London: Edward Arnold, 1962), 9-36.

Elizabeth Salter, *Fourteenth-Century English Poetry: Contexts and Readings* (Oxford: Clarendon Press, 1983), 141-81.

A. V. C. Schmidt, "The Tragedy of Arcite: A Reconsideration of the *Knight's Tale*," *EIC* 19 (April 1969): 107-17.

Spearing, *Medieval to Renaissance*, 46-58.

Lorraine Kochanske Stock, "The Two Mayings in Chaucer's *Knight's Tale*: Convention and Invention," *JEGP* 85 (April 1986): 206-21.

Theodore A. Stroud, "Chaucer's Structural Balancing of *Troilus* and 'Knight's Tale,'" *AnM* 21 (1981): 31-45.

Linda Tatelbaum, "Venus' *Citole* and the Restoration of Harmony in Chaucer's *Knight's Tale*," *NM* 74 (1973): 649-64.

Paul Thayer Thurston, *Artistic Ambivalence in Chaucer's Knight's Tale* (Gainesville: University of Florida Press, 1968).

Traversi, *The Canterbury Tales*, 37-61.

Philippa Tristram, *Figures of Life and Death in Medieval English Literature* (London: Paul Elek, 1976), 87-91 and *passim*.

Frederick Turner, "A Structuralist Analysis of the *Knight's Tale*," *ChauR* 8 (1974): 279-96.

Dale Underwood, "The First of the Canterbury Tales," *ELH* 26 (1959): 455-69.

Joseph Westlund, "The 'Knight's Tale' as an Impetus for Pilgrimage," *PQ* 43 (October 1964): 526-37.

Whittock, *A Reading of the Canterbury Tales*, 57-76.

H. S. Wilson, "The *Knight's Tale* and the *Teseida* Again," *UTQ* 18 (January 1949): 139-46.

Chauncey Wood, *Chaucer and the Country of the Stars: Poetic Uses of Astrological Imagery* (Princeton, N.J.: Princeton University Press, 1970), 69-76.

William F. Woods, "Chivalry and Nature in *The Knight's Tale*," *PQ* 66 (Summer 1987): 287-301.

"Lak of Stedfastnesse"

Jane Chance, "Chaucerian Irony in the Boethian Short Poems: The Dramatic Tension between Classical and Christian," *ChauR* 20 (1986): 238-39.

Jean Klene, C. S. C., "Chaucer's Contributions to a Popular Topos: The World Upside-Down," *Viator* 11 (1980): 331-32.

Mogan, *Chaucer and the Theme*, 88-89.

Legend of Dido

George Sanderlin, "Chaucer's *Legend of Dido* – A Feminist Exemplum," *ChauR* 20 (1986): 331-40.

Legend of Good Women

Peter L. Allen, "Reading Chaucer's *Good Women*," *ChauR* 21 (1987): 419-34.

Ruth M. Ames, "The Feminist Connections of Chaucer's *Legend of Good Women*," in Wasserman and Blanch, *Chaucer in the Eighties*, 57-74.

Paull F. Baum, "Chaucer's 'Glorious Legende,'" *MLN* 60 (June 1945): 377-81.

Paul M. Clogan, "Chaucer's Cybele and the *Liber Imaginum Deorum*," *PQ* 43 (April 1964): 272-74.

Davenport, *Chaucer: Complaint and Narrative*, 74-87.

Sheila Delany, "Rewriting Woman Good: Gender and the Anxiety of Influence in Two Late-Medieval Texts," in Wasserman and Blanch, *Chaucer in the Eighties*, 77-82.

Robert Worth Frank, Jr., *Chaucer and "The Legend of Good Women"* (Cambridge, Mass.: Harvard University Press, 1972).

Fyler, *Chaucer and Ovid*, 96-115.

Gardner, *The Poetry of Chaucer*, 191-215.

Elaine Tuttle Hansen, "Irony and the Antifeminist Narrator in Chaucer's *Legend of Good Women*," *JEGP* 82 (1983): 11-31.

Lisa J. Kiser, *Telling Classical Tales: Chaucer and the "Legend of Good Women"* (Ithaca and London: Cornell University Press, 1983).

V. A. Kolve, "From Cleopatra to Alceste: An Iconographic Study of *The Legend of Good Women*," in Hermann and Burke, *Signs and Symbols*, 130-78.

Steven F. Kruger, "Passion and Order in Chaucer's *Legend of Good Women*," *ChauR* 23 (1989): 219-35.

McCall, *Chaucer among the Gods*, 113-23.

Ann McMillan, "Introduction" to *The Legend of Good Women* (Houston: Rice University Press, 1987): 1-51.

Mehl, *Geoffrey Chaucer*, 98-119.

North, *Chaucer's Universe*, 469-83.

Norton-Smith, *Geoffrey Chaucer*, 62-78.

Pat Trefzger Overbeck, "Chaucer's Good Woman," *ChauR* 2 (1967): 75-94.

Russell A. Peck, "Chaucerian Poetics and the *Prologue to the Legend of Good Women*," in Wasserman and Blanch, *Chaucer in the Eighties*, 39-55.

D. W. Robertson, Jr., "Historical Criticism," in *English Institute Essays, 1950*, ed. Alan S. Downer (New York: Columbia University Press, 1951). Reprinted in Robertson, *Essays in Medieval Culture*, 3-20.

Donald W. Rowe, *Through Nature to Eternity: Chaucer's Legend of Good Women* (Lincoln and London: University of Nebraska Press, 1988).

Gale C. Schricker, "On the Relation of Fact and Fiction in Chaucer's Poetic Endings," *PQ* 60 (Winter 1981): 13-27.

Sklute, *Virtue of Necessity*, 85-92.

"Lenvoy de Chaucer a Bukton"

Jane Chance, "Chaucerian Irony in the Verse Epistles 'Wordes Unto Adam,' 'Lenvoy a Scogan,' and 'Lenvoy a Bukton,'" *PLL* 21 (Spring 1985): 124-28.

Norton-Smith, *Geoffrey Chaucer*, 220-23.

John Stephens, "The Uses of Personae and the Art of Obliqueness in Some Chaucer Lyrics, Part II," *ChauR* 21 (1987): 449-64.

"Lenvoy de Chaucer a Scogan"

Jane Chance, "Chaucerian Irony in the Verse Epistles 'Wordes Unto Adam,' 'Lenvoy a Scogan,' and 'Lenvoy a Bukton,'" *PLL* 21 (Spring 1985): 120-24.

Alfred David, "Chaucer's Good Counsel to Scogan," *ChauR* 3 (1969): 265-74.

Walter H. French, "The Meaning of Chaucer's 'Envoy to Scogan,'" *PMLA* 48 (1933): 289-92.

Kean, *Love Division and Debate*, 33-36.

R. T. Lenaghan, "Chaucer's *Envoy to Scogan*: The Uses of Literary Convention," *ChauR* 10 (1975): 55-56.

Norton-Smith, *Geoffrey Chaucer*, 216-19.

Marion L. Polzella, "'The Craft so Long to Lerne': Poet and Lover in Chaucer's 'Envoy to Scogan' and *Parliament of Fowls*," *ChauR* 10 (1976): 279-86.

Jay Ruud, "Chaucer's *Envoy to Scogan*: 'Tullius Kyndenesse' and the Law of Kynde," *ChauR* 20 (1986): 323-30.

John Stephens, "The Uses of Personae and the Art of Obliqueness in Some Chaucer Lyrics, Part II," *ChauR* 21 (1987): 459-62 *passim*, 464-68.

The Manciple's Tale

Earle Birney, "Chaucer's 'Gentil' Manciple and his 'Gentil' Tale," *NM* 61 (1960): 257-67. Reprinted in Earle Birney, *Essays on Chaucerian Irony*, ed. Beryl Rowland (Toronto: University of Toronto Press, 1985), 125-33.

Alexander H. Brodie, "Hodge of Ware and Geber's Cook: Wordplay in the 'Manciple's Prologue,'" *NM* 72 (1971): 62-68.

J. A. Burrow, "Chaucer's Canterbury Pilgrimage," *EIC* 36 (1986): 97-119.

Arnold E. Davidson, "The Logic of Confusion in Chaucer's *Manciple's Tale*," *AnM* 19 (1979): 5-12.

James Dean, "Dismantling the Canterbury Book," *PMLA* 100 (1985): 752-54.

James Dean, "The Ending of the *Canterbury Tales*, 1952-1976," *TSLL* 21 (Spring 1979): 16-33.

J. D. Elliott, "The Moral of the *Manciple's Tale*," *N&Q* 1 (December 1954): 511-12.

Louise Fradenburg, "The Manciple's Servant Tongue: Politics and Poetry in *The Canterbury Tales*," *ELH* 52 (1985): 85-118.

R. D. Fulk, "Reinterpreting the *Manciple's Tale*," *JEGP* 78 (1979): 485-93.

Gardner, *The Poetry of Chaucer*, 332-35.

Britton J. Harwood, "Language and the Real: Chaucer's Manciple," *ChauR* 6 (1972): 268-79.

Gustaf E. Karsten, "Is the *Manciple's Tale* a Success?" *JEGP* 51 (1952): 1-16.

Stephen Thomas Knight, *Rymyng Craftily: Meaning in Chaucer's Poetry* (Sydney and London: Angus and Robertson, 1973), 161-83.

McCall, *Chaucer among the Gods*, 129-31, 148-52.

John J. McGavin, "How Nasty Is Phoebus's Crow?" *ChauR* 21 (1987): 444-58.

Rogers, *Upon the Ways*, 117-19.

V. J. Scattergood, "The Manciple's Manner of Speaking," *EIC* 24 (April 1974): 124-46.

Wayne Shumaker, "Chaucer's *Manciple's Tale* as Part of a Canterbury Group," *UTQ* 22 (January 1953): 147-56.

A. C. Spearing, "*The Canterbury Tales* IV: Exemplum and Fable," in Boitani and Mann, *The Cambridge Chaucer Companion*, 172-75.

Derek Traversi, *The Literary Imagination: Studies in Dante, Chaucer, and Shakespeare* (Newark: University of Delaware Press; London and Toronto: Associated University Presses, 1982), 120-44.

L. A. Westervelt, "The Mediaeval Notion of Janglery and Chaucer's *Manciple's Tale*," *SoRA* 14 (July 1981): 107-15.

Whittock, *A Reading of the Canterbury Tales*, 281-85.

The Man of Law's Tale

Morton W. Bloomfield, "*The Man of Law's Tale*: A Tragedy of Victimization and a Christian Comedy," *PMLA* 87 (1972): 384-90.

Brewer, *An Introduction to Chaucer*, 185-88.

Susan L. Clark and Julian N. Wasserman, "Constance as Romance and Folk Heroine in Chaucer's *Man of Law's Tale*," *RUS* 64, no. 1 (1978): 13-24.

Eugene Clasby, "Chaucer's Constance, Womanly Virtue and the Heroic Life," *ChauR* 13 (1979): 221-33.

Paul M. Clogan, "The Narrative Style of *The Man of Law's Tale*," *M&H* 8 (1977): 217-33.

T. D. Culver, "The Imposition of Order: A Measure of Art in the *Man of Law's Tale*," *YES* 2 (1972): 13-20.

Sheila Delany, "Womanliness in the *Man of Law's Tale*," *ChauR* 9 (1974): 63-72.

Robert T. Farrell, "Chaucer's Man of Law and His Tale: The Eccentric Design," in Salu and Farrell, *J. R. R. Tolkien*, 159-72.

Robert T. Farrell, "Chaucer's Use of the Theme of the Help of God in the *Man of Law's Tale*," *NM* 71 (1970): 239-43.

A. J. Fletcher, "Line 30 of *The Man of Law's Tale* and the Medieval Malkyn," *ELN* 24 (December 1986): 15-20.

Gardner, *The Poetry of Chaucer*, 265-74.

Joseph E. Grennen, "Chaucer's Man of Law and the Constancy of Justice," *JEGP* 84 (1985): 498-514.

Kevin J. Harty, "Chaucer's Man of Law and the 'Muses that men clepe Pierides,'" *SSF* 18 (Winter 1981): 75-77.

Kevin J. Harty, "The Tale and Its Teller: The Case of Chaucer's Man of Law," *ABR* 34 (1983): 361-71.

Hornsby, *Chaucer and the Law*, 145-48.

Huppé, *A Reading of the "Canterbury Tales,"* 91-107.

William C. Johnson, Jr., "The *Man of Law's Tale*: Aesthetics and Christianity in Chaucer," *ChauR* 16 (1982): 201-21.

Kean, *The Art of Narrative*, 114-22.

Knight, *The Poetry of the Canterbury Tales*, 43-48.

Kolve, *Chaucer and the Imagery of Narrative*, 285-358.

Albert C. Labriola, "The Doctrine of Charity and the Use of Homiletic 'Figures' in the *Man of Law's Tale*," *TSLL* 12 (Spring 1970): 5-14.

Arthur Norman, "The Man of Law's Tale," in *Studies in Language, Literature, and Culture of the Middle Ages and Later*, ed. E. Bagby Atwood and Archibald A. Hill (Austin: University of Texas at Austin, 1969), 312-23.

McCall, *Chaucer among the Gods*, 110-12.

Makarewicz, *The Patristic Influence*, 203-6, 218-22.

North, *Chaucer's Universe*, 484-98.

Michael R. Paull, "The Influence of the Saint's Legend Genre in the *Man of Law's Tale*," *ChauR* 5 (1971): 179-94.

Kevin Roddy, "Mythic Sequence in the *Man of Law's Tale*," *JMRS* 10 (1980): 1-22.

Ruggiers, *The Art of the Canterbury Tales*, 167-74.

Walter Scheps, "Chaucer's Man of Law and the Tale of Constance," *PMLA* 89 (1974): 285-95.

Hope Phyllis Weissman, "Late Gothic Pathos in the *Man of Law's Tale*," *JMRS* 9 (1979): 133-53.

Chauncey Wood, *Chaucer and the Country of the Stars: Poetic Uses of Astrological Imagery* (Princeton, N.J.: Princeton University Press, 1970), 192-244.

Chauncey Wood, "Chaucer's Man of Law as Interpreter," *Traditio* 23 (1967): 149-90.

Douglas Wurtele, "Chaucer's 'Man of Law's Tale,'" *Neophil* 60 (October 1976): 577-93.

The Merchant's Tale

David Aers, *Chaucer, Langland, and the Creative Imagination* (London, Boston and Henley: Routledge & Kegan Paul, 1980), 153-60.

Leigh A. Arrathoon, "Antinomic Cluster Analysis and the Boethian Verbal Structure of Chaucer's *Merchant's Tale*," *Lang&S* 17 (Winter 1984): 92-120.

Leigh A. Arrathoon, "'For craft is al, whoso that do it kan': The Genre of *The Merchant's Tale*," in Arrathoon, *Chaucer and the Craft*, 241-328.

Peter B. Beidler, "The Climax in the *Merchant's Tale*," *ChauR* 6 (1971): 38-43.

C. David Benson, *Chaucer's Drama of Style: Poetic Variety and Contrast in the "Canterbury Tales"* (Chapel Hill and London: University of North Carolina Press, 1986), 116-30.

Bishop, *The Narrative Art*, 134-39.

Kenneth A. Bleeth, "The Image of Paradise in the *Merchant's Tale*," in Benson, *The Learned and the Lewed*, 45-60.

Kenneth Bleeth, "Joseph's Doubting of Mary and the Conclusion of the *Merchant's Tale*," *ChauR* 21 (1986): 58-66.

Brewer, *An Introduction to Chaucer*, 221-25.

Bertrand H. Bronson, "Afterthoughts on the 'Merchant's Tale,'" *SP* 58 (October 1961): 583-96.

Emerson Brown, Jr., "Biblical Women in the *Merchant's Tale*: Feminism, Antifeminism, and Beyond," *Viator* 5 (1974): 387-412.

Emerson Brown, Jr., "Chaucer, the Merchant, and Their Tale: Getting Beyond Old Controversies, I," *ChauR* 13 (1978): 141-56.

Emerson Brown, Jr., "*Hortus Inconclusus*: The Significance of Priapus and Pyramus and Thisbe in the *Merchant's Tale*," *ChauR* 4 (1969): 31-40.

Emerson Brown, Jr., "*The Merchant's Tale*: Januarie's 'Unlikly Elde,'" *NM* 74 (1973): 92-106.

John Bugge, "Damyan's Wanton *Clyket* and an Ironic New *Twiste* to the *Merchant's Tale*," *AnM* 14 (1973): 53-62.

Douglas A. Burger, "Deluding Words in the *Merchant's Tale*," *ChauR* 12 (1977): 103-10.

Burlin, *Chaucerian Fiction*, 207-16.

J. D. Burnley, "The Morality of *The Merchant's Tale*," *YES* 6 (1976): 16-25.

J. A. Burrow, "Irony in the *Merchant's Tale*," *Anglia* 75 (1957): 199-208. Reprinted in Burrow, *Essays on Medieval Literature*, 49-59.

Michael A. Calabrese, "May Devoid of All Delight: January, the *Merchant's Tale* and the *Romance of the Rose*," *SP* 87 (1990): 261-84.

Michael D. Cherniss, "The *Clerk's Tale* and *Envoy*, the Wife of Bath's Purgatory and the *Merchant's Tale*," *ChauR* 6 (1972): 246-53.

Edward I. Condren, "Transcendent Metaphor or Banal Reality: Three Chaucerian Dilemmas," *PLL* 21 (Summer 1985): 239-47.

Thomas D. Cooke, *The Old French and Chaucerian Fabliaux: A Study of Their Comic Climax* (Columbia and London: University of Missouri Press, 1978), 185-94.

Helen Cooper, "The Girl with Two Lovers: Four Canterbury Tales," in *Medieval Studies for J. A. W. Bennett*, ed. P. L. Heyworth (Oxford: Clarendon Press, 1981), 65-79.

Corsa, *Chaucer: Poet of Mirth*, 155-66.

Craik, *The Comic Tales*, 133-53.

David, *The Strumpet Muse*, 170-81.

E. Talbot Donaldson, "The Effect of the *Merchant's Tale*," in Donaldson, *Speaking of Chaucer*, 30-45. Reprinted in *Geoffrey Chaucer: Modern Critical Views*, ed. Harold Bloom (New York: Chelsea House Publishers, 1985), 37-48.

E. Talbot Donaldson, "The Masculine Narrator and Four Women of Style," in Donaldson, *Speaking of Chaucer*, 50-53.

Mortimer J. Donovan, "The Image of Pluto and Proserpine in the *Merchant's Tale*," *PQ* 36 (January 1957): 49-60.

George D. Economou, "January's Sin Against Nature: *The Merchant's Tale* and *The Roman de la Rose*," *CL* 17 (Summer 1965): 251-57.

Robert Emmett Finnegan, "The Man of Law, His Tale, and the Pilgrims," *NM* 77 (1976): 227-40.

Gardner, *The Poetry of Chaucer*, 285-88.

Barbara T. Gates, "'A Temple of False Goddis': Cupidity and Mercantile Values in Chaucer's Fruit-tree Episode," *NM* 77 (1976): 369-75.

Philip Mahone Griffith, *Expl* 16 (December 1957): 13.

Albert E. Hartung, "The Non-Comic *Merchant's Tale*, Maximianus, and the Sources," *MS* 29 (1967): 1-25.

Carol Falvo Heffernan, "Wells and Streams in Three Chaucerian Gardens," *PLL* 15 (Fall 1979): 347-50.

C. Hugh Holman, "Courtly Love in the Merchant's and the Franklin's Tales," *ELH* 18 (1951): 241-52. Reprinted in Wagenknecht, *Chaucer*, 240-49.

Huppé, *A Reading of the "Canterbury Tales,"* 147-62.

Hussey, *Chaucer*, 147-56.

Jordan, *Chaucer and the Shape of Creation*, 132-51.

Robert M. Jordan, "The Non-Dramatic Disunity of the *Merchant's Tale*," *PMLA* 78 (1963): 293-99.

Kean, *The Art of Narrative*, 157-64.

Kenneth Kee, "Two Chaucerian Gardens," *MS* 23 (1961): 159-61.

George R. Keiser, "Chaucer's *Merchant's Tale*, E 2412-16," *SSF* 15 (Spring 1978): 191-92.

Robert J. Kloss, "Chaucer's *The Merchant's Tale*: Tender Youth and Stooping Age," *AI* 31 (Spring 1974): 65-79.

Knight, *The Poetry of the Canterbury Tales,* 88-101.

Koff, *Chaucer*, 110-18.

Bernard S. Levy, "*Gentilesse* in Chaucer's *Clerk's* and *Merchant's Tales*," *ChauR* 11 (1977): 309-16.

Joanna Lloyd, *Expl* 47 (Summer 1989): 3-4.

Lumiansky, *Of Sondry Folk*, 156-71.

William W. Main, *Expl* (November 1955): 13.

Makarewicz, *The Patristic Influence*, 54-75 *passim*, 108-13.

Mehl, *Geoffrey Chaucer*, 178-83.

Richard Neuse, "Marriage and the Question of Allegory in the *Merchant's Tale*," *ChauR* 24 (1989): 115-31.

North, *Chaucer's Universe*, 443-55.

Paul A. Olson, "Chaucer's Merchant and January's 'Hevene in Erthe Heere,'" *ELH* 28 (September 1961): 203-14.

Charles A. Owen, Jr., "The Crucial Passages in Five of *The Canterbury Tales*: A Study in Irony and Symbol," *JEGP* 52 (1953): 294-311. Reprinted in Wagenknecht, *Chaucer*, 252-68.

Owen, *Pilgrimage and Storytelling*, 189-200.

George B. Pace, "The Scorpion of Chaucer's 'Merchant's Tale,'" *MLQ* 26 (September 1965): 369-74.

Roy J. Pearcy, "The Genre of Chaucer's Fabliau-Tales," in Arrathoon, *Chaucer and the Craft*, 358-66.

Derek Pearsall, "*The Canterbury Tales* II: Comedy," in Boitani and Mann, *The Cambridge Chaucer Companion*, 137-39.

Malcolm Pittock, "The Merchant's Tale," *EIC* 17 (January 1967): 26-40.

Richardson, *Blameth Nat Me*, 123-46.

Velma Bourgeois Richmond, "'Pacience in Adversitee': Chaucer's Presentation of Marriage," *Viator* 10 (1979): 340-48.

D. W. Robertson, Jr., "The Doctrine of Charity in Medieval Literary Gardens: A Topical Approach through Symbolism and Allegory," *Speculum* 26 (1951): 24-59. Reprinted in Robertson, *Essays in Medieval Culture*, 21-50.

Rogers, *Upon the Ways*, 65-69.

Wolfgang E. H. Rudat, "Chaucer's Spring of Comedy: *The Merchant's Tale* and Other 'Games' with Augustinian Theology," *AnM* 21 (1981): 111-20.

Wolfgang E. H. Rudat, *Expl* 35 (Summer 1977): 25-26.

Ruggiers, *The Art of the Canterbury Tales*, 109-20.

Jay Schleusener, "The Conduct of the *Merchant's Tale*," *ChauR* 14 (1980): 237-50.

Gary D. Schmidt, "The Marriage Irony in the Tales of the Merchant and Franklin," in *Portraits of Marriage in Literature*, ed. Ann C. Hargrove and Maurine Magliocco (Macomb: Western Illinois University, 1984), 97-101.

Mary C. Schroeder, "Fantasy in the 'Merchant's Tale,'" *Criticism* 12 (Summer 1970): 167-79.

G. G. Sedgwick, "The Structure of *The Merchant's Tale*," *UTQ* 17 (July 1948): 337-45.

David L. Shores, "*The Merchant's Tale*: Some Lay Observations," *NM* 71 (1970): 119-33.

Speirs, *Chaucer the Maker*, 155-62.

Traversi, *The Canterbury Tales*, 135-58.

Nicolai von Kreisler, "An Aesopic Allusion in the *Merchant's Tale*," *ChauR* 6 (1971): 30-37.

Karl P. Wentersdorf, "Imagery, Structure, and Theme in Chaucer's *Merchant's Tale*," in Arrathoon, *Chaucer and the Craft*, 35-62.

Karl P. Wentersdorf, "Theme and Structure in *The Merchant's Tale*: The Function of the Pluto Episode," *PMLA* 80 (1965): 522-27.

Whittock, *A Reading of the Canterbury Tales*, 153-62.

Robert A. Wichert, *Expl* 25 (December 1966): 32.

Wimsatt, *Allegory and Mirror*, 84-86.

James I. Wimsatt, "Chaucer and the Canticle of Canticles," in Mitchell and Provost, *Chaucer the Love Poet*, 84-88.

Rosemary Woolf, "Moral Chaucer and Kindly Gower," in Salu and Farrell, *J. R. R. Tolkien*, 235-39.

Douglas Wurtele, "The Blasphemy of Chaucer's Merchant," *AnM* 21 (1981): 91-110.

The Miller's Tale

W. P. Albrecht, *Expl* 9 (February 1951): 25.

Paul E. Beichner, C. S. C., "Chaucer's Hende Nicholas," *MS* 14 (1952): 151-53.

Peter G. Beidler, "Art and Scatology in the *Miller's Tale*," *ChauR* 12 (1977): 90-102.

C. David Benson, *Chaucer's Drama of Style: Poetic Variety and Contrast in the "Canterbury Tales"* (Chapel Hill and London: University of North Carolina Press, 1986), 64-88, 90-103.

Joseph Bentley, "Chaucer's Fantastic Miller," *SAQ* 64 (Spring 1965): 247-53.

Dennis Biggins, "Sym(e)kyn/*simia*: The Ape in Chaucer's Millers," *SP* 65 (January 1968): 44-50.

Earle Birney, "The Inhibited and the Uninhibited: Ironic Structure in the *Miller's Tale*," *Neophil* 44 (1960): 333-38. Reprinted in Earle Birney, *Essays on Chaucerian Irony*, ed. Beryl Rowland (Toronto: University of Toronto Press, 1985), 77-83.

Bishop, *The Narrative Art*, 55-70.

Michael Harry Blechner, "Chaucer's Nicholas and Saint Nicholas," *NM* 79 (1978): 367-71.

E. D. Blodgett, "Chaucerian *Pryvetee* and the Opposition to Time," *Speculum* 51 (1976): 482-84.

Morton W. Bloomfield, "*The Miller's Tale*–An UnBoethian Interpretation," in *Medieval Literature and Folklore Studies: Essays in Honor of Francis Lee Utley*, ed. Jerome Mandel and Bruce A. Rosenberg (New Brunswick, N.J.: Rutgers University Press, 1970), 205-11.

W. F. Bolton, "'The Miller's Tale': An Interpretation," *MS* 24 (1962): 83-94.

Brewer, *An Introduction to Chaucer*, 177-80.

Derek Brewer, "The Poetry of Chaucer's 'Fabliaux,'" in Derek S. Brewer, *Chaucer: The Poet as Storyteller* (London and Basingstoke: Macmillan, 1984), 112-13.

Derek Brewer, "Structures and Character-types of Chaucer's Popular Comic Tales," in *Estudios sobre los generos literarios*, ed. Javier Coy and Javier De Hoz, Acta Salmanticensia, Filosofia y Letras, no. 89 (Salamanca: Universidad de Salamanca, 1975), 107-18. Reprinted in Derek S. Brewer, *Chaucer: The Poet as Storyteller* (London and Basingstoke: Macmillan, 1984), 81-83.

Saul N. Brody, "The Comic Rejection of Courtly Love," in *In Pursuit of Perfection: Courtly Love in Medieval Literature*, ed. Joan M. Ferrante and George D. Economou (London: National University Publications; Port Washington, N.Y.: Kennikat Press, 1975), 250-52.

Roy Peter Clark, "Christmas Games in Chaucer's 'The Miller's Tale,'" *SSF* 13 (Summer 1976): 277-87.

Edward I. Condren, "Transcendent Metaphor or Banal Reality: Three Chaucerian Dilemmas," *PLL* 21 (Summer 1985): 235-39.

Thomas D. Cooke, *The Old French and Chaucerian Fabliaux: A Study of Their Comic Climax* (Columbia and London: University of Missouri Press, 1978), 176-84.

Helen Cooper, "The Girl with Two Lovers: Four Canterbury Tales," in *Medieval Studies for J. A. W. Bennett*, ed. P. L. Heyworth (Oxford: Clarendon, 1981), 65-79.

Geoffrey Cooper, "'Sely John' in the 'Legende' of the *Miller's Tale*," *JEGP* 79 (1980): 1-12.

Corsa, *Chaucer: Poet of Mirth*, 108-14.

Craik, *The Comic Tales*, 1-29.

Joseph A. Dane, "The Mechanics of Comedy in Chaucer's *Miller's Tale*," *ChauR* 14 (1980): 215-24.

David, *The Strumpet Muse*, 92-107.

Christopher Dean, "Imagery in the *Knight's Tale* and the *Miller's Tale*," *MS* 31 (1969): 149-63.

E. Talbot Donaldson, "Idiom of Popular Poetry in the *Miller's Tale,*" in *English Institute Essays, 1950*, ed. A. S. Downer (New York: Columbia University Press, 1951), 116-40. Reprinted in *Explication as Criticism, Selected Papers from the English Institute, 1941-1952*, ed. W. K. Wimsatt, Jr. (New York and London: Columbia University Press, 1963), 27-51; Donaldson, *Speaking of Chaucer*, 13-29.

Gardner, *The Poetry of Chaucer*, 254-59.

Robert V. Graybill, "Chaucer's 'The Miller's Tale': Exemplum of *Caritas*," in *Proceedings of the Illinois Medieval Association*, no. 2, ed. Mark D. Johnston and Samuel M. Riley (Normal, Ill.: Illinois State University, 1985), 51-65.

Thomas B. Hanson, "Physiognomy and Characterization in the *Miller's Tale*," *NM* 72 (1971): 477-82.

Kelsie Harder, "Chaucer's Use of the Mystery Plays in the *Miller's Tale*," *MLQ* 17 (September 1956): 193-98.

Britton J. Harwood, "The 'Nether Ye' and Its Antitheses: A Structuralist Reading of 'The Miller's Tale,'" *AnM* 21 (1981): 5-30.

Ann S. Haskell, *Essays on Chaucer's Saints* (The Hague and Paris: Mouton, 1976), 38-43.

John C. Hirsh, "Why Does the *Miller's Tale* Take Place on Monday?" *ELN* 13 (December 1976): 86-90.

Huppé, *A Reading of the "Canterbury Tales,"* 75-88.

Hussey, *Chaucer*, 140-46.

Jordan, *Chaucer and the Shape of Creation*, 185-97.

R. E. Kaske, "The *Canticum Canticorum* in the *Miller's Tale*," *SP* 59 (July 1962): 479-500.

R. E. Kaske, "The Defense," in *Critical Approaches to Medieval Literature: Selected Papers from the English Institute, 1958-1959,* ed. Dorothy Bethurum (New York and London: Columbia University Press, 1960), 52-60.

Kolve, *Chaucer and the Imagery of Narrative*, 158-216.

Lawrence, Seifter, and Ratner, *McGraw-Hill Guide*, 41-43.

Robert E. Lewis, "The English Fabliau Tradition and Chaucer's *Miller's Tale*," *MP* 79 (February 1982): 241-55.

John Leyerle, "The Heart and the Chain," in Benson, *The Learned and the Lewed*, 122-23.

Garth A. McCann, "Chaucer's First Three Tales: Unity in Trinity," *BRMMLA* 27 (1973): 15-16.

Mehl, *Geoffrey Chaucer*, 172-76.

Robert P. Miller, "The *Miller's Tale* as Complaint," *ChauR* 5 (1970): 147-60.

Charles Muscatine, *Chaucer and the French Tradition* (Berkeley and Los Angeles: University of California Press, 1957), 223-30.

Paula Neuss, "Double-Entendre in *The Miller's Tale*," *EIC* 24 (October 1974): 325-40.

Norton-Smith, *Geoffrey Chaucer*, 136-45.

Cornclius Novclli, "Absolon's 'Freend so Deere': A Pivotal Point in the *Miller's Tale*," *Neophil* 52 (January 1968): 65-69.

John J. O'Connor, "The Astrological Background of the *Miller's Tale*," *Speculum* 31 (1956): 120-25.

Paul A. Olson, "Poetic Justice in the 'Miller's Tale,'" *MLQ* 24 (September 1963): 227-36.

Charles A. Owen, Jr., "Chaucer's *Canterbury Tales*: Aesthetic Design in Stories of the First Day," *ES* 35 (1954): 51-55.

Owen, *Pilgrimage and Storytelling*, 99-106.

George B. Pace, "Physiognomy and Chaucer's Summoner and Alisoun," *Traditio* 18 (1962): 417-20.

Roy J. Pearcy, "The Genre of Chaucer's Fabliau-Tales," in Arrathoon, *Chaucer and the Craft*, 341-50.

Derek Pearsall, "*The Canterbury Tales* II: Comedy," in Boitani and Mann, *The Cambridge Chaucer Companion* 130-33.

Sandra Pierson Prior, "Parodying Typology and the Mystery Plays in the *Miller's Tale*," *JMRS* 16 (Spring 1986): 57-73.

Edmund Reiss, "Chaucer's Parodies of Love," in Mitchell and Provost, *Chaucer the Love Poet*, 40-42.

Edmund Reiss, "Daun Gerveys in the *Miller's Tale*," *PLL* 6 (Spring 1970): 115-24.

Alain Renoir, "The Inept Lover and the Reluctant Mistress: Remarks on Sexual Inefficiency in Medieval Literature," in *Chaucerian Problems and Perspectives: Essays Presented to Paul E. Beichner, C. S. C.*, ed. Edward Vasta and Zacharias P. Thundy (Notre Dame and London: University of Notre Dame, 1979), 184-90.

Carter Revard, "The Tow on Absalom's Distaff and the Punishment of Lechers in Medieval London," *ELN* 17 (March 1980): 168-70.

Richardson, *Blameth Nat Me*, 159-69.

Rogers, *Upon the Ways*, 38-41.

Thomas W. Ross, "Notes on Chaucer's *Miller's Tale*, A 3216 and 3320," *ELN* 13 (June 1976): 256-58.

Beryl Rowland, "Chaucer's Blasphemous Churl: A New Interpretation of the *Miller's Tale*," in Rowland, *Chaucer and Middle English Studies*, 43-55.

Beryl B. Rowland, "The Play of the *Miller's Tale*: A Game Within a Game," *ChauR* 5 (1970): 140-46.

Ruggiers, *The Art of The Canterbury Tales*, 53-65.

Edward C. Schweitzer, "The Misdirected Kiss and the Lover's Malady in Chaucer's *Miller's Tale*," in Wasserman and Blanch, *Chaucer in the Eighties*, 223-33.

Roger D. Sell, "Tellability and Politeness in 'The Miller's Tale': First Steps in Literary Pragmatics," *ES* 66 (December 1985): 496-512.

A. Booker Thro, "Chaucer's Creative Comedy: A Study of the *Miller's Tale* and the *Shipman's Tale*," *ChauR* 5 (1970): 98-106.

E. M. W. Tillyard, *Poetry Direct and Oblique* (London: Chatto & Windus, 1948), 85-92.

Traversi, *The Canterbury Tales*, 62-82.

Raymond P. Tripp, Jr., "The Darker Side to Absolon's Dawn Visit," *ChauR* 20 (1986): 210-11.

M. F. Vaughan, "Chaucer's Imaginative One-Day Flood," *PQ* 60 (Winter 1981): 117-23.

Whittock, *A Reading of the Canterbury Tales*, 77-95.

David Williams, "Radical Therapy in the *Miller's Tale*," *ChauR* 15 (1981): 227-35.

The Monk's Tale

Burlin, *Chaucerian Fiction*, 182-85.

Thomas J. Hatton, "Chauntecleer and the Monk, Two False Knights," *PLL* 3 (Summer supplement 1967): 31-39.

Knight, *The Poetry of the Canterbury Tales*, 151-56.

Jack B. Oruch, "Chaucer's Worldly Monk," *Criticism* 8 (Summer 1966): 280-88.

Jay Ruud, "'In Meetre in Many a Sondry Wyse': Fortune's Wheel and the *Monk's Tale*," *ELN* 26 (June 1989): 6-11.

William C. Strange, "The *Monk's Tale*: A Generous View," *ChauR* 1 (1967): 167-80.

The Nun's Priest's Tale

Aers, *Chaucer*, 8-13.

Judith H. Anderson, "'Nat Worth a Boterflye': *Muiopotmos* and *The Nun's Priest's Tale*," *JMRS* 1 (1971): 90-94.

Bishop, *The Narrative Art*, 164-76.

Ian Bishop, "The *Nun's Priest's Tale* and the Liberal Arts," *RES*, n.s. 30 (1979): 257-67.

Morton W. Bloomfield, "The Wisdom of the *Nun's Priest's Tale*," in *Chaucerian Problems and Perspectives: Essays Presented to Paul E. Beichner, C. S. C.*, ed. Edward Vasta and Zacharias P. Thundy (Notre Dame and London: University of Notre Dame, 1979), 70-82.

W. F. Bolton, "Structural Meaning in *The Pardoner's Tale* and *The Nun's Priest's Tale*," *Lang&S* 11 (Fall 1978): 206-10.

Brewer, *An Introduction to Chaucer*, 197-200.

Saul Nathaniel Brody, "Truth and Fiction in the 'Nun's Priest's Tale,'" *ChauR* 14 (1979): 34-47. Reprinted in *Geoffrey Chaucer: Modern Critical Views*, ed. Harold Bloom (New York: Chelsea House Publishers, 1985), 111-22.

Arthur T. Broes, "Chaucer's Disgruntled Cleric: *The Nun's Priest's Tale*," *PMLA* 78 (1963): 156-62.

Burlin, *Chaucerian Fiction*, 228-34.

David S. Chamberlain, "The *Nun's Priest's Tale* and Boethius's *De Musica*," *MP* 68 (November 1970): 188-91.

Corsa, *Chaucer: Poet of Mirth*, 211-22.

Craik, *The Comic Tales*, 71-87.

Dolores L. Cullen, *Expl* 38 (Fall 1979): 11.

David, *The Strumpet Muse*, 224-31.

Davidoff, *Beginning Well*, 126-27.

Nancy Dean, "Chaucerian Attitudes toward Joy with Particular Consideration of the *Nun's Priest's Tale*," *MÆ* 44 (1975): 1-13.

E. Talbot Donaldson, "Patristic Exegesis in the Criticism of Medieval Literature: The Opposition," in *Critical Approaches to Medieval Literature: Selected Papers from the English Institute, 1958-1959*, ed. Dorothy Bethurum (New York: Columbia University Press, 1960), 16-20. Reprinted in Donaldson, *Speaking of Chaucer*, 147-50.

Peter H. Elbow, *Oppositions in Chaucer* (Middletown, Conn.: Wesleyan University Press, 1973), 95-113, 116-21.

Ralph W. V. Elliott, *The Nun's Priest's Tale and the Pardoner's Tale* (New York: Barnes & Noble, 1965), 7-39.

John Block Friedman, "The *Nun's Priest's Tale*: The Preacher and the Mermaid's Song," *ChauR* 7 (1973): 250-66.

Fyler, *Chaucer and Ovid*, 148-63.

Patrick Gallacher, "Food, Laxatives, and Catharsis in Chaucer's *Nun's Priest's Tale*," *Speculum* 51 (1976): 49-68.

Gardner, *The Poetry of Chaucer*, 311-15.

Susan Gallick, "A Look at Chaucer and His Preachers," *Speculum* 50 (1975): 471-76.

Thomas J. Hatton, "Chauntecleer and the Monk, Two False Knights," *PLL* 3 (Summer supplement 1967): 31-39.

Constance B. Hieatt, "The Moral of *The Nun's Priest's Tale*," *SN* 42 (1970): 3-8.

Hieatt, *The Realism of Dream Visions*, 40-43.

John Hollander, *Melodius Guile: Fictive Pattern in Poetic Language* (New Haven and London: Yale University Press, 1988), 202-5.

Huppé, *A Reading of the "Canterbury Tales,"* 174-84.

Hussey, *Chaucer*, 183-88.

Maurice Hussey, "Introduction" to *The Nun's Priest's Prologue & Tale* (Cambridge: Cambridge University Press, 1965), 1-42.

Eric Jager, "Croesus and Chauntecleer: The Royal Road of Dreams," *MLQ* 49 (March 1988): 3-18.

Lynn Staley Johnson, "'To Make in Som Comedye': Chauntecleer, Son of Troy," *ChauR* 19 (1985): 225-44.

Corinne E. Kauffman, "Dame Pertelote's Parlous Parle," *ChauR* 4 (1969): 41-48.

J. Kieran Kealy, *Expl* 33 (October 1974): 12.

Kean, *The Art of Narrative*, 131-39.

Alfred L. Kellogg, *Chaucer, Langland, Arthur: Essays in Middle English Literature* (New Brunswick, N.J.: Rutgers University Press, 1972), 180-87.

Knight, *The Poetry of the Canterbury Tales,* 157-72.

Stephen Thomas Knight, *Rymyng Craftily: Meaning in Chaucer's Poetry* (Sydney and London: Angus and Robertson, 1973), 206-35.

Rama Rani Lall, *Satiric Fable in English: A Critical Study of the Animal Tales of Chaucer, Spenser, Dryden, and Orwell* (New Delhi: New Statesman Publishing Company, 1979), 24-39.

Lawrence, Seifter, and Ratner, *McGraw-Hill Guide*, 43-48.

R. T. Lenaghan, "The Nun's Priest's Tale," *PMLA* 78 (1963): 300-307.

Bernard S. Levy and George R. Adams, "Chauntecleer's Paradise Lost and Regained," *MS* 29 (1967): 178-92.

R. M. Lumiansky, "The Nun's Priest in *The Canterbury Tales*," *PMLA* 68 (1953): 896-906.

McCall, *Chaucer among the Gods*, 140-43.

Mehl, *Geoffrey Chaucer*, 200-204.

Peter Meredith, "Chauntecleer and the Mermaids," *Neophil* 54 (January 1970): 81-83.

D. E. Myers, "Focus and 'Moralite' in the *Nun's Priest's Tale*," *ChauR* 7 (1973): 210-20.

North, *Chaucer's Universe*, 456-68.

Charles A. Owen, Jr., "The Crucial Passages in Five of *The Canterbury Tales*: A Study in Irony and Symbol," *JEGP* 52 (1953): 294-311. Reprinted in Wagenknecht, *Chaucer*, 252-68.

Owen, *Pilgrimage and Storytelling*, 134-42.

F. Anne Payne, *Chaucer and Menippean Satire* (Madison: University of Wisconsin Press, 1981), 159-206.

F. Anne Payne, "Foreknowledge and Free Will: Three Theories in the *Nun's Priest's Tale*," *ChauR* 10 (1976): 201-19.

Robert A. Pratt, "Some Latin Sources of the Nonnes Preest on Dreams," *Speculum* 52 (1977): 538-70.

Thomas L. Reed, Jr., "Nebuchadnezzar and Chauntecleer: Chaucer's Fortunate Fowl," *NM* 89 (1988): 44-56.

Rogers, *Upon the Ways*, 98-107.

Beryl Rowland, "'Owles and Apes' in Chaucer's *Nun's Priest's Tale*, 3092," *MS* 27 (1965): 322-25.

Ruggiers, *The Art of the Canterbury Tales*, 184-96.

J. Burke Severs, "Chaucer's Originality in the *Nun's Priest's Tale*," *SP* 43 (January 1946): 22-41.

A. Paul Shallers, "*The Nun's Priest's Tale*: An Ironic Exemplum," *ELH* 42 (1975): 319-37.

Speirs, *Chaucer the Maker*, 185-93.

John M. Steadman, "Flattery and the Moralitas of the *Nonne Preestes Tale*," *MÆ* 28 (1959): 172-79.

Paul R. Thomas, "Cato on Chauntecleer: Chaucer's Sophisticated Audience," *Neophil* 72 (April 1988): 278-83.

Traversi, *The Canterbury Tales*, 210-36.

Peter W. Travis, "Chaucer's Trivial Fox Chase and the Peasants' Revolt of 1381," *JMRS* 18 (Fall 1988): 195-220 *passim*.

Whittock, *A Reading of the Canterbury Tales*, 228-50.

Richard Zacharias, *Expl* 32 (April 1974): 60.

The Pardoner's Tale

Janet Adelman, "That We May Leere Som Wit," in Faulkner, *Twentieth Century Interpretations*, 96-106.

Aers, *Chaucer*, 45-51.

David Aers, *Chaucer, Langland, and the Creative Imagination* (London, Boston, and Henley: Routledge & Kegan Paul, 1980), 89-106.

David M. Anderson, "The Pardoner's True Profession," *NM* 75 (1974): 630-39.

Stephen A. Barney, "An Evaluation of the *Pardoner's Tale*," in Faulkner, *Twentieth Century Interpretations*, 83-95.

Paul C. Bauschatz, "Chaucer's Pardoner's Beneficent Lie," *Assays* 2 (1983): 19-43.

Paul E. Beichner, C. S. C., "Chaucer's Pardoner as Entertainer," *MS* 25 (1963): 160-72.

Peter G. Beidler, "The Plague and Chaucer's Pardoner," *ChauR* 16 (1982): 257-69.

C. David Benson, *Chaucer's Drama of Style: Poetic Variety and Contrast in the "Canterbury Tales"* (Chapel Hill and London: University of North Carolina Press, 1986), 44-63.

Bishop, *The Narrative Art*, 91-105.

Ian Bishop, "The Narrative Art of *The Pardoner's Tale*," *MÆ* 36 (1967), 15-24.

Robert Boenig, "Musical Irony in the *Pardoner's Tale*," *ChauR* 24 (1990): 253-62.

W. F. Bolton, "Structural Meaning in *The Pardoner's Tale* and *The Nun's Priest's Tale*," *Lang&S* 11 (Fall 1978): 202-6.

Bertrand H. Bronson, *In Search of Chaucer* (Toronto: University of Toronto Press, 1960), 78-87. Reprinted in Faulkner, *Twentieth Century Interpretations*, 15-22.

Burlin, *Chaucerian Fiction*, 169-75.

James L. Calderwood, "Parody in *The Pardoner's Tale*," *ES* 45 (1964): 302-9.

Jane Chance, "'Disfigured is thy face': Chaucer's Pardoner and the Protean Shape-Shifter Fals Semblant (A Response to Britton Harwood)," *PQ* 67 (Fall 1988): 423-35.

Carolyn P. Collette, "'Ubi Peccaverant, Ibi Punirentur': The Oak Tree and the *Pardoner's Tale*," *ChauR* 19 (1984): 39-45.

Edward I. Condren, "The Pardoner's Bid for Existence," *Viator* 4 (1973): 177-205.

Corsa, *Chaucer: Poet of Mirth*, 190-96.

Alfred David, "Criticism and 'The Pardoner's Tale,'" *CE* 27 (October 1965): 39-44.

David, *The Strumpet Muse*, 193-206.

Christopher Dean, "Salvation, Damnation and the Role of the Old Man in the *Pardoner's Tale*," *ChauR* 3 (1968): 44-49.

James Dean, "Spiritual Allegory and Chaucer's Narrative Style: Three Test Cases," *ChauR* 18 (1984): 277-81.

Rodney Delasanta, "Sacrament and Sacrifice in the *Pardoner's Tale*," *AnM* 14 (1973): 43-52.

A. Leigh DeNeef, "Chaucer's *Pardoner's Tale* and the Irony of Misinterpretation," *JNT* 3 (May 1973): 85-96.

Russell Duino, "The Tortured Pardoner," *EJ* 46 (1957): 320-25.

Ralph W. V. Elliott, *The Nun's Priest's Tale and the Pardoner's Tale* (New York: Barnes & Noble: 1964), 40-71. Reprinted in Faulkner, *Twentieth Century Interpretations*, 23-32.

Garland Ethel, "Chaucer's Worst Shrewe: The Pardoner," *MLQ* 20 (September 1959): 211-27.

Dewey R. Faulkner, "Introduction," in Faulkner, *Twentieth Century Interpretations*, 1-14.

Susan Gallick, "A Look at Chaucer and His Preachers," *Speculum* 50 (1975): 467-71.

Gardner, *The Poetry of Chaucer*, 299-303.

John Halverson, "Chaucer's Pardoner and the Progress of Criticism," *ChauR* 4 (1970): 184-202.

David V. Harrington, "Narrative Speed in the *Pardoner's Tale*," *ChauR* 3 (1968-69): 50-59. Reprinted in Faulkner, *Twentieth Century Interpretations*, 33-42.

Britton J. Harwood, "Chaucer's Pardoner: The Dialectics of Inside and Outside," *PQ* 67 (Fall 1988): 409-22.

Ann S. Haskell, *Essays on Chaucer's Saints* (The Hague and Paris: Mouton, 1976), 17-22.

Elizabeth R. Hatcher, "Life Without Death: The Old Man in Chaucer's *Pardoner's Tale*," *ChauR* 9 (1975): 246-52.

N. R. Havely, "Introduction" to *The Friar's, Summoners's and Pardoner's Tales from the Canterbury Tales* (London: University of London Press, 1975), 28-39.

Masayuki Higuchi, "On the Integration of the *Pardoner's Tale*," *ChauR* 22 (1987): 161-69.

Huppé, *A Reading of the "Canterbury Tales,"* 209-19.

Hussey, *Chaucer*, 177-83.

Robert E. Jungman, "The Pardoner's Quarrel with the Host," *PQ* 55 (Spring 1976): 279-81.

Stewart Justman, "Literal and Symbolic in 'The Canterbury Tales,'" *ChauR* 14 (1980): 199-214. Reprinted in *Geoffrey Chaucer: Modern Critical Views*, ed. Harold Bloom (New York: Chelsea House Publishers, 1985), 130ff.

Alfred L. Kellogg, "An Augustinian Interpretation of Chaucer's Pardoner," *Speculum* 26 (1951): 465-81. Reprinted in Alfred L. Kellogg, *Chaucer, Langland, Arthur: Essays in Middle English Literature* (New Brunswick, N.J.: Rutgers University Press, 1972), 245-68.

Stephan A. Khinoy, "Inside Chaucer's Pardoner," *ChauR* 6 (1972): 255-67.

Knight, *The Poetry of the Canterbury Tales*, 123-35.

Koff, *Chaucer*, 156-73.

H. Marshall Leicester, Jr., "'Synne Horrible': The Pardoner's Exegesis of His Tale, and Chaucer's," in Carruthers and Kirk, *Acts of Interpretation*, 25-50.

R. M. Lumiansky, "A Conjecture Concerning Chaucer's Pardoner," *TSE* 1 (1949): 11-28.

Lumiansky, *Of Sondry Folk*, 212-19.

Monica E. McAlpine, "The Pardoner's Homosexuality and How It Matters," *PMLA* 95 (1980): 8-22.

Makarewicz, *The Patristic Influence*, 214-17.

Robert P. Merrix, "Sermon Structure in the *Pardoner's Tale*," *ChauR* 17 (1983): 235-49.

Clarence H. Miller and Roberta Bux Bosse, "Chaucer's Pardoner and the Mass," *ChauR* 6 (1972): 171-84.

Robert P. Miller, "Chaucer's Pardoner, the Scriptural Eunuch, and the Pardoner's Tale," *Speculum* 30 (1955): 180-99. Reprinted in Faulkner, *Twentieth Century Interpretations*, 43-69.

Joseph R. Millichap, "Transubstantiation in the *Pardoner's Tale*," *BRMMLA* 28 (December 1974): 102-8.

Charles Mitchell, "The Moral Superiority of Chaucer's Pardoner," *CE* 27 (March 1966): 437-44.

Gerald Morgan, "The Self-Revealing Tendencies of Chaucer's Pardoner," *MLR* 71 (April 1976): 241-55.

Robert E. Nichols, Jr., "The Pardoner's Ale and Cake," *PMLA* 82 (1967): 498-504.

Alicia K. Nitecki, "The Convention of the Old Man's Lament in the *Pardoner's Tale*," *ChauR* 16 (1981): 76-84.

N. E. Osselton, "Chaucer's 'Clumsy Transition' in the *Pardoner's Tale*," *ES* 49 (February 1968): 36-38.

Charles A. Owen, "The Crucial Passages in Five of *The Canterbury Tales*: A Study in Irony and Symbol," *JEGP* 52 (1953): 294-311. Reprinted in Wagenknecht, *Chaucer*, 252-68.

Charles A. Owen, *Pilgrimage and Storytelling*, 170-83.

Nancy H. Owen, "The Pardoner's Introduction, Prologue, and Tale: Sermon and Fabliau," *JEGP* 66 (1967): 541-49. Reprinted in Faulkner, *Twentieth Century Interpretations*, 114-17.

Malcolm Pittock, "The *Pardoner's Tale* and the Quest for Death," *EIC* 24 (April 1974): 107-23.

Robert A. Pratt, *Expl* 21 (October 1962): 14.

Edmund Reiss, "The Final Irony of 'The Pardoner's Tale,'" *CE* 25 (January 1964): 260-66.

James F. Rhodes, "Motivation in Chaucer's *Pardoner's Tale*: Winner Take Nothing," *ChauR* 17 (1982): 40-61.

Janette Richardson, "Intention and the Pardoner," in Arrathoon, *Chaucer and the Craft*, 85-95.

D. W. Robertson, Jr., *A Preface to Chaucer* (London: Oxford University Press, 1962), 332-34 and *passim*.

Rogers, *Upon the Ways*, 82-85.

Ruggiers, *The Art of the Canterbury Tales*, 121-30.

A. C. Spearing, "The *Canterbury Tales* IV; Exemplum and Fable," in Boitani and Mann, *The Cambridge Chaucer Companion*, 165-69.

Speirs, *Chaucer the Maker*, 169-77.

John Speirs, "Chaucer III," *Scrutiny* 12 (Winter 1944): 35-37.

John M. Steadman, *Nature into Myth: Medieval and Renaissance Moral Symbols* (Pittsburgh, Penn.: Duquesne University Press, 1979), 104-14.

John M. Steadman, "Old Age and *Contemptus Mundi* in *The Pardoner's Tale*," *MÆ* 33 (1964): 121-30. Reprinted in Faulkner, *Twentieth Century Interpretations*, 70-82.

Martin Stevens and Kathleen Falvey, "Substance, Accident, and Transformations: A Reading of the *Pardoner's Tale*," *ChauR* 17 (1982): 142-58.

P. B. Taylor, "Peynted Confessiouns: Boccaccio and Chaucer," *CL* 34 (Spring 1982), 116-29.

Robert E. Todd, "The Magna Mater Archetype in 'The Pardoner's Tale,'" *L&P* 15 (Winter 1965): 32-40.

William B. Toole, "Chaucer's Christian Irony: The Relationship of Character and Action in the *Pardoner's Tale*," *ChauR* 3 (1968): 37-43.

Traversi, *The Canterbury Tales*, 161-94.

Philippa Tristram, *Figures of Life and Death in Medieval English Literature* (London: Paul Elek, 1976), 70-71.

Katherine B. Trower, "Spiritual Sickness in the Physician's and Pardoner's Tales: Thematic Unity in Fragment VI of the *Canterbury Tales*," *ABR* 29 (March 1978): 67-86.

Whittock, *A Reading of the Canterbury Tales*, 185-94.

Douglas J. Wurtele, "The Concept of Healing in Chaucer's *Pardoner's Tale*," *ABR* 41 (March 1990): 59-79.

The Parlement of Foules

Aers, *Chaucer*, 15-17.

David Aers, "The *Parliament of Fowls*: Authority, the Knower and the Known," *ChauR* 16 (1981): 1-17.

Ross G. Arthur, "Chaucer's Use of *The Dream of Scipio* in *The Partliament of Fowls*," *ABR* 38 (March 1987): 29-48.

Donald C. Baker, "The Parliament of Fowls," in Rowland, *Companion to Chaucer Studies*, 355-69.

Donald C. Baker, "The Poet of Love and the *Parlement of Foules*," *UMSE* 2 (1961): 79-110.

Barbara Bartholomew, *Fortuna and Natura: A Reading of Three Chaucer Narratives* (The Hague: Mouton, 1966), 39-44.

J. A. W. Bennett, *The Parlement of Foules: An Interpretation* (Oxford: Clarendon Press, 1957).

J. A. W. Bennett, "Some Second Thoughts on *The Parlement of Foules*," in *Chaucerian Problems and Perspectives: Essays Presented to Paul E. Beichner, C. S. C.*, ed. Edward Vasta and Zacharias P. Thundy (Notre Dame and London: University of Notre Dame, 1979), 132-46.

Larry D. Benson, "The Occasion of the *Parliament of Fowls*," in Benson and Wenzel, *The Wisdom of Poetry*, 123-49.

Dorothy Bethurum, "Chaucer's Point of View as Narrator in the Love Poems," *PMLA* 75 (1959): 514-15.

Bishop, *The Narrative Art*, 29-34.

Boitani, *English Medieval Narrative*, 168-92 and *passim*.

Piero Boitani, "Old Books Brought to Life in Dreams: The *Book of the Duchess*, the *House of Fame*, the *Parliament of Fowls*," in Boitani and Mann, *The Cambridge Chaucer Companion*, 47-52.

Brewer, *An Introduction to Chaucer*, 79-86 and *passim*.

D. S. Brewer, *Chaucer*, 3d ed. (London: Longman, 1973), 58-68.

D. S. Brewer, "Introduction" to *The Parlement of Foulys* (London: Thomas Nelson & Sons, 1960), 13-25.

D. S. Brewer, "Natural Love in *The Parlement of Foules* II," *EIC* 5 (October 1955): 407-13.

D. S. Brewer, "The Parlement of Foules," *EIC* 6 (1956): 248.

Saul N. Brody, "The Comic Rejection of Courtly Love," in *In Pursuit of Perfection: Courtly Love in Medieval Literature*, ed. Joan M. Ferrante and George D. Economou (London: National University Publications; Washington, N.Y.: Kennikat Press, 1975), 247-49.

Bertrand H. Bronson, *In Search of Chaucer* (Toronto: University of Toronto Press, 1960), 43-48.

Emerson Brown, Jr., "Priapus and the *Parlement of Foulys*," *SP* 72 (July 1975): 258-74.

Burlin, *Chaucerian Fiction*, 83-94.

David Chamberlain, "The Music of the Spheres and *The Parlement of Foules*," *ChauR* 5 (1970): 32-56.

Cherniss, *Boethian Apocalypse*, 119-47.

Cecily Clark, "Natural Love in *The Parlement of Foules* I," *EIC* 5 (October 1955): 405-7.

Wolfgang Clemen, *Chaucer's Early Poetry*, trans. C. A. M. Sym (New York: Barnes & Noble, 1964), 122-69.

Corsa, *Chaucer: Poet of Mirth*, 19-29.

Bruce Kent Cowgill, "The *Parlement of Foules* and the Body Politic," *JEGP* 74 (1975): 315-35.

James Dean, "Artistic Conclusiveness in Chaucer's *Parliament of Fowls*," *ChauR* 21 (1986): 16-25.

Robert R. Edwards, *The Dream of Chaucer: Representation and Reflection in the Early Narratives* (Durham and London: Duke University Press, 1989), 123-46.

Norman E. Eliason, "Chaucer the Love Poet," in Mitchell and Provost, *Chaucer the Love Poet*, 13.

Macdonald Emslie, "Codes of Love and Class Distinctions," *EIC* 5 (January 1955): 1-17. Further discussion by Cecily Clark, D. S. Brewer, and Macdonald Emslie, *EIC* 5 (April 1955): 405-18.

Macdonald Emslie, "Natural Love in *The Parlement of Foules* III," *EIC* 5 (October 1955): 413-18.

Robert L. Entzminger, "The Pattern of Time in *The Parlement of Foules*," *JMRS* 5 (1975): 1-11.

Dorothy Everett, *Essays on Middle English Literature*, ed. Patricia Kean (Oxford: Clarendon Press, 1955), 102-14.

Judith Ferster, *Chaucer on Interpretation* (Cambridge: Cambridge University Press, 1985), 46-68.

Fowler, *The Bible in Middle English Literature*, 128-70.

R. W. Frank, Jr., "Structure and Meaning in the *Parlement of Foules*," *PMLA* 71 (1957): 530-39.

Fyler, *Chaucer and Ovid*, 81-95.

Gardner, *The Poetry of Chaucer*, 42-64.

Gradon, *Form and Style*, 77-82.

Carrie Esther Hammil, *The Celestial Journey and the Harmony of the Spheres in English Literature, 1300-1700* (Fort Worth: Texas Christian University Press, 1980), 51-59.

Carol Falvo Heffernan, "Wells and Streams in Three Chaucerian Gardens," *PLL* 15 (Fall 1979): 339-46.

A. Kent Hieatt, *Chaucer, Spenser, Milton: Mythopoeic Continuities and Transformations* (Montreal and London: McGill-Queen's University Press, 1975), 47-58.

Constance B. Hieatt, *The Realism of Dream Visions*, 78-84.

Bernard F. Huppé and D. W. Robertson, Jr., *Fruyt and Chaf: Studies in Chaucer's Allegories* (Princeton, N.J.: Princeton University Press, 1963), 101-48.

Hussey, *Chaucer*, 41-46.

Judith Hutchinson, "*The Parliament of Fowls*: A Literary Entertainment?" *Neophil* 61 (January 1977): 143-51.

George Kane, *Chaucer* (Oxford and New York: Oxford University Press, 1984), 56-62.

Kean, *Love Division and Debate*, 67-85.

Stephen Thomas Knight, *Rymyng Craftily: Meaning in Chaucer's Poetry* (Sydney and London: Angus and Robertson, 1973), 24-46.

John Lawlor, "The Earlier Poems," in *Chaucer & Chaucerians: Critical Studies in Middle English Literature*, ed. D. S. Brewer (University: University of Alabama Press, 1966), 50-57.

H. M. Leicester, Jr., "The Harmony of Chaucer's *Parlement*: A Dissonant Voice," *ChauR* 9 (1974): 15-34.

Leonard, *Laughter in the Courts of Love*, 47-52.

R. M. Lumiansky, "Chaucer's *Parlement of Foules*: A Philosophical Interpretation," *RES* 24 (April 1948): 81-89.

McCall, *Chaucer among the Gods*, 59-64 and *passim*.

John P. McCall, "The Harmony of Chaucer's *Parliament*," *ChauR* 5 (1970): 22-31.

Charles O. McDonald, "An Interpretation of Chaucer's *Parlement of Foules*," *Speculum* 30 (1955): 444-57. Reprinted in Schoeck and Taylor, *Chaucer Criticism* II, 275-93; Wagenknecht, *Chaucer*, 309-27.

Kemp Malone, *Chapters on Chaucer* (Baltimore, Md.: Johns Hopkins Press, 1951), 61-79.

Mehl, *Geoffrey Chaucer*, 37-53.

Tony Millns, "Chaucer's Suspended Judgements," *EIC* 27 (January 1977): 8-11.

Mogan, *Chaucer and the Theme*, 106-15.

North, *Chaucer's Universe*, 326-41, 351-66.

Kurt Olsson, "Poetic Invention and Chaucer's *Parlement of Foules*," *MP* 87 (August 1989): 13-35.

Jack B. Oruch, "Nature's Limitations and the Demande D'Amour of Chaucer's *Parlement*," *ChauR* 18 (1983): 23-37.

C. A. Owen, Jr., "The Role of the Narrator in the *Parlement of Foules*," *CE* 14 (1953): 264-68.

Robert O. Payne, *Geoffrey Chaucer*, 2d ed. (Boston: Twayne, 1986), 68-75.

Payne, *The Key of Remembrance*, 139-44.

Russell A. Peck, "Love, Politics, and Plot in the *Parlement of Foules*," *ChauR* 24 (1990): 290-305.

Marc M. Pelen, "Form and Meaning of the Old French Love Vision: The *Fableau dou Dieu d'Amors* and Chaucer's *Parliament of Fowls*," *JMRS* 9 (Fall 1979): 297-305.

Paul Piehler, "Myth, Allegory, and Vision in the *Parlement of Foules*: A Study in Chaucerian Problem Solving," in *Allegorisis: The Craft of Allegory in Medieval Literature*, ed. J. Stephen Russell (New York and London: Garland, 1988), 187-214.

Marion L. Polzella, "'The Craft so Long to Lerne': Poet and Lover in Chaucer's 'Envoy to Scogan' and *Parliament of Fowls*," *ChauR* 10 (1976): 279-86.

Victoria Rothschild, "*The Parliament of Fowls*: Chaucer's Mirror up to Nature?" *RES*, n.s. 35 (May 1984): 164-84.

Elizabeth Salter, *Fourteenth-Century English Poetry: Contexts and Readings* (Oxford: Clarendon Press, 1983), 127-40.

Gale C. Schricker, "On the Relation of Fact and Fiction in Chaucer's Poetic Endings," *PQ* 60 (Winter 1981): 13-27.

Rhoda Hurwitt Selvin, "Shades of Love in the *Parlement of Foules*," *SN* 37 (1965): 146-60.

Larry M. Sklute, "The Inconclusive Form of the *Parliament of Fowls*," *ChauR* 16 (1981): 119-28.

Sklute, *Virtue of Necessity*, 47-57.

Spearing, *Medieval Dream-Poetry*, 89-101.

Gardiner Stillwell, "Unity and Comedy in Chaucer's *Parlement of Foules*," *JEGP* 49 (1950): 470-95.

Derek Traversi, *Chaucer, the Earlier Poetry: A Study in Poetic Development* (London and Toronto: Associated University Presses; Newark: University of Delaware Press, 1987), 78-101.

Philippa Tristram, *Figures of Life and Death in Medieval English Literature* (London: Paul Elek, 1976), 58-60.

Robert W. Uphaus, "Chaucer's *Parlement of Foules*: Aesthetic Order and Individual Experience," *TSLL* 10 (Fall 1968): 349-58.

Nicolai von Kreisler, "The Locus Amoenus and Eschatological Lore in the *Parliament of Fowls*, 204-210," *PQ* 50 (January 1971): 16-22.

F. H. Whitman, "Exegesis and Chaucer's Dream Visions," *ChauR* 3 (1969): 229-38.

George Williams, *A New View of Chaucer* (Durham, N.C.: Duke University Press, 1965), 82-104.

James Winny, *Chaucer's Dream-Poems* (New York: Barnes & Noble, 1973), 113-43.

The Physician's Tale

Barbara Bartholomew, *Fortuna and Natura: A Reading of Three Chaucer Narratives* (The Hague: Mouton, 1966), 46-57.

Bishop, *The Narrative Art*, 149-55.

Emerson Brown, Jr., "What Is Chaucer Doing with the Physician and His Tale?" *PQ* 60 (Spring 1982): 129-49.

J. D. W. Crowther, "Chaucer's *Physician's Tale* and Its 'Saint,'" *ESC* 8 (June 1982): 125-37.

Gardner, *The Poetry of Chaucer*, 294-98.

Hornsby, *Chaucer and the Law*, 149-58.

Kean, *The Art of Narrative*, 181-85.

Daniel Kempton, "The *Physician's Tale*: The Doctor of Physic's Diplomatic 'Cure,'" *ChauR* 19 (1984): 24-38.

Knight, *The Poetry of the Canterbury Tales*, 119-22.

Brian S. Lee, "The Position and Purpose of the *Physician's Tale*," *ChauR* 22 (1987): 141-60.

Robert Longworth, "The Doctor's Dilemma: A Comic View of the 'Physician's Tale,'" *Criticism* 13 (Summer 1971): 223-33.

McCall, *Chaucer among the Gods*, 105-8.

Makarewicz, *The Patristic Influence*, 21-30.

Jerome Mandel, "Governance in the *Physician's Tale*," *ChauR* 10 (1976): 316-25.

Jeanne T. Mathewson, "For Love and Not for Hate: The Value of Virginity in Chaucer's *Physician's Tale*," *AnM* 14 (1973): 35-42.

D. W. Robertson, Jr., "The Physician's Comic Tale," *ChauR* 23 (1988): 129-39.

Rogers, *Upon the Ways*, 80-82.

Katherine B. Trower, "Spiritual Sickness in the *Physician's* and *Pardoner's Tales*: Thematic Unity in Fragment VI of the *Canterbury Tales*," *ABR* 29 (1978): 67-86.

Whittock, *A Reading of the Canterbury Tales*, 179-84.

The Prioress's Tale

C. David Benson, *Chaucer's Drama of Style: Poetic Variety and Contrast in the "Canterbury Tales"* (Chapel Hill and London: University of North Carolina Press, 1986), 131-46.

Bishop, *The Narrative Art*, 147-58 *passim*.

Burlin, *Chaucerian Fiction*, 185-94.

Carolyn P. Collette, "Sense and Sensibility in the *Prioress's Tale*," *ChauR* 15 (1980): 138-50.

Edward I. Condren, "The Prioress: A Legend of Spirit, a Life of Flesh," *ChauR* 23 (1989): 192-218.

David, *The Strumpet Muse*, 206-15.

Charles Clay Doyle, "The Avenging Voice from the Depths," *WF* 47 (January 1988): 21-37.

Sumner Ferris, "The Mariology of *The Prioress's Tale*," *ABR* 32 (September 1981): 232-54.

Gardner, *The Poetry of Chaucer*, 304-6.

Ann S. Haskell, *Essays on Chaucer's Saints* (The Hague and Paris: Mouton, 1976), 51-55.

Sherman Hawkins, "Chaucer's Prioress and the Sacrifice of Praise," *JEGP* 63 (1964): 599-624.

John C. Hirsh, "Reopening the *Prioress's Tale*," *ChauR* 10 (1975): 30-45.

Kean, *The Art of Narrative*, 205-9.

Edward H. Kelly, "By Mouth of Innocentz: The Prioress Vindicated," *PLL* 5 (Fall 1969): 362-74.

Knight, *The Poetry of the Canterbury Tales*, 139-43.

Koff, *Chaucer*, 204-19.

Sister Nicholas Maltman, O. P., "The Divine Granary, or the End of the Prioress's 'Greyn,'" *ChauR* 17 (1982): 163-70.

Owen, *Pilgrimage and Storytelling*, 119-21.

Ruggiers, *The Art of the Canterbury Tales*, 175-83.

G. H. Russell, "Chaucer: The Prioress's Tale," in *Medieval Literature and Civilization: Studies in Memory of G. N. Garmonsway*, ed. D. A. Pearsall and R. A. Waldron (London: Athlone Press, 1969), 211-27.

J. C. Wenk, "On the Sources of *The Prioress's Tale*," *MS* 17 (1955): 214-19.

Whittock, *A Reading of the Canterbury Tales*, 202-8.

Prologue to *Legend of Good Women*

Judson Boyce Allen, *The Ethical Poetic of the Later Middle Ages: A Decorum of Convenient Distinction* (Toronto: University of Toronto Press, 1982), 266-75.

Dorothy Bethurum, "Chaucer's Point of View as Narrator in the Love Poems," *PMLA* 74 (1959): 515-16.

A. Blamires, "A Chaucer Manifesto," *ChauR* 24 (1989): 29-44.

Burlin, *Chaucerian Fiction*, 33-44.

Michael D. Cherniss, "Chaucer's Last Dream Vision: The *Prologue* to the *Legend of Good Women*," *ChauR* 20 (1986): 183-99.

David, *The Strumpet Muse*, 37-51.

Fyler, *Chaucer and Ovid*, 115-23.

Margaret Galway, "Lylye Floures Newe," *TLS*, 29 September 1945, 468.

Hieatt, *The Realism of Dream Visions*, 84-88.

B. G. Koonce, "Satan the Fowler," *MS* 21 (1959): 176-84.

Leonard, *Laughter in the Courts of Love*, 52-56.

Ann McMillan, "Introduction" to *The Legend of Good Women* (Houston: Rice University Press, 1987), 27-36.

Robert O. Payne, *Geoffrey Chaucer*, 2d ed. (Boston: Twayne, 1986), 75-79.

D. W. Robertson, Jr., "Historical Criticism," in *English Institute Essays, 1950*, ed. Alan S. Downer (New York: Columbia University Press, 1951), 28-30. Reprinted in Robertson, *Essays in Medieval Culture*, 18-19.

Donald W. Rowe, *Through Nature to Eternity: Chaucer's "Legend of Good Women"* (Lincoln and London: University of Nebraska Press, 1988), 15-46 and *passim*.

Spearing, *Medieval Dream-Poetry*, 101-10.

George Williams, *A New View of Chaucer* (Durham, N.C.: Duke University Press, 1965), 130-44.

Prologue to *The Parson's Tale*

Russell A. Peck, "Number Symbolism in the *Prologue* to Chaucer's *Parson's Tale*," *ES* 48 (June 1967): 205-15.

The Reeve's Tale

Joseph L. Baird, "Law and the *Reeve's Tale*," *NM* 70 (1969): 679-83.

Gay L. Balliet, "The Wife in Chaucer's *Reeve's Tale*: Siren of Sweet Vengeance," *ELN* 28 (September 1990): 1-6.

Jeffrey Baylor, "The Failure of the Intellect in Chaucer's *Reeve's Tale*," *ELN* 28 (September 1990): 17-19.

C. David Benson, *Chaucer's Drama of Style: Poetic Variety and Contrast in the "Canterbury Tales"* (Chapel Hill and London: University of North Carolina Press, 1986), 90-103.

Brewer, *An Introduction to Chaucer*, 180-84.

Peter Brown, "The Containment of Symkyn: The Function of Space in the *Reeve's Tale*," *ChauR* 14 (1980): 225-36.

Roger T. Burbridge, "Chaucer's *Reeve's Tale* and the Fabliau 'Le meunier et les deux clercs,'" *AnM* 12 (1971): 30-36.

M. Copland, "The *Reeve's Tale*: Harlotrie or Sermonyng?" *MÆ* 31 (1962): 14-32.

Corsa, *Chaucer: Poet of Mirth*, 115-20.

Craik, *The Comic Tales*, 30-47.

David, *The Strumpet Muse*, 108-18.

Robert W. Frank, Jr., "The *Reeve's Tale* and the Comedy of Limitations," in *Directions in Literary Criticism: Contemporary Approaches to Literature*, ed. Stanley Weintraub and Philip Young (University Park: Pennsylvania State University Press, 1973), 53-65.

John Block Friedman, "A Reading of Chaucer's *Reeve's Tale*," *ChauR* 2 (1967): 8-19.

Gardner, *The Poetry of Chaucer*, 259-61.

Joseph E. Grennen, "The Calculating Reeve and His *Camera Obscura*," *JMRS* 14 (Fall 1984): 245-59.

Carol Falvo Heffernan, "A Reconsideration of the Cask Figure in the *Reeve's Prologue*," *ChauR* 15 (Summer 1980): 37-43.

Ronald B. Herzman, "The *Reeve's Tale*, Symkyn, and Simon the Magician," *ABR* 33 (1982): 325-33.

Knight, *The Poetry of the Canterbury Tales*, 37-40.

Kolve, *Chaucer and the Imagery of Narrative*, 217-56.

Ian Lancashire, "Sexual Innuendo in the *Reeve's Tale*," *ChauR* 6 (1972): 159-70.

Garth A. McCann, "Chaucer's First Three Tales: Unity in Trinity," *BRMMLA* 27 (1973):13-15.

Bruce Moore, "The Reeve's 'Rusty Blade,'" *MÆ* 58 (1989): 304-12.

Glending Olson, "The *Reeve's Tale* as a Fabliau," *MLQ* 35 (September 1974): 219-30.

Paul A. Olson, "The *Reeve's Tale*: Chaucer's *Measure for Measure*," *SP* 59 (January 1962): 1-17.

Owen, *Pilgrimage and Storytelling*, 106-9.

Payne, *The Key of Remembrance*, 91-111.

Roy J. Pearcy, "The Genre of Chaucer's Fabliau-Tales," in Arrathoon, *Chaucer and the Craft*, 350-58.

Derek Pearsall, "The *Canterbury Tales* II: Comedy," in Boitani and Mann, *The Cambridge Chaucer Companion*, 133-35.

John F. Plummer, "'Hooly Chirches Blood': Simony and Patrimony in Chaucer's *Reeve's Tale*," *ChauR* 18 (1983): 49-60.

Edmund Reiss, "Chaucer's Parodies of Love," in Mitchell and Provost, *Chaucer the Love Poet*, 42.

Richardson, *Blameth Nat Me*, 86-99.

Rogers, *Upon the Ways*, 41-45.

Ruggiers, *The Art of the Canterbury Tales*, 66-79.

Traversi, *The Canterbury Tales*, 82-88.

W. Arthur Turner, "Chaucer's 'Lusty Malyne,'" *N&Q*, n.s. 1 (June 1954): 232.

Whittock, *A Reading of the Canterbury Tales*, 96-105.

Robert C. Wilson, *Expl* 24 (December 1965): 32.

The Second Nun's Tale

C. David Benson, *Chaucer's Drama of Style: Poetic Variety and Contrast in the "Canterbury Tales"* (Chapel Hill and London: University of North Carolina Press, 1986), 131-46.

Paul M. Clogan, "The Figural Style and Meaning of *The Second Nun's Prologue* and *Tale*," *M&H*, n.s. 3 (1972): 213-40.

Carolyn P. Collette, "A Closer Look at Seinte Cecile's Special Vision," *ChauR* 10 (1976): 337-49.

James Dean, "Dismantling the Canterbury Book," *PMLA* 100 (1985): 747-49.

Anne Eggebroten, "Laughter in the *Second Nun's Tale*: A Redefinition of the Genre," *ChauR* 19 (1984): 55-61.

Gardner, *The Poetry of Chaucer*, 316-19.

Kean, *The Art of Narrative*, 201-4.

V. A. Kolve, "Chaucer's *Second Nun's Tale* and the Iconography of Saint Cecilia," in *New Perspectives in Chaucer Criticism*, ed. Donald M. Rose (Norman, Okla.: Pilgrim Books, 1981), 137-74.

McCall, *Chaucer among the Gods*, 108-10.

Russell A. Peck, "The Ideas on 'Entente' and Translation in Chaucer's *Second Nun's Tale*," *AnM* 8 (1967): 17-37.

Sherry L. Reames, "The Cecilia Legend as Chaucer Inherited It and Retold It: The Disappearance of an Augustinian Ideal," *Speculum* 55 (1980): 38-57.

Rogers, *Upon the Ways*, 111-13.

Bruce A. Rosenberg, "The Contrary Tales of the Second Nun and the Canon's Yeoman," *ChauR* 2 (1968): 278-91.

Whittock, *A Reading of the Canterbury Tales*, 251-61.

The Shipman's Tale

David H. Abraham, "*Cosyn* and *Cosynage*: Pun and Structure in the *Shipman's Tale*," *ChauR* 11 (1977): 319-27.

Aers, *Chaucer*, 20-23.

C. David Benson, *Chaucer's Drama of Style: Poetic Variety and Contrast in the "Canterbury Tales"* (Chapel Hill and London: University of North Carolina Press, 1986), 104-16.

Mary Flowers Braswell, "Chaucer's 'Queinte Termes of Lawe': A Legal View of the *Shipman's Tale*," *ChauR* 22 (1988): 295-304.

Theresa Coletti, "Biblical Wisdom: Chaucer's *Shipman's Tale* and the *Mulier Fortis*," *ChauR* 15 (1982): 236-49. Reprinted in *Chaucer and Scriptural Tradition*, ed. David Lyle Jeffrey (Ottawa: University of Ottawa Press, 1984), 171-82.

Thomas D. Cooke, *The Old French and Chaucerian Fabliaux: A Study of Their Comic Climax* (Columbia and London: University of Missouri Press, 1978), 172-76.

Murray Copland, "*The Shipman's Tale*: Chaucer and Boccaccio," *MÆ* 35 (1966): 11-28.

Craik, *The Comic Tales*, 48-70.

Gail McMurray Gibson, "Resurrection as Dramatic Icon in the *Shipman's Tale*," in Hermann and Burke, *Signs and Symbols*, 102-12.

John P. Hermann, "Dismemberment, Dissemination, Discourse: Sign and Symbol in the *Shipman's Tale*," *ChauR* 19 (1985): 302-37.

Hornsby, *Chaucer and the Law*, 96-101.

George R. Keiser, "Language and Meaning in Chaucer's *Shipman's Tale*," *ChauR* 12 (1978): 147-61.

William W. Lawrence, "The Wife of Bath and the Shipman," *MLN* 72 (February 1957): 87-88.

B. S. Levy, "The Quaint World of *The Shipman's Tale*," *SSF* 4 (Winter 1967): 112-18.

Richard Lock, *Aspects of Time in Medieval Literature* (New York and London: Garland Publishing, 1985), 105-8, 234-39.

Michael W. McClintock, "Games and the Players of Games: Old French Fabliaux and the *Shipman's Tale*," *ChauR* 5 (1970): 112-36.

Peter Nicholson, "The 'Shipman's Tale' and the Fabliaux," *ELH* 45 (1978): 583-96.

Owen, *Pilgrimage and Storytelling*, 115-18.

Roy J. Pearcy, "The Genre of Chaucer's Fabliau-Tales," in Arrathoon, *Chaucer and the Craft*, 366-71.

Derek Pearsall, "The *Canterbury Tales* II: Comedy," in Boitani and Mann, *The Cambridge Chaucer Companion*, 135-37.

Richardson, *Blameth Nat Me*, 100-122.

Janette Richardson, "The Facade of Bawdry: Image Patterns in Chaucer's *Shipman's Tale*," *ELH* 32 (1965): 303-13.

Rogers, *Upon the Ways*, 86-91.

Ruggiers, *The Art of the Canterbury Tales*, 80-89.

Paul Stephen Schneider, "'Taillynge Ynough': The Function of Money in the *Shipman's Tale*," *ChauR* 11 (1977): 201-9.

Albert H. Silverman, "Sex and Money in Chaucer's *Shipman's Tale*," *PQ* 32 (July 1953): 329-36.

Lorraine Kochanske Stock, "The Meaning of 'Chevyssaunce': Complicated Word Play in Chaucer's *Shipman's Tale*," *SSF* 18 (Summer 1981): 245-49.

A. Booker Thro, "Chaucer's Creative Comedy: A Study of the *Miller's Tale* and the *Shipman's Tale*," *ChauR* 5 (1970): 106-11.

Whittock, *A Reading of the Canterbury Tales*, 195-201.

Wimsatt, *Allegory and Mirror*, 178-81.

William F. Woods, "A Professional Thyng: The Wife as Merchant's Apprentice in the *Shipman's Tale*," *ChauR* 24 (1989): 139-49.

Michael Yots, *Expl* 36 (Summer 1978): 23-24.

The Squire's Tale

Marie Cornelia, "Chaucer's Tartarye," *DR* 47 (Spring 1977): 81-89.

Davenport, *Chaucer: Complaint and Narrative*, 40-50.

John M. Fyler, "Domesticating the Exotic in the *Squire's Tale*," *ELH* 55 (1988): 1-26.

Renate Haas, "Chaucer's Use of the Lament for the Dead," in Wasserman and Blanch, *Chaucer in the Eighties*, 26-28.

Robert S. Haller, "Chaucer's *Squire's Tale* and the Uses of Rhetoric," *MP* 62 (May 1965): 285-95.

John P. McCall, "The Squire in Wonderland," *ChauR* 1 (1966): 103-9.

Robert P. Miller, "Chaucer's Rhetorical Rendition of Mind: The *Squire's Tale*," in Arrathoon, *Chaucer and the Craft*, 219-40.

North, *Chaucer's Universe*, 263-88.

J. R. Osgerby, "Set Books XIV; Chaucer's *Squire's Tale*," *Use of English*, 11 (Winter 1959): 102-7.

D. A. Pearsall, "The Squire as Story-Teller," *UTQ* 34 (October 1964): 82-92.

Joyce E. Peterson, "The Finished Fragment: A Reassessment of the *Squire's Tale*," *ChauR* 5 (1970): 62-74.

Whittock, *A Reading of the Canterbury Tales*, 163-69.

The Summoner's Tale

John F. Adams, "The Structure of Irony in *The Summoner's Tale*," *EIC* 12 (April 1962): 126-32.

Aers, *Chaucer*, 37-45.

John A. Alford, "Scriptural Testament in *The Canterbury Tales*: The Letter Takes Its Revenge," in *Chaucer and Scriptural Tradition*, ed. David Lyle Jeffrey (Ottawa: University of Ottawa Press, 1984), 197-203.

Earle Birney, "Structural Irony within the *Summoner's Tale*," *Anglia* 78 (1960): 204-18. Reprinted in Earle Birney, *Essays on Chaucer*, ed. Beryl Rowland (Toronto: University of Toronto Press, 1985), 109-23.

Bishop, *The Narrative Art*, 110-13.

Roy Peter Clark, "Doubting Thomas in Chaucer's *Summoner's Tale*," *ChauR* 11 (1976): 164-78.

Roy Peter Clark, "Wit and Witsunday in Chaucer's *Summoner's Tale*," *AnM* 17 (1976): 48-57.

Corsa, *Chaucer: Poet of Mirth*, 186-90.

Craik, *The Comic Tales*, 116-32.

Susan Gallick, "A Look at Chaucer and His Preachers," *Speculum* 50 (1975): 465-66.

Gardner, *The Poetry of Chaucer*, 281-82.

Ann S. Haskell, *Essays on Chaucer's Saints* (The Hague and Paris: Mouton, 1976), 58-68.

Ann S. Haskell, "St. Simon in the *Summoner's Tale*," *ChauR* 5 (1971): 218-24.

N. R. Havely, "Introduction" to *The Friar's, Summoner's and Pardoner's Tales from the Canterbury Tales* (London: University of London Press, 1975), 16-25.

Hornsby, *Chaucer and the Law*, 46-51, 89-90.

Huppé, *A Reading of the "Canterbury Tales,"* 202-9.

Knight, *The Poetry of the Canterbury Tales,* 70-77.

Ian Lancashire, "Moses, Elijah and the Back Parts of God: Satiric Scatology in Chaucer's *Summoner's Tale*," *Mosaic* 14 (Summer 1981): 17-30.

Alan Levitan, "The Parody of Pentecost in Chaucer's *Summoner's Tale*," *UTQ* 40 (Spring 1971): 236-46.

Edward A. Malone, *Expl* 47 (Summer 1989): 4-5.

Thomas F. Merrill, "Wrath and Rhetoric in 'The Summoner's Tale,'" *TSLL* 4 (1962): 341-50.

Owen, *Pilgrimage and Storytelling*, 161-67.

George B. Pace, "Physiognomy and Chaucer's Summoner and Alisoun," *Traditio* 18 (1962): 417-20.

Richardson, *Blameth Nat Me*, 147-58.

D. W. Robertson, Jr., *A Preface to Chaucer* (London: Oxford University Press, 1962), 331-32.

Rogers, *Upon the Ways*, 58-61.

Ruggiers, *The Art of the Canterbury Tales*, 98-108.

J. Burke Severs, *Expl* 23 (November 1964): 20.

James G. Southworth, *Expl* 11 (March 1953): 29.

Penn R. Szittya, *The Antifraternal Tradition in Medieval Literature* (Princeton, N.J.: Princeton University Press, 1986), 231-46.

Penn R. Szittya, "The Friar as False Apostle: Antifraternal Exegesis and the *Summoner's Tale*," *SP* 71 (January 1974): 19-46.

Whittock, *A Reading of the Canterbury Tales*, 136-42.

Stephen K. Wright, "Jankyn's Boethian Learning in the *Summoner's Tale*," *ELN* 26 (September 1988): 4-7.

Paul N. Zietlow, "In Defense of the Summoner," *ChauR* 1 (1966): 4-19.

The Tale of Sir Thopas

Brewer, *An Introduction to Chaucer*, 192-94.

T. L. Burton, *Expl* 40 (Summer 1982): 6.

John Conley, "The Peculiar Name *Thopas*," *SP* 73 (1976): 42-61.

Dolores L. Cullen, *Expl* 32 (January 1974): 35.

Mortimer J. Donovan; "*Sir Thopas*, 772-774," *NM* 57 (1956): 237-46.

A. Wigfall Green, "Chaucer's 'Sir Thopas': Meter, Rhyme and Contrast," *UMSE* 1 (1960): 1-11.

Ann S. Haskell, "*Sir Thopas*: The Puppet's Puppet," *ChauR* 9 (1975): 253-61.

John L. Melton, "Sir Thopas' 'Charboncle,'" *PQ* 35 (April 1956): 215-17.

Owen, *Pilgrimage and Storytelling*, 122-24.

Ramsey, *Chivalric Romances*, 211-13.

George Williams, *A New View of Chaucer* (Durham, N.C.: Duke University Press, 1965), 145-51.

Chauncey Wood, "Chaucer and 'Sir Thopas': Irony and Concupiscence," *TSLL* 14 (Fall 1972): 389-403.

"To Rosemounde"

Albright, *Lyricality*, 82-83.

Saul N. Brody, "The Comic Rejection of Courtly Love," in *In Pursuit of Perfection: Courtly Love in Medieval Literature*, ed. Joan M. Ferrante and George D. Economou (London: National University Publications; Port Washington, N.Y.: Kennikat Press, 1975), 246-47.

Helge Kokentz, "Chaucer's 'Rosemounde,'" *MLN* 63 (May 1948): 310-18.

Moore, *The Secular Lyric in Middle English*, 132-33.

John Stephens, "The Uses of Personae and the Art of Obliqueness in Some Chaucer Lyrics, Part III," *ChauR* 22 (1987): 42-45.

Edward Vasta, "To Rosemounde: Chaucer's 'Gentil' Dramatic Monologue," in *Chaucerian Problems and Perspectives: Essays Presented to Paul E. Beichner, C. S. C.*, ed. Edward Vasta and Zacharias P. Thundy (Notre Dame and London: University of Notre Dame, 1979), 97-113.

Troilus and Criseyde

John F. Adams, "Irony in Troilus' Apostrophe to the Vacant House of Criseyde," *MLQ* 24 (March 1963): 61-65.

Aers, *Chaucer*, 94-102.

David Aers, *Chaucer, Langland, and the Creative Imagination* (London, Boston, and Henley: Routledge & Kegan Paul, 1980), 117-42.

David Aers, *Community, Gender, and Individual Identity: English Writing 1360-1430* (London and New York: Routledge, 1988), 117-52.

Malcolm Andrew, "The Fall of Troy in *Sir Gawain and the Green Knight* and *Troilus and Criseyde*," in *The European Tragedy of Troilus*, ed. Piero Boitani (Oxford: Clarendon Press, 1989), 85-93.

Robert P. apRoberts, "The Boethian God and the Audience of the *Troilus*," *JEGP* 69 (1970): 425-36.

Robert P. apRoberts, "The Central Episode in Chaucer's *Troilus*," *PMLA* 77 (1962): 373-85.

Robert P. apRoberts, "Criseyde's Infidelity and the Moral of the *Troilus*," *Speculum* 44 (1969): 383-402.

Robert P. apRoberts, "The Growth of Criseyde's Love," in *Medieval Studies Conference Aachen 1983: Language and Literature*, ed. Wolf-Dietrich Bald and Horst Weinstock (Frankfurt am Main: Verlag Peter Lang, 1984), 131-41.

Ann W. Astell, "Orpheus, Eurydice, and the 'Double Sorwe' of Chaucer's *Troilus*," *ChauR* 23 (1989): 283-99.

Susan E. Bailey, "Controlled Partial Confusion: Concentrated Imagery in *Troilus and Criseyde*," *ChauR* 20 (1985): 83-89.

Stephen A. Barney, "Troilus Bound," *Speculum* 47 (1972): 445-58.

F. Xavier Baron, "Chaucer's *Troilus* and Self-Renunciation in Love," *PLL* 10 (Winter 1974): 5-14.

Barbara Bartholomew, *Fortuna and Natura: A Reading of Three Chaucer Narratives* (The Hague: Mouton, 1966), 31-39.

Christopher C. Baswell and Paul Beekman Taylor, "The *Faire Queene Eleyne* in Chaucer's *Troilus*," *Speculum* 63 (1988): 301-11.

Paull F. Baum, *Chaucer: A Critical Appreciation* (New York: Octagon Books, 1982), 143-67.

C. David Benson and David Rollman, "Wynkyn de Worde and the Ending of Chaucer's *Troilus and Criseyde*," *MP* 78 (February 1981): 275-79.

Charles Berryman, "The Ironic Design of Fortune in *Troilus and Criseide*," *ChauR* 2 (1967): 1-7.

Benjamin R. Bessent, "The Puzzling Chronology of Chaucer's *Troilus*," *SN* 41 (1969): 99-111.

Dorothy Bethurum, "Chaucer's Point of View as Narrator in the Love Poems," *PMLA* 74 (1959): 516-18.

Ian Bishop, *Chaucer's "Troilus and Criseyde": A Critical Study* (Bristol: University of Bristol, 1981).

Morton W. Bloomfield, "Distance and Predestination in *Troilus and Criseyde*," *PMLA* 72 (1957): 14-26. Reprinted in Schoeck and Taylor, *Chaucer Criticism II*, 196-210; Barney, *Chaucer's "Troilus,"* 75-90.

Morton W. Bloomfield, "Troilus' Paraclaus: Thyron and Its Setting: *Troilus and Criseyde* V, 519-602," *NM* 73 (1972): 15-24.

Boitani, *English Medieval Narrative*, 193-226.

Sister Mary Charlotte Borthwick, F. C. S. P., "Antigone's Song as 'Mirour' in Chaucer's *Troilus and Criseyde*," *MLQ* 22 (September 1961): 227-35.

John M. Bowers, "How Criseyde Falls in Love," in *The Expansion and Transformations of Courtly Literature*, ed. Nathaniel B. Smith and Joseph T. Snow (Athens: University of Georgia Press, 1980), 140-55.

Gerry Brenner, "Narrative Structure in Chaucer's *Troilus and Criseyde*," AnM 6 (1965): 5-18. Reprinted in Barney, *Chaucer's "Troilus,"* 131-44.

D. S. Brewer, *Chaucer*, 3d ed. (London: Longman, 1973), 76-95.

Derek Brewer, "Comedy and Tragedy in *Troilus and Criseyde*," in *European Tragedy of Troilus*, ed. Piero Boitani (Oxford: Clarendon Press, 1989), 95-109.

Brewer, *An Introduction to Chaucer*, 115-50 *passim*.

D. M. Burjorjee, "The Pilgrimage of Troilus's Sailing Heart in Chaucer's *Troilus and Criseyde*," *AnM* 13 (1972): 14-31.

Burlin, *Chaucerian Fiction*, 113-35.

J. D. Burnley, "Proude Bayard: 'Troilus and Criseyde,' I.218," *N&Q* 23 (April 1976): 148-52.

Nan Cooke Carpenter, *Expl* 30 (February 1972): 51.

Evan Carton, "Complicity and Responsibility in Pandarus' Bed and Chaucer's Art," *PMLA* 94 (1979): 47-61.

Peter Christmas, "*Troilus and Criseyde*: The Problems of Love and Necessity," *ChauR* 9 (1975): 285-96.

Gloria Cigman, "Amphibologies and Heresy: *Troilus and Criseyde*," *EA* 42 (October-December 1989): 385-400.

Caron Ann Cioffi, "Criseyde's Oaths of Love: Do They Really Belong to the Tradition of Lying-Songs?" *JEGP* 87 (1988): 522-34.

S. L. Clark and Julian N. Wasserman, "The Heart in *Troilus and Criseyde*: The Eye of the Breast, the Mirror of the Mind, the Jewel in Its Setting," *ChauR* 18 (1984): 316-27.

Paul M. Clogan, "The Theban Scenes in Chaucer's *Troilus*," *M&H*, n.s. 12 (1984): 176-83.

Andrea Clough, "Medieval Tragedy and the Genre of *Troilus and Criseyde*," *M&H*, n.s. 11 (1982): 211-27.

Nevill Coghill, *The Poet Chaucer* (London: Oxford University Press, 1949; reprint, 1960), 65-85.

Edward I. Condre, "Transcendent Metaphor or Banal Reality: Three Chaucerian Dilemmas," *PLL* 21 (Summer 1985): 247-56.

Robert G. Cook, "Chaucer's Pandarus and the Medieval Ideal of Friendship," *JEGP* 69 (1970): 407-24.

John D. Cormican, "Motivation of Pandarus in *Troilus and Criseyde*," *LangQ* 18, no. 3-4 (1980): 43-48.

Corsa, *Chaucer: Poet of Mirth*, 40-70.

Georgia Ronan Crampton, "Action and Passion in Chaucer's *Troilus*," *MÆ* 43 (1974): 22-36.

Walter Clyde Curry, "Destiny in *Troilus and Criseyde*," in *Chaucer and the Mediaeval Sciences*, ed. Walter Clyde Curry, 2d ed. (New York: Barnes & Noble, 1960), 241-98. Reprinted in Schoeck and Taylor, *Chaucer Criticism II*, 34-70.

Charles Dahlberg, *The Literature of Unlikeness* (Hanover and London: University Press of New England, 1988), 129-48.

Davenport: *Chaucer: Complaint and Narrative*, 129-77.

Alfred David, "Chaucerian Comedy and Criseyde," in Salu, *Essays on Troilus and Criseyde*, 90-104.

Alfred David, "The Hero of the Troilus," *Speculum* 37 (1962): 566-81.

Alfred David, "Narrative Structure in Chaucer's *Troilus and Criseyde*," *AnM* 6 (1965): 5-27.

David, *The Strumpet Muse*, 27-36.

James Dean, "Chaucer's *Troilus*, Boccaccio's *Filostrato*, and the Poetics of Closure," *PQ* 64 (Spring 1985): 175-84.

Alexander J. Denomy, C. S. B., "The Two Moralities of Chaucer's *Troilus and Criseyde*," Transactions of the Royal Society of Canada Series 3, no. 44:2, June 1950, 35-46. Reprinted in Schoeck and Taylor, *Chaucer Criticism* II, 147-59.

James A. Devereaux, S. J., "A Note on *Troilus and Criseyde*, Book III, Line 1309," *PQ* 44 (October 1965): 550-52.

F. C. DeVries, "*Troilus and Criseyde*, Book III, Stanza 251, and Boethius," *ES* 52 (December 1971): 502-7.

P. Di Pasquale, Jr., "Sikernesse and Fortune in *Troilus and Criseyde*," *PQ* 49 (April 1970): 152-63.

E. Talbot Donaldson, "Chaucer and the Elusion of Clarity," *E&S* 25 (1972): 28-42.

E. T. Donaldson, "Commentary" in *Chaucer's Poetry: An Anthology for the Modern Reader*, 2d ed. (New York: Ronald Press, 1975), 1129-44.

E. Talbot Donaldson, "Creseide and Her Narrator," in Donaldson, *Speaking of Chaucer*, 65-83.

E. Talbot Donaldson, "Cressid False, Criseyde Untrue: An Ambiguity Revisited," in Mack and Lord, *Poetic Traditions*, 67-83.

E. Talbot Donaldson, "The Ending of 'Troilus,'" in *Early English and Norse Studies Presented to Hugh Smith*, eds. Arthur Brown and Peter Foote (London: Methuen, 1963), 26-45. Reprinted in Donaldson, *Speaking of Chaucer*, 84-100; *Geoffrey Chaucer: Modern Critical Views*, ed. Harold Bloom (New York: Chelsea House, 1985), 22-36.

E. Talbot Donaldson, "The Masculine Narrator and Four Women of Style," in Donaldson, *Speaking of Chaucer*, 53-59.

Philip Drew, *The Meaning of Freedom* (Aberdeen: Aberdeen University Press, 1982), 29-46.

Peter Dronke, "The Conclusion of *Troilus and Criseyde*," *MÆ* 38 (1964): 47-52.

Lonnie J. Durham, "Love and Death in *Troilus and Criseyde*," *ChauR* 3 (1968): 1-11.

E. F. Dyck, "Ethos, Pathos, and Logos in *Troilus and Criseyde*," *ChauR* 20 (1986): 169-82.

Julia Ebel, "Troilus and Oedipus: The Genealogy of an Image," *ES* 55 (February 1974): 15-21.

George D. Economou, "The Two Venuses and Courtly Love," in *In Pursuit of Perfection: Courtly Love in Medieval Literature*, ed. Joan M. Ferrante and George D. Economou (London: National University Publications; Port Washington, N.Y.: Kennikat Press, 1975), 39-46.

Peter H. Elbow, *Oppositions in Chaucer* (Middletown, Conn.: Wesleyan University Press, 1973; reprint, 1975), 49-72.

Norman E. Eliason, *The Language of Chaucer's Poetry: An Appraisal of the Verse, Style, and Structure*, Anglistica, no. 18 (Copenhagen: Rosenkilde and Bugger, 1972), 121-35.

William Empson, *Seven Types of Ambiguity* (London: Chatto and Windus, 1930; reprint New York: New Directions, 1966), 57-68. Reprinted in Barney, *Chaucer's "Troilus,"* 25-35.

Lawrence G. Evans, "A Biblical Allusion in *Troilus and Criseyde*," *MLN* 74 (November 1959): 584-87.

Murray J. Evans, "'Making Strange': The Narrator (?), the Ending (?), and Chaucer's 'Troilus,'" *NM* 87 (1986): 218-28.

Dorothy Everett, *Essays on Middle English Literature*, ed. Patricia Kean (Oxford: Clarendon Press, 1955), 115-38.

Anne Falke, "The Comic Function of the Narrator in *Troilus and Criseyde*," *Neophil* 68 (January 1984): 134-41.

Anthony E. Farnham, "Chaucerian Irony and the Ending of the *Troilus*," *ChauR* 1 (1967): 207-16.

William J. Farrell, "Chaucer's Use of the Catalogue," *TSLL* 5 (Spring 1963): 74-77.

John Frankis, "Paganism and Pagan Love in *Troilus and Criseyde*," in Salu, *Essays on Troilus and Criseyde*, 57-72.

Allen J. Frantzen, "The 'Joie and Tene' of Dreams in *Troilus and Criseyde*," in Wasserman and Blanch, *Chaucer in the Eighties*, 105-19.

Michael H. Frost, "Narrative Devices in Chaucer's *Troilus and Criseyde*," *THOTH* 14, no. 2/3 (1974): 29-38.

Fyler, *Chaucer and Ovid*, 129-38.

Joseph E. Gallagher, "Criseyde's Dream of the Eagle: Love and War in *Troilus and Criseyde*," *MLQ* 36 (June 1975): 115-32.

John M. Ganim, *Style and Consciousness in Middle English Narrative* (Princeton, N.J.: Princeton University Press, 1983), 79-102.

Gardner, *The Poetry of Chaucer*, 96-147.

Alan T. Gaylord, "Friendship in Chaucer's *Troilus*," *ChauR* 3 (1969): 239-64.

Alan T. Gaylord, "*Gentilesse* in Chaucer's *Troilus*," *SP* 61 (January 1964): 19-34.

Alan T. Gaylord, "The Lesson of the *Troilus*: Chastisement and Correction," in Salu, *Essays on Troilus and Criseyde*, 23-42.

Albert Gérard, "Meaning and Structure in *Troilus and Cressida*," *ES* 40 (1959): 144-57.

Sister Anne Barbara Gill, *Paradoxical Patterns in Chaucer's Troilus: An Explanation of the Palinode* (Washington, D.C.: Catholic University of America Press, 1960).

Ida L. Gordon, *The Double Sorrow of Troilus: A Study of Ambiguities in "Troilus and Criseyde"* (Oxford: Clarendon Press, 1970).

Gradon, *Form and Style*, 325-28.

D. H. Green, *Irony in the Medieval Romance* (Cambridge: Cambridge University Press, 1979), 35-37, 341-42.

Stanley B. Greenfield, "The Role of Calkas in *Troilus and Criseyde*," *MÆ* 36 (1967): 141-51.

Joseph E. Grennen, "Aristotelian Ideas in Chaucer's *Troilus*: A Preliminary Study," *M&H*, n.s. 14 (1986): 125-38.

Laila Gross, "The Two Wooings of Criseyde," *NM* 74 (1973): 113-25.

Carrie Esther Hammil, *The Celestial Journey and the Harmony of the Spheres in English Literature, 1300-1700* (Fort Worth: Texas Christian University Press, 1980), 59-69.

Ann S. Haskell, "The Doppelgängers in Chaucer's *Troilus*," *NM* 72 (1971): 723-34.

Carol Falvo Heffernan, "Chaucer's *Troilus and Criseyde*: The Disease of Love and Courtly Love," *Neophil* 74 (April 1990): 300-306.

Jeffrey Helterman, "The Masks of Love in *Troilus and Criseyde*," *CL* 26 (Winter 1974): 14-31.

Linda Tarte Holley, "Medieval Optics and the Framed Narrative in Chaucer's *Troilus and Criseyde*," *ChauR* 21 (1986): 26-44.

Linda T. Holley, "The Narrative Speculum in *Troilus and Criseyde*," *CLAJ* 25 (1981): 212-24.

Hornsby, *Chaucer and the Law*, 56-68 and *passim*.

Donald R. Howard, "The Philosophies of Chaucer's *Troilus*," in Benson and Wenzel, *The Wisdom of Poetry*, 151-75.

Donald R. Howard, *The Three Temptations: Medieval Man in Search of the World* (Princeton, N.J.: Princeton University Press, 1966): 79-160.

Edwin J. Howard, *Geoffrey Chaucer* (New York: Twayne, 1964), 105-17.

Bernard F. Huppé, "The Unlikely Narrator: The Narrative Strategy of the *Troilus*," in Hermann and Burke, *Signs and Symbols*, 179-94.

Hussey, *Chaucer*, 55-95.

Jordan, *Chaucer and the Shape of Creation*, 61-110.

Robert M. Jordan, "The Narrator in Chaucer's *Troilus*," *ELH* 25 (December 1958): 237-57.

Bertram Joseph, "*Troilus and Criseyde*: 'a most admirable and inimitable, Epicke poeme,'" *E&S* 7 (1954): 42-61.

Alice R. Kaminsky, Chaucer's *"Troilus and Criseyde" and the Critics* (Athens: Ohio University Press, 1980).

George Kane, *Chaucer* (Oxford and New York: Oxford University Press, 1984), 71-87.

Kean, *Love Division and Debate*, 112-78.

Milo Kearney and Mimosa Schraer, "The Flaw in Troilus," *ChauR* 22 (1988): 185-91.

Edward Hanford Kelly, "Myth as Paradigm in *Troilus and Criseyde*," *PLL* 3 (Summer supplement 1967): 28-30.

Henry Ansgar Kelly, "Clandestine Marriage and Chaucer's 'Troilus,'" *Viator* 4 (1973): 446-57.

Henry Ansgar Kelly, *Love and Marriage in the Age of Chaucer* (Ithaca and London: Cornell University Press), *passim*.

K. S. Kiernan, "Hector the Second: The Lost Face of Troilustratus," *AnM* 16 (1975): 52-62.

Thomas A. Kirby, *Chaucer's "Troilus": A Study in Courtly Love* (University: Louisiana State University Press, 1940), 121-284.

Elizabeth D. Kirk, "'Paradis Stood Formed in Hire Yën': Courtly Love and Chaucer's Re-Vision of Dante," in Carruthers and Kirk, *Acts of Interpretation*, 257-77.

George Lyman Kittredge, *Chaucer and His Poetry* (Cambridge, Mass.: Harvard University Press, 1915; reprint, 1970), 108-45. Reprinted in Barney, *Chaucer's "Troilus,"* 1-23.

Stephen Thomas Knight, *Rymyng Craftily: Meaning in Chaucer's Poetry* (Sydney and London: Angus and Robertson, 1973), 49-97.

Sherron E. Knopp, "The Narrator and His Audience in Chaucer's *Troilus and Criseyde*," *SP* 78 (Fall 1981): 323-40.

Allen D. Lackey, *Expl* 32 (September 1973): 5.

Mark Lambert, "Telling the Story in *Troilus and Criseyde*," in Boitani and Mann, *The Cambridge Chaucer Companion*, 59-73.

Mark Lambert, "*Troilus*, Books I-III: A Criseydan Reading," in Salu, *Essays on Troilus and Criseyde*, 105-25.

David Lawton, "Irony and Sympathy in *Troilus and Criseyde*: A Reconsideration," *LeedsSE*, n.s. 14 (1983): 94-115.

Robert Levine, "Restraining Ambiguities in Chaucer's *Troilus and Criseyde*," *NM* 87 (1986): 558-64.

C. S. Lewis, *The Allegory of Love* (London: Oxford University, 1936), 176-97.

John Leyerle, "The Heart and the Chain," in Benson, *The Learned and the Lewed*, 124-37. Reprinted in Barney, *Chaucer's "Troilus,"* 181-209.

Adrienne Lockhart, "Semantic, Moral, and Aesthetic Degeneration in *Troilus and Criseyde*," *ChauR* 8 (1973): 100-118.

R. M. Lumiansky, "The Function of the Proverbial Monitory Elements in Chaucer's *Troilus and Criseyde*," *TSE* 2 (1950): 5-48.

Monica E. McAlpine, *The Genre of "Troilus and Criseyde"* (Ithaca and London: Cornell University Press, 1978).

McCall, *Chaucer among the Gods*, 22-41, 45-46, 95-104.

John P. McCall, "Five-Book Structure in Chaucer's *Troilus*," *MLQ* 23 (December 1962): 297-308.

John P. McCall, "Troilus and Criseyde," in Rowland, *Companion to Chaucer Studies*, 370-84.

John P. McCall, "The Trojan Scene in Chaucer's *Troilus*," *ELH* 29 (1962): 263-75. Reprinted in McCall, *Chaucer among the Gods*, 93-104; Barney, *Chaucer's "Troilus,"* 101-13.

John McKinnell, "Letters as a Type of the Formal Level in *Troilus and Criseyde*," in Salu, *Essays on Troilus and Criseyde*, 73-89.

Samuel L. Macey, "Dramatic Elements in Chaucer's *Troilus*," *TSLL* 12 (Fall 1970): 307-23.

Makarewicz, *The Patristic Influence*, 116-41.

John Maguire, "The Clandestine Marriage of *Troilus and Criseyde*," *ChauR* 8 (1974): 262-78.

Kemp Malone, *Chapters on Chaucer* (Baltimore, Md.: Johns Hopkins Press, 1951), 100-143.

Colin Manlove, "'Rooteles moot grene soone deye': The Helplessness of Chaucer's *Troilus and Criseyde*," *E&S* 31 (1978): 1-22.

Jill Mann, "Chance and Destiny in *Troilus and Criseyde* and the *Knight's Tale*," in Boitani and Mann, *The Cambridge Chaucer Companion*, 75-87.

Jill Mann, "Shakespeare and Chaucer: 'What is Criseyde Worth?'" *CQ* 18 (1989): 110-16.

Jill Mann, "Troilus' Swoon," *ChauR* 14 (1980): 319-35.

Thomas E. Maresca, *Three English Epics: Studies of "Troilus and Criseyde," "The Faerie Queene," and "Paradise Lost"* (Lincoln and London: University of Nebraska Press, 1979), 143-96.

Murray F. Markland, "*Troilus and Criseyde*: The Inviolability of the Ending," *MLQ* 31 (June 1970): 147-59.

Michael Masi, "*Troilus*: A Medieval Psychoanalysis," *AnM* 11 (1970): 81-88.

Sanford B. Meech, *Design in Chaucer's Troilus* (Syracuse, N.Y.: Syracuse University Press, 1959).

Sanford B. Meech, "Figurative Contrasts in Chaucer's *Troilus and Criseyde*," in *English Institute Essays, 1950*, ed. Alan S. Downer (New York: Columbia University Press, 1951), 57-88.

Mehl, *Geoffrey Chaucer*, 65-97.

Tony Millns, "Chaucer's Suspended Judgements," 27 *EIC* (January 1977): 1-8.

A. J. Minnis, *Chaucer and Pagan Antiquity* (Cambridge: D. S. Brewer; Totowa, N.J.: Rowman & Littlefield, 1982), 61-107.

Arthur Mizener, "Character and Action in the Case of Criseyde," *PMLA* 54 (1939): 65-81. Reprinted in Barney, *Chaucer's "Troilus,"* 55-74; Wagenknecht, *Chaucer*, 348-65.

Mogan, *Chaucer and the Theme*, 116-44.

Joseph J. Mogan, Jr., "Further Aspects of Mutability in Chaucer's *Troilus*," *PLL* 1 (Winter 1965): 72-77.

Gerald Morgan, "The Ending of *Troilus and Criseyde*," *MLR* 77 (April 1982): 257-71.

Gerald Morgan, "The Significance of the Aubades in *Troilus and Criseyde*," *YES* 9 (1979): 221-35.

Marvin Mudrick, "Chaucer's Nightingales," *HudR* 10 (1957): 88-95. Reprinted in Marvin Mudrick, *On Culture and Literature* (New York: Horizon Press, 1970), 69-77; Barney, *Chaucer's "Troilus,"* 91-99.

Charles Muscatine, *Chaucer and the French Tradition* (Berkeley and Los Angeles: University of California Press, 1957), 125-65.

S. Nagarajan, "The Conclusion to Chaucer's *Troilus and Criseyde*," *EIC* 13 (January 1963): 1-8.

Barbara Newman, "'Feynede Loves,' Feigned Lore, and Faith in Trouthe," in Barney, *Chaucer's "Troilus,"* 257-75.

North, *Chaucer's Universe*, 367-401.

Norton-Smith, *Geoffrey Chaucer*, 90-93, 160-212.

Richard H. Osberg, "Between the Motion and the Act: Intentions and Ends in Chaucer's *Troilus*," *ELH* 48 (Summer 1981): 257-70.

Charlotte F. Otten, "The Love-Sickness of *Troilus*," in Arrathoon, *Chaucer and the Craft*, 23-33.

Charles A. Owen, "The Problem of Free Will in Chaucer's Narratives," *PQ* 46 (October 1967): 439-49.

Charles A. Owen, "Significance of a Day in *Troilus and Criseyde*," *MS* 22 (1960): 366-70.

Howard Rollin Patch, *On Rereading Chaucer* (Cambridge, Mass.: Harvard University Press, 1939), 56-122.

F. Anne Payne, *Chaucer and Menippean Satire* (Madison: University of Wisconsin Press, 1981), 86-158.

Robert O. Payne, *Geoffrey Chaucer*, 2d ed. (Boston: Twayne, 1986), 80-101.

Payne, *The Key of Remembrance*, 171-232.

Russell A. Peck, "Numerology and Chaucer's *Troilus and Criseyde*," *Mosaic* 5 (Summer 1972): 1-29.

Raymond Preston, *Chaucer* (London and New York: Sheed and Ward, 1952), 55-112.

William Provost, *The Structure of Chaucer's "Troilus and Criseyde,"* Anglistica, no. 20 (Copenhagen: Rosenkilde and Bugger, 1974).

Martin Puhvel, *Expl* 42 (Summer 1984): 7-9.

Edmund Reiss, "*Troilus* and the Failure of Understanding," *MLQ* 29 (September 1968): 131-44.

Alain Renoir, "The Inept Lover and the Reluctant Mistress: Remarks on Sexual Inefficiency in Medieval Literature," in *Chaucerian Problems and Perspectives: Essays Presented to Paul E. Beichner, C. S. C.*, eds. Edward Vasta and Zacharias P. Thundy (Notre Dame and London: University of Notre Dame, 1979), 185-90.

D. W. Robertson, Jr., "Chaucerian Tragedy," *ELH* 19 (1952): 1-37. Reprinted in Schoeck and Taylor, *Chaucer Criticism II*, 86-121.

D. W. Robertson, Jr., "The Concept of Courtly Love as an Impediment to the Understanding of Medieval Texts," in *The Meaning of Courtly Love*, ed. F. X. Newman (Albany: State University of New York Press, 1968), 1-18. Reprinted in Robertson, *Essays in Medieval Culture*, 257-72.

D. W. Robertson, Jr., *A Preface to Chaucer* (London: Oxford University Press, 1962), 472-502.

Donald W. Rowe, *O Love, O Charite!: Contraries Harmonized in Chaucer's "Troilus"* (Carbondale and Edwardsville: Southern Illinois University Press; London and Amsterdam: Feffer & Simons, 1976).

Beryl Rowland, "Chaucer's Speaking Voice and Its Effect on His Listener's Perception of Criseyde," *ESC* 7 (Summer 1981): 129-40.

Beryl Rowland, "The Horse and the Rider Figure in Chaucer's Works," *UTQ* 35 (April 1966): 252-53.

Charles S. Rutherford, "Pandarus as Lover: 'A Joly Wo' or 'Loves Shotes Keene'?" *AnM* 13 (1972): 5-13.

Charles S. Rutherford, "Troilus' Farewell to Criseyde: The Idealist as Clairvoyant and Rhetorician," *PLL* 17 (Summer 1981): 245-54.

Joseph S. Salemi, "Playful Fortune and Chaucer's Criseyde," *ChauR* 15 (Winter 1980): 209-23.

Elizabeth Salter, *English and International Studies in the Literature, Art and Patronage of Medieval England*, ed. Derek Pearsall and Nicolette Zeeman (Cambridge: Cambridge University Press, 1988), 215-38 *passim*.

Henry W. Sams, "The Dual Time-Scheme in Chaucer's *Troilus*," *MLN* 56 (1941): 94-100. Reprinted in Schoeck and Taylor, *Chaucer Criticism II*, 180-85.

Claes Schaar, "Troilus' Elegy and Criseyde's," *SN* 24 (1951/52): 185-91.

Susan Schibanoff, "Criseyde's 'Impossible' *Aubes*," *JEGP* 76 (1977): 326-33.

Michael Schmidt, *A Reader's Guide to Fifty British Poets – 1300-1900* (London: Heinemann, 1980), 35-39.

Gale C. Schricker, "On the Relation of Fact and Fiction in Chaucer's Poetic Endings," *PQ* 60 (Winter 1981): 13-27.

Samuel Schuman, "The Circle of Nature: Patterns of Imagery in Chaucer's *Troilus and Criseyde*," *ChauR* 10 (1975): 99-112.

James Lyndon Shanley, "The *Troilus* and Christian Love," *ELH* 6 (1939): 271-81. Reprinted in Schoeck and Taylor, *Chaucer Criticism II*, 136-46.

Roger Sharrock, "C. S. Lewis on Chaucer's *Troilus*," *EIC* 8 (April 1958): 123-37.

G. T. Shepherd, "*Troilus and Criseyde*," in *Chaucer & Chaucerians: Critical Studies in Middle English Literature*, ed. D. S. Brewer (University: University of Alabama Press, 1966), 65-87.

R. Allen Shoaf, "Dante's *Commedia* and Chaucer's Theory of Mediation: A Preliminary Sketch," in *New Perspectives in Chaucer Criticism*, ed. Donald M. Rose (Norman, Okla.: Pilgrim Books, 1981), 83-103.

David Sims, "An Essay on the Logic of *Troilus and Criseyde*," *CQ* 4 (Spring 1969): 125-49.

Sklute, *Virtue of Necessity*, 64-84.

Eugene E. Slaughter, "Chaucer's Pandarus: Virtuous Uncle and Friend," *JEGP* 48 (1949): 186-95.

Sally K. Slocum, "Criseyde among the Greeks," *NM* 87 (1986): 365-74.

A. C. Spearing, *Chaucer: Troilus and Criseyde* (London: Edward Arnold, 1976).

Spearing, *Readings in Medieval Poetry*, 107-33.

Speirs, *Chaucer the Maker*, 49-82.

John Stevens, *Medieval Romance: Themes and Approaches* (London: Hutchinson University Library, 1973), *passim*.

Martin Stevens, "The Winds of Fortune in the *Troilus*," *ChauR* 13 (1979): 285-307.

Myra Stokes, "Wordes White: Disingenuity in *Troilus and Criseyde*," *ES* 64 (February 1983): 18-29.

Melvin Storm, "Troilus, Mars, and Late Medieval Chivalry," *JMRS* 12 (1982): 45-65.

Theodore A. Stroud, "Boethius' Influence on Chaucer's *Troilus*," *MP* 49 (1951-52): 1-9. Reprinted in Schoeck and Taylor, *Chaucer Criticism II*, 122-37.

Theodore A. Stroud, "Chaucer's Structural Balancing of *Troilus* and 'Knight's Tale,'" *AnM* 21 (1981): 31-45.

J. S. P. Tatlock, *The Mind and Art of Chaucer* (Syracuse, N.Y.: Syracuse University Press, 1950), 38-50.

Ann M. Taylor, "Troilus' Rhetorical Failure (4: 1440-1526)," *PLL* 15 (Fall 1979): 357-69.

Davis Taylor, "The Terms of Love: A Study of Troilus's Style," *Speculum* 51 (1976): 69-90. Reprinted in Barney, *Chaucer's "Troilus,"* 231-56.

Karla Taylor, *Chaucer Reads "The Divine Comedy"* (Stanford, Calif.: Stanford University Press, 1988), 40-209.

Karla Taylor, "A Text and Its Afterlife: Dante and Chaucer," *CL* 35 (Winter 1983): 1-20.

Zacharias P. Thundy, "Chaucer's *Corones Tweyne* and Matheolus," *NM* 86 (1985): 343-47.

William B. Toole, III, "The Imagery of Fortune and Religion in *Troilus and Criseyde*," in *A Fair Day in the Affections: Literary Essays in Honor of Robert B. White, Jr.*, ed. Jack D. Durant and M. Thomas Hester (Raleigh, N.C.: Winston Press, 1980), 25-35.

Derek Traversi, *Chaucer, the Earlier Poetry: A Study in Poetic Development* (London and Toronto: Associated University Presses; Newark: University of Delaware Press, 1987), 102-44.

Francis Lee Utley, "Chaucer's Troilus and St. Paul's Charity," in Rowland, *Chaucer and Middle English Studies*, 272-87.

Thomas A. Van, "Chaucer's Pandarus as an Earthly Maker," *SHR* 12 (1978): 89-97.

Thomas A. Van, *Expl* 34 (November 1975): 20.

Thomas A. Van, *Expl* 40 (Spring 1982): 8-10.

Eugene Vance, "Marvelous Signals: Poetics, Sign Theory, and Politics in Chaucer's Troilus," *NLH* 10 (Winter 1979): 293-337.

Carolynn Van Dyke, "The Errors of Good Men: Hamartia in Two Middle English Poems," in *Hamartia: The Concept of Error in the Western Tradition, Essays in Honor of John M. Crossett*, ed. Donald V. Stump, James A. Arieti, Lloyd Gerson, and Eleonore Stump, Texts and Studies in Religion, no. 16 (New York and Toronto: Edwin Mellen Press, 1983), 171-91.

Richard Waswo, "The Narrator of *Troilus and Criseyde*," *ELH* 50 (1983): 1-25.

Karl P. Wentersdorf, "Some Observations on the Concept of Clandestine Marriage in *Troilus and Criseyde*," *ChauR* 15 (1980): 101-26.

Winthrop Wetherbee, *Chaucer and the Poets: An Essay on "Troilus and Criseyde"* (Ithaca and London: Cornell University Press, 1984).

Bonnie Wheeler, "Dante, Chaucer, and the Ending of *Troilus and Criseyde*," *PQ* 61 (Spring 1982): 105-23.

George Williams, *A New View of Chaucer* (Durham, N.C.: Duke University Press, 1965), 66-81, 175-95.

Wimsatt, *Allegory and Mirror*, 61-84 *passim*, 100-02.

James I. Wimsatt, "Medieval and Modern in Chaucer's *Troilus and Criseyde*," *PMLA* 92 (March 1977): 203-16.

Chauncey Wood, *Chaucer and the Country of the Stars: Poetic Uses of Astrological Imagery* (Princeton, N.J.: Princeton University Press, 1970), 83-92.

Chauncey Wood, *The Elements of Chaucer's "Troilus"* (Durham, N.C.: Duke University Press, 1984).

Marjorie Curry Woods, "Chaucer the Rhetorician: Criseyde and Her Family," *ChauR* 20 (1985): 28-39.

Stephenie Yearwood, "The Rhetoric of Narrative Rendering in Chaucer's *Troilus*," *ChauR* 12 (1977): 27-37.

Rose A. Zimbardo, "Creator and Created: The Generic Perspective of Chaucer's *Troilus and Criseyde*," *ChauR* 11 (1977): 283-98.

Troilus and Criseyde, Book 2

Heiner Gillmeister, "Chaucer's *Kan Ke Dort* (*Troilus*, II, 1752), and the 'Sleeping Dogs' of the Trouvéres," *ES* 59 (August 1978): 310-23.

Donald R. Howard, "Experience, Language, and Consciousness: *Troilus and Criseyde*, II, 596-931," in *Medieval Literature and Folklore Studies: Essays in Honor of Francis Lee Utley*, ed. Jerome Mandel and Bruce A. Rosenberg (New Brunswick, N.J.: Rutgers University Press, 1970). Reprinted in Barney, *Chaucer's "Troilus,"* 159-80.

Joseph A. Longo, "The Double Time Scheme in Book II of Chaucer's *Troilus and Criseyde*," *MLQ* 22 (March 1961): 37-40.

Charles A. Owen, Jr., *Expl* 9 (February 1951): 25.

Troilus and Criseyde, Book 3

Patricia Brückmann, "*Troilus and Criseyde*, III, 1226-1232: A Clandestine Topos," *ELN* 18 (March 1981): 166-70.

Mark J. Glenson, "Nicholas Trevet, Boethius, Boccaccio: Contexts of Cosmic Love in *Troilus*, Book III," *M&H*, n.s. 15 (1987): 176-79.

John V. Hagopian, *Expl* 10 (October 1951): 2.

Winthrop Wetherbee, "The Descent from Bliss: *Troilus* III.1310-1582," in Barney, *Chaucer's "Troilus,"* 297-317.

Troilus and Criseyde, Book 4

Kathleen Skubikowski, *Expl* 40 (Spring 1982): 7-8.

Siegfried Wenzel, "Chaucer's *Troilus* of Book IV,' *PMLA* 79 (1964): 542-47.

Troilus and Criseyde, Book 5

S. S. Hussey, "The Difficult Fifth Book of 'Troilus and Criseyde,'" *MLR* 67 (October 1972): 721-29.

Stephen Manning, "*Troilus*, Book V: Invention and the Poem as Process," *ChauR* 18 (1984): 288-303.

M. Stokes, "The Moon in Leo in Book V of *Troilus and Criseyde*," *ChauR* 17 (1982): 116-29.

Troilus and Criseyde, Epilogue

Gertrude C. Drake, "The Moon and Venus: Troilus's Havens in Eternity," *PLL* 11 (Winter 1975): 3-17.

"Truth, Balade de Bon Conseyl"

Jane Chance, "Chaucerian Irony in the Boethian Short Poems: The Dramatic Tension Between Classical and Christian," *ChauR* 20 (1986): 241-43.

Charles Dahlberg, *The Literature of Unlikeness* (Hanover and London: University Press of New England, 1988), 17-23.

Alfred David, "The Truth about 'Vache,'" *ChauR* 11 (1977): 334-37.

Gardner, *The Poetry of Chaucer*, 67-68.

Heiner Gillmeister, *Chaucer's Conversion: Allegorical Thought in Medieval Literature* (Frankfurt am Main: Verlag Peter Lang, 1984), 1-128 *passim*.

Heiner Gillmeister, "The Whole Truth about *Vache*," *Chaucer Newsletter* 2 (Winter 1980): 13-14.

David E. Lampe, "The Truth of a 'Vache': The Homely Homily of Chaucer's 'Truth,'" *PLL* 9 (Summer 1973): 311-14.

Mogan, *Chaucer and the Theme*, 85-87.

The Wife of Bath's Prologue

David Aers, *Chaucer, Langland, and the Creative Imagination* (London, Boston, and Henley: Routledge & Kegan Paul, 1980), 83-88, 147-51.

Steven Axelrod, "The Wife of Bath and the Clerk," *AnM* 15 (1974): 109-24.

Dennis Biggins, *Expl* 32 (February 1974): 44.

James L. Boren, "Alysoun of Bath and the Vulgate 'Perfect Wife,'" *NM* 76 (1975): 247-56.

Robert Cook, "Another Biblical Echo in the *Wife of Bath's Prologue*?" *ES* 59 (October 1978): 390-94.

Rodney Delesanta, "*Quoniam* and the Wife of Bath," *PLL* 8 (Spring 1972): 202-6.

Gardner, *The Poetry of Chaucer*, 274-75.

Barbara Gottfried, "Conflict and Relationship, Sovereignty and Survival: Parables of Power in the *Wife of Bath's Prologue*," *ChauR* 19 (1985): 202-24.

Jordan, *Chaucer and the Shape of Creation*, 208-26.

Koff, *Chaucer*, 106-10, 129-36, 138-49.

Lumiansky, *Of Sondry Folk*, 120-25.

Marjorie M. Malvern, "'Who peyntede the leon, tel me who?': Rhetorical and Didactic Roles Played by an Aesopic Fable in the *Wife of Bath's Prologue*," *SP* 80 (Spring 1983): 238-52.

William Matthews, "The Wife of Bath and All Her Sect," *Viator* 5 (1974): 434-43.

Mehl, *Geoffrey Chaucer*, 147-48.

Richard Rex, "'Spiced Conscience' in the *Canterbury Tales*," *MP* 80 (August 1982): 53-54.

Beryl Rowland, "Chaucer's Dame Alys: Critics in Blunderland?" *NM* 73 (1972): 381-95.

Beryl Rowland, "The Wife of Bath's 'Unlawfull Philtrum,'" *Neophil* 56 (April 1972): 201-6.

D. S. Silvia, *Expl* 28 (January 1970): 44.

Speirs, *Chaucer the Maker*, 136-48.

June Verbillion, *Expl* 24 (March 1966): 58.

D. J. Wurtele, "Chaucer's Wife of Bath and the Problem of the Fifth Husband," *ChauR* 23 (1988): 117-28.

The Wife of Bath's Tale

Michael Atkinson, "Soul's Time and Transformations: *The Wife of Bath's Tale*," *SoRA* 13 (1980): 72-78.

Ian Bishop, "Chaucer and the Rhetoric of Consolation," *MÆ* 52 (1983): 47-49.

Bishop, *The Narrative Art*, 120-29.

W. F. Bolton, "The Wife of Bath: Narrator as Victim," *W&L*, n.s. 1 (1980): 54-65.

Brewer, *An Introduction to Chaucer*, 204-10.

D. S. Brewer, *Chaucer*, 3d ed. (London: Longman, 1973), 139-41, 179-82.

Burlin, *Chaucerian Fiction*, 217-27.

Mary Carruthers, "The Wife of Bath and the Painting of Lions," *PMLA* 94 (March 1979): 209-22.

Meredith Cary, "Sovereignty and Old Wife," *PLL* 5 (Fall 1969): 375-88.

Gloria Cigman, "Introduction" to *The Wife of Bath's Prologue and Tale and The Clerk's Prologue and Tale from The Canterbury Tales* (London: University of London Press, 1975), 2-14.

George R. Coffman, "Chaucer and Courtly Love Once More – 'The Wife of Bath's Tale,'" *Speculum* 20 (1945): 43-50.

Dorothy Colmer, "Character and Class in *The Wife of Bath's Tale*," *JEGP* 72 (1973): 329-39.

Susan Crane, "Alison's Incapacity and Poetic Instability in the *Wife of Bath's Tale*," *PMLA* 102 (1987): 20-28.

David, *The Strumpet Muse*, 135-58.

Patrick J. Gallacher, "Dame Alice and the Nobility of Pleasure," *Viator* 13 (1982): 275-93.

Gardner, *The Poetry of Chaucer*, 276-78.

Robert S. Haller, "The Wife of Bath and the Three Estates," *AnM* 6 (1965): 47-64.

Britton J. Harwood, "The Wife of Bath and the Dream of Innocence," *MLQ* 33 (September 1972): 257-73.

Norman N. Holland, "Meaning as Transformation: *The Wife of Bath's Tale*," *CE* 28 (January 1967): 279-90.

Huppé, *A Reading of the "Canterbury Tales,"* 107-35.

R. E. Kaske, "Chaucer's Marriage Group," in Mitchell and Provost, *Chaucer the Love Poet*, 50-53.

Kean, *The Art of Narrative*, 149-56.

Peggy A. Knapp, "Alisoun of Bathe and the Reappropriation of Tradition," *ChauR* 24 (1989): 45-52.

Knight, *The Poetry of the Canterbury Tales*, 51-64.

Charles Koban, "Hearing Chaucer Out: The Art of Persuasion in the *Wife of Bath's Tale*," *ChauR* 5 (1971): 225-39.

Bernard S. Levy, "The Wife of Bath's *Queynte Fantasye*," *ChauR* 4 (1969): 106-22.

McCall, *Chaucer among the Gods*, 137-40 and *passim*.

Makarewicz, *The Patristic Influence*, 12-20, 34-52 *passim*, 217-18.

Kemp Malone, "*The Wife of Bath's Tale*," *MLR* 57 (October 1962): 481-91.

Robert J. Meger, "Chaucer's Tandem Romances: A Generic Approach to the *Wife of Bath's Tale* as Palinode," *ChauR* 18 (1984): 221-38.

Robert P. Miller, "Allegory in *The Canterbury Tales*," in Rowland, *Companion to Chaucer Studies*, 287-88.

Robert P. Miller, "The *Wife of Bath's Tale* and Mediaeval Exempla," *ELH* 32 (December 1965): 442-456.

Charles A. Owen, "The Crucial Passages in Five of *The Canterbury Tales*: A Study in Irony and Symbol," *JEGP* 52 (1953): 294-311. Reprinted in Wagenknecht, *Chaucer*, 252-68.

Owen, *Pilgrimage and Storytelling*, 144-57.

Robert A. Pratt, "Chaucer and Isidore on Why Men Marry," *MLN* 74 (April 1959): 293-95.

Velma Bourgeois Richmond, "'Pacience in Adversitee': Chaucer's Presentation of Marriage," *Viator* 10 (1979): 332-36.

Rogers, *Upon the Ways*, 53-55.

Joseph P. Roppolo, "The Converted Knight in Chaucer's 'Wife of Bath's Tale,'" *CE* 12 (February 1951): 263-69.

Ruggiers, *The Art of the Canterbury Tales*, 197-215.

Gloria K. Shapiro, "Dame Alice as Deceptive Narrator," *ChauR* 6 (Fall 1971): 130-41.

Tony Slade, "Irony in *The Wife of Bath's Tale*," *MLR* 64 (April 1969): 241-47.

Aaron Steinberg, "'The Wife of Bath's Tale' and the Fantasy of Fulfillment," *CE* 26 (December 1964): 187-91.

John Stevens, *Medieval Romance: Themes and Approaches* (London: Hutchinson University Library, 1973), 58-62.

Traversi, *The Canterbury Tales*, 91-121.

P. Verdonk, "'Sire Knyght, heer forth ne lith no wey': A Reading of Chaucer's *The Wife of Bath's Tale*," *Neophil* 60 (April 1976): 297-308.

Whittock, *A Reading of the Canterbury Tales*, 118-28.

"Womanly Noblesse"

Moore, *The Secular Lyric in Middle English*, 131-32.

"Wordes unto Adam"

Jane Chance, "Chaucerian Irony in the Verse Epistles 'Wordes unto Adam,' 'Lenvoy a Scogan,' and 'Lenvoy a Bukton,'" *PLL* 21 (Spring 1985): 117-20.

Russell A. Peck, "Public Dreams and Private Myths: Perspective in Middle English Literature," *PMLA* 90 (1975): 467.

CHESTRE, THOMAS

Sir Launfal

Ramsey, *Chivalric Romances*, 133-50 *passim*.

Speirs, *Medieval English Poetry*, 161-67.

CLANVOWE, SIR JOHN

The Cuckoo and the Nightingale (or *The Boke of Cupide*)

David E. Lampe, "Tradition and Meaning in *The Cuckoo and the Nightingale*," *PLL* 3 (Summer 1967): 49-62.

Charles S. Rutherford, "*The Boke of Cupide* Reopened," *NM* 78 (1977): 350-58.

Spearing, *Medieval Dream-Poetry*, 176-81.

CYNEWULF

Christ II

R. W. Adams, "Christ II: Cynewulfian *Heilsgeschichte*," *ELN* 12 (December 1974): 73-79.

Earl R. Anderson, *Cynewulf: Structure, Style, and Theme in His Poetry* (London: Associated University Presses; Rutherford, N.J.: Fairleigh Dickinson University Press, 1983), 45-67.

George Hardin Brown, "The Descent-Ascent Motif in *Christ II* of Cynewulf," *JEGP* 73 (1974): 1-12.

Daniel G. Calder, *Cynewulf* (Boston: Twayne, 1981), 42-74.

Colin Chase, "God's Presence Through Grace as the Theme of Cynewulf's *Christ II* and the Relationship of This Theme to *Christ I* and *Christ III*," *ASE* 3 (1974): 87-101.

Cherniss, *Ingeld and Christ*, 221-26.

Peter Clemoes, "Cynewulf's Image of the Ascension," in *England Before the Conquest: Studies in Primary Sources Presented to Dorothy Whitelock*, ed. Peter Clemoes and Kathleen Hughes (Cambridge: Cambridge University Press, 1971), 293-304.

Gardner, *The Construction of Christian Poetry in Old English*, 111-12.

Greenfield, *A Critical History*, 128-31.

Greenfield and Calder, *A New Critical History*, 188-93.

Oliver J. H. Grosz, "Man's Imitation of the Ascension: The Unity of *Christ II*," *Neophil* 54 (October 1970): 398-408.

Kennedy, *The Earliest English Poetry*, 220-30.

Lee, *The Guest-Hall*, 70-73 and *passim*.

Raw, *The Art and Background of Old English Poetry*, 40-41 and *passim*.

Schaar, *Critical Studies*, 31-34, 124-26.

Elene

Earl R. Anderson, *Cynewulf: Structure, Style, and Theme in His Poetry* (London: Associated University Presses; Rutherford, N.J.: Fairleigh Dickinson University Press, 1983), 103-75.

Bridges, *Generic Contrast*, 69-84, 212-52.

Daniel G. Calder, *Cynewulf* (Boston: Twayne, 1981), 104-38.

Daniel G. Calder, "Strife, Revelation, and Conversion: The Thematic Structure of *Elene*," *ES* 53 (June 1972): 201-10.

Jackson J. Campbell, "Cynewulf's Multiple Revelations," *M&H*, n.s. 3 (1972): 257-77.

Chance, *Woman as Hero*, 46-52.

James Doubleday, "The Speech of Stephen and the Tone of *Elene*," in Nicholson and Frese, *Anglo-Saxon Poetry*, 116-23.

Vard Fish, "Theme and Pattern in Cynewulf's *Elene*," *NM* 76 (1975): 1-25.

Gardner, *The Construction of Christian Poetry in Old English*, 86-98.

J. Gardner, "Cynewulf's *Elene*: Sources and Structure," *Neophil* 54 (January 1970), 65-76.

Greenfield, *A Critical History*, 113-18.

Greenfield and Calder, *A New Critical History*, 171-76.

Hermann, *Allegories of War*, 91-118.

Thomas D. Hill, "Bread and Stone, Again, *Elene* 611-18," *NM* 81 (1980): 252-57.

Thomas D. Hill, "Sapiential Structure and Figural Narrative in the Old English *Elene*," *Traditio* 27 (1971): 159-77.

Martin Irvine, "Anglo-Saxon Literary Theory Exemplified in Old English Poems: Interpreting the Cross in *The Dream of the Rood* and *Elene*," *Style* 20 (Summer 1986): 157-81.

Lee, *The Guest-Hall*, 95-99.

Alexandra Hennessey Olsen, *Speech, Song, and Poetic Craft: The Artistry of the Cynewulf Canon* (New York: Peter Lang, 1984), 48-81.

Catharine A. Regan, "Evangelicalism as the Informing Principle of Cynewulf's 'Elene,'" *Traditio* 29 (1973): 27-52.

Schaar, *Critical Studies*, 24-27, 60-71, 120-23.

Robert Stepsis and Richard Rand, "Contrast and Conversion in Cynewulf's *Elene*," *NM* 70 (1969): 273-82.

W. A. M. van der Wurff, "Cynewulf's *Elene*: The First Speech to the Jews," *Neophil* 66 (April 1982): 301-12.

E. Gordon Whatley, "Bread and Stone: Cynewulf's 'Elene' 611-618," *NM* 76 (1975): 550-60.

E. Gordon Whatley, "The Figure of Constantine the Great in Cynewulf's 'Elene,'" *Traditio* 37 (1981): 161-202.

E. Gordon Whatley, "Old English Onomastics and Narrative Art: *Elene* 1062," *MP* 73 (November 1975): 109-20.

Woolf, *Art and Doctrine*, 227-29.

Ellen F. Wright, "Cynewulf's *Elene* and the 'Sinȝal Sacu,'" *NM* 76 (1975): 538-49.

Fates of the Apostles

Earl R. Anderson, *Cynewulf: Structure, Style, and Theme in His Poetry* (London: Associated University Presses; Rutherford, N.J.: Fairleigh Dickinson University Press, 1983), 73-83.

James L. Boren, "Form and Meaning in Cynewulf's *Fates of the Apostles*," *PLL* 5 (Spring 1969): 115-22.

Daniel G. Calder, *Cynewulf* (Boston: Twayne, 1981), 27-41.

Daniel G. Calder, "*The Fates of the Apostles*, the Latin Martyrologies, and the Litany of the Saints," *MÆ* 44 (1975): 219-24.

Warren Ginsberg, "Cynewulf and His Sources: *The Fates of the Apostles*," *NM* 78 (1977): 108-14.

Constance B. Hieatt, "*The Fates of the Apostles*: Imagery, Structure, and Meaning," *PLL* 10 (Spring 1974): 115-25.

D. R. Howlett, "Se Giddes Begang of *The Fates of the Apostles*," *ES* 56 (October 1975): 385-89.

Robert C. Rice, "The Penitential Motif in Cynewulf's *Fates of the Apostles* and in His Epilogues," *ASE* 6 (1977): 105-19.

Geoffrey R. Russom, "Artful Avoidance of the Useful Phrase in *Beowulf*, *The Battle of Maldon*, and *Fates of the Apostles*," *SP* 75 (October 1978): 371-90.

Juliana

Earl R. Anderson, *Cynewulf: Structure, Style, and Theme in His Poetry* (London: Associated University Presses; Rutherford, N.J.: Fairleigh Dickinson University Press, 1983), 84-102.

Kenneth A. Bleeth, "*Juliana*, 647-52," *MÆ* 38 (1969): 119-22.

Bridges, *Generic Contrast*, 23-35, 85-116.

Donald G. Bzdyl, "*Juliana*: Cynewulf's Dispeller of Delusion," *NM* 86 (1985): 165-75.

Daniel G. Calder, "The Art of Cynewulf's *Juliana*," *MLQ* 34 (December 1973): 355-71.

Daniel G. Calder, *Cynewulf* (Boston: Twayne, 1981), 75-103.

Chance, *Woman as Hero*, 40-46.

Cherniss, *Ingeld and Christ*, 194-207.

Greenfield and Calder, *A New Critical History*, 167-71.

Hermann, *Allegories of War*, 151-71.

John P. Hermann, "Language and Spirituality in Cynewulf's *Juliana*," *TSLL* 26 (Fall 1984): 263-81.

Lee, *The Guest-Hall*, 99-103.

Marie Nelson, "*The Battle of Maldon* and *Juliana*: The Language of Confrontation," in Brown, Crampton, and Robinson, *Modes of Interpretation*, 137-50.

Alexandra Hennessey Olsen, *Speech, Song, and Poetic Craft: The Artistry of the Cynewulf Canon* (New York: Peter Lang, 1984), 88-112.

Claude Schneider, "Cynewulf's Devaluation of Heroic Tradition in *Juliana*," *ASE* 7 (1978): 107-18.

Raymond C. St. Jacques, "The Cosmic Dimensions of Cynewulf's *Juliana*," *Neophil* 64 (January 1980): 134-39.

Raymond C. St. Jacques, *Expl* 39 (Spring 1981): 4-5.

Schaar, *Critical Studies*, 27-31, 123-24.

Joseph Wittig, "Figural Narrative in Cynewulf's *Juliana*," *ASE* 4 (1975): 37-55.

Woolf, *Art and Doctrine*, 225-27.

DOUGLAS, GAVIN

Eneados Prologues

Ebin, *Illuminator, Makar, Vates*, 97-106.

Lois Ebin, "The Role of the Narrator in the Prologues to Gavin Douglas's *Eneados*," *ChauR* 14 (1980): 353-65.

Gerald B. Kinneavy, "An Analytical Approach to Literature in the Late Middle Ages: The 'Prologues' of Gavin Douglas," *NM* 75 (1974): 126-42.

Alicia K. Nitecki, "Mortality and Poetry in Douglas' Prologue 7," *PLL* 18 (Winter 1982): 81-87.

Palice of Honour

Ebin, *Illuminator, Makar, Vates*, 92-97.

Denton Fox, "The Scottish Chaucerians," in *Chaucer & Chaucerians: Critical Studies in Middle English Literature*, ed. D. S. Brewer (University: University of Alabama Press, 1966): 193-99.

Gerald B. Kinneavy, "The Poet in *The Palice of Honour*," *ChauR* 3 (1969): 280-303.

Leonard, *Laughter in the Courts of Love*, 107-15.

C. S. Lewis, *The Allegory of Love* (London: Oxford University Press, 1936), 290-92.

Spearing, *Medieval Dream-Poetry*, 202-11.

DUNBAR, WILLIAM

"All Erdly Joy Returnis in Pane" ("Off Lentren in the First Mornyng")

Reiss, *William Dunbar*, 75-76.

Ross, *William Dunbar*, 132-33.

Scott, *Dunbar*, 241-43.

"Amang Thir Freiris Within Ane Cloister" ("Ane Ballat of the Passioun of Christ")

J. A. W. Bennett, *Poetry of the Passion: Studies in Twelve Centuries of English Verse* (Oxford: Clarendon Press, 1982), 121-27.

Reiss, *William Dunbar*, 89-91.

Scott, *Dunbar*, 284-88.

"Ane Ballat of the Fenȝeit Freir of Tungland" ("The Fenyet Freir of Tungland")

Davidoff, *Beginning Well*, 170-74.

Ross, *William Dunbar*, 200-203.

"Ane Ballat of Our Lady"
("Haile, Sterne Superne! Haile, in Eterne")

Manning, *Wisdom and Number*, 63-64.

Reiss, *William Dunbar*, 94-96.

Karen Swenson, "Mary as *Wall* in Dunbar's 'Ane Ballat of Our Lady,'" *ELN* 27 (September 1989): 1-6.

"Be Dyvers Wayis"
("Aganis the Solistaris in Court")

Scott, *Dunbar*, 92-93.

"The Beistly Lust, the Furious Appatite"
("Ballate Against Evil Women")

Scott, *Dunbar*, 68-70.

"Betuix Twell Houris and Ellevin"
("Amendis to the Tailyeouris and Sowtaris")

Scott, *Dunbar*, 237-38.

"Bewty and the Presoneir"
("Sen That I Am a Presoneir")

Ross, *William Dunbar*, 102-5.

"Be Ye ane Luvar, Think Ye Nocht Ye Suld"
("Gude Counsale")

Reiss, *William Dunbar*, 98-99.

"Blyth Aberdeane"
("To Aberdein" or "The Queinis Reception at Aberdein")

Scott, *Dunbar*, 16.

"Complane I Wald, Wist I Quhone Till"
("To the King" or "Dunbar's Complaint")

Ross, *William Dunbar*, 143-44.

"Complaint to the King Aganis Mure"
("Schir, I Complane of Iniuris")

Reiss, *William Dunbar*, 31-33.

"Dance in the Quenis Chalmer"
("Schir Jhon Sinclair Begowthe to Dance")

Reiss, *William Dunbar*, 23-25.

"The Dance of the Sevin Deidly Synnis"
("Off Februar the Fyiftene Nycht")

Reiss, *William Dunbar*, 79-82.

Ross, *William Dunbar*, 126-27, 168-75.

Scott, *Dunbar*, 229-31.

"Doverrit with Dreme"
("A Generall Satyre")

Scott, *Dunbar*, 84-88.

"Exces of Thocht Dois Me Mischeif"
("To the King")

Scott, *Dunbar*, 115-18.

"The Flyting of Dunbar and Kennedie"

Ross, *William Dunbar*, 184-92.

Scott, *Dunbar*, 171-78.

"The Golden Targe"

Ebin, *Illuminator, Makar, Vates*, 75-79.

Lois A. Ebin, "The Theme of Poetry in Dunbar's 'Goldyn Targe,'" *ChauR* 7 (1972): 147-59.

Denton Fox, "Dunbar's 'The Golden Targe,'" *ELH* 26 (1959): 311-34 *passim*.

Gradon, *Form and Style*, 356-60.

Gerald B. Kinneavy, "Metaphors of the Poet and His Craft in William Dunbar," in *Aeolian Harps: Essays in Honor of Maurice Browning Cramer*, ed. Donna G. Fricke and Douglas C. Fricke (Bowling Green, Ohio: Bowling Green University Press, 1976), 61-63.

Leonard, *Laughter in the Courts of Love*, 81-87.

R. J. Lyall, "Moral Allegory in Dunbar's 'Golden Targe,'" *SSL* 11 (July-October 1973): 47-65.

Reiss, *William Dunbar*, 105-10.

Ross, *William Dunbar*, 250-69.

Walter Scheps, "'The Golden Targe': Dunbar's Comic 'Psychomachia,'" *PLL* 11 (Fall 1975): 339-56.

Scott, *Dunbar*, 40-46.

E. Allen Tilley, "The Meaning of Dunbar's 'The Golden Targe,'" *SSL* 10 (April 1973): 221-31.

"How Sowld I Rewill Me"
("How Sall I Governe Me")

Scott, *Dunbar*, 142-44.

"In Secreit Place This Hyndir Nycht"
("Ane Brash Wowing")

Reiss, *William Dunbar*, 110-12.

Ross, *William Dunbar*, 166.

Scott, *Dunbar*, 63-65.

"Lament for the Makaris"
("I That in Heill Wes and Gladnes")

Cunningham, *Tradition and Poetic Structure*, 50-53.

Gerald B. Kinneavy, "Metaphors of the Poet and His Craft in William Dunbar," in *Aeolian Harps: Essays in Honor of Maurice Browning Cramer*, ed. Donna G. Fricke and Doublas C. Fricke (Bowling Green, Ohio: Bowling Green University Press, 1976), 58-60.

Reiss, *William Dunbar*, 28-31, 70-71.

Scott, *Dunbar*, 247-53.

"Lucina Schynning in Silence of the Nicht"
("The Birth of Antechrist" or "Dream of the Abbot of Tungland")

Davidoff, *Beginning Well*, 174-75.

Ross, *William Dunbar*, 198-99.

Scott, *Dunbar*, 130-34.

"Madame, Your Men Said Thai Wald Ryd"
("To the Quene")

Scott, *Dunbar*, 163-65.

"May na Man Now Undemit Be"

Ross, *William Dunbar*, 157.

"Meditatioun in Wyntir"
("In to Thir Dirk and Drublie Dayis")

Gerald B. Kinneavy, "Metaphors of the Poet and His Craft in William Dunbar," in *Aeolian Harps: Essays in Honor of Maurice Browning Cramer*, ed. Donna G. Fricke and Douglas C. Fricke (Bowling Green, Ohio: Bowling Green University Press, 1976), 61.

Moore, *The Secular Lyric in Middle English*, 107-9.

Reiss, *William Dunbar*, 133-35.

Ross, *William Dunbar*, 157-58.

Scott, *Dunbar*, 244-47.

John Speirs, "William Dunbar," *Scrutiny* 7 (June 1938): 67-68.

"Memento, Homo, Quod Cinis Es!"
("Of Manis Mortalitie")

Reiss, *William Dunbar*, 73-74.

Scott, *Dunbar*, 243-44.

"The Merle and the Nychtingaill"
("In May as That Aurora Did Vpspring" or "The Twa Luves")

J. A. Burrow, "'Young Saint, Old Devil': Reflections on a Medieval Proverb," *RES*, n.s. 30 (1979): 385-86. Reprinted in Burrow, *Essays on Medieval Literature*, 177-78.

Davidoff, *Beginning Well*, 167-68.

Reiss, *William Dunbar*, 112-14.

Scott, *Dunbar*, 278-82.

"Musing Allone This Hinder Nicht"
("Of Deming")

Reiss, *William Dunbar*, 77.

Scott, *Dunbar*, 37-42.

"My Hartis Tresure, and Swete Assured Fo"

Reiss, *William Dunbar*, 99-100.

"My Heid Did Yak Yesternicht"
("On His Heid-Ake")

Moore, *The Secular Lyric in Middle English*, 205-7.

Reiss, *William Dunbar*, 25-28.

"A New Year's Gift to the King"
("My Prince in God Gif the Guid Grace")

Reiss, *William Dunbar*, 43-45.

"Now Culit Is Dame Venus Brand"
("Of Luve Erdly and Divine" or "Now Cumis Aige Quhair")

Scott, *Dunbar*, 275-78.

"Now Lythis off ane Gentill Knycht"
("Of Sir Thomas Norray")

Reiss, *William Dunbar*, 52-54.

"Now of Wemen"
("In Prays of Woman")

Reiss, *William Dunbar*, 116-17.

"Of ane Blak-Moir"
("Lang Heff I Maid")

Reiss, *William Dunbar*, 57-58.

"Of Covetyce"
("Ffredome, Honour and Nobilnes")

Scott, *Dunbar*, 88-91.

"Off Benefice, Schir, at Everie Feist"
("To the King" or "Quha Nathing Hes Can Get Nathing")

Scott, *Dunbar*, 101-2.

"Of the Resurrection of Christ"

Reiss, *William Dunbar*, 93-94.

"Petition of the Gray Horse, Auld Dunbar"
("Schir, Lat It Nevir in Toun Be Tald" or
"Now Lufferis Cummis with Largess Lowd")

Moore, *The Secular Lyric in Middle English*, 209-13.

Reiss, *William Dunbar*, 37.

Scott, *Dunbar*, 109-15.

"Quha Will Behald of Luve the Chance"
("Inconstancy of Luve")

Scott, *Dunbar*, 60-62.

"Quhome to Sall I Compleine My Wo"
("None May Assure in This World")

Ross, *William Dunbar*, 142-43.

Scott, *Dunbar*, 94-96.

"Sanct Salvatour! Send Silver Sorrow"
("To the King")

Reiss, *William Dunbar*, 42-43.

Scott, *Dunbar*, 93-94.

"Schir, for Your Grace"
("To the King That He War John Thomosunis Man")

Scott, *Dunbar*, 156-57.

"Schir, Ye Have Mony Servitouris"
("Dunbar's Remonstrance to the King")

Scott, *Dunbar*, 11-12, 105-7.

"Schir, Yit Remembir as of Befoir"
("To the King")

Reiss, *William Dunbar*, 38-40.

Ross, *William Dunbar*, 146-48.

"Sic Tydingis Hard I at the Sessioun"
("Tydingis fra the Sessioun")

Scott, *Dunbar*, 73-76.

"Sweit Rois of Vertew and of Gentilnes"
("To a Ladye")

Reiss, *William Dunbar*, 100-102.

"The Testament of Maister Andro Kennedy"
("I, Maister Andro Kennedy")

Reiss, *William Dunbar*, 58-59.

Ross, *William Dunbar*, 163-65.

Scott, *Dunbar*, 220-28.

"This Hinder Nycht, Halff Sleiping as I Lay"
("Dunbar's Dream")

Reiss, *William Dunbar*, 86-89.

Scott, *Dunbar*, 151-54.

"This Nycht, Befoir the Dawing Cleir"
("How Dunbar Wes Desyrd to Be ane Freir")

R. J. Lyall, "Dunbar and the Franciscans," *MÆ* 46 (1977): 253-58.

Reiss, *William Dunbar*, 136-37.

Scott, *Dunbar*, 269-75.

"This Nycht in My Sleip I Wes Agast"
("The Devillis Inquest" or "Renunce They God and Cum to Me")

Scott, *Dunbar*, 81-84.

"This Warld Unstabille"

Ross, *William Dunbar*, 156.

"This Waverand Worldis Wretchidnes"
("Of the Warldis Instabilitie")

Alasdiar A. MacDonald, "William Dunbar, Mediaeval Cosmography, and the Alleged First Reference to the New Word in English Literature," *ES* 68 (1987): 377-91.

Scott, *Dunbar*, 103-5.

"The Thrissil and the Rois"

J. C. Nitzsche, "The Role of Kingship in William Dunbar's *Thrissil and the Rois*," *UMSE*, n.s. 2 (1981): 25-34.

Reiss, *William Dunbar*, 49-51.

Ross, *William Dunbar*, 239-50.

Scott, *Dunbar*, 46-52.

Spearing, *Medieval Dream-Poetry*, 192-96, 206-15.

"Thyne Awin Gude"
("Advice to Spend Anis Awin Gude")

Scott, *Dunbar*, 258-60.

"To the King"

Spearing, *Medieval to Renaissance*, 201-6.

"To the Merchantis of Edinburgh"
("Quhy Will Ye, Merchantis of Renoun" or "Satire on Edinburgh")

Ross, *William Dunbar*, 139-40.

Scott, *Dunbar*, 15-16, 76-78.

"To a Lady"

Walter Gierasch, *Expl* 6 (December, 1947): 21. Reprinted in *The Explicator Cyclopedia*, 2:132-33.

Reiss, *William Dunbar*, 100-102.

"The Turnament"
("Next That a Turnament Wes Tryid")

Davidoff, *Beginning Well*, 169-70.

Reiss, *William Dunbar*, 82-84.

Scott, *Dunbar*, 234-37.

"To The, O Mercifull Salviour, Jesus"
("The Tabill of Confessioun" or "I Cry Mercy")

Scott, *Dunbar*, 288-98.

"The Tretis of the Tua Mariit Wemen and the Wedo"

Priscilla Bawcutt, "Aspects of Dunbar's Imagery," in Rowland, *Chaucer and Middle English Studies*, 196-99.

Deanna Delmar Evans, "Dunbar's *Tretis*: The Seven Deadly Sins in Carnivalesque Disguise," *Neophil* 73 (January 1989): 130-41.

A. D. Hope, *A Midsummer Eve's Dream: Variations on a Theme by William Dunbar* (New York: Viking, 1970).

James Kinsley, "The Tretis of the Tua Mariit Wemen and the Wedo," *MÆ* 23 (1954): 31-35.

Roy J. Pearcy, "The Genre of William Dunbar's *Tretis of the Tua Mariit Wemen and the Wedow*," *Speculum* 55 (1980): 58-74.

Reiss, *William Dunbar*, 117-25.

Allan Rodway, *English Comedy: Its Role and Nature from Chaucer to the Present Day* (London: Chatto & Windus, 1975), 76-79.

Ross, *William Dunbar*, 217-36.

Thomas W. Ross, "William Dunbar's *Dialogus Obscoenus* in *Locus Amoenus*," *UMSE*, n.s. 1 (1980): 32-49.

Scott, *Dunbar*, 179-211.

Spearing, *Medieval to Renaissance*, 215-23.

John Speirs, "William Dunbar," *Scrutiny* 7 (June 1938): 59-61.

"The Twa Cummeris"
("This Lang Lentern Makis Me Lene" or "Rycht Airlie on Ask Weddinsday")

Scott, *Dunbar*, 65-67.

"We That Ar Heir in Hevins Glory"
("The Dregy of Dunbar Maid to King James")

Reiss, *William Dunbar*, 65-68.

Ross, *William Dunbar*, 162-63.

Scott, *Dunbar*, 218-20.

"Wowing of the King Quhen He Wes in Dumfermeling" ("This Hinder Nicht in Dumfermeling")

Ross, *William Dunbar*, 166-68.

Scott, *Dunbar*, 212-16.

FRIAR JOHN OF GRIMESTONE

"Als I Lay Vpon a Nith"

Wenzel, *Preachers, Poets*, 137-39.

"Lullay, Lullay, Litel Child"

Wenzel, *Preachers, Poets*, 164-66.

"Maiden and Moder, Cum and Se"

Wenzel, *Preachers, Poets*, 156-58.

" þu Sikest Sore"

Wenzel, *Preachers, Poets*, 135-37.

"Water und Blod for þe Isuet"

Wenzel, *Preachers, Poets*, 154-55.

GOWER, JOHN

Confessio Amantis

J. A. W. Bennet, "Gower's 'Honest Love,'" in *Patterns of Love and Courtesy: Essays in Memory of C. S. Lewis*, ed. John Lawlor (London: Edward Arnold, 1966), 107-21.

Bennett, *Middle English Literature*, 408-29.

Boitani, *English Medieval Narrative*, 117-32 *passim*.

J. A. Burrow, "The Portrayal of Amans in *Confessio Amantis*," in Minnis, *Gower's "Confessio Amantis,"* 5-24.

David G. Byrd, *Expl* 29 (September 1970): 2.

Michael D. Cherniss, "The Allegorical Figures in Gower's *Confessio Amantis*," *Res Publica Litterarum* 1 (1978): 7-20.

Cherniss, *Boethian Apocalypse*, 99-118.

Paul M. Clogan, "From Complaint to Satire: The Art of the *Confessio Amantis*," *M&H* 4 (1963): 217-22.

Samuel T. Cowling, "Gower's Ironic Self-Portrait in the *Confessio Amantis*," *AnM* 16 (1975): 63-70.

Dove, *The Perfect Age*, 126-33.

Anthony E. Farnham, "The Art of High Prosaic Seriousness: John Gower as Didactic Raconteur," in Benson, *The Learned and the Lewed*, 160-73.

John H. Fisher, *John Gower: Moral Philosopher and Friend of Chaucer* (New York: New York University Press, 1964), 185-203.

Patrick J. Gallacher, *Love, the Word, and Mercury: A Reading of John Gower's "Confessio Amantis"* (Albuquerque: University of New Mexico Press, 1975).

Katharine S. Gittes, "Gower's Helen of Troy and the Contemplative Way of Life," *ELN* 27 (September 1989): 19-24.

Katharine S. Gittes, "Ulysses in Gower's *Confessio Amantis*: The Christian Soul as Silent Rhetorician," *ELN* 24 (December 1986): 7-14.

Thomas J. Hatton, "The Role of Venus and Genius in John Gower's *Confessio Amantis*: A Reconsideration," *Greyfriar* 16 (1975): 29-40.

David W. Hiscoe, "The Ovidian Comic Strategy of Gower's *Confessio Amantis*," *PQ* 64 (Summer 1985): 367-85.

Henry Ansgar Kelly, *Love and Marriage in the Age of Chaucer* (Ithaca and London: Cornell University Press, 1975), 121-60.

Leonard, *Laughter in the Courts of Love*, 62-79.

C. S. Lewis, *The Allegory of Love* (London: Oxford University Press, 1936), 213-22.

Alastair Minnis, "'Moral Gower' and Medieval Literary Theory," in Minnis, *Gower's "Confessio Amantis,"* 50-78.

Jane Chance Nitzsche, *The Genius Figure in Antiquity and the Middle Ages* (New York: Columbia University Press, 1975), *passim*.

Kurt O. Olsson, "Natural Law and John Gower's *Confessio Amantis*," *M&H*, n.s. 11 (1982): 229-61.

Kurt O. Olsson, "Rhetoric, John Gower, and the Late Medieval *Exemplum*," *M&H*, n.s. 8 (1977): 194-98.

Derek Pearsall, *Gower and Lydgate*, ed. Geoffrey Bullough (Essex: Longmans, Green & Co., 1969), 10-22.

Russell A. Peck, "Introduction" to *Confessio Amantis* (New York: Holt, Rinehart and Winston, 1968; reprint, Toronto, Buffalo, London: University of Toronto Press, 1980), xi-xxix.

Russell A. Peck, *Kingship & Common Profit in Gower's "Confessio Amantis"* (Carbondale and Edwardsville: Southern Illinois University Press; London and Amsterdam: Feffer & Simons, 1978).

Elizabeth Porter, "Gower's Ethical Microcosm and Political Macrocosm," in Minnis, *Gower's "Confessio Amantis,"* 135-62.

Christopher Ricks, "Metamorphosis in Other Words," in Minnis, *Gower's "Confessio Amantis,"* 25-49.

Charles Runacres, "Art and Ethics in the 'Exempla' of *Confessio Amantis*," in Minnis, *Gower's "Confessio Amantis,"* 106-34.

Donald G. Schueler, "The Age of the Lover in Gower's *Confessio Amantis*," *MÆ* 36 (1967): 152-58.

Donald G. Schueler, "Gower's Characterization of Genius in the *Confessio Amantis*," *MLQ* 33 (September 1972): 240-56.

Judith Davis Shaw, "Gower's Art in Transforming His Sources into Exempla of the Seven Deadly Sins," Ph.D. Diss., University of Pennsylvania, 1977.

Judith Shaw, "John Gower's Illustrative Tales," *NM* 84 (1983): 437-47.

Paul Strohm, "Form and Social Statement in *Confessio Amantis* and *The Canterbury Tales*," *SAC* 1 (1979): 17-40.

Hugh White, "Division and Failure in Gower's *Confessio Amantis*," *Neophil* 72 (October 1988): 600-616.

Maria Wickert, *Studies in John Gower*, trans. Robert J. Meindl (Washington, D.C.: University Press of America, 1981).

Wimsatt, *Allegory and Mirror*, 156-58.

Confessio Amantis, Prologue and Book 1

James Simpson, "Ironic Incongruence in the Prologue and Book I of Gower's *Confessio Amantis*," *Neophil* 72 (October 1988): 617-32.

Confessio Amantis, Book 1 "Tale of Florent"

Walter S. Phelan, "Beyond the Concordance: Semantic and Mythic Structures in Gower's *Tale of Florent*," *Neophil* 61 (July 1977): 461-79.

Confessio Amantis, Book 2 "Tale of Acis and Galatea"

Peter G. Beidler, "The Tale of Acis and Galatea," in Beidler, *John Gower's Literary Transformations*, 11-14.

Confessio Amantis, Book 2 "Tale of Deianira and Nessus"

Carole Koepke Brown, "The Tale of Deianira and Nessus," in Beidler, *John Gower's Literary Transformations*, 15-19.

Confessio Amantis, Book 3 "Tale of Canace and Machaire"

Kurt O. Olsson, "Natural Law and John Gower's *Confessio Amantis*," *M&H*, n.s. 11 (1982): 229-61.

Confessio Amantis, Book 3 "Tale of Pyramus and Thisbe"

Judith C. G. Moran, "The Tale of Pyramus and Thisbe," in Beidler, *John Gower's Literary Transformations*, 21-24.

Confessio Amantis, Book 4
"Tale of Argus and Mercury"

Douglas L. Lepley, "The Tale of Argus and Mercury," in Beidler, *John Gower's Literary Transformations*, 45-49.

Confessio Amantis, Book 4
"The Tale of Icarus"

Karl A. Zipf, Jr., "The Tale of Icarus," in Beidler, *John Gower's Literary Transformations*, 37-39.

Confessio Amantis, Book 4
"Tale of Iphis and Araxarathen"

Nicolette Stasko, "The Tale of Iphis and Araxarathen," in Beidler, *John Gower's Literary Transformations*, 51-54.

Confessio Amantis, Book 4
"Tale of Pygmalion"

Carole Koepke Brown, "The Tale of Pygmalion," in Beidler, *John Gower's Literary Transformations*, 29-32.

Confessio Amantis, Book 5
"Tale of Midas"

Judith C. G. Moran, "The Tale of Midas," in Beidler, *John Gower's Literary Transformations*, 55-58.

Confessio Amantis, Book 5
"Tale of Neptune and Cornix"

Natalie Epinger Ruyak, "The Tale of Neptune and Cornix," in Beidler, *John Gower's Literary Transformations*, 71-74.

Confessio Amantis, Book 5
"Tale of Tereus"

Bruce Harbert, "The Myth of Tereus in Ovid and Gower," *MÆ* 41 (1972): 208-14.

Douglas L. Lepley, "The Tale of Tereus," in Beidler, *John Gower's Literary Transformations*, 63-69.

Confessio Amantis, Book 6
"Tale of Nectanabus"

Peter G. Beidler, "Diabolical Treachery in the *Tale of Nectanabus*," in Beidler, *John Gower's Literary Transformations*, 83-90.

Confessio Amantis, Book 7

M. A. Manzalaoui, "'Noght in the Registre of Venus': Gower's English Mirror for Princes," in *Medieval Studies for J. A. W. Bennett*, ed. P. L. Heyworth (Oxford: Clarendon, 1985), 159-83.

Confessio Amantis, Book 7
"The Jew and the Pagan"

Ruth M. Ames, "The Source and Significance of 'The Jew and the Pagan,'" *MS* 19 (1957): 37-47.

Confessio Amantis, Book 8
"Apollonius of Tyre"

Peter Goodall, "John Gower's Apollonius of Tyre: *Confessio Amantis*, Book VIII," *SoRA* 15 (November 1982): 243-53.

HARY

Wallace

Matthew P. McDiarmid, "Introduction" to *Hary's "Wallace"* (Edinburgh and London: William Blackwood & Sons, 1968), lxxv-civ.

HAWES, STEPHEN

The Conforte of Louers

Ebin, *Illuminator, Makar, Vates*, 147-61.

The Pastime of Pleasure

Ebin, *Illuminator, Makar, Vates*, 135-45.

Leonard, *Laughter in the Courts of Love*, 115-25.

Spearing, *Medieval to Renaissance*, 253-55.

HAWGHTON, JOHN

Poem 74

Davidoff, *Beginning Well*, 183-85.

HENRYSON, ROBERT

"The Annunciation"

Charles A. Hallett, "Theme and Structure in Henryson's 'The Annunciation,'" *SSL* 10 (January 1973): 165-74.

John Stephens, "Devotion and Wit in Henryson's 'The Annunciation,'" *ES* 51 (August 1970): 323-31.

"The Cok and the Jasp"

Ian Bishop, "Lapidary Formulas as Topics of Invention From Thomas of Hales to Henryson," *RES*, n.s. 37 (November 1986): 475-77.

George Clark, "Henryson and Aesop: The Fable Transformed," *ELH* 43 (1976): 18.

Denton Fox, "Henryson's *Fables*," *ELH* 29 (1962): 341-48.

MacQueen, *Robert Henryson*, 100-110.

"The Fox and the Wolf"
("How this foirsaid Tod maid his Confessioun to Freir Wolf Waitskaith")

John Block Friedman, "Henryson, the Friars, and the *Confessio Reynardi*," *JEGP* 66 (1967): 550-61.

MacQueen, *Robert Henryson*, 145-48.

"The Fox, the Wolf, and the Cadger"
("Of the Wolf that gat the Nekhering throw the Wrinkis of the Foxe that begilit the Cadgear")

MacQueen, *Robert Henryson*, 177-84.

"The Fox, the Wolf, and the Husbandman"
("Of the Foxe that beylit the Wolf in the Schadow of the Mone")

Craig McDonald, "The Perversion of Law in Robert Henryson's Fable of the *Fox, the Wolf, and the Husbandman*," *MÆ* 49 (1980): 244-53.

MacQueen, *Robert Henryson*, 173-77.

"The Lyoun and the Mous"

MacQueen, *Robert Henryson*, 165-73.

A. C. Spearing, "Central and Displaced Sovereignty in Three Medieval Poems," *RES*, n.s. 33 (August 1982): 252-57.

Spearing, *Medieval Dream-Poetry*, 188-89.

Nicolai von Kreisler, "Henryson's Visionary Fable: Tradition and Craftsmanship in *The Lyoun and the Mous*," *TSLL* 15 (Fall 1973): 391-403.

Morall Fabillis

Ebin, *Illuminator, Makar, Vates*, 58-70.

George D. Gopen, "Addendum to *SP*, LXXXII, 51," *SP* 82 (Summer 1985): 399.

George D. Gopen, "The Essential Seriousness of Robert Henryson's Moral Fables: A Study in Structure," *SP* 82 (Winter 1985): 42-59.

Matthew P. McDiarmid, *Robert Henryson* (Edinburgh: Scottish Academic Press, 1981), 62-87.

MacQueen, *Robert Henryson*, 94-188.

Spearing, *Medieval to Renaissance*, 187-99.

"Orpheus and Eurydice"

Ebin, *Illuminator, Makar, Vates*, 56-58.

Kenneth R. R. Gros Louis, "Robert Henryson's *Orpheus and Eurydice* and the Orpheus Traditions of the Middle Ages," *Speculum* 41 (1966): 643-55.

Matthew P. McDiarmid, *Robert Henryson* (Edinburgh: Scottish Academic Press, 1981), 43-61.

MacQueen, *Robert Henryson*, 24-44.

"The Paddok and the Mous"

MacQueen, *Robert Henryson*, 110-21.

Daniel M. Murtaugh, "Henryson's Animals," *TSLL* 14 (Fall 1972): 416-21 *passim*.

Robert Pope, "A Sly Toad, Physiognomy and the Problem of Deceit: Henryson's *The Paddok and the Mous*," *Neophil* 63 (July 1979): 461-68.

"The Preiching of the Swallow"

J. A. Burrow, "Henryson: *The Preaching of the Swallow*," *EIC* 25 (1975): 25-37. Reprinted in Burrow, *Essays on Medieval Literature*, 148-60.

George Clark, "Henryson and Aesop: The Fable Transformed," *ELH* 43 (1976): 10-17.

Denton Fox, "Henryson's Fables," *ELH* 29 (1962): 348-55.

Matthew P. McDiarmid, *Robert Henryson* (Edinburgh: Scottish Academic Press, 1981), 76-80.

MacQueen, *Robert Henryson*, 153-65.

Daniel M. Murtaugh, "Henryson's Animals," *TSLL* 14 (Fall 1972): 405-13.

Prolog to *Morall Fabillis*

Denton Fox, "Henryson's Fables," *ELH* 29 (1962): 338-41.

Spearing, *Medieval to Renaissance*, 187-92.

"The Ressoning Betuix Aige and Yowth"

Davidoff, *Beginning Well*, 180-81.

"Robene and Makyne"

Moore, *The Secular Lyric in Middle English*, 188-94.

"The Scheip and the Doig"

MacQueen, *Robert Henryson*, 127-31.

Robert Pope, "Henryson's *The Sheep and the Dog*," *EIC* 30 (July 1980): 205-14.

"Schir Chantecleir and the Foxe"

Morton W. Bloomfield, "The Wisdom of the Nun's Priest's Tale," in *Chaucerian Problems and Perspectives: Essays Presented to Paul E. Beichner, C. S. C.*, ed. Edward Vasta and Zacharias P. Thundy (Notre Dame and London: University of Notre Dame, 1979), 73-74.

Denton Fox, "The Scottish Chaucerians," in *Chaucer & Chaucerians: Critical Studies in Middle English Literature*, ed. D. S. Brewer (University: University of Alabama Press, 1966), 173-76.

MacQueen, *Robert Henryson*, 135-44.

"Sum Practysis of Medecyne"

Denton Fox, "Henryson's 'Sum Practysis of Medecyne,'" *SP* 69 (October 1972): 453-60.

The Testament of Cresseid

E. Duncan Aswell, "The Role of Fortune in *The Testament of Cresseid*," *PQ* 46 (1967): 471-87.

C. David Benson, "Troilus and Cresseid in Henryson's *Testament*," *ChauR* 13 (1979): 263-71.

Cherniss, *Boethian Apocalypse*, 211-31.

Christopher Dean, *Expl* 31 (November 1972): 21.

Douglas Duncan, "Henryson's *Testament of Cresseid*," *EIC* 11 (April 1961): 128-35.

Ebin, *Illuminator, Makar, Vates*, 70-73.

Denton Fox, "Introduction" to *Testament of Cresseid* (London: Thomas Nelson & Sons, 1968), 20-58.

Denton Fox, "The Scottish Chaucerians," in *Chaucer & Chaucerians: Critical Studies in Middle English Literature*, ed. D. S. Brewer (University: University of Alabama Press, 1966), 178.

John B. Friedman, "Henryson's *Testament of Cresseid* and the *Judicio Solis in Conviviis Saturni* of Simon of Couvin," *MP* 83 (August 1985): 12-21.

John M. Ganim, *Style and Consciousness in Middle English Narrative* (Princeton, N.J.: Princeton University Press, 1983), 123-41.

Peter Godman, "Henryson's Masterpiece," *RES*, n.s. 35 (August 1984): 291-300.

Ralph Hanna, III, "Cresseid's Dream and Henryson's *Testament*," in Rowland, *Chaucer and Middle English Studies*, 288-97.

Sydney Harth, "Henryson Reinterpreted," *EIC* 11 (October 1961): 471-80.

Matthew P. McDiarmid, *Robert Henryson* (Edinburgh: Scottish Academic Press, 1981), 88-116.

MacQueen, *Robert Henryson*, 45-93.

Alicia K. Nitecki, "'Fenȝeit of the New': Authority in *The Testament of Cresseid*," *JNT* 15 (Spring 1985): 120-32.

Florence H. Ridley, "A Plea for the Middle Scots," in Benson, *The Learned and the Lewed*, 179-96.

Götz Schmitz, "Cresseid's Trial: A Revision. Fame and Defamation in Henryson's '*Testament of Cresseid*,'" *E&S* 32 (1979): 44-56.

Larry Sklute, "Phoebus Descending: Rhetoric and Moral Vision in Henryson's *Testament of Cresseid*," *ELH* 44 (1977): 189-204.

Spearing, *Medieval to Renaissance*, 165-87.

Nikki Stiller, "Robert Henryson's Cresseid and Sexual Backlash," *L&P* 31 (1981): 88-95.

Ann Torti, "From 'History' to 'Tragedy': The Story of Troilus and Criseyde in Lydgate's *Troy Book* and Henryson's *Testament of Cresseid*," in *European Tragedy of Troilus*, ed. Piero Boitani (Oxford: Clarendon Press, 1989), 184-96.

Philippa Tristram, *Figures of Life and Death in Medieval English Literature* (London: Paul Elek, 1976), 147-51.

Kurt Wittig, *The Scottish Tradition in Literature* (Westport, Conn.: Greenwood Press, 1958. Reprint, 1972), 37-39 and *passim*.

"The Trial of the Fox"
("Of the Sone and Air of the foirsaid Foxe, callit Fatherwer: alswa the Parliament of fourfuttit Beistis haldin be the Lyoung")

MacQueen, *Robert Henryson*, 149-53.

"The Uponlandis Mous and the Burges Mous"

MacQueen, *Robert Henryson*, 121-27.

Daniel M. Murtaugh, "Henryson's Animals," *TSLL* 14 (Fall 1972): 416-19.

"The Wolf and the Lamp"

MacQueen, *Robert Henryson*, 131-35.

"The Wolf and the Wedder"

MacQueen, *Robert Henryson*, 184-88.

HOCCLEVE, THOMAS

"Epistle of Cupid"

William A. Quinn, *Expl* 45 (Fall 1986): 7-10.

La Male Regle

Spearing, *Medieval to Renaissance*, 110-19.

Eva M. Thornley, "The Middle English Penitential Lyric and Hoccleve's Autobiographical Poetry," *NM* 68 (1967): 295-321.

"Of My Lady, Wel Me Reioise"

Jan Ziolkowski, "Avatars of Ugliness in Medieval Literature," *MLR* 79 (January 1984): 10-11.

The Regement of Princes

Douglas J. McMillan, "The Single Most Popular of Thomas Hoccleve's Poems: *The Regement of Princes*," *NM* 89 (1988): 63-71.

HOLLAND, RICHARD

Buke of the Howlat

Matthew P. McDiarmid, "Richard Holland's *Buke of the Howlat*: An Interpretation," *MÆ* 38 (1969): 277-90.

KING JAMES I OF SCOTLAND

The Kingis Quair

Cherniss, *Boethian Apocalypse*, 193-210.

Lois A. Ebin, "Boethius, Chaucer, and *The Kingis Quair*," *PQ* 53 (1974): 321-41.

Ebin, *Illuminator, Makar, Vates*, 50-55.

Matthew P. McDiarmid, "Introduction" to *The Kingis Quair of James Stewart* (Totowa, N.J.: Rowman and Littlefield, 1973), 60-77.

John MacQueen, "Tradition and the Interpretation of the *Kingis Quair*," *RES*, n.s. 12 (May 1961): 117-31.

M. F. Markland, "The Structure of 'The Kingis Quair,'" *RS*, 25 (1957): 273-86.

Alice Miskimin, "Patterns in *The Kingis Quair* and the *Temple of Glas*," *PLL* 13 (Fall 1977): 339-61.

John Preston, "Fortunys Exiltree: A Study of *The Kingis Quair*," *RES*, n.s. 7 (November 1956): 339-47.

William Quinn, "Memory and the Matrix of Unity in *The Kingis Quair*," *ChauR* 15 (1981): 332-35.

Mary Rohrberger, "*The Kingis Quair*, an Evaluation," *TSLL* 2 (1960): 292-302.

Spearing, *Medieval Dream-Poetry*, 181-87.

KENNEDY, WALTER

"Passioun of Crist"

J. A. W. Bennett, *Poetry of the Passion: Studies in Twelve Centuries of English Verse* (Oxford: Clarendon Press, 1982), 123-36.

LANGLAND, WILLIAM

Piers Plowman

John F. Adams, "*Piers Plowman* and the Three Ages of Man," *JEGP* 61 (1962): 23-41.

David Aers, *Chaucer, Langland, and the Creative Imagination* (London, Boston, and Henley: Routledge & Kegan Paul, 1980), 1-79.

David Aers, *Community, Gender, and Individual Identity: English Writing 1360-1430* (London and New York: Routledge, 1988), 35-72.

David Aers, *Piers Plowman and Christian Allegory* (London: Edward Arnold, 1975), 71-131 *passim*.

David Aers, "*Piers Plowman* and Problems in the Perception of Poverty: A Culture in Transition," *LeedsSE*, n.s. 14 (1983): 5-25.

David Aers, "Reflections on the 'Allegory of the Theologians,' Ideology and *Piers Plowman*," in Aers, *Medieval Literature*, 65-71.

John A. Alford, "The Design of the Poem," in *A Companion to "Piers Plowman,"* ed. John A. Alford (Berkeley, Los Angeles, and London: University of California Press, 1988): 29-66.

John A. Alford, "Haukyn's Coat: Some Observations on *Piers Plowman* B.XIV.22-7," *MÆ* 43 (1974): 133-38.

John A. Alford, "The Idea of Reason in *Piers Plowman*," in *Medieval English Studies Presented to George Kane*, ed. Edward Donald Kennedy, Ronald Waldron, and Joseph S. Wittig (Wolfeboro, N.H.: D. S. Brewer, 1988), 199-215.

John A. Alford, "The Role of Quotations in *Piers Plowman*," *Speculum* 52 (1977): 80-99.

David G. Allen, "The Premature Hermeneutics of *Piers Plowman* B," in *Allegoresis: The Craft of Allegory in Medieval Literature*, ed. J. Stephen Russell (New York and London: Garland, 1988), 49-65.

Judson Boyce Allen, *The Ethical Poetic of the Later Middle Ages: A Decorum of Convenient Distinction* (Toronto: University of Toronto Press, 1982), 275-83 *passim*.

Margaret Amassian and James Sadowsky, "Mede and Mercede: A Study of the Grammatical Metaphor in 'Piers Plowman' C:IV:335-409," *NM* 72 (1971): 457-76.

Ruth M. Ames, *The Fulfillment of the Scriptures: Abraham, Moses, and Piers* (Evanston, Ill.: Northwestern University Press, 1970), 75-92, 161-200, and *passim*.

Ruth M. Ames, "The Pardon Impugned by the Priest," in Levy and Szarmach, *The Alliterative Tradition*, 47-68.

Judith H. Anderson, *The Growth of a Personal Voice: "Piers Plowman" and "The Faerie Queene"* (New Haven and London: Yale University Press, 1976).

Mary-Jo Arn, "Langland's Triumph of Grace in *Do Best*," *ES* 63 (December 1982): 506-16.

Denise N. Baker, "Dialectic Form in *Pearl* and *Piers Plowman*," *Viator* 15 (1984): 267-73.

Denise N. Baker, "From Plowing to Penitence: *Piers Plowman* and Fourteenth-Century Theology," *Speculum* 55 (1980): 715-25.

Denise Baker, "The Pardons of *Piers Plowman*," *NM* 85 (1984): 462-72.

Anna P. Baldwin, "The Double Duel in *Piers Plowman* B XVIII and CXXI," *MÆ* 50 (1981): 64-78.

Anna P. Baldwin, *The Theme of Government in Piers Plowman* (Cambridge: D. S. Brewer, 1981).

Stephen A. Barney, "The Plowshare of the Tongue: The Progress of a Symbol from the Bible to *Piers Plowman*," *MS* 35 (1973): 261-93.

Alexandra Barratt, "The Characters 'Civil' and 'Theology' in 'Piers Plowman,'" *Traditio* 38 (1982): 352-64.

Bennett, *Middle English Literature*, 431-55.

J. A. W. Bennett, *Poetry of the Passion: Studies in Twelve Centuries of English Verse* (Oxford: Clarendon, 1982).

C. David Benson, "The Function of Lady Meed in *Piers Plowman*," *ES* 61 (June 1980): 193-205.

Douglas Bertz, "Prophecy and Apocalypse in Langland's *Piers Plowman*, B-Text, Passus XVI to XIX," *JEGP* 84 (1985): 313-27.

William J. Birnes, "Christ as Advocate: The Legal Metaphor of *Piers Plowman*," *AnM* 16 (1975): 71-93.

Ian Bishop, "Relatives at the Court of Heaven: Contrasted Treatments of an Idea in *Piers Plowman* and *Pearl*," in Stokes and Burton, *Medieval Literature*, 111-18.

Morton W. Bloomfield, "The Allegories of *Dobest* (*Piers Plowman* B XIX-XX)," *MÆ* 50 (1981): 30-39.

Morton W. Bloomfield, "*Piers Plowman* and the Three Grades of Chastity," *Anglia* 76 (1958): 227-53.

Morton W. Bloomfield, "*Piers Plowman* as a Fourteenth-Century Apocalypse," *CRAS* 5 (1961): 281-95. Reprinted in Vasta, *Interpretations of Piers Plowman*, 339-54.

Morton W. Bloomfield, *"Piers Plowman" as a Fourteenth-Century Apocalypse* (New Brunswick, N.J.: Rutgers University Press, 1961).

Boitani, *English Medieval Narrative*, 72-96 *passim*.

A. Joan Bowers, "The Tree of Charity in *Piers Plowman*: Its Allegorical and Structural Significance," *Literary Monographs*, ed. Eric Rothstein and Joseph Anthony Wittreich, Jr., No. 6 (Madison: University of Wisconsin Press, 1975): 1-34.

John M. Bowers, *The Crisis of Will in Piers Plowman* (Washington, D.C.: Catholic University of America Press, 1986), *passim*.

Derek Brewer, *English Gothic Literature* (London and Basingstoke: Macmillan, 1983), 181-212.

J. A. Burrow, "The Action of Langland's Second Vision," *EIC* 15 (1965): 247-68. Reprinted in Burrow, *Essays on Medieval Literature*, 79-101; Blanch, *Style and Symbolism*, 209-27.

J. A. Burrow, "Langland *Nel Mezzo Del Cammin*," in *Medieval Studies for J. A. W. Bennett*, ed. P. L. Heyworth (Oxford: Clarendon, 1981), 21-41.

J. A. Burrow, "Words, Works, and Will: Theme and Structure in *Piers Plowman*," in Hussey, *Piers Plowman: Critical Approaches*, 111-24.

Mary J. Carruthers, *The Search for St. Truth: A Study of Meaning in Piers Plowman* (Evanston, Ill.: Northwestern University Press, 1973).

Mary J. Carruthers, "Time, Apocalypse, and the Plot of *Piers Plowman*," in Carruthers and Kirk, *Acts of Interpretation*, 175-88.

Ladislav Cejp, "An Interpretation of *Piers the Plowman*," *Philologica*, supplement to *Casopis pro Moderni Filologii* 7 (1955): 17-29.

Ladislav Cejp, *An Introduction to the Study of Langland's Piers Plowman: B Text*, Acta Universitatis Palackianae Olomucensis, no. 9 (Palackého Universita v. Olomouci, 1956).

R. W. Chambers, *Man's Unconquerable Mind* (London: Jonathan Cape, 1952), 88-171.

Lawrence M. Clopper, "The Contemplative Matrix of *Piers Plowman* B," *MLQ* 46 (March 1985): 3-28.

Lawrence M. Clopper, "Langland's Trinitarian Analogies as Key to Meaning and Structure," *M&H* 9 (1979): 87-110.

Lawrence M. Clopper, "The Life of the Dreamer, the Dreams of the Wanderer in *Piers Plowman*," *SP* 86 (Summer 1989): 261-85.

Charlotte Clutterbuck, "Hope and Good Works: *Leaute* in the C-Text of *Piers Plowman*," *RES*, n.s. 28 (May 1977): 129-40.

Nevill K. Coghill, "The Character of *Piers Plowman* Considered from the B Text," *MÆ* 2 (1933): 108-35. Reprinted in Vasta, *Interpretations of Piers Plowman*, 54-86.

Nevill K. Coghill, "The Pardon of *Piers Plowman*," *PBA* 30 (1944): 303-57. Abridged in Blanch, *Style and Symbolism*, 40-86.

A. J. Colaianne, "Structure and 'Foreconceit' in *Piers Plowman* B: Some Observations on Langland's Psychology of Composition," *AnM* 22 (1982): 102-11.

J. V. Crewe, "Langland's Vision of Society in *Piers Ploughman*," *Theoria* 39 (1973): 1-16.

Sister Mary Clemente Davlin, O. P., *A Game of Heuene: Word Play and the Meaning of "Piers Plowman" B* (Cambridge: D. S. Brewer, 1989).

Sister Mary Clemente Davlin, O. P., "*Kynde Knowying* as a Major Theme in *Piers Plowman* B," *RES*, n.s. 22 (February 1971): 1-19.

Sister Mary Clemente Davlin, O. P., "*Kynde Knowying* as a Middle English Equivalent for 'Wisdom' in *Piers Plowman* B," *MÆ* 50 (1981): 5-17.

Sister Mary Clemente Davlin, O. P., "*Petrus Id Est, Christus*: Piers the Plowman as 'The Whole Christ,'" *ChauR* 6 (1972): 280-92.

Pandelis Demedis, *Expl* 33 (November 1974): 27.

Janette Dillon, "Piers Plowman: A Particular Example of Wordplay and Its Structural Significance," *MÆ* 50 (1981): 40-48.

E. Talbot Donaldson, "Apocalyptic Style in *Piers Plowman* B XIX-XX," *LeedsSE*, n.s. 14 (1983): 74-81.

E. Talbot Donaldson, "Patristic Exegesis in the Criticism of Medieval Literature: The Opposition," in *Critical Approaches to Medieval Literature: Selected Papers from the English Institute, 1958-1959,* ed. Dorothy Bethurum (New York: Columbia University Press, 1960), 5-16. Reprinted in Donaldson, *Speaking of Chaucer*, 138-46.

E. Talbot Donaldson, *Piers Plowman: The C-Text and Its Poet* (Hamden, Conn.: Archon Books, 1966), 121-98. Pp. 156-98 reprinted in Vasta, *Interpretations of Piers Plowman*, 130-89.

Dove, *The Perfect Age,* 104-24.

Elizabeth Doxsee, "'Trew Treuthe' and Canon Law: The Orthodoxy of Trojan's Salvation in *Piers Plowman* C-Text," *NM* 89 (1988): 295-311.

Peter Dronke, "Arbor Caritatis," in *Medieval Studies for J. A. W. Bennett*, ed. P. L. Heyworth (Oxford: Clarendon, 1981), 209-14.

T. P. Dunning, "Action and Contemplation in *Piers Plowman*," in Hussey, *Piers Plowman: Critical Approaches*, 213-25.

T. P. Dunning, *Piers Plowman: An Interpretation of the A-Text* (London: Longmans, Green, & Co.; Dublin: Talbot Press, 1937); rev. ed., ed. T. P. Dolan (Oxford, 1980). Pp. 16-23, 167, 169-86 reprinted in Vasta, *Interpretations of Piers Plowman*, 87-114.

T. P. Dunning, C. M., "The Structure of the B-Text of *Piers Plowman*," *RES*, n.s. 7 (1956): 225-37. Reprinted in Blanch, *Style and Symbolism*, 87-100; Vasta, *Interpretations of Piers Plowman*, 259-77.

J. T. Durkin, "Kingship in the Vision of *Piers Plowman*," *Thought* 14 (1939): 413-21.

George D. Economou, "The Vision's Aftermath in *Piers Plowman*: The Poetics of the Middle English Dream Vision," *Genre* 18 (Winter 1985): 313-21.

W. O. Evans, "Charity in *Piers Plowman*," in Hussey, *Piers Plowman*: *Critical Approaches*, 245-78.

Fowler, *The Bible in Middle English Literature*, 226-96.

David C. Fowler, "A Pointed Personal Allusion in *Piers the Plowman*," *MP* 77 (November 1979): 158-59.

Robert Worth Frank, Jr., "The Conclusion of '*Piers Plowman*,'" *JEGP* 49 (1950): 309-16.

Robert Worth Frank, Jr., *Piers Plowman and the Scheme of Salvation: An Interpretation of Dowel, Dobet, and Dobest* (New Haven, Conn.: Yale University Press, 1957; reprint, Hamden, Conn.: Shoestring Press, 1969; reprint, New Haven, Conn.: Yale University Press, 1975). Pp. 19-33 reprinted in Vasta, *Interpretations of Piers Plowman*, 298-318.

Robert Worth Frank, Jr., "The Pardon Scene in *Piers Plowman*," *Speculum* 26 (1951): 317-31.

Lavon B. Futwiler, "The Pardon Episode of *Piers the Plowman*: Some Rhetorical Considerations," *CEA* 47 (Summer 1985): 22-26.

G. H. Gerould, "The Structural Integrity of 'Piers Plowman B,'" *SP* 45 (1948): 60-75.

Beverly Brian Gilbert, "'Civil' and the Notaries in *Piers Plowman*," *MÆ* 50 (1981): 49-63.

Malcolm Godden, "Plowmen and Hermits in Langland's *Piers Plowman*," *RES*, n.s. 35 (May 1984): 129-63.

Margaret E. Goldsmith, *The Figure of Piers Plowman: The Image on the Coin* (Cambridge: D. S. Brewer, 1981).

Margaret E. Goldsmith, "Will's Pilgrimage in *Piers Plowman* B," in Stokes and Burton, *Medieval Literature*, 119-32.

Gradon, *Form and Style*, 74-77, 84-90, 99-113.

Pamela Gradon, "*Trajanus Redivivus*: Another Look at Trajan in *Piers Plowman*," in *Middle English Studies Presented to Norman Davis in Honour of His Seventieth Birthday*, ed. Douglas Gray and Eric Gerald Stanley (Oxford: Clarendon, 1983), 93-114.

Nick Gray, "The Clemency of Cobblers: A Reading of 'Glutton's Confession' in *Piers Plowman*," *LSE*, n.s. 17 (1986): 61-75.

Nick Gray, "Langland's Quotations from the Penitential Tradition," *MP* 84 (August 1986): 53-60.

Eugene Green, "Patterns of the Negative in *Piers Plowman*," in *Allegoresis: The Craft of Allegory in Medieval Literature*, ed. J. Stephen Russell (New York and London: Garland, 1988), 67-88.

Lavinia Griffiths, *Personification in Piers Plowman* (Cambridge: D. S. Brewer, 1985).

Bruce Harbert, "Truth, Love, and Grace in the B-Text of 'Piers Plowman,'" in *Literature in Fourteenth-Century England*, ed. Piero Boitani and Anna Torti (Cambridge: D. S. Brewer, 1983), 33-48.

Britton J. Harwood, "'Clergye' and the Action of the Third Vision in *Piers Plowman*," *MP* 70 (May 1973): 279-90.

Britton J. Harwood, "Dame Study and the Place of Orality in *Piers Plowman*," *ELH* 57 (1990): 1-17.

Britton J. Harwood, "Imaginative in *Piers Plowman*," *MÆ* 44 (1975): 249-63.

Britton J. Harwood, "Langland's *Kynde Knowyng* and the Quest for Christ," *MP* 80 (February 1983): 242-55.

Britton J. Harwood and Ruth F. Smith, "Inwit and the Castle of Caro in *Piers Plowman*," *NM* 71 (1970): 648-54.

James E. Hicks, "The Eremitic Ideal and the Dreamer's Quest in *Piers Plowman*," in *Proceedings of the Illinois Medieval Association*, no. 2, ed. Mark D. Johnston and Samuel M. Riley (Normal, Ill.: Illinois State University Press, 1985), 107-30.

Hieatt, *The Realism of Dream Visions*, 89-97.

Elton D. Higgs, "The Path to Involvement: The Centrality of the Dreamer in *Piers Plowman*," *TSE* 21 (1974): 1-34.

Thomas D. Hill, "Davidic Typology and the Characterization of Christ: 'Piers Plowman B.XIX, 95-103," *N&Q* 23 (July 1976): 291-94.

Thomas D. Hill, "The Light That Blew the Saints to Heaven: *Piers Plowman* B, V.495-503," *RES*, n.s. 24 (November 1973): 444-49.

Thomas D. Hill, "Two Notes on Exegetical Allusion in Langland: *Piers Plowman* XI, 161-167, and B, I, 115-124," *NM* 75 (1974): 92-97.

Richard L. Hoffman, "The Burning of 'Boke' in *Piers Plowman*," *MLQ* 25 (March 1964): 57-65.

J. V. Holleran, "The Role of the Dreamer in *Piers Plowman*," *AnM* 7 (1966): 33-50.

Donald R. Howard, *The Three Temptations: Medieval Man in Search of the World* (Princeton, N.J.: Princeton University Press, 1966), 163-214.

Bernard F. Huppé, "*Petrus Id Est Christus*: Word Play in *Piers Plowman*, the B-Text," *ELH* 17 (1950): 163-90.

S. S. Hussey, "Langland and Hilton and the Three Lives," *RES*, n.s. 7 (1956): 132-50. Reprinted in Vasta, *Interpretations of Piers Plowman*, 232-58.

Priscilla Jenkins, "Conscience: The Frustration of Allegory," in Hussey, *Piers Plowman: Critical Approaches*, 125-42.

Margaret Jennings, C. S. J., "*Piers Plowman* and the Holychurch," *Viator* 9 (1978): 367-74.

Steven Justice, "The Genres of *Piers Plowman*," *Viator* 19 (1988): 291-306.

George Kane, "The Perplexities of William Langland," in Benson and Wenzel, *The Wisdom of Poetry*, 73-89.

R. E. Kaske, "The Character Hunger in *Piers Plowman*," in *Medieval English Studies Presented to George Kane*, ed. Edward Donald Kennedy, Ronald Waldron, and Joseph S. Wittig (Wolfeboro, N.H.: D. S. Brewer, 1988), 187-97.

R. E. Kaske, "The Defense," in *Critical Approaches to Medieval Literature: Selected Papers from the English Institute, 1958-1959,* ed. Dorothy Bethurum (New York and London: Columbia University Press, 1960), 32-49.

R. E. Kaske, "*Ex vi transicionis* and Its Passage in *Piers Plowman*," *JEGP* 62 (1963): 32-60. Reprinted in Blanch, *Style and Symbolism*, 228-63.

R. E. Kaske, "Holy Church's Speech and the Structure of *Piers Plowman*," in Rowland, *Chaucer and Middle English Studies*, 320-27.

R. E. Kaske, "Patristic Exegesis in the Criticism of Medieval Literature: The Defense," in *Critical Approaches to Medieval Literature: Selected Papers from the English Institute, 1958-1959*, ed. Dorothy Bethurum (New York and London: Columbia University Press, 1960), 27-48. Reprinted in Vasta, *Interpretations of Piers Plowman*, 319-38.

R. E. Kaske, "The Speech of 'Book' in *Piers Plowman*," *Anglia* 77 (1959): 117-44.

Ernest N. Kaulbach, "The 'Vis Imaginativa' and the Reasoning Powers of Ymaginatif in the B-Text of *Piers Plowman*," *JEGP* 84 (1985): 16-29.

Ernest N. Kaulbach, "The 'Vis Imaginative Secundum Avicennam' and the Naturally Prophetic Powers of Ymaginatif in the B-Text of *Piers Plowman*," *JEGP* 86 (1987): 496-514.

Patricia Margaret Kean, "Justice, Kingship, and the Good Life in the Second Part of *Piers Plowman*," in Hussey, *Piers Plowman: Critical Approaches*, 76-110.

Patricia Margaret Kean, "Love, Law, and *Lewte* in *Piers Plowman*," *RES*, n.s. 15 (1964): 241-61. Reprinted in Blanch, *Style and Symbolism*, 132-55.

Elizabeth D. Kirk, *The Dream Thought of "Piers Plowman"* (New Haven and London: Yale University Press, 1972).

Stephen Thomas Knight, "Satire in *Piers Plowman*," in Hussey, *Piers Plowman*: *Critical Approaches*, 279-309.

Traugott Lawler, "The Gracious Imagining of Redemption in '*Piers Plowman*,'" *English* 28 (Autumn 1979): 203-16.

John Lawlor, "The Imaginative Unity of *Piers Plowman*," *RES*, n.s. 8 (1957): 113-26. Reprinted in Blanch, *Style and Symbolism*, 101-16; Vasta, *Interpretations of Piers Plowman*, 278-97.

John Lawlor, *Piers Plowman: An Essay in Criticism* (London: Edward Arnold, 1962).

Lawrence, Seifter, and Ratner, *McGraw-Hill Guide*, 27-33.

David A. Lawton, "*Piers Plowman*: On Tearing – and not Tearing – the Pardon," *PQ* 60 (Summer 1981): 414-22.

David A. Lawton, "The Unity of Middle English Alliterative Poetry," *Speculum* 58 (1982): 77-80.

Joseph A. Longo, "*Piers Plowman* and the Tropological Matrix: Passus XI and XII," *Anglia* 82 (1964): 291-308.

Anthony Low, *The Georgic Revolution* (Princeton, N.J.: Princeton University Press, 1985), 183-87 *passim*.

Elizabeth Lunz, "The Valley of Jehoshaphat in *Piers Plowman*," *TSE* 20 (1972): 1-10.

Alan C. Lupack, *Expl* 34 (December 1975): 31.

Stella Maguire, "The Significance of Haukyn, *Activa Vita*, in *Piers Plowman*," *RES*, 25 (1949): 97-109. Reprinted in Blanch, *Style and Symbolism*, 194-208.

Jill Mann, "Eating and Drinking in 'Piers Plowman,'" *E&S* 32 (1979): 26-43.

Stephen Manning, "A Psychological Interpretation of *Sir Gawain and the Green Knight*," *Criticism* 6 (1964): 165-77.

Stephen Manning, "William Langland and Jean Piaget," in *Allegoresis: The Craft of Allegory in Medieval Literature*, ed. J. Stephen Russell (New York and London: Garland, 1988), 89-106.

Jay Martin, "Wil as Fool and Wanderer in *Piers Plowman*," *TSLL* 3 (Winter 1962): 535-48.

Priscilla Martin, *Piers Plowman: The Field and the Tower* (London and Basingstoke: Macmillan, 1979).

Gervase Matthew, "Justice and Charity in the Vision of *Piers Plowman*," *Dominican Studies* 1 (1948): 360-66.

Michael H. Means, "*Piers Plowman*: The Fragmented Consolatio," in *The Consolatio Genre in Medieval English Literature*, University of Florida Monographs, no. 36 (Gainesville: University of Florida Press, 1972), 66-90.

H. Meroney, "The Life and Death of Long Wille," *ELH* 17 (1950) 1-35 *passim*.

Anne Middleton, "Narration and the Invention of Experience: Episodic Form in *Piers Plowman*," in Benson and Wenzel, *The Wisdom of Poetry*, 91-122.

Anne Middleton, "Two Infinites: Grammatical Metaphor in *Piers Plowman*," *ELH* 39 (1972): 169-88.

David Mills, "The Role of the Dreamer in *Piers Plowman*," in Hussey, *Piers Plowman: Critical Approaches*, 180-212.

Alexander G. Mitchell, "Lady Meed and the Art of *Piers Plowman*," Chambers Memorial Lecture, London, 1956, in Blanch, *Style and Symbolism*, 174-93.

Gerald Morgan, "Langland's Conception of Favel, Guile, Liar, and False in the First Vision of *Piers Plowman*," *Neophil* 71 (October 1987): 626-33.

Gerald Morgan, "The Meaning of Kind Wit, Conscience, and Reason in the First Vision of *Piers Plowman*," *MP* 84 (May 1987): 351-58.

Gerald Morgan, "The Status and Meaning of Meed in the First Vision of *Piers Plowman*," *Neophil* 72 (July 1988): 449-63.

Daniel M. Murtaugh, *"Piers Plowman" and the Image of God* (Gainesville: University Presses of Florida, 1978).

Charles Muscatine, *Poetry and Crisis in the Age of Chaucer* (Notre Dame and London: University of Notre Dame Press, 1972), 71-109.

Barbara Nolan, *The Gothic Visionary Perspective* (Princeton, N.J.: Princeton University Press, 1977), 205-58.

John Norton-Smith, *William Langland* (Leiden: E. J. Brill, 1983), 46-89.

Philomena O'Driscoll, "The *Dowel* Debate in *Piers Plowman B*," *MÆ* 50 (1981): 18-29.

Elisabeth M. Orsten, "The Ambiguities in Langland's Rat Parliament," *MS* 23 (1961): 216-39.

Elisabeth M. Orsten, "*Patientia* in the B-Text of 'Piers Plowman,'" *MS* 31 (1969): 317-33.

Samuel A. Overstreet,"'Grammaticus Ludens': Theological Aspects of Langland's Grammatical Allegory," *Traditio* 40 (1984): 251-96.

Michael R. Paull, "Mahomet and the Conversion of the Heathen in *Piers Plowman*," *ELN* 10 (September 1972): 1-8.

Derek Pearsall, *Old English and Middle English Poetry*, Routledge History of English Poetry, Vol. 1 (London: Routledge & Kegan Paul, 1977), 177-81.

Conrad Pepler, *The English Religious Heritage* (St. Louis, Mo.: B. Herder & Co., 1958).

Maureen Quilligan, "Langland's Literal Allegory," *EIC* 28 (April 1978): 95-111.

Maureen Quilligan, *The Language of Allegory: Defining the Genre* (Ithaca, N.Y.: Cornell University Press, 1979), 58-79.

Barbara Raw, "Piers and the Image of God in Man," in Hussey, *Piers Plowman: Critical Approaches*, 143-79.

Mary Riach, "Langland's Dreamer and the Transformation of the Third Vision," *EIC* 19 (January 1969): 6-18.

D. W. Robertson, Jr., and Bernard F. Huppé, *Piers Plowman and Scriptural Tradition* (Princeton, N.J.: Princeton University Press; London: Geoffrey Cumberlege, Oxford University Press, 1951), 1-16, 234-48. Reprinted in Vasta, *Interpretations of Piers Plowman*, 190-216.

William M. Ryan, *William Langland* (New York: Twayne, 1968), 64-99.

Raymond C. St. Jacques, "Conscience's Final Pilgrimage in *Piers Plowman* and the Cyclical Structure of the Liturgy," *RUO* 40 (1970): 210-23.

Raymond C. St. Jacques, "The Liturgical Associations of Langland's Samaritan," *Traditio* 25 (1969): 217-30.

Elizabeth Salter, *English and International Studies in the Literature, Art, and Patronage of Medieval England*, ed. Derek Pearsall and Nicolette Zeeman (Cambridge: Cambridge University Press, 1988), 111-57 *passim*.

Elizabeth Salter, *Piers Plowman: An Introduction* (Cambridge, Mass.: Harvard University Press; Oxford: Basil Blackwell, 1962).

Elizabeth Zeeman (Salter), "*Piers Plowman* and the Pilgrimage to Truth," *E&S*, n.s. 11 (1958): 1-16. Reprinted in Blanch, *Style and Symbolism*, 117-31.

A. V. C. Schmidt, "The Inner Dreams in *Piers Plowman*," *MÆ* 55 (1986): 24-40.

A. V. C. Schmidt, "Langland and Scholastic Philosophy," *MÆ* 38 (1969): 134-56.

A. V. C. Schmidt, "Langland's Structural Imagery," *EIC* 30 (October 1980): 311-25.

Mary C. Schroeder, "*Piers Plowman*: The Tearing of the Pardon," *PQ* 49 (January 1970): 8-18.

Edward C. Schweitzer, "'Half a Laumpe Lyne in Latyne,' and Patience's Riddle in *Piers Plowman*," *JEGP* 73 (1974): 313-27.

John L. Selzer, "Topical Allegory in *Piers Plowman*: Lady Meed's B-Text Debate with Conscience," *PQ* 59 (Summer 1980): 257-67.

James Simpson, "From Reason to Affective Knowledge: Modes of Thought and Poetic Form in *Piers Plowman*," *MÆ* 55 (1986): 1-23.

James Simpson, "The Role of *Scientia* in *Piers Plowman*," in *Medieval English Religious and Ethical Literature: Essays in Honour of G. H. Russell*, ed. Gregory Kratzmann and James Simpson (Cambridge: D. S. Brewer, 1986), 49-65.

James Simpson, "Spiritual and Earthly Nobility in *Piers Plowman*," *NM* 86 (1985): 467-81.

James Simpson, "The Transformation of Meaning: A Figure of Thought in *Piers Plowman*," *RES*, n.s. 37 (May 1986): 161-83.

A. H. Smith, "*Piers Plowman* and the Pursuit of Poetry," in Blanch, *Style and Symbolism*, 26-39.

Ben H. Smith, Jr., *Traditional Imagery of Charity in "Piers Plowman"* (The Hague and Paris: Mouton, 1966).

A. C. Spearing, "The Development of a Theme in *Piers Plowman*," *RES*, n.s. 11 (August 1960): 241-53.

Spearing, *Medieval Dream-Poetry*, 138-62.

Spearing, *Readings in Medieval Poetry*, 216-45.

Lorraine Kochanske Stock, "Will, Actyf, Pacience, and *Liberum Arbitrium*: Two Recurring Quotations in Langland's Revisions of *Piers Plowman* C Text, Passus V, XV, XVI," *TSLL* 30 (Winter 1988): 461-77.

Myra Stokes, *Justice and Mercy in Piers Plowman: A Reading of the B Text Visio* (London and Canberra: Croom Helm, 1984).

William C. Strange, "The Willful Trope: Some Notes on Personification with Illustrations from *Piers* (A)," *AnM* 9 (1968): 26-39.

Penn R. Szittya, *The Antifraternal Tradition in Medieval Literature* (Princeton, N.J.: Princeton University Press, 1986), 247-87.

M. Teresa Tavormina, "'Bothe two ben gode': Marriage and Virginity in *Piers Plowman* C.18.68-100," *JEGP* 81 (1982): 320-30.

M. Teresa Tavormina, "Kindly Similitude: Langland's Matrimonial Trinity," *MP* 80 (November 1982): 117-28.

M. Teresa Tavormina, "*Piers Plowman* and the Liturgy of St. Lawrence: Composition and Revision in Langland's Poetry," *SP* 84 (1987): 245-71.

Claud A. Thompson, "Structural, Figurative, and Thematic Trinities in *Piers Plowman*," *Mosaic* 9 (Winter 1976): 105-14.

E. M. W. Tillyard, *The English Epic and Its Background* (London: Chatto and Windus, 1954), 151-71 *passim*.

Philippa Tristram, *Figures of Life and Death in Medieval English Literature* (London: Paul Elek, 1976), 197-201.

Katherine B. Trower, "The Figure of Hunger in *Piers Plowman*," *ABR* 24 (June 1973): 238-60.

Katherine B. Trower, "Temporal Tensions in the *Visio* of *Piers Plowman*," *MS* 35 (1973): 389-412.

Howard William Troyer, "Who Is Piers Plowman?" *PMLA* 47 (1932): 368-84. Reprinted in Blanch, *Style and Symbolism*, 156-73.

Edward Vasta, *The Spiritual Basis of Piers Plowman* (The Hague: Mouton, 1965).

Edward Vasta, "Truth, The Best Treasure in *Piers Plowman*," *PQ* 44 (January 1964), 17-29.

Marshall Walker, "Piers Plowman's Pardon: A Note," *ESA* 8 (1965): 64-70.

James F. G. Weldon, "The Structure of Dream Visions in *Piers Plowman*," *MS* 49 (1987): 254-81.

Henry W. Wells, "The Construction of *Piers Plowman*," *PMLA* 44 (1929): 123-40. Reprinted in Vasta, *Interpretations of Piers Plowman*, 1-21.

Henry W. Wells, "The Philosophy of *Piers Plowman*," *PMLA* 53 (1938): 339-49. Reprinted in Vasta, *Interpretations of Piers Plowman*, 115-29.

Thomas J. Wertenbaker, Jr., *Expl* 34 (March 1976): 51.

Donald Wesling, "Eschatology and the Language of Satire in *Piers Plowman*," *Criticism* 10 (1968): 277-89.

Gordon Whatley, "*Piers Plowman* B 12.277-94: Notes on Language, Text, and Theology," *MP* 82 (August 1984): 1-12.

Hugh White, "Langland's Ymaginatif, Kynde and the *Benjamin Major*," *MÆ* 55 (1986): 241-48.

Hugh White, *Nature and Salvation in Piers Plowman* (Cambridge: D. S. Brewer, 1988).

Margaret Williams, "Introduction" to *Piers the Plowman* (New York: Random House, 1971), 23-60.

Wimsatt, *Allegory and Mirror*, 49-54, 105-12, 128-30.

Joseph S. Wittig, "The Dramatic and Rhetorical Development of Long Will's Pilgrimage," *NM* 76 (1975): 52-76.

Joseph S. Wittig, "*Piers Plowman* B Passus IX-XII: Elements in the Design of the Inward Journey," *Traditio* 28 (1972): 211-80.

Rosemary Woolf, "Some Non-Medieval Qualities of *Piers Plowman*," *EIC* 12 (1962): 111-25. Reprinted in Woolf, *Art and Doctrine*, 85-97.

Rosemary Woolf, "The Tearing of the Pardon," in Hussey, *Piers Plowman: Critical Approaches*, 50-75. Reprinted in Woolf, *Art and Doctrine*, 131-56.

LAȜAMON

Brut

W. R. J. Barron, "Arthurian Romance: Traces of an English Tradition," *ES* 61 (February 1980): 6-10.

Swanton, *English Literature*, 175-87.

LYDGATE, JOHN

"Balade in Commendation of Our Lady"

Gradon, *Form and Style*, 353-55.

"The Child Jesus to Mary, the Rose"

Wenzel, *Preachers, Poets*, 251-52.

"Complaint of the Black Knight" (or "A Complaynt of a Loveres Lyfe")

Derek Pearsall, *John Lydgate* (Charlottesville: University Press of Virginia, 1970), 84-97.

Dance Macabre

Wimsatt, *Allegory and Mirror*, 168-70.

"The Debate of the Horse, Goose, and Sheep"

David Lampe, "Lydgate's Laughter: 'Horse, Goose, and Sheep' as Social Satire," *AnM* 15 (1974): 150-58.

Derek Pearsall, *John Lydgate* (Charlottesville: University Press of Virginia, 1970), 200-202.

"Erly on Morwe, and Toward Nyght Also"

Woolf, *The English Religious Lyric*, 198-201.

Fall of Princes

Derek Pearsall, *John Lydgate* (Charlottesville: University Press of Virginia, 1970), 223-54 *passim*.

Walter F. Schirmer, *John Lydgate: A Study in the Culture of the XVth Century*, trans. Ann E. Keep (*John Lydgate: Ein Kulturbild aus dem 15. Jahrhundert* [Tübingen: Max Neineyer Verlag, 1952]; Berkeley and Los Angeles: University of California Press, 1961), 206-27.

Fall of Princes, Book 6

Ebin, *Illuminator, Makar, Vates*, 44-48.

"Flower of Courtesy"

Derek Pearsall, *John Lydgate* (Charlottesville: University Press of Virginia, 1970), 97-103.

"The Life of Our Lady"

Walter F. Schirmer, *John Lydgate: A Study in the Culture of the XVth Century*, trans. Ann E. Keep (1952; Berkeley and Los Angeles: University of California Press, 1961), 150-54.

The Lyfe of Seint Albon and the Lyfe of Saint Amphabel

Walter F. Schirmer, *John Lydgate: A Study in the Culture of the XVth Century*, trans. Ann E. Keep (1952; Berkeley and Los Angeles: University of California Press, 1961), 166-70.

Reason and Sensuality

Edgar Schell, *Strangers and Pilgrims: From "The Castle of Perseverance" to "King Lear"* (Chicago and London: University of Chicago Press, 1983), 15-25 *passim*.

"A Seying of the Nightingale"

Davidoff, *Beginning Well*, 66-70.

Walter F. Schirmer, *John Lydgate: A Study in the Culture of the XVth Century*, trans. Ann E. Keep (1952; Berkeley and Los Angeles: University of California Press, 1961), 180-82.

Siege of Thebes

R. W. Ayers, "Medieval History, Moral Purpose, and the Structure of Lydgate's 'Siege of Thebes,'" *PMLA* 73 (1958): 463-74.

Ebin, *Illuminator, Makar, Vates*, 42-44.

John M. Ganim, *Style and Consciousness in Middle English Narrative* (Princeton, N.J.: Princeton University Press, 1983), 103-22.

Derek Pearsall, *John Lydgate* (Charlottesville: University Press of Virginia, 1970), 151-56.

Alain Renoir, *The Poetry of John Lydgate* (Cambridge, Mass.: Harvard University Press, 1967): 110-35.

Temple of Glas

Davidoff, *Beginning Well*, 135-46.

Derek Pearsall, *John Lydgate* (Charlottesville: University Press of Virginia, 1970), 104-15 *passim*.

Spearing, *Medieval Dream-Poetry*, 171-76.

"Testament of Lydgate"

Walter F. Schirmer, *John Lydgate: A Study in the Culture of the XVth Century*, trans. Ann E. Keep (1952; Berkeley and Los Angeles: University of California Press, 1961), 182-84.

Troy Book

Derek Pearsall, *John Lydgate* (Charlottesville: University Press of Virginia, 1970), 125-51 *passim*.

Alain Renoir, *The Poetry of John Lydgate* (Cambridge, Mass.: Harvard University Press, 1967), 96-100.

Anna Torti, "From 'History' to 'Tragedy': The Story of Troilus and Criseyde in Lydgate's *Troy Book* and Henryson's *Testament of Cresseid*," in *European Tragedy of Troilus*, ed. Piero Boitani (Oxford: Clarendon, 1989), 171-84.

"The Virtues of the Mass"

Walter F. Schirmer, *John Lydgate: A Study in the Culture of the XVth Century*, trans. Ann E. Keep (1952; Berkeley and Los Angeles: University of California Press, 1961), 175-77.

MAIDSTONE, RICHARD

"Mercy God of Mysdede"
The Fifty-first Psalm

Rogers, *Image and Abstraction*, 107-24.

Penitential Psalms

Valerie Edden, "Richard Maidstone's *Penitential Psalms*," *LeedsSE*, n.s. 17 (1986): 77-94.

MANNYNG, ROBERT

Handlyng Synne

Boitani, *English Medieval Narrative*, 23-27.

Fritz Kemmler, *Context: A Historical and Critical Study of Robert Mannyng of Brunne's "Handlyng Synne"* (Tubingen: Narr, 1984).

Wimsatt, *Allegory and Mirror*, 150-55.

MASTER THOMAS

Romance of Horn

Ramsey, *Chivalric Romances*, 26-43 *passim*.

NICHOLAS OF GUILFORD

The Owl and the Nightingale

Anne W. Baldwin, "Henry II and *The Owl and the Nightingale*," *JEGP* 66 (1967): 207-29.

Bennett, *Middle English Literature*, 1-10.

Derek Brewer, *English Gothic Literature* (London and Basingstoke: Macmillan, 1983), 30-35.

M. Angela Carson, O. S. U., "Rhetorical Structure in *The Owl and the Nightingale*," *Speculum* 42 (1967): 92-103.

A. C. Cawley, "Astrology in 'The Owl and the Nightingale,'" *MLR* 46 (April 1951): 161-74.

Mortimer J. Donovan, "The Owl as Religious Altruist in *The Owl and the Nightingale*," *MS* 18 (1956): 207-14.

W. G. East, "The Owl and the Nightingale, Lines 427-8," *ES* 59 (October 1978): 442-43.

John Gardner, "*The Owl and the Nightingale*: A Burlesque," *PLL* 2 (Winter 1966): 3-12.

Jane Gottschalk, "*The Owl and the Nightingale*: Lay Preachers to a Lay Audience," *PQ* 45 (October 1966): 657-67.

Constance B. Hieatt, "The Subject of the Mock-Debate Between the Owl and the Nightingale," *SN* 40 (1968): 155-60.

Kathryn Huganir, *"The Owl and the Nightingale": Sources, Date, Author* (New York: Haskell House, 1966), 9-61.

Kathryn Hume, *"The Owl and the Nightingale": The Poem and Its Critics* (Toronto and Buffalo: University of Toronto Press, 1975).

Gerald B. Kinneavy, "Fortune, Providence, and the Owl," *SP* 64 (October 1967): 655-64.

Seth Lerer, "The Owl, the Nightingale, and the Apes," *ES* 64 (April 1983): 102-5.

Irene Moran, "Two Notes on *The Owl and the Nightingale*," *ES* 59 (December 1978): 499-507.

Kurt Olsson, "Character and Truth in *The Owl and the Nightingale*," *ChauR* 11 (1977): 351-68.

R. Barton Palmer, "The Narrator in *The Owl and the Nightingale*: A Reader in the Text," *ChauR* 22 (1988): 305-321.

Douglas L. Peterson, "*The Owl and the Nightingale* and Christian Dialectic," *JEGP* 55 (1956): 13-26.

Nancy M. Reale, "Rhetorical Strategies in *The Owl and the Nightingale*," *PQ* 63 (Fall 1984): 417-29.

D. W. Robertson, Jr., "Historical Criticism," in *English Institute Essays, 1950*, ed. Alan S. Downer (New York: Columbia University Press, 1951), 23-26. Reprinted in Robertson, *Essays in Medieval Culture*, 3-20.

Jay Schleusener, "*The Owl and the Nightingale*: A Matter of Judgment," *MP* 70 (1973): 185-89.

Swanton, *English Literature*, 262-80.

Elizabeth Williams, "Blossom in the Breach: Some Comments on the Language of Spring in *The Owl and the Nightingale*," *LeedsSE*, n.s. 12 (1981): 170-74.

Michael A. Witt, "*The Owl and the Nightingale* and English Law Court Procedure of the Twelfth and Thirteenth Centuries," *ChauR* 16 (1982): 282-92.

PEARL-POET

(also Gawain-Poet)

Cleanness (or *Purity*)

Elizabeth Armstrong, *Expl* 36 (Fall 1977): 29-31.

Bennett, *Middle English Literature*, 226-36.

Boitani, *English Medieval Narrative*, 12-18.

Derek Brewer, *English Gothic Literature* (London and Basingstoke: Macmillan, 1983), 170-73.

Monica Brzezinski, "Conscience and Covenant: The Sermon Structure of *Cleanness*," *JEGP* 89 (1990): 166-80.

A. C. Cawley and J. J. Anderson, "Introduction" to *Pearl, Cleanness, Patience, Sir Gawain and the Green Knight* (London: J. M. Dent & Sons; New York: E. P. Dutton & Co., 1976), xiv-xviii.

S. L. Clark and Julian N. Wasserman, "*Purity*: The Cities of the Dove and the Raven," *ABR* 29 (September 1978): 284-306.

W. A. Davenport, *The Art of the Gawain-Poet* (London: University of London, Athlone Press, 1978), 55-102.

Fowler, *The Bible in Middle English Literature*, 172-86.

John Gardner, *The Complete Works of the Gawain-Poet* (Chicago and London: University of Chicago Press, 1965), 61-69.

Jonathan A. Glenn, "Dislocation of *Kynde* in the Middle English *Cleanness*," *ChauR* 18 (1983): 77-91.

Gradon, *Form and Style*, 119-23.

Ruth E. Hamilton, "Repeating Narrative and Anachrony in *Cleanness*," *Style* 20 (Summer 1986): 182-88.

Johnson, *The Voice*, 97-143.

T. D. Kelly and John T. Irwin, "The Meaning of *Cleanness*: Parable as Effective Sign," *MS* 35 (1973): 232-60.

Charles Moorman, *The "Pearl"-Poet* (New York: Twayne, 1968), 78-87.

Charlotte C. Morse, "The Image of the Vessel in *Cleanness*," *UTQ* 40 (Spring 1971): 202-16.

Jonathan Nicholls, *The Matter of Courtesy: Medieval Courtesy Books and the Gawain-Poet* (Woodbridge, Suffolk, and Dover, N.H.: D. S. Brewer, 1985), 85-102.

Daniel W. O'Bryan, "Sodom and Gomorrah: The Use of the Vulgate in *Cleanness*," *JNT* 12 (Winter 1982): 15-23.

Derek Pearsall, *Old English and Middle English Poetry*, Routledge History of English Poetry, Vol. 1 (London: Routledge & Kegan Paul, 1977), 170-71.

Earl G. Schreiber, "The Structures of *Clannesse*," in Levy and Szarmach, *The Alliterative Tradition*, 131-52.

A. C. Spearing, *The Gawain-Poet: A Critical Study* (Cambridge: Cambridge University Press, 1969), 4-73.

A. C. Spearing, "*Purity* and Danger," *EIC* 30 (October 1980): 293-310.

Spearing, *Readings in Medieval Poetry*, 173-94.

Theresa Tinkle, "The Heart's Eye: Beatific Vision in *Purity*," *SP* 85 (Fall 1988): 451-70.

William Vantuono, "*Cleanness* and *Le Roman de la Rose*," *ELN* 26 (December 1988): 1-6.

William Vantuono, "*Patience*, *Cleanness*, *Pearl*, and *Gawain*: the Case for Common Authorship," *AnM* 12 (1971): 37-69.

Edward Wilson, *The Gawain-Poet* (Leiden: E. J. Brill, 1976), 72-112.

Patience

J. J. Anderson, "Introduction" to *Patience* (Manchester: Manchester University Press; New York: Barnes & Noble, 1969), 7-19.

J. J. Anderson, "The Prologue of *Patience*," *MP* 63 (May 1966): 283-87.

Malcolm Andrew, "The Diabolical Chapel: A Motif in *Patience* and *Sir Gawain and the Green Knight*," *Neophil* 66 (April 1982): 313-19.

Malcolm Andrew, "*Patience*: The 'Munster Dor,'" *ELN* 14 (March 1977): 164-67.

Bennett, *Middle English Literature*, 217-26.

Morton W. Bloomfield, "*Patience* and the Mashal," in *Medieval Studies in Honor of Lillian Herlands Hornstein*, ed. Jess B. Bessinger, Jr., and Robert R. Raymo (New York: New York University Press, 1976), 41-49.

Boitani, *English Medieval Narrative*, 8-12 *passim*.

John M. Bowers, "*Patience* and the Ideal of the Mixed Life," *TSLL* 28 (Spring 1986): 1-23.

Susan L. Clark and Julian N. Wasserman, "Jews, Gentiles, and Prophets: The Sense of Community in *Patience*," *ABR* 37 (September 1986): 230-55.

W. A. Davenport, *The Art of the Gawain-Poet* (London: University of London, Athlone Press, 1978), 103-35.

F. N. M. Diekstra, "Jonah and *Patience*: The Psychology of a Prophet," *ES* 55 (June 1974): 205-17.

R. J. Dingley, *Expl* 46 (Winter 1988): 3-4.

Laurence Eldredge, "Sheltering Space and Cosmic Space in the Middle English *Patience*," *AnM* 21 (1981): 121-33.

Fowler, *The Bible in Middle English Literature*, 186-94.

John B. Friedman, "Figural Typology in the Middle English *Patience*," in Levy and Szarmach, *The Alliterative Tradition*, 99-129.

John Gardner, *The Complete Works of the Gawain-Poet* (Chicago and London: University of Chicago Press, 1965), 69-70.

Victor Yelverton Haines, *The Fortunate Fall of Sir Gawain: The Typology of "Sir Gawain and the Green Knight"* (Washington, D.C.: University Press of America, 1982), 70-71.

John T. Irwin and T. D. Kelly, "The Way and the End Are One: *Patience* as a Parable of the Contemplative Life," *ABR* 25 (March 1974): 33-53.

Lynn Staley Johnson, "An Examination of the Middle English *Patience*," *ABR* 32 (December 1981): 336-64.

Johnson, *The Voice*, 3-36.

Charles Moorman, *The "Pearl"-Poet* (New York: Twayne, 1968), 64-77.

Charles Moorman, "The Role of the Narrator in *Patience*," *MP* 61 (November 1963): 90-95.

Jonathan Nicholls, *The Matter of Courtesy: Medieval Courtesy Books and the Gawain-Poet* (Woodbridge, Suffolk and Dover, N.H.: D. S. Brewer, 1985), 79-84.

Sandra Pierson Prior, "*Patience* – Beyond Apocalypse," *MP* 83 (May 1986): 337-48.

James Rhodes, "Vision and History in *Patience*," *JMRS* 19 (Spring 1989): 1-13.

N. P. Robinson, "The Middle English *Patience*: The Preacher-Poet, Jonah, and Their Common Mission," *ABR* 37 (June 1986): 130-42.

George Sanderlin, "The *Gawain*-poet's Heroes – ¿Human or 'Something More Than Man'?" *LangQ* 23 (Spring-Summer, 1985): 36-38.

George Sanderlin, "The Role of Jonah in *Patience*," *LangQ* 16 (Fall-Winter 1977): 39-40.

Jay Schleusener, "History and Action in *Patience*," *PMLA* 86 (1971): 959-65.

R. A. Shoaf, "God's 'Malyse': Metaphor and Conversion in *Patience*," *JMRS* 11 (Fall 1981): 261-79.

A. C. Spearing, *The Gawain-Poet: A Critical Study* (Cambridge: Cambridge University Press, 1969), 74-95.

A. C. Spearing, "*Patience* and the *Gawain*-Poet," *Anglia* 84 (1966): 307-20.

Sarah Stanbury, "Space and Visual Hermeneutics in the *Gawain*-Poet," *ChauR* 21 (1987): 482-85.

Myra Stokes, "'Suffering' in *Patience*," *ChauR* 18 (1984): 354-63.

William Vantuono, "*Patience*, *Cleanness*, *Pearl*, and *Gawain*: Thc Case for Common Authorship," *AnM* 12 (1971): 37-69.

William Vantuono, "The Structure and Sources of *Patience*," *MS* 34 (1972): 401-21.

David J. Williams, "The Point of *Patience*," *MP* 68 (November 1970): 127-36.

Edward Wilson, *The Gawain-Poet* (Leiden: E. J. Brill, 1976), 46-71.

Pearl

Malcolm Andrew, *Expl* 40 (Fall 1981): 4-5.

Ross G. Arthur, "The Day of Judgment Is Now: A Johannine Pattern in the Middle English *Pearl*," *ABR* 38 (September 1987): 227-42.

Denise N. Baker, "Dialectic Form in *Pearl* and *Piers Plowman*," *Viator* 15 (1984): 264-67.

Bennett, *Middle English Literature*, 236-58.

Ian Bishop, *Pearl in Its Setting: A Critical Study of the Structure and Meaning of the Middle English Poem* (New York: Barnes & Noble, 1968).

Ian Bishop, "Relatives at the Court of Heaven: Contrasted Treatments of an Idea in *Piers Plowman* and *Pearl*," in Stokes and Burton, *Medieval Literature*, 111-18.

Ian Bishop, "The Significance of the 'Garlande Gay' in the Allegory of *Pearl*," *RES*, n.s. 8 (February 1957): 12-21.

Robert J. Blanch, "Precious Metal and Gem Symbolism in *Pearl*," *The Lock Haven Review*, 7 (1965): 1-12. Reprinted in Blanch, *"Sir Gawain" and "Pearl,"* 86-97.

Louis Blenkner, O. S. B., "The Pattern of Traditional Images in *Pearl*," *SP* 68 (January 1971): 26-49.

Louis Blenkner, O. S. B., "The Theological Structure of *Pearl*," *Traditio* 24 (1968): 43-75. Reprinted in Conley, *The Middle English "Pearl,"* 220-71.

Boitani, *English Medieval Narrative*, 96-113 *passim*.

Marie Borroff, "Introduction" to *Pearl: A New Verse Translation* (New York: W. W. Norton & Co., 1977), viii-xix.

Marie Borroff, "*Pearl's* 'Maynful Mone': Crux, Simile, and Structure," in Carruthers and Kirk, *Acts of Interpretation*, 159-72.

Derek Brewer, *English Gothic Literature* (London and Basingstoke: Macmillan, 1983), 165-70.

Stephen M. Burke, "Temporal Metaphor in *Pearl*: 'In augoste in a hyȝ seysoun,'" *FCS* 3 (1980): 41-54.

Mother Angela Carson, "Aspects of Elegy in the Middle English *Pearl*," *SP* 62 (January 1964): 17-27.

A. C. Cawley and J. J. Anderson, "Introduction" to *Pearl, Cleanness, Patience, Sir Gawain and the Green Knight* (London: J. M. Dent & Sons; New York: E. P. Dutton & Co., 1976), x-xiv.

Cherniss, *Boethian Apocalypse*, 151-68.

John Conley, "*Pearl* and a Lost Tradition," *JEGP* 54 (1955): 332-47. Reprinted in Conley, *The Middle English "Pearl,"* 50-72.

Edwin Dodge Cuffe, S. J., "An Interpretation of *Patience*, *Cleanness*, and *The Pearl* from the Viewpoint of Imagery," Ph.D. diss., University of North Carolina, 1951.

William A. Davenport, *The Art of the Gawain-Poet* (London: University of London, Athlone Press, 1978), 7-54.

William A. Davenport, "Desolation, Not Consolation: *Pearl* 19-22," *ES* 55 (October 1974): 421-23.

W. A. Davenport, "Patterns in Middle English Dialogues," in *Medieval English Studies Presented to George Kane*, ed. Edward Donald Kennedy, Ronald Waldron, and Joseph S. Wittig (Suffolk: D. S. Brewer, 1988), 140-41.

E. Talbot Donaldson, "Oysters, Forsooth: Two Readings in *Pearl*," *NM* 73 (1972): 75-82.

Morton Donner, "A Grammatical Perspective on Word Play in *Pearl*," *ChauR* 22 (1988): 322-31.

James W. Earl, "Saint Margaret and the Pearl Maiden," *MP* 70 (August 1972): 1-8.

Dorothy Everett, *Essays on Middle English Literature*, ed. Patricia Kean (Oxford: Clarendon, 1955), 85-96.

Rosalind Field, "The Heavenly Jerusalem in *Pearl*," *MLR* 81 (January 1986): 7-17.

Dorothee Metlitzki Finkelstein, "The *Pearl*-Poet as Bezalel," *MS* 35 (1973): 413-32.

John Finlayson, "*Pearl*: Landscape and Vision," *SP* 71 (July 1974): 314-43.

J. Finlayson, "*Pearl*, Petrarch's *Trionfo della Morte*, and Boccaccio's *Olympia*," *ESC* 9 (March 1983): 1-13.

John V. Fleming, "The Centuple Structure of the *Pearl*," in Levy and Szarmach, *The Alliterative Tradition*, 81-98.

J. B. Fletcher, "The Allegory of the *Pearl*," *JEGP* 20 (1921): 1-21.

Fowler, *The Bible in Middle English Literature*, 200-225.

David C. Fowler, "On the Meaning of *Pearl*, 139-40," *MLQ* 21 (March 1960), 27-29.

David C. Fowler, "*Pearl* 558: 'waning,'" *MLN* 74 (November 1959): 581-84.

Donald W. Fritz, "*The Pearl*: The Sacredness of Numbers," *ABR* 31 (September 1980): 314-34.

John Gardner, *The Complete Works of the Gawain-Poet* (Chicago and London: University of Chicago Press, 1965), 50-60.

Robert Max Garrett, "*The Pearl*: An Interpretation," *University of Washington Studies in English* 4 (1918): 1-48.

John Gatta, Jr., "Transformation, Symbolism and the Liturgy of the Mass in *Pearl*," *MP* 71 (February 1974); 243-56.

Gradon, *Form and Style*, 193-211.

W. K. Greene, "The 'Pearl' – A New Interpretation," *PMLA* 40 (1925): 814-27.

Victor Yelverton Haines, *The Fortunate Fall of Sir Gawain: The Typology of "Sir Gawain and the Green Knight"* (Washington, D.C.: University Press of America, 1982), 71-73.

Marie P. Hamilton, "The Meaning of the Middle English *Pearl*," *PMLA* 70 (1955): 805-24. Reprinted in Blanch, *"Sir Gawain" and "Pearl,"* 37-59.

Arthur R. Heiserman, "The Plot of *Pearl*," *PMLA* 80 (1965): 164-71.

Howard V. Hendrix, "Reasonable Failure: 'Pearl' Considered as a Self-Consuming Artifact of 'Gostly Porpose,'" *NM* 86 (1985): 458-66.

Constance B. Hieatt, "*Pearl* and the Dream-Vision Tradition," *SN* 37 (1965): 139-45.

Hieatt, *The Realism of Dream Visions*, 61-67.

Sister Mary Vincent Hillmann, *The Pearl: A New Translation and Interpretation* (New York: University Publishers, 1960) and *The Pearl: Mediaeval Text with a Literal Translation and Interpretation* (Rahway, N.J.: College of Saint Elizabeth Press, 1961), xi-xii.

Sister Mary Vincent Hillman, "Some Debatable Words in *Pearl* and Its Theme," *MLN* 60 (1945): 241-48. Reprinted in Conley, *The Middle English "Pearl,"* 9-17.

Stanton De Voren Hoffman, "*The Pearl*: Notes for an Interpretation," *MP* 58 (1960): 73-80. Reprinted in Conley, *The Middle English "Pearl,"* 86-102.

S. S. Hussey, "*Sir Gawain* and Romance Writing," *SN* 40 (1968): 161-74.

Lynn Staley Johnson, "The Motif of the *Noli Me Tangere* and Its Relation to *Pearl*," *ABR* 30 (March 1979): 93-106.

Johnson, *The Voice*, 144-210.

Wendell Stacy Johnson, "The Imagery and Diction of The *Pearl*: Toward an Interpretation," *ELH* 20 (1953): 161-80. Reprinted in Conley, *The Middle English "Pearl,"* 27-49.

R. E. Kaske, "Two Cruxes in 'Pearl': 596 and 609-10," *Traditio* 15 (1959): 418-28.

P. M. Kean, *The Pearl: An Interpretation* (London: Routledge & Kegan Paul, 1967).

Peter J. Lucas, "Pearl's Free-Flowing Hair," *ELN* 15 (December 1977): 94-95.

C. A. Luttrell, "The Introduction to the Dream in *Pearl*," *MÆ* 47 (1978): 274-91.

C. A. Luttrell, "*Pearl*: Symbolism in a Garden Setting," *Neophil* 49 (1965): 160-76. Reprinted in Blanch, *"Sir Gawain" and "Pearl,"* 60-85; Conley, *The Middle English "Pearl,"* 297-324.

John C. McGalliard, "Links, Language, and Style in *The Pearl*," in *Studies in Language, Literature, and Culture of the Middle Ages and Later*, ed. E. Bagby Atwood and Archibald A. Hill (Austin: University of Texas at Austin, 1969), 279-99.

O. D. Macrae-Gibson, "*Pearl*: The Link-Words and the Thematic Structure," *Neophil* 52 (1968): 54-64. Reprinted in Conley, *The Middle English "Pearl,"* 203-19.

Sister M. Madeleva, *"Pearl": A Study in Spiritual Dryness* (New York and London: D. Appleton, 1925).

C. Manes, "A Plum for the *Pearl*-Poet," *ELN* 23 (June 1986): 4-6.

James Milroy, "The Verbal Texture and the Linguistic Theme," *Neophil* 55 (April 1971): 195-208.

Charles Moorman, *The "Pearl"-Poet* (New York: Twayne, 1968), 35-63.

Charles Moorman, "The Role of the Narrator in *Pearl*," *MP* 53 (1955): 73-81. Reprinted in Conley, *The Middle English "Pearl,"* 103-21.

Daniel M. Murtaugh, "*Pearl* 462: ' þe mayster of myste,'" *Neophil* 55 (April 1971): 191-94.

Charles Muscatine, *Poetry and Crisis in the Age of Chaucer* (Notre Dame and London: University of Notre Dame Press, 1972), 45-55.

Cary Nelson, *The Incarnate Word: Literature as Verbal Space* (Urbana: University of Illinois Press, 1973), 25-49.

Jonathan Nicholls, *The Matter of Courtesy: Medieval Courtesy Books and the Gawain-Poet* (Woodbridge, Suffolk, and Dover, N.H.: D. S. Brewer, 1985), 103-11.

Barbara Nolan, *The Gothic Visionary Perspective* (Princeton, N.J.: Princeton University Press, 1977), 156-204.

Michael Olmert, "Game-Playing, Moral Purpose, and the Structure of *Pearl*," *ChauR* 21 (1987): 383-403.

Charlotte Otten, "A Note on 'Gyltes Felle' in *Pearl*," *ES* 52 (June 1971): 209-11.

Derek Pearsall, *Old English and Middle English Poetry*, Routledge History of English Poetry, Vol. 1 (London: Routledge & Kegan Paul, 1977), 172-73.

Derek Pearsall and Elizabeth Salter, *Landscapes and Seasons of the Medieval World* (London: Elek Books, 1973), 102-8.

Elizabeth Petroff, "Landscape in *Pearl*: The Transformation of Nature," *ChauR* 16 (Fall 1981): 181-93.

Heather Phillips, "The Eucharistic Allusions of *Pearl*," *MS* 47 (1985): 474-86.

Thomas A. Reisner, "The 'Cortaysye' Sequence in *Pearl*: A Legal Interpretation," *MP* 72 (May 1975): 400-403.

Thomas A. Reisner, *Expl* 31 (March 1973): 55.

D. W. Robertson, Jr., "The 'Heresy' of *The Pearl*," *MLN* 65 (1950): 152-54. Reprinted in Conley, *The Middle English "Pearl,"* 291-96.

D. W. Robertson, Jr., "The *Pearl* as a Symbol," *MLN* 65 (1950): 155-61. Reprinted in Conley, *The Middle English "Pearl,"* 18-26; Robertson, *Essays in Medieval Culture*, 209-17.

J. Stephen Russell, *The English Dream Visions: Anatomy of a Form* (Columbus: Ohio State University Press, 1988), 159-74.

J. Stephen Russell, "*Pearl's* 'Courtesy': A Critique of Eschatology," *Renascence* 35 (Spring 1983): 183-95.

George Sanderlin, "The *Gawain*-poet's Heroes – ¿Human or 'Something More Than Man'?" *LangQ* 23 (Spring-Summer 1985): 36-38.

Howard H. Schless, "*Pearl's* 'Princes Paye' and the Law," *ChauR* 24 (1989): 183-85.

W. H. Scholfield, "The Nature and Fabric of *The Pearl*," *PMLA* 19 (1904): 154-215.

W. H. Scholfield, "Symbolism, Allegory, and Autobiography in *The Pearl*," *PMLA* 24 (1909): 585-675.

Anne Howland Schotter, "The Paradox of Equality and Hierarchy of Reward in *Pearl*," *Renascence* 33 (Spring 1981): 172-79.

A. C. Spearing, *The Gawain-Poet: A Critical Study* (Cambridge: Cambridge University Press, 1969), 96-170.

Spearing, *Medieval Dream-Poetry*, 111-29.

A. C. Spearing, "*Patience* and the *Gawain*-Poet," *Anglia* 84 (1966): 322-25.

Spearing, *Readings in Medieval Poetry*, 207-15.

A. C. Spearing, "Symbolic and Dramatic Development in *Pearl*," *MP* 60 (1962): 1-12. Reprinted in Conley, *The Middle English "Pearl,"* 122-48; Blanch, *"Sir Gawain" and "Pearl,"* 98-119.

Sarah Stanbury, "Space and Visual Hermeneutics in the *Gawain*-Poet," *ChauR* 21 (1987): 480-82.

Milton R. Stern, "An Approach to *The Pearl*," *JEGP* 54 (1955): 684-92. Reprinted in Conley, *The Middle English "Pearl,"* 73-85.

John Stevens, *Medieval Romance: Themes and Approaches* (London: Hutchinson University Library, 1973), 233-35.

Nikki Stiller, "The Transformation of the Physical in the Middle English *Pearl*," *ES* 63 (October 1982); 402-9.

Sylvia Tomasch, "A *Pearl* Punnology," *JEGP* 88 (1989): 1-20.

Anna Torti, "Auenture, Cnawyng and Lote in 'Pearl,'" in *Literature in Fourteenth-Century England*, ed. Piero Boitani and Anna Torti (Cambridge: D. S. Brewer, 1983), 49-63.

Richard Tristman, "Some Consolatory Strategies in *Pearl*," in Conley, *The Middle English "Pearl,"* 272-87.

William Vantuono, "*Patience*, *Cleanness*, *Pearl*, and *Gawain*: The Case for Common Authorship," *AnM* 12 (1971): 37-69.

Edward Vasta, "*Pearl*: Immortal Flowers and the Pearl's Decay," *JEGP* 66 (1967): 519-31. Reprinted in Conley, *The Middle English "Pearl,"* 185-202.

Ann Chalmers Watts, "*Pearl*, Inexpressibility and Poems of Human Loss," *PMLA* 99 (1984): 26-40.

René Wellek, "*The Pearl*: An Interpretation of the Middle English Poem," *Studies in English by Members of the English Seminar of Charles University*, 4 (1933): 5-33. Revised in Blanch, *"Sir Gawain" and "Pearl,"* 3-36.

Hugh White, "Blood in *Pearl*," *RES*, n.s. 38 (February 1987): 5-13.

Edward Wilson, *The Gawain-Poet* (Leiden: E. J. Brill, 1976), 1-45.

Edward Wilson, "The 'Gostly Drem' in *Pearl*," *NM* 69 (1968): 90-101.

Edward Wilson, "Word Play and the Interpretation of *Pearl*," *MÆ* 40 (1971): 116-34.

Wimsatt, *Allegory and Mirror*, 122-27, 130-33.

Ann Douglas Wood, "The *Pearl*-Dreamer and the 'Hyne' in the Vineyard Parable," *PQ* 52 (January 1973): 9-19.

Sir Gawain and the Green Knight

David Aers, *Community, Gender, and Individual Identity: English Writing 1360-1430* (London and New York: Routledge, 1988), 153-78.

J. J. Anderson, "The Three Judgments and the Ethos of Chivalry in *Sir Gawain and the Green Knight*," *ChauR* 24 (1990): 337-55.

Malcolm Andrew, "The Diabolical Chapel: A Motif in *Patience* and *Sir Gawain and the Green Knight*," *Neophil* 66 (April 1982): 313-19.

Malcolm Andrew, "The Fall of Troy in *Sir Gawain and the Green Knight* and *Troilus and Criseyde*," in *The European Tragedy of Troilus*, ed. Piero Boitani (Oxford: Clarendon, 1989), 77-85, 92-93.

Ross G. Arthur, *Medieval Sign Theory and "Sir Gawain and the Green Knight"* (Toronto, Buffalo, London: University of Toronto Press, 1987), *passim*.

Ann W. Astell, "*Sir Gawain and the Green Knight*: A Study in the Rhetoric of Romance," *JEGP* 84 (April 1985): 188-202.

W. Bryant Bachman, Jr., "*Sir Gawain and the Green Knight*: The Green and the Gold Once More," *TSLL* 23 (Winter 1981): 495-516.

Sylvan Barnet, "A Note on the Structure of *Sir Gawain and the Green Knight*," *MLN* 71 (May 1956): 319.

Barron, *English Medieval Romance*, 166-73.

W. R. J. Barron, "Arthurian Romances: Traces of an English Tradition," *ES* 61 (February 1980): 17-20.

W. R. J. Barron, *Trawthe and Treason: The Sin of Gawain Reconsidered: A Thematic Study of "Sir Gawain and the Green Knight"* (Manchester: Manchester University Press, 1980).

Peter Barry, *Expl* 37 (Fall 1978): 29-30.

Robert Joyce Barton, "A Figural Reading of *Sir Gawain and the Green Knight*," Ph. D. diss., Stanford University, 1969.

Denver Ewing Baughan, "The Role of Morgan le Fay in *Sir Gawain and the Green Knight*," *ELH* 17 (1950): 241-51.

Bennett, *Middle English Literature*, 202-17.

Larry D. Benson, *Art and Tradition in "Sir Gawain and the Green Knight"* (New Brunswick, N.J.: Rutgers University Press, 1965). Pp. 158-64, 240-48 reprinted in Fox, *Twentieth Century Interpretations*, 23-34; pp. 207-18 Howard and Zacher, *Critical Studies*, 295-306.

Sacvan Bercovitch, "Romance and Anti-Romance in *Sir Gawain and the Green Knight*," *PQ* 44 (1965): 30-37. Reprinted in Howard and Zacher, *Critical Studies*, 257-66.

Sidney E. Berger, "Gawain's Departure from the *Pereginatio*," in *Proceedings of the Illinois Medieval Association*, Vol. 2, ed. Mark D. Johnston and Samuel M. Riley (Normal, Ill.: Illinois State University, 1985), 86-106.

Lawrence Besserman, "Gawain's Green Girdle," *AnM* 22 (1987): 84-100.

Lawrence Besserman, "The Idea of the Green Knight," *ELH* 53 (1986): 219-39.

Ian Bishop, "Time and Tempo in *Sir Gawain and the Green Knight*," *Neophil* 69 (October 1985): 611-19.

Robert J. Blanch, "The Game of Invoking Saints in *Sir Gawain and the Green Knight*," *ABR* 31 (June 1980): 237-62.

Robert J. Blanch, "The Legal Framework of 'A Twelmonyth and a Day' in *Sir Gawain and the Green Knight*," *NM* 84 (1983): 347-52.

Robert J. Blanch, "Religion and Law in *Sir Gawain and the Green Knight*," in *Approaches to Teaching Sir Gawain and the Green Knight*, ed. Miriam Youngerman Miller and Jane Chance (New York: Modern Language Association, 1986), 93-101.

Robert J. Blanch and Julian N. Wasserman, "Medieval Contrasts and Covenants: The Legal Coloring of *Sir Gawain and the Green Knight*," *Neophil* 68 (October 1984): 598-610.

Robert J. Blanch and Julian N. Wasserman, "To 'Overtake Your Wylle': Volition and Obligation in *Sir Gawain and the Green Knight*," *Neophil* 70 (January 1986): 119-29.

Louis Blenkner, O. S. B., "The Three Hunts and Sir Gawain's Triple Fault," *ABR* 29 (September 1978): 227-46.

Boitani, *English Medieval Narrative*, 60-70 *passim*.

Marie Borroff, "*Sir Gawain and the Green Knight*: The Passing of Judgment," in *The Passing of Arthur: New Essays in Arthurian Tradition*, ed. Christopher Baswell and William Sharpe (New York and London: Garland Publishing, 1988), 105-28.

Marie Borroff, *Sir Gawain and the Green Knight: A Stylistic and Metrical Study*, Yale Studies in English, no. 152 (New Haven and London: Yale University Press, 1962). Pp. 91-94, 100, 102-5, 110-12, 115-18, 120, 128-29 reprinted as "The Criticism of Style" in Fox, *Twentieth Century Interpretations*, 57-67.

Lois Bragg, "*Sir Gawain and the Green Knight* and the Elusion of Clarity," *NM* 86 (1985): 482-88.

Derek Brewer, *English Gothic Literature* (London and Basingstoke: Macmillan, 1983), 155-65.

Derek Brewer, "The Interpretation of Dream, Folktale, and Romance with Special Reference to *Sir Gawain and the Green Knight*," *NM* 77 (1976): 569-81.

Derek Brewer, *Symbolic Stories: Traditional Narratives of the Family Drama in English Literature* (Cambridge: D. S. Brewer; Totowa, N.J.: Rowman & Littlefield, 1980), 72-91.

J. A. Burrow, "'Cupiditas' in *Sir Gawain and the Green Knight*: A Reply to D. F. Hills," *RES*, n.s. 15 (1964), 56. Reprinted in Howard and Zacher, *Critical Studies*, 325-26.

Burrow, *Essays on Medieval Literature*, 117-31.

J. A. Burrow, *A Reading of Sir Gawain and the Green Knight* (London: Routledge & Kegan Paul, 1965). Pp. 96-104 reprinted in Fox, *Twentieth Century Interpretations*, 35-43.

J. A. Burrow, "The Two Confession Scenes in *Sir Gawain and the Green Knight*," *MP* 57 (1959): 73-79. Reprinted in Blanch, *"Sir Gawain" and "Pearl,"* 123-34.

Douglas R. Butturff, "Laughter and Discovered Aggression in *Sir Gawain and the Green Knight*," *L&P* 22 (1972): 139-49.

Mother Angela Carson, O. S. U., "The Green Chapel: Its Meaning and Its Function," *SP* 60 (1963): 598-605. Reprinted in Howard and Zacher, *Critical Studies*, 245-54.

Mother Angela Carson, O. S. U., "The Green Knight's Name," *ELN* 1 (December 1963): 84-90.

Mother Angela Carson, O. S. U., "Morgain La Fée as the Principle of Unity in 'Gawain and the Green Knight,'" *MLQ* 23 (March 1962): 3-16.

Richard Cavendish, *King Arthur and the Grail: The Arthurian Legends and Their Meaning* (London: Granada, 1978), 95-98.

Larry S. Champion, "Grace Versus Merit in *Sir Gawain and the Green Knight*," *MLQ* 28 (December 1967): 413-25.

Peter Christmas, "A Reading of *Sir Gawain and the Green Knight*," *Neophil* 58 (April 1974): 238-46.

Cecily Clark, "*Sir Gawain and the Green Knight*: Its Artistry and Its Audience," *MÆ* 40 (1971): 10-20.

S. L. Clark and Julian N. Wasserman, "The Passing of the Seasons and the Apocalyptic in *Sir Gawain and the Green Knight*," *SCRev* 3 (Spring 1986): 5-22.

Wendy Clein, *Concepts of Chivalry in "Sir Gawain and the Green Knight"* (Norman, Okla.: Pilgrim Books, 1987), 75-129.

Robert G. Cook, "The Play-Element in *Sir Gawain and the Green Knight*," *TSE* 13 (1963): 5-32.

Martin Coyle, *Expl* 42 (Spring 1984): 4-5.

John Kenny Crane, "The Four Levels of Time in *Sir Gawain and the Green Knight*," *AnM* 10 (1969): 65-80.

Michael J. Curley, "A Note on Bertilak's Beard," *MP* 73 (August 1975): 69-73.

W. A. Davenport, *The Art of the Gawain-Poet* (London: University of London, Athlone Press, 1978), 136-220.

Alfred David, "Gawain and Aeneas," *ES* 49 (October 1968): 402-9.

Christopher Dean, *Expl* 22 (April 1964): 67.

Paul Delany, "The Role of the Guide in *Sir Gawain and the Green Knight*," *Neophil* 49 (1965): 250-55. Reprinted in Howard and Zacher, *Critical Studies*, 227-35.

Morton Donner, "Tact as Criterion of Reality in *Sir Gawain and the Green Knight*," *PLL* 1 (Fall 1965): 306-15.

Mary Dove, "Gawain and the *Blasme des Femmes* Tradition," *MÆ* 41 (1972): 20-26.

Dove, *The Perfect Age,* 134-40.

Vincent A. Dunn, *Cattle-Raids and Courtships: Medieval Narrative Genres in a Traditional Context* (New York and London: Garland Publishing, 1989), 195-205.

John Eadie, "Morgain La Fée and the Conclusion of *Sir Gawain and the Green Knight,*" *Neophil* 52 (July 1968): 299-304.

John Eadie, "Sir Gawain and the Ladies of Ill-Repute," *AnM* 20 (1981): 52-66.

Joseph F. Eagan, "The Import of Color Symbolism in *Sir Gawain and the Green Knight,*" *Saint Louis University Studies*, Series A, 1 (November 1949): 11-86.

George J. Engelhardt, "The Predicament of Gawain," *MLQ* 16 (1955): 218-25.

W. O. Evans, "The Case for Sir Gawain Re-Opened," *MLR* 68 (October 1973): 721-33.

Dorothy Everett, "The Alliterative Revival," in *Essays on Middle English Literature*, ed. Patricia Kean (Oxford: Clarendon, 1955), 74-85. Reprinted in Fox, *Twentieth Century Interpretations*, 13-22.

P. J. C. Field, "A Rereading of *Sir Gawain and the Green Knight,*" *SP* 68 (July 1971): 255-69.

John Finlayson, "The Expectations of Romance in *Sir Gawain and the Green Knight,*" *Genre* 12 (Spring 1974): 1-24.

John Finlayson, "Sir Gawain, Knight of the Queen, in *Sir Gawain and the Green Knight,*" *ELN* 27 (September 1989): 7-13.

Sheila Fisher, "Leaving Morgan Aside: Women, History, and Revisionism in *Sir Gawain and the Green Knight,*" in *The Passing of Arthur: New Essays in Arthurian Tradition*, ed. Christopher Baswell and William Sharpe (New York and London: Garland Publishing, 1988), 129-51.

Michael Foley, "Gawain's Two Confessions Reconsidered," *ChauR* 9 (1974): 73-79.

Adam Freeman and Janet Thormann, "*Sir Gawain and the Green Knight*: An Anatomy of Chastity," *AI* 45 (Winter 1988): 389-410.

Albert B. Friedman, "Morgan le Fay in *Sir Gawain and the Green Knight,*" *Speculum* 35 (1960): 260-74. Reprinted in Blanch, *"Sir Gawain" and "Pearl,"* 135-58.

Maureen Fries, "The Characterization of Women in the Alliterative Tradition," in Levy and Szarmach, *The Alliterative Tradition*, 33-38.

Joseph E. Gallagher, "'Trawþe' and 'Luf-Talkyng' in *Sir Gawain and the Green Knight*," *NM* 78 (1977): 362-76.

Gerald Gallant, "The Three Beasts: Symbols of Temptation in *Sir Gawain and the Green Knight*," *AnM* 11 (1970): 35-50.

John M. Ganim, "Disorientation, Style, and Consciousness in *Sir Gawain and the Green Knight*," *PMLA* 91 (1976): 376-84.

John M. Ganim, *Style and Consciousness in Middle English Narrative* (Princeton, N.J.: Princeton University Press, 1983), 55-78.

John Gardner, *The Complete Works of the Gawain-Poet* (Chicago and London: University of Chicago Press, 1965), 70-84.

Enrico Giaccherini, "Gawain's Dream of Emancipation," in *Literature in Fourteenth-Century England*, ed. Piero Boitani and Anna Torti (Cambridge: D. S. Brewer, 1983), 65-82.

Doreen M. E. Gillan, *Expl* 45 (Fall 1986): 3-7.

William Goldhurst, "The Green and the Gold: The Major Theme of *Gawain and the Green Knight*," *CE* 20 (November 1958): 61-65.

Gradon, *Form and Style*, 131-38.

Peter Graham, "The Comedy of *Sir Gawain and the Green Knight*," *The Use of English* 30 (Summer 1979): 45-50.

D. H. Green, *Irony in the Medieval Romance* (Cambridge: Cambridge University Press, 1979), 352-57.

Richard Firth Green, "Gawain's Five Fingers," *ELN* 27 (September 1989): 14-18.

Richard Hamilton Green, "Gawain's Shield and the Quest for Perfection," *ELH* 29 (1962): 121-39. Reprinted in Blanch, *"Sir Gawain" and "Pearl,"* 176-94.

Victor Yelverton Haines, *The Fortunate Fall of Sir Gawain: The Typology of "Sir Gawain and the Green Knight"* (Washington, D.C.: University Press of America, 1982), 74-162 and *passim*.

Victor Yelverton Haines, "Morgan and the Missing Day in *Sir Gawain and the Green Knight*," *MS* 33 (1971): 354-59.

R. A. Halpern, "The Last Temptation of Gawain: 'Hony Soyt Qui Mal Pence,'" *ABR* 23 (September 1972): 353-84.

John Halverson, "Template, Criticism: *Sir Gawain and the Green Knight*," *MP* 67 (November 1969): 133-39.

Ralph Hanna, III, "Unlocking What's Locked: Gawain's Green Girdle," *Viator* 14 (1983): 289-302.

Robert W. Hanning, "Sir Gawain and the Red Herring: The Perils of Interpretation," in Carruthers and Kirk, *Acts of Interpretation*, 5-23.

Hans Häsmann, "Numerical Structure in Fitt III of *Sir Gawain and the Green Knight*," in Rowland, *Chaucer and Middle English Studies*, 131-39.

A. Kent Hieatt, "*Sir Gawain*: Pentangle, *Luf-Lace*, Numerical Structure," *PLL* 4 (Fall 1968): 339-59.

David Farley Hills, "Gawain's Fault in *Sir Gawain and the Green Knight*," *RES* 14 (1963): 124-31. Reprinted in Howard and Zacher, *Critical Studies*, 311-24.

Stephanie J. Hollis, "The Pentangle Knight: *Sir Gawain and the Green Knight*," *ChauR* 15 (1981): 267-81.

A. D. Horgan, "Gawain's *pure pentaungel* and the Virtue of Faith," *MÆ* 56 (1987): 300-316.

Donald R. Howard, "Structure and Symmetry in *Sir Gawain*," *Speculum* 39 (1964): 425-33. Reprinted in Fox, *Twentieth Century Interpretations*, 44-56; Howard and Zacher, *Critical Studies*, 159-73; Blanch, *"Sir Gawain" and "Pearl,"* 195-208.

Donald R. Howard, *The Three Temptations: Medieval Man in Search of the World* (Princeton, N.J.: Princeton University Press, 1966), 217-54.

Derek W. Hughes, "The Problem of Reality in *Sir Gawain and the Green Knight*," *UTQ* 40 (Spring 1971): 217-35.

Nicolas Jacobs, "Gawain's False Confession," *ES* 51 (October 1970): 433-35.

Johnson, *The Voice*, 37-96.

Frederick B. Jonassen, "Elements from the Traditional Drama of England in *Sir Gawain and the Green Knight*," *Viator* 17 (1986): 221-54.

Edward Trostle Jones, "The Sound of Laughter in *Sir Gawain and the Green Knight*," *MS* 31 (1969): 343-45.

Sally P. Kennedy, "Vestiges of Rule Ritual in *Sir Gawain and the Green Knight*," Ph.D. diss., University of Tennessee, 1968.

Robert L. Kindrick, "Gawain's Ethics: Shame and Guilt in *Sir Gawain and the Green Knight*," *AnM* 20 (1981): 5-32.

John F. Kiteley, "The *De Arte Honeste Amandi* of Andreas Capellanus and the Concept of Courtesy in *Sir Gawain and the Green Knight*," *Anglia* 79 (1961): 7-16.

John F. Kiteley, "'The Endless Knot': Magical Aspects of the Pentangle in *Sir Gawain and the Green Knight*," *SLitI* 4 (1971): 41-50.

Stephen Thomas Knight, "The Social Function of the Middle English Romances," in *Medieval Literature: Criticism, Ideology & History*, ed. David Aers (Brighton: Harvester Press, 1986), 115-17.

A. H. Kroppe, "Who *Was* the Green Knight?" *Speculum* 13 (1938): 206-15.

B. P. Lamba and R. Jeet, *Expl* 27 (February 1969): 47.

Roger Lass, "'Man's Heaven': The Symbolism of Gawain's Shield," *MS* 28 (1966): 354-60.

Lawrence, Seifter, and Ratner, *McGraw-Hill Guide*, 19-23.

David A. Lawton, "The Unity of Middle English Alliterative Poetry," *Speculum* 58 (1983): 89-92.

Joseph M. Lenz, *The Promised End: Romance Closure in the Gawain-poet, Malory, Spenser, and Shakespeare* (New York: Peter Lang, 1986), 31-44.

Bernard S. Levy, "Gawain's Spiritual Journey: *Imitatio Christ* in *Sir Gawain and the Green Knight*," *AnM* 6 (1965): 65-106.

John Leyerle, "The Game and Play of Hero," in *Concepts of the Hero in the Middle Ages and the Renaissance*, ed. Norman T. Burns and Christopher J. Reagen (Albany: State University of New York Press, 1975), 50-64.

Richard Lock, *Aspects of Time in Medieval Literature* (New York and London: Garland Publishing, 1985), 79-88, 206-21.

Charles Long, "Was the Green Knight Really Merlin?" *Interpretations* 7 (1975): 1-7.

Joseph A. Longo, "*Sir Gawain and the Green Knight*: The Christian Quest for Perfection," *NMS* 11 (1967): 57-85.

Claude Luttrell, "The Folk-Tale Element in *Sir Gawain and the Green Knight*," *SP* 77 (1980): 105-27. Reprinted in *Studies in Medieval English Romances: Some New Approaches*, ed. Derek Brewer (Cambridge: D. S. Brewer, 1988), 92-112.

Peter McClure, "Gawain's Mesure and the Significance of the Three Hunts in *Sir Gawain and the Green Knight*," *Neophil* 57 (October 1973): 375-87.

Stoddard Malarkey and J. Barre Toelken, "Gawain and the Green Girdle," *JEGP* 63 (1964): 14-20. Reprinted in Howard and Zacher, *Critical Studies*, 236-44.

Jill Mann, "Price and Value in *Sir Gawain and the Green Knight*," *EIC* 36 (1986): 294-318.

Stephen Manning, "A Psychological Interpretation of *Sir Gawain and the Green Knight*," *Criticism* 6 (1964): 165-77. Reprinted in Howard and Zacher, *Critical Studies*, 279-94.

Robert W. Margeson, "Structure and Meaning in *Sir Gawain and the Green Knight*," *PLL* 13 (Winter 1977): 16-24.

Alan M. Markman, "The Meaning of *Sir Gawain and the Green Knight*," *PMLA* 72 (1957): 574-86. Reprinted in Blanch, *"Sir Gawain" and "Pearl,"* 159-75.

Madeline M. Maxwell, "Ritual and Aggression in *Gawain and the Green Knight*," *LangQ* 23 (Spring-Summer 1985): 33-35.

Mehl, *The Middle English Romances*, 193-206.

Allan Metcalf, "Gawain's Number," in *Essays in Numerical Criticism of Medieval Literature*, ed. Caroline D. Eckhardt (Lewisburg, Pa.: Bucknell University Press; London: Associated University Presses, 1980), 141-55.

David Mills, "An Analysis of the Temptation Scenes in *Sir Gawain and the Green Knight*," *JEGP* 67 (October 1968): 612-30.

David Mills, "The Rhetorical Function of Gawain's Antifeminism?" *NM* 72 (1970): 635-46.

M. Mills, "Christian Significance and Romance Tradition in 'Sir Gawain and the Green Knight,'" *MLN* 60 (October 1965): 483-93.

Douglas M. Moon, "Clothing Symbolism in *Sir Gawain and the Green Knight*," *NM* 66 (1965): 334-47.

Douglas M. Moon, "The Role of Morgain la Fée in *Sir Gawain and the Green Knight*," *NM* 67 (1966): 31-57.

Charles Moorman, *A Knyght There Was: The Evolution of the Knight in Literature* (Lexington: University of Kentucky Press, 1967), 58-75.

Charles Moorman, "Myth and Mediaeval Literature: *Sir Gawain and the Green Knight*," *MS* 18 (1956): 158-72. Reprinted in Blanch, *"Sir Gawain" and "Pearl,"* 209-35.

Charles Moorman, *The "Pearl"-Poet* (New York: Twayne, 1968), 88-112.

Gerald Morgan, "The Action of the Hunting and Bedroom Scenes in *Sir Gawain and the Green Knight*," *MÆ* 56 (1987): 200-216.

Gerald Morgan, "The Significance of the Pentangle Symbolism in 'Sir Gawain and the Green Knight,'" *MLR* 74 (October 1979): 769-90.

Gerald Morgan, "The Validity of Gawain's Confession in *Sir Gawain and the Green Knight*," *RES*, n.s. 36 (February 1985): 1-18.

Charles Muscatine, *Poetry and Crisis in the Age of Chaucer* (Notre Dame and London: University of Notre Dame Press, 1972), 55-69.

Robert Neale, "*Sir Gawain and the Green Knight*," *The Use of English* 20 (Autumn 1968): 41-46.

Jonathan Nicholls, *The Matter of Courtesy: Medieval Courtesy Books and the Gawain-Poet* (Woodbridge, Suffolk, and Dover, N.H.: D. S. Brewer, 1985), 112-38.

Margaret Anne Nossel, "Christian Commitment and Romance Ideals in *Sir Gawain and the Green Knight*," Ph.D. diss., Cornell University, 1968.

Ingeborg Oppel, "The Endless Knot: An Interpretation of *Sir Gawain and the Green Knight* Through Its Myth," Ph.D. diss., University of Washington, 1960.

Walter S. Phelan, "Playboy of the Medieval World: Nationalism and Internationalism in *Sir Gawain and the Green Knight*," *LitR* 23 (Summer 1980): 542-58.

Dale B. J. Randall, "A Note on Structure in *Sir Gawain and the Green Knight*," *MLN* 72 (March 1957): 161-63.

Dale B. J. Randall, "Was the Green Knight a Fiend?" *SP* 57 (July 1960): 479-91.

Thomas L. Reed, Jr., "'Boþe Blysse and Blunder': *Sir Gawain and the Green Knight* and the Debate Tradition," *ChauR* 23 (1988): 140-61.

Paul F. Reichardt, "Gawain and the Image of the Wound," *PMLA* 99 (March 1984): 154-61.

Paul F. Reichardt, "A Note on Structural Symmetry in *Gawain and the Green Knight*," *NM* 72 (1971): 276-82.

Alain Renoir, "An Echo to the Sense: The Patterns of Sound in *Sir Gawain and the Green Knight*," *EM* 13 (1962): 9-23. Reprinted in Howard and Zacher, *Critical Studies*, 144-58.

Michael Robertson, "Stanzaic Symmetry in *Sir Gawain and the Green Knight*," *Speculum* 57 (1982): 779-85.

L. Y. Roney, *Expl* 37 (Fall 1978): 33-34.

Anne Samson, *"Sir Gawain," EIC* 18 (July 1968): 343-47.

George Sanderlin, "The *Gawain*-poet's Heroes – ¿Human or 'Something More Than Man'?" *LangQ* 23 (Spring-Summer 1985): 36-38.

Henry Lyttleton Savage, *Expl* 3 (June 1945): 58.

Henry Lyttelton Savage, *The Gawain-Poet: Studies in His Personality and Background* (Chapel Hill: University of North Carolina Press, 1956), 31-48 and *passim*.

V. J. Scattergood, "'Sir Gawain and the Green Knight' and the Sins of the Flesh," *Traditio* 37 (1981): 347-71.

A. V. C. Schmidt, "'Latent Content' and 'The Testimony in the Text': Symbolic Meaning in *Sir Gawain and the Green Knight*," *RES*, n.s. 38 (May 1987): 145-68.

Hans Schnyder, "Aspects of Kingship in *Sir Gawain and the Green Knight*," *ES* 60 (1959): 289-94.

Hans Schnyder, *Sir Gawain and the Green Knight: An Essay in Interpretation*, The Cooper Monographs on English and American Literature, no. 6, ed. H. Lüdeke (Bern: A. Franke Verlag, 1961).

Gordon M. Shedd, "Knight in Tarnished Armour: The Meaning of 'Sir Gawain and the Green Knight,'" *MLR* 62 (January 1967): 3-13.

Martin B. Shichtman, "*Sir Gawain and the Green Knight*: A Lesson in the Terror of History," *PLL* 22 (Winter 1986): 3-15.

R. A. Shoaf, *The Poem as Green Girdle: "Commercium" in "Sir Gawain and the Green Knight,"* Humanities Monographs (Gainesville: University Presses of Florida, 1984), *passim*.

Theodore Silverstein, "The Art of *Sir Gawain and the Green Knight*," *UTQ* 33 (April 1964): 258-78.

Theodore Silverstein, "*Sir Gawain*, Dear Brutus, and Britain's Fortunate Founding: A Study in Comedy and Convention," *MP* 62 (February 1965): 189-206.

G. V. Smithers, "What *Sir Gawain and the Green Knight* Is About," *MÆ* 32 (1963): 171-89.

Jan Solomon, "The Lesson of *Sir Gawain*," *Papers of the Michigan Academy of Science, Arts, and Letters* 48 (1963): 599-608. Reprinted in Howard and Zacher, *Critical Studies*, 267-78.

A. Francis Soucy, "Gawain's Fault 'Angardez Pryde,'" *ChauR* 13 (1978): 166-76.

A. C. Spearing, "Central and Displaced Sovereignty in Three Medieval Poems," *RES*, n.s. 33 (August 1982): 257-61.

A. C. Spearing, *Criticism and Medieval Poetry* (London: Arnold; New York: Barnes & Noble, 1964), 38-45. Reprinted in Howard and Zacher, *Critical Studies*, 174-81.

A. C. Spearing, *The Gawain-Poet: A Critical Study* (Cambridge: Cambridge University Press, 1969), 171-236.

A. C. Spearing, "Patience and the *Gawain*-Poet," *Anglia* 84 (1966): 325-29. Reprinted in Fox, *Twentieth Century Interpretations*, 101-5.

Spearing, *Readings in Medieval Poetry*, 196-207.

Speirs, *Medieval English Poetry*, 215-51.

John Speirs, *"Sir Gawain and the Green Knight," Scrutiny* 16 (1949): 274-90. Reprinted in Fox, *Twentieth Century Interpretations*, 79-94.

Ralph J. Spendal, "The Fifth Pentad in 'Sir Gawain and the Green Knight,'" *N&Q* 23 (April 1976): 147-48.

Martin Stevens, "Laughter and Game in *Sir Gawain and the Green Knight*," *Speculum* 47 (1972): 65-78.

Ronald Tamplin, "The Saints in *Sir Gawain and the Green Knight*," *Speculum* 44 (1969): 403-20.

Paul B. Taylor, "'Blysse and blunder,' Nature and Ritual in *Sir Gawain and the Green Knight*," *ES* 50 (April 1969): 165-75.

Paul B. Taylor, "Commerce and Comedy in *Sir Gawain*," *PQ* 50 (January 1971): 1-15.

Paul B. Taylor, "Gawain's Garland of Girdle and Name," *ES* 55 (February 1974): 6-14.

J. R. R. Tolkien, *"The Monsters and the Critics" and Other Essays*, ed. Christopher Tolkien (London: George Allen & Unwin, 1983), 72-108.

Richard M. Trask, "Sir Gawain's Unhappy Fault," *SSF* 16 (Winter 1979): 1-9.

Philippa Tristram, *Figures of Life and Death in Medieval English Literature* (London: Paul Elek, 1976), 28-34 and *passim*.

Carolynn Van Dyke, "The Errors of Good Men: *Hamartia* in Two Middle English Poems," in *Hamartia: The Concept of Error in the Western Tradition, Essays in Honor of John M. Crossett*, ed. Donald V. Stump, James A. Arieti, Lloyd Gerson, and Eleonore Stump, Text and Studies in Religion, no. 16 (New York and Toronto: Edwin Mellen Press, 1983), 171-91.

William Vantuono, "*Patience*, *Cleanness*, *Pearl*, and *Gawain*: The Case for Common Authorship," *AnM* 12 (1971): 37-69.

Sidney Wade, "An Analysis of the Similes and Their Function in the Characterization of the Green Knight," *NM* 87 (1986): 375-81.

R. A. Waldron, "Introduction" to *Sir Gawain and the Green Knight* (Evanston, Ill.: Northwestern University Press, 1970), 1-25.

Elizabeth Porges Watson, "The Arming of Gawain: *Vrysoun* and *Cercle*," *LeedsSE*, n.s. 18 (1987): 31-41.

Victoria L. Weiss, "Gawain's First Failure: The Beheading Scene in *Sir Gawain and the Green Knight*," *ChauR* 10 (Spring 1976): 361-66.

Victoria L. Weiss, "The Medieval Knighting Ceremony in *Sir Gawain and the Green Knight*," *ChauR* 12 (Winter 1978): 183-89.

Hugh White, "Blood in *Pearl*," *RES*, n.s. 38 (February 1987): 2-5.

Robert B. White, Jr., "A Note on the Green Knight's Red Eyes," *ELN* 2 (1965): 250-52. Reprinted in Howard and Zacher, *Critical Studies*, 223-26.

Gregory J. Wilkin, "The Dissolution of the Templar Ideal in *Sir Gawain and the Green Knight*," *ES* 63 (April 1982): 109-21.

Anne Wilson, *Traditional Romance and Tale: How Stories Mean* (Cambridge and Ipswich: D. S. Brewer, 1976), 80-82, 96-108.

Wimsatt, *Allegory and Mirror*, 194-95, 198-202.

Hanneke Wirtjes, "Bertilak De Hautdesert and the Literary Vavasour," *ES* 65 (August 1984): 291-301.

Thomas L. Wright, "*Luf-Talking* in *Sir Gawain and the Green Knight*," in *Approaches to Teaching Sir Gawain and the Green Knight*, ed. Miriam Youngerman Miller and Jane Chance (New York: Modern Language Association, 1986), 79-86.

Christopher Wrigley, "*Sir Gawain and the Green Knight*: The Underlying Myth," in *Studies in Medieval English Romances: Some New Approaches*, ed. Derek Brewer (Cambridge: D. S. Brewer, 1988), 113-28.

ROLLE, RICHARD

"Jhesu, God Sonn"

Rogers, *Image and Abstraction*, 70-81.

"Luf Es Lyf þat Lastes Ay"

Woolf, *The English Religious Lyric*, 169-72.

RYMAN, JACOB

"O Cruell Deth Paynfull and Smert"

Woolf, *The English Religious Lyric*, 341-42.

RYMAN, JAMES

"Amende We Vs, While We Haue Space"

David L. Jeffrey, *The Early English Lyric & Franciscan Spirituality* (Lincoln: University of Nebraska Press, 1975), 255-57.

SKELTON, JOHN

"Against Venemous Tongues"

Kinney, *John Skelton*, 124-30.

"The Auncient Acquaintance, Madam"

Fish, *John Skelton's Poetry*, 46-49.

Bernard Sharratt, "John Skelton: Finding a Voice – Notes After Bakhtin," in Aers, *Medieval Literature*, 200-201.

Boke of Phyllyp Sparowe

F. W. Brownlow, "*The Boke of Phyllyp Sparowe* and the Liturgy," *ELR* 9 (Winter 1979): 5-20.

Carpenter, *John Skelton*, 59-66.

Ebin, *Illuminator, Makar, Vates*, 167-72.

H. L. R. Edwards, *Skelton: The Life and Times of an Early Tudor Poet* (London: Jonathan Cape, 1949), 107-11.

Fish, *John Skelton's Poetry*, 98-125.

Kinney, *John Skelton*, 98-116.

R. S. Kinsman, "Phyllyp Sparowe: *Titulus*," *SP* 47 (1950): 473-84.

Susan Schibanoff, "Taking Jane's Cue: *Phyllyp Sparowe* as a Primer for Women Readers," *PMLA* 101 (1986): 832-47.

Bernard Sharratt, "John Skelton: Finding a Voice – Notes After Bakhtin," in Aers, *Medieval Literature*, 205-9.

J. Swart, "John Skelton's *Philip Sparrow*," *ES* 45 (1964): 161-64.

The Bowge of Court

Carpenter, *John Skelton*, 47-50.

Ebin, *Illuminator, Makar, Vates*, 166-67.

Fish, *John Skelton's Poetry*, 54-81.

Heiserman, *Skelton and Satire*, 14-28.

Kinney, *John Skelton*, 3-15.

Stanley J. Kozikowski, "Allegorical Meanings in Skelton's *The Bowge of Court*," *PQ* 61 (Summer 1982): 305-15.

Judith Sweitzer Larson, "What Is *The Bowge of Courte*?" *JEGP* 61 (1962): 288-95.

Leonard, *Laughter in the Courts of Love*, 88-96.

Paul D. Psilos, "'Dulle' Drede and the Limits of Prudential Knowledge in Skelton's *Bowge of Courte*," *JMRS* 6 (Fall 1976): 297-317.

Bernard Sharratt, "John Skelton: Finding a Voice – Notes after Bakhtin," in Aers, *Medieval Literature*, 197-200.

Spearing, *Medieval Dream-Poetry*, 197-202, 261-65.

Collyn Clout

Carpenter, *John Skelton*, 89-93.

H. L. R. Edwards, *Skelton: The Life and Times of an Early Tudor Poet* (London: Jonathan Cape, 1949), 210-19.

Fish, *John Skelton's Poetry*, 176-205.

Heiserman, *Skelton and Satire*, 192-208, 239-41.

Kinney, *John Skelton*, 139-49.

Lawrence, Seifter, and Ratner, *McGraw-Hill Guide*, 72-74.

P. E. McLane, "Prince Lucifer and the Fitful 'Lanternes of Lyght': Wolsey and the Bishops in Skelton's *Colyn Cloute*," *HLQ* 43 (Summer 1980): 159-79.

William Nelson, *John Skelton, Laureate* (New York: Columbia University Press, 1939), 192-96.

Bernard Sharratt, "John Skelton: Finding a Voice–Notes after Bakhtin," in Aers, *Medieval Literature*, 212-13.

Spearing, *Medieval to Renaissance*, 230-33.

"Epitaphes of Two Knaves at Diss"

Kinney, *John Skelton*, 95-98.

Garlande of Laurell

Carpenter, *John Skelton*, 102-7.

Ebin, *Illuminator, Makar, Vates*, 182-87.

H. L. R. Edwards, *Skelton: The Life and Times of an Early Tudor Poet* (London: Jonathan Cape, 1949), 227-40 *passim*.

Fish, *John Skelton's Poetry*, 225-39.

David A. Loewenstein, "Skelton's Triumph: The *Garland of Laurel* and Literary Fame," *Neophil* 68 (October 1984): 611-22.

Spearing, *Medieval Dream-Poetry*, 211-18.

Leigh Winser, "'The Garlande of Laurell': Masque Spectacular," *Criticism* 19 (Winter 1977): 51-69.

"Knolege, Aquayntance, Resort"

Fish, *John Skelton's Poetry*, 19-23.

"Lullay, Lullay"

Fish, *John Skelton's Poetry*, 49-53.

Frankenberg, *Invitation to Poetry*, 151-52.

"Manerly Margery Mylk and Ale"

Fish, *John Skelton's Poetry*, 42-46.

David V. Harrington, *Expl* 25 (January 1967): 42.

"A Replycacion"

Kinney, *John Skelton*, 197-204.

Speke Parott

F. W. Brownlow, "The Boke Compiled by Maister Skelton, Poet Laureate, Called *Speake Parrot*," *ELR* 1 (Winter 1971): 3-26.

Carpenter, *John Skelton*, 83-89.

Ebin, *Illuminator, Makar, Vates*, 175-80.

H. L. R. Edwards, *Skelton: The Life and Times of an Early Tudor Poet* (London: Jonathan Cape, 1949), 184-93.

Fish, *John Skelton's Poetry*, 135-76.

Heiserman, *Skelton and Satire*, 126-68.

Kinney, *John Skelton*, 15-30.

David Lawton, "Skelton's Use of *Persona*," *EIC* 30 (January 1980): 19-27.

William Nelson, *John Skelton, Laureate* (New York: Columbia University Press, 1939), 158-84.

William Nelson, "Skelton's 'Speak, Parrot,'" *PMLA* 51 (1936): 59-82.

John Richardson, "Generational Conflict in John Skelton's *Speke Parott*," *Neophil* 74 (July 1990): 444-52.

Bernard Sharratt, "John Skelton: Finding a Voice – Notes after Bakhtin," in Aers, *Medieval Literature*, 209-12.

Spearing, *Medieval to Renaissance*, 265-77.

Greg Walker, *John Skelton and the Politics of the 1520s* (Cambridge: Cambridge University Press, 1988), 60-100 *passim*.

Nathaniel O. Wallace, "The Responsibilities of Madness: John Skelton, 'Speke, Parrot,' and Homeopathetic Satire," *SP* 82 (Winter 1985): 60-80.

The Tunnyng of Elynour Rummyng

Kinney, *John Skelton*, 167-87.

Deborah Baker Wyrick, "Withinne That Develes Temple: An Examination of Skelton's *The Tunnyng of Elynour Rummyng*," *JMRS* 10 (Fall 1980): 239-54.

"Uppon a Deedmans Hed"

Kinney, *John Skelton*, 79-81.

Ware the Hauke

Fish, *John Skelton's Poetry*, 88-98.

David Lawton, "Skelton's Use of *Persona*," *EIC* 30 (January 1980): 13-16.

Kinney, *John Skelton*, 83-94.

John Scattergood, "Skelton and Traditional Satire: *Ware the Hauke*," *MÆ* 55 (1986): 203-16.

Bernard Sharratt, "John Skelton: Finding a Voice – Notes after Bakhtin," in Aers, *Medieval Literature*, 203-5.

Janet Wilson, "Skelton's *Ware the Hauke* and the 'Circumstances' of Sin," *MÆ* 58 (1989): 243-57.

Why Come Ye Nat to Courte?

Carpenter, *John Skelton*, 97-102.

Fish, *John Skelton's Poetry*, 207-25.

Heiserman, *Skelton and Satire*, 262-71.

Kinney, *John Skelton*, 151-67.

"Womanhod, Wanton, Ye Want"

Fish, *John Skelton's Poetry*, 40-42.

THOMAS OF HALES

"A Luve Ron"

Ian Bishop, "Lapidary Formulas as Topics of Invention – From Thomas of Hales to Henryson," *RES*, n.s. 37 (November 1986): 469-77.

Fowler, *The Bible in Middle English Literature*, 73-74.

Manning, *Wisdom and Number*, 122-24.

Rogers, *Image and Abstraction*, 28-40.

Swanton, *English Literature*, 24.

ST. GODRIC

"Crist and Sainte Marie"

Dronke, *The Medieval Lyric*, 63-64.

Main Sources Consulted

Books listed as main sources are those in which we have found numerous explications – usually five or more. Citations for books with fewer explications are included with full publication information in the Checklist itself. Periodicals listed as main sources are those that frequently publish explications of Old English or Medieval poetry. For a complete list of periodicals cited, see the list of periodical abbreviations on pages xi-xix.

ABAD, GEMINO H. *A Formal Approach to Lyric Poetry*. Quezon City, Philippines: University of the Philippines Press, 1978.

ADAMS, ROBERT M. *Strains of Discord: Studies in Literary Openness*. Ithaca, N.Y.: Cornell University Press, 1958.

AERS, DAVID. *Chaucer*. Brighton, Sussex: Harvester Press, 1986.

_____, ed. *Medieval Literature: Criticism, Ideology & History*. Brighton, Sussex: Harvester Press, 1986.

ALBRIGHT, DANIEL. *Lyricality in English Literature*. Lincoln and London: University of Nebraska Press, 1985.

American Benedictine Review 16 (1965)-41, no. 1 (March 1990).

ANDERSON, JAMES E. *Two Literary Riddles in the Exeter Book: Riddle 1 and "The Easter Riddle," A Critical Edition with Full Translations*. Norman and London: University of Oklahoma Press, 1986.

Anglo-Saxon England 1 (1972)-18 (1989).

ARRATHOON, LEIGH A., ed. *Chaucer and the Craft of Fiction*. Rochester, Mich.: Solaris Press, 1986.

BARNEY, STEPHEN A., ed. *Chaucer's "Troilus": Essays in Criticism*. Hamden, Conn.: Archon Books, 1980.

BARRON, W. R. J. *English Medieval Romance*. London and New York: Longman, 1987.

BATESON, F. W. *English Poetry: A Critical Introduction*. London and New York: Longmans, Green, 1950.

BEATY, JEROME, and WILLIAM H. MATCHETT. *Poetry: From Statement to Meaning*. New York: Oxford University Press, 1965.

BEIDLER, PETER G., ed. *John Gower's Literary Transformations in the "Confessio Amantis": Original Articles and Translations*. Washington, D.C.: University Press of America, 1982.

BENNETT, J. A. W. *Middle English Literature*. Oxford: Clarendon, 1986.

BENSON, LARRY D., ed. *The Learned and the Lewed: Studies in Chaucer and Medieval Literature*. Harvard English Studies, no. 5. Cambridge, Mass.: Harvard University Press, 1974.

BENSON, LARRY D., and SIEGFRIED WENZEL, eds. *The Wisdom of Poetry: Essays in Early English Literature in Honor of Morton W. Bloomfield*. Kalamazoo, Mich.: Medieval Institute Publications, 1982.

BESSINGER, JESS B., Jr., and STANLEY J. KAHRL, eds. *Essential Articles for the Study of Old English Poetry*. Hamden, Conn.: Archon Books, 1968.

BISHOP, IAN. *The Narrative Art of the "Canterbury Tales": A Critical Study of the Major Poems*. London and Melbourne: Everyman's Library, 1988.

BLANCH, ROBERT J., ed. *"Sir Gawain" and "Pearl": Critical Essays*. Bloomington and London: Indiana University Press, 1966.

_____. *Style and Symbolism in "Piers Plowman": A Modern Critical Anthology*. Knoxville: University of Tennessee Press, 1969.

BOITANI, PIERO. *English Medieval Narrative in the Thirteenth and Fourteenth Centuries*. Translated by Joan Krakover Hall. Cambridge: Cambridge University Press, 1982.

BOITANI, PIERO, and JILL MANN, eds. *The Cambridge Chaucer Companion*. Cambridge: Cambridge University Press, 1986.

BREWER, DEREK. *An Introduction to Chaucer*. London and New York: Longman, 1984.

BRIDGES, MARGARET ENID. *Generic Contrast in Old English Hagiographical Poetry*, Anglistica, no. 22. Copenhagen: Rosenkilde and Bagger, 1984.

BROOKS, CLEANTH, Jr., JOHN THIBAUT PURSER, and ROBERT PENN WARREN. *An Approach to Literature*. Rev. ed. New York: F. S. Crofts & Co., 1942. 3d ed., 1952. 4th ed., 1964.

BROOKS, CLEANTH, Jr., and ROBERT PENN WARREN. *Understanding Poetry: An Anthology for College Students*. New York: Henry Holt & Co., 1938. Rev. ed., 1950. 4th ed., 1964.

BROWN, PHYLLIS RUGG, GEORGIA RONAN CRAMPTON, and FRED C. ROBINSON, eds. *Modes of Interpretation in Old English Literature: Essays in Honour of Stanley B. Greenfield*. Toronto: University of Toronto Press, 1986.

BURLIN, ROBERT B. *Chaucerian Fiction*. Princeton, N.J.: Princeton University Press, 1977.

BURLIN, ROBERT B., and EDWARD B. IRVING, Jr., eds. *Old English Studies in Honour of John C. Pope*. Toronto: University of Toronto Press, 1974.

BURROW, J. A. *Essays on Medieval Literature*. Oxford: Clarendon, 1984.

The Cambridge Quarterly 1 (1965)-18 (1989).

CARPENTER, NAN COOKE. *John Skelton*. New York: Twayne, 1967.

CARRUTHERS, MARY J., and ELIZABETH D. KIRK, eds. *Acts of Interpretation: The Text in Its Contexts, 700-1600: Essays on Medieval and Renaissance Literature*. Norman, Okla.: Pilgrim Books, 1982.

The CEA Critic 1 (1939)-52 (1989).

CHANCE, JANE. *Woman as Hero in Old English Literature*. Syracuse, N.Y.: Syracuse University Press, 1986.

The Chaucer Review 1 (1966)-24, no. 4 (1990).

CHERNISS, MICHAEL D. *Boethian Apocalypse: Studies in Middle English Vision Poetry*. Norman, Okla.: Pilgrim Books, 1987.

_____. *Ingeld and Christ: Heroic Concepts and Values in Old English Christian Poetry*. The Hague and Paris: Mouton, 1972.

CIARDI, JOHN. *How Does a Poem Mean?* Boston: Houghton Mifflin, 1959.

CONLEY, JOHN, ed. *The Middle English "Pearl": Critical Essays*. Notre Dame and London: University of Notre Dame Press, 1970.

CORSA, HELEN STORM. *Chaucer: Poet of Mirth and Morality*. Notre Dame, Ind.: University of Notre Dame Press, 1964.

CRAIK, T. W. *The Comic Tales of Chaucer*. New York: Barnes & Noble, 1964.

Critical Quarterly 1 (1959)-31 (1989).

Criticism: A Quarterly for Literature and the Arts 1 (1959)-31 (1989).

CROSSLEY-HOLLAND, KEVIN, trans., and BRUCE MITCHELL, ed. *The Battle of Maldon and Other Old English Poems*. London and Basingstoke: Macmillan; New York: St. Martin's Press, 1965.

DAICHES, DAVID. *A Study of Literature for Readers and Critics*. Ithaca, N.Y.: Cornell University Press, 1948.

DANIELS, EARL. *The Art of Reading Poetry*. New York: Farrar & Rinehart, 1941.

DAVENPORT, W. A. *Chaucer: Complaint and Narrative*. Cambridge: D. S. Brewer, 1988.

DAVID, ALFRED. *The Strumpet Muse: Art and Morals in Chaucer's Poetry*. Bloomington and London: Indiana University Press, 1976.

DAVIDOFF, JUDITH M. *Beginning Well: Framing Fictions in Late Middle English Poetry*. Rutherford, N.J.: Fairleigh Dickinson University Press; London and Toronto: Associated University Presses, 1988.

DONALDSON, E. TALBOT. *Speaking of Chaucer*. Durham, N.C.: Labyrinth Press, 1983.

DOVE, MARY. *The Perfect Age of Man's Life*. Cambridge: Cambridge University Press, 1986.

DREW, ELIZABETH. *Poetry: A Modern Guide to Its Understanding and Enjoyment*. New York: W. W. Norton & Co., 1959.

DRONKE, PETER. *The Medieval Lyric*. London: Hutchinson University Library, 1968.

EBIN, LOIS A. *Illuminator, Makar, Vates: Visions of Poetry in the Fifteenth Century*. Lincoln and London: University of Nebraska Press, 1988.

ELH: A Journal of English Literary History 1 (1934)-56, no. 1 (1990).

English 1 (1936)-38 (Autumn 1989).

English Language Notes 1 (1963)-28 (September 1990).

Essays and Studies by Members of the English Association 11 (1925)-33 (1947); n.s. 3 (1950)-42 (1989).

Essays in Criticism 1 (1951)-40 (January 1990).

Essays in Literature (Western Illinois University) 1 (1974)-17 (Spring 1990).

The Explicator 1 (1942)-48 (Summer 1990).

The Explicator Cyclopedia. Vol. 2, edited by Charles Child Walcutt and J. Edwin Whitesell. Chicago: Quadrangle Books, 1968.

FAULKNER, DEWEY R., ed. *Twentieth Century Interpretations of "The Pardoner's Tale": A Collection of Critical Essays*. Englewood Cliffs, N.J.: Prentice-Hall, 1973.

FISH, STANLEY EUGENE. *John Skelton's Poetry*. New Haven, Conn.: Yale University Press, 1965.

FOWLER, DAVID C. *The Bible in Middle English Literature*. Seattle: University of Washington Press, 1984.

FOX, DENTON, ed. *Twentieth Century Interpretations of Sir Gawain and the Green Knight*. Englewood Cliffs, N.J.: Prentice-Hall, 1968.

FRANKENBERG, LLOYD. *Invitation to Poetry*. New York: Doubleday & Co., 1956.

FRY, DONALD K., ed. *The Beowulf Poet: A Collection of Critical Essays*. Englewood Cliffs, N.J.: Prentice-Hall, 1968.

FYLER, JOHN M. *Chaucer and Ovid*. New Haven and London: Yale University Press, 1979.

GARDNER, JOHN. *The Construction of Christian Poetry in Old English*. Carbondale: Southern Illinois University Press, 1975.

_____. *The Poetry of Chaucer.* Carbondale and Edwardsville: Southern Illinois University Press; London and Amsterdam: Fetter & Simons, 1977.

Genre 1 (1968)-22 (1989).

GÖLLER, KARL HEINZ, ed. *The Alliterative Morte Arthure: A Reassessment of the Poem*. Cambridge: D. S. Brewer, 1981.

GORDEN, EDWARD J., and EDWARD S. NOYES. *Essays on the Teaching of English: Reports of the Yale Conference on the Teaching of English*. New York: Appleton-Century-Crofts, 1960.

GRADON, PAMELA. *Form and Style in Early English Literature*. London: Methuen, 1971.

GRAY, DOUGLAS. *Themes and Images in the Medieval English Religious Lyric*. London and Boston: Routledge & Kegan Paul, 1972.

GREEN, MARTIN, ed. *The Old English Elegies: New Essays in Criticism and Research*. Rutherford, N.J.: Fairleigh Dickinson University Press, 1983.

GREENFIELD, STANLEY B. *A Critical History of Old English Literature*. New York: New York University Press, 1965.

____. *Hero and Exile: The Art of Old English Poetry*. London and Ronceverte: Hambledon Press, 1989.

GREENFIELD, STANLEY, B., and DANIEL G. CALDER. *A New Critical History of Old English Literature*. New York and London: New York University Press, 1986.

GREENFIELD, STANLEY B., and A. KINGSLEY WEATHERHEAD, eds. *The Poem: An Anthology*. New York: Appleton-Century-Crofts, 1968.

GWYNN, FREDERICK L., RALPH W. CONDEE, and ARTHUR O. LEWIS. *The Case for Poetry*. Englewood Cliffs, N.J.: Prentice-Hall, 1954.

HANSEN, ELAINE TUTTLE. *The Solomon Complex: Reading Wisdom in Old English Poetry*. Toronto, Buffalo, and London: University of Toronto Press, 1988.

HARDY, JOHN EDWARD. *The Curious Frame: Seven Poems in Text and Context*. Notre Dame, Ind.: University of Notre Dame Press, 1962.

HEISERMAN, A. R. *Skelton and Satire*. Chicago: University of Chicago Press; Toronto: University of Toronto Press, 1961.

HERMANN, JOHN P. *Allegories of War: Language and Violence in Old English Poetry*. Ann Arbor: University of Michigan Press, 1989.

HERMANN, JOHN P., and JOHN J. BURKE, Jr., eds. *Signs and Symbols in Chaucer's Poetry*. University: University of Alabama Press, 1981.

HIEATT, CONSTANCE B. *The Realism of Dream Visions: The Poetic Exploitation of the Dream-Experience in Chaucer and His Contemporaries*. The Hague and Paris: Mouton, 1967.

HORNSBY, JOSEPH ALLEN. *Chaucer and the Law*. Norman, Okla.: Pilgrim Books, 1988.

HOWARD, DONALD R., and CHRISTIAN ZACHER, eds. *Critical Studies of "Sir Gawain and the Green Knight."* Notre Dame and London: University of Notre Dame Press, 1968.

HUPPÉ, BERNARD F. *Doctrine and Poetry: Augustine's Influence on Old English Poetry*. New York: State University of New York Press, 1959.

_____. *A Reading of the "Canterbury Tales."* Albany: State University of New York Press, 1964.

_____. *The Web of Words: Structural Analyses of Four Old English Poems*. Albany: State University of New York Press, 1970.

HUSSEY, S. S. *Chaucer: An Introduction*, 2d ed. London and New York: Methuen, 1981.

_____, ed. *Piers Plowman: Critical Approaches*. London: Methuen, 1969.

ISAACS, NEIL D. *Structural Principles in Old English Poetry*. Knoxville: University of Tennessee Press, 1968.

JOHNSON, LYNN STALEY. *The Voice of the "Gawain"-Poet*. Madison: University of Wisconsin Press, 1984.

JORDAN, ROBERT M. *Chaucer and the Shape of Creation: The Aesthetic Possibilities of Inorganic Structure*. Cambridge, Mass.: Harvard University Press, 1967.

Journal of English and Germanic Philology 24 (1925)-89, no. 3 (1990).

Journal of Medieval and Renaissance Studies 1 (1971)-19 (1989).

Journal of Narrative Technique 3 (1973)-20, no. 1 (Winter 1990).

KEAN, PATRICIA MARGARET. *The Art of Narrative.* Vol. 2 of *Chaucer and the Making of English Poetry*. London and Boston: Routledge & Kegan Paul, 1972.

_____. *Love Division and Debate*. Vol. 1 of *Chaucer and the Making of English Poetry*. London and Boston: Routledge & Kegan Paul, 1972.

KENNEDY, CHARLES W. *The Earliest English Poetry: A Critical Survey*. London: Oxford University Press, 1943.

KINNEY, ARTHUR K. *John Skelton: Priest as Poet*. Chapel Hill and London: University of North Carolina Press, 1987.

KNIGHT, STEPHEN THOMAS. *The Poetry of the Canterbury Tales*. Sydney: Angus and Robertson, 1973.

KOFF, LEONARD MICHAEL. *Chaucer and the Art of Storytelling*. Berkeley: University of California Press, 1988.

KOLVE, V. A. *Chaucer and the Imagery of Narrative: The First Five Canterbury Tales*. Stanford, Calif.: Stanford University Press, 1984.

LAWRENCE, KAREN, BETSEY SEIFTER, and LOIS RATNER. *The McGraw-Hill Guide to English Literature*, Vol. 1. New York: McGraw-Hill, 1985.

LEE, ALVIN A. *The Guest-Hall of Eden: Four Essays on the Design of Old English Poetry*. New Haven and London: Yale University Press, 1972.

LEONARD, FRANCES McNEELY. *Laughter in the Courts of Love: Comedy in Allegory from Chaucer to Spenser*. Norman, Okla.: Pilgrim Books, 1981.

LEVY, BERNARD S., and PAUL E. SZARMACH, eds. *The Alliterative Tradition in the Fourteenth Century*. Kent, Ohio: Kent State University Press, 1981.

LOCKE, LOUIS G., WILLIAM M. GIBSON, and GEORGE ARMS. *Introduction to Literature*. 3d ed. New York: Rinehart & Co., 1957. 4th ed., 1962. 5th ed., 1967.

LOCKE, LOUIS G., WILLIAM M. GIBSON, and GEORGE ARMS, eds. *Readings for Liberal Education*. New York: Rinehart & Co., 1948.

LUMIANSKY, R. M. *Of Sondry Folk: The Dramatic Principle in the Canterbury Tales*. Austin: University of Texas Press, 1955.

McCALL, John P. *Chaucer among the Gods: The Poetics of Classical Myth*. University Park and London: Pennsylvania State University Press, 1979.

MACK, MAYNARD, and GEORGE DE FOREST LORD, eds. *Poetic Traditions of the English Renaissance*. New Haven and London: Yale University Press, 1982.

MacQUEEN, JOHN. *Robert Henryson: A Study of the Major Narrative Poems*. Oxford: Clarendon, 1967.

MAKAREWICZ, SISTER MARY RAYNELDA. *The Patristic Influence on Chaucer*. Washington, D.C.: Catholic University of America Press, 1953.

MANDEL, JEROME. *Alternative Readings in Old English Poetry*. New York: Peter Lang, 1987.

MANNING, STEPHEN. *Wisdom and Number: Toward a Critical Appraisal of the Middle English Lyric*. Lincoln: University of Nebraska Press, 1962.

Medievalia et Humanistica n.s. 1 (1970)-n.s. 15 (1987).

Mediaeval Studies 1 (1939)-52 (1990).

Medium Ævum 1-2 (1932-33)-58 (1989).

MEHL, DIETER. *Geoffrey Chaucer: An Introduction to His Narrative Poetry*. Cambridge: Cambridge University Press, 1986.

____. *The Middle English Romances of the Thirteenth and Fourteenth Centuries*. New York: Barnes & Noble, 1969.

MINNIS, ALASTAIR, J., ed. *Gower's "Confessio Amantis": Responses and Reassessments*. Cambridge: D. S. Brewer, 1983.

MITCHELL, JEROME, and WILLIAM PROVOST, eds. *Chaucer the Love Poet*. Athens: University of Georgia Press, 1973.

Modern Language Notes 40 (1925)-104 (1989).

Modern Language Quarterly 1 (1940)-49 (1988).

Modern Philology 22 (1924)-88, no. 1 (August 1990).

MOGAN, JOSEPH J., Jr. *Chaucer and the Theme of Mutability*. The Hague and Paris: Mouton, 1969.

MOORE, ARTHUR K. *The Secular Lyric in Middle English*. Lexington: University of Kentucky Press, 1951.

Neuphilologische Mitteilungen 51 (1950)-91 (1990).

Neophilologus 1-2 (1916-17)-74, no. 3 (1990).

NICHOLSON, LEWIS E., ed. *An Anthology of Beowulf Criticism*. Notre Dame, Ind.: Notre Dame University Press, 1963. Reprint. Freeport, N.Y.: Books for Libraries Press, 1972.

NICHOLSON, LEWIS E., and DOLORES WARWICK FRESE, eds. *Anglo-Saxon Poetry: Essays in Appreciation, for John C. McGalliard*. Notre Dame, Ind.: Notre Dame University Press, 1975.

NORTH, J. D. *Chaucer's Universe*. Oxford: Clarendon, 1988.

NORTON-SMITH, JOHN. *Geoffrey Chaucer*. London and Boston: Routledge & Kegan Paul, 1974.

OLIVER, RAYMOND. *Poems without Names: The English Lyric, 1200-1500*. Berkeley: University of California Press, 1970.

OWEN, CHARLES A., Jr., *Pilgrimage and Storytelling in the Canterbury Tales: The Dialectic of "Earnest" and "Game."* Norman: University of Oklahoma Press, 1977.

Papers on Language & Literature 1 (1965)-26, no. 3 (1990).

PAYNE, ROBERT O. *The Key of Remembrance: A Study of Chaucer's Poetics*. New Haven, Conn.: Yale University Press, 1963. Reprint. Westport, Conn.: Greenwood Press, 1973.

Philological Quarterly 1 (1922)-69, no. 2 (Spring 1990).

Publications of the Modern Language Association of America 40 (1925)-105 (October 1990).

RAMSEY, LEE C. *Chivalric Romances: Popular Literature in Medieval England*. Bloomington: Indiana University Press, 1983.

RANSOM, JOHN CROWE, ed. *The Kenyon Critics: Studies in Modern Literature from the "Kenyon Review."* Cleveland and New York: World Publishing Company, 1951.

RAW, BARBARA C. *The Art and Background of Old English Poetry*. London: Edward Arnold, 1978.

REISS, EDMUND. *The Art of the Middle English Lyric*. Athens: University of Georgia Press, 1972.

____. *William Dunbar.* Boston: Twayne, 1979.

Review of English Studies o.s. 1 (1925)-n.s. 41 (August 1990).

RIBNER, IRVING, and HARRY MORRIS. *Poetry: A Critical and Historical Introduction*. Chicago: Scott, Foresman, & Co., 1962.

RICHARDSON, JANETTE. *Blameth Nat Me: A Study of Imagery in Chaucer's Fabliaux*. The Hague and Paris: Mouton, 1970.

RICHMOND, VELMA BOURGEOIS. *The Popularity of Middle English Romance*. Bowling Green, Ohio: Bowling Green University Popular Press, 1975.

ROBERTSON, D. W., Jr. *Essays in Medieval Culture*. Princeton, N.J.: Princeton University Press, 1980.

ROGERS, WILLIAM ELFORD. *Image and Abstraction: Six Middle English Religious Lyrics*. Copenhagen: Rosenkilde and Bagger, 1972.

____. *Upon the Ways: The Structure of "The Canterbury Tales,"* English Literary Studies Monograph Series, no. 36. Victoria, B.C.: University of Victoria, 1986.

ROSENTHAL, M. L., and A. J. M. SMITH. *Exploring Poetry*. New York: Macmillan, 1955.

ROSS, IAN SIMPSON. *William Dunbar*. Leiden: E. J. Brill, 1981.

ROWLAND, BERYL, ed., *Chaucer and Middle English Studies in Honor of Rossell Hope Robbins*. London: Allen & Unwin, 1974.

____. *Companion to Chaucer Studies*. Rev. ed. Toronto, New York, and London: Oxford University Press, 1979.

RUGGIERS, PAUL G. *The Art of the Canterbury Tales*. Madison, Milwaukee, and London: University of Wisconsin Press, 1965.

SALU, MARY, ed. *Essays on Troilus and Criseyde*. Cambridge: D. S. Brewer; Totowa, N.J.: Rowman and Littlefield, 1979.

SALU, MARY, and ROBERT T. FARRELL, eds. *J. R. R. Tolkien, Scholar and Storyteller: Essays in Memoriam*. Ithaca and London: Cornell University Press, 1979.

SANDERS, THOMAS E. *The Discovery of Poetry*. Glenview, Ill.: Scott, Foresman & Co., 1967.

SAVAGE, D. S. *The Personal Principle: Studies in Modern Poetry*. London: George Routledge & Sons, 1944.

SCHAAR, CLAES. *Critical Studies in the Cynewulf Group*, Lund Studies in English, no. 17, ed. Olof Arngart. Lund: C. W. K. Gleerup; Copenhagen: Ejnar Munksgaard, 1949.

SCHMIDT, A. V. C., and NICOLAS JACOBS. "Introduction" to *Medieval English Romances*. Vol. 1 and 2. London: Hodder and Stoughton, 1980.

SCHOECK, RICHARD J., and JEROME TAYLOR, eds. *Chaucer Criticism, II: "Troilus and Criseyde" and the Minor Poems*. Notre Dame, Ind.: University of Notre Dame Press, 1961.

SCHORER, MARK, JOSEPHINE MILES, and GORDON McKENZIE. *Criticism: The Foundations of Modern Literary Judgment*. New York: Harcourt, Brace, & Co., 1948.

SCOTT, TOM. *Dunbar: A Critical Exposition of the Poems*. London and Edinburgh: Oliver & Boyd, 1966.

SHIPPEY, T. A. "Introduction" to *Poems of Wisdom and Learning in Old English*. Cambridge: D. S. Brewer; Totowa, N.J.: Rowman and Littlefield, 1976.

SKLUTE, LARRY. *Virtue of Necessity: Inconclusiveness and Narrative Form in Chaucer's Poetry*. Columbus: Ohio State University Press, 1984.

South Central Review 1 (1984)-7 (Fall 1990).

SPEARING, A. C. *Medieval Dream-Poetry*. Cambridge: Cambridge University Press, 1976.

_____. *Medieval to Renaissance in English Poetry*. Cambridge: Cambridge University Press, 1985.

_____. *Readings in Medieval Poetry*. Cambridge: Cambridge University Press, 1987.

Speculum: A Journal of Medieval Studies 1 (1926)-65, no. 3 (1990).

SPEIRS, JOHN. *Chaucer the Maker*. London: Faber and Faber, 1951.

_____. *Medieval English Poetry: The Non-Chaucerian Tradition*. London: Faber and Faber, 1958.

SPITZER, LEO. *Essays on English and American Literature by Leo Spitzer*, edited by Anna Hatcher. Princeton, N.J.: Princeton University Press, 1962.

STALLMAN, ROBERT WOOSTER, ed. *Critiques and Essays in Criticism, 1920-1948*. New York: Ronald Press, 1949.

STANLEY, ERIC GERALD, ed. *Continuations and Beginnings: Studies in Old English Literature*. London: Thomas Nelson & Sons, 1966.

STAUFFER, DONALD A. *The Nature of Poetry*. New York: W. W. Norton & Co., 1946.

STEVENS, MARTIN, and JEROME MANDEL, eds. *Old English Literature: Twenty-two Analytical Essays*. Lincoln: University of Nebraska Press, 1968.

STOKES, MYRA, and T. L. BURTON, eds. *Medieval Literature and Antiquities: Studies in Honour of Basil Cottle*. Cambridge: D. S. Brewer, 1987.

Studies in Philology 20 (1924)-87, no. 3 (Summer 1990).

Style 1 (1967)-24 (Spring 1990).

SWANTON, MICHAEL. *English Literature before Chaucer*. London and New York: Longman, 1987.

Texas Studies in Literature and Language 1 (1959)-31 (1989).

Traditio: Studies in Ancient and Medieval History, Thought, and Religion 10 (1945)-43 (1987).

TRAVERSI, DEREK. *The Canterbury Tales: A Reading*. London, Sydney, and Toronto: Bodley Head, 1983.

UNGER, LEONARD, and WILLIAM VAN O'CONNOR. *Poems for Study*. New York: Rinehart & Co., 1953.

University of Mississippi Studies in English n.s. 1 (1980)-7 (1989).

University of Toronto Quarterly 13 (1943-44)-59 (1989).

VAN DOREN, MARK. *Introduction to Poetry*. New York: William Sloane Associates, 1951.

VASTA, EDWARD, ed. *Interpretations of Piers Plowman*. Notre Dame and London: University of Notre Dame Press, 1968.

Viator: Medieval and Renaissance Studies 1 (1970)-20 (1989).

WAGENKNECHT, EDWARD, ed. *Chaucer: Modern Essays in Criticism*. New York: Oxford University Press, 1959.

WALSH, WILLIAM. *The Use of Imagination: Educational Thought and the Literary Mind*. London: Chatto & Windus, 1959.

WASSERMAN, JULIAN N., and ROBERT J. BLANCH, eds. *Chaucer in the Eighties*. Syracuse, N.Y.: Syracuse University Press, 1986.

WEBER, SARAH APPLETON. *Theology and Poetry in the Middle English Lyric: A Study of Sacred History and Aesthetic Form*. Columbus: Ohio State University Press, 1969.

WENZEL, SIEGFRIED. *Preachers, Poets, and the Early English Lyric*. Princeton, N.J.: Princeton University Press, 1986.

WEST, RAY B. *Essays in Modern Literary Criticism*. New York: Rinehart & Co., 1952.

WHEELER, CHARLES B. *The Design of Poetry*. New York: W. W. Norton & Co., 1966.

WHITTOCK, TREVOR. *A Reading of the Canterbury Tales*. Cambridge: Cambridge University Press, 1968.

WILLIAMSON, CRAIG. *A Feast of Creatures: Anglo-Saxon Riddle Songs*. Philadelphia: University of Pennsylvania Press, 1982.

WIMSATT, JAMES I. *Allegory and Mirror: Tradition and Structure in Middle English Literature*. New York: Pegasus, 1970.

WOOLF, ROSEMARY. *Art and Doctrine: Essays on Medieval Literature*, ed. Heather O'Donoghue. London and Ronceverte: Hambledon Press, 1986.

____. *The English Religious Lyric in the Middle Ages*. Oxford: Clarendon, 1968.